To
Read
Poetry

Daniel White

Donald Hall

1) Read it more than once
2) Keep a dictionary handy
3) Read it alone + listen to it,

feel the rythm
who is speaking it
Always reduce poem to what is happening
assume there is a reason for everything

Thursday
p. 38
p. 41

Tuesday - p. 126-128
look over p. 75 + 76 in preparation for in class paper

Friday p. 97 "Easter Wings"

Also by Donald Hall

Poetry

Exiles and Marriages
The Dark Houses
A Roof of Tiger Lilies
The Alligator Bride: Poems New and Selected
The Yellow Room
The Town of Hill
Kicking the Leaves

Prose

String Too Short to Be Saved
Henry Moore
Writing Well
Playing Around (with G. McCauley et al.)
Dock Ellis in the Country of Baseball
Goatfoot Milktongue Twinbird
Remembering Poets
Ox Cart Man

Editions

New Poets of England and America (with R. Pack and L. Simpson)
The Poetry Sampler
New Poets of England and America (Second Selection) (with R. Pack)
Contemporary American Poets
A Concise Encyclopedia of English and American Poetry and Poets
    (with Stephen Spender)
Poetry in English (with Warren Taylor)
The Modern Stylists
A Choice of Whitman's Verse
Man and Boy
American Poetry
A Writer's Reader (with D. L. Emblen)
To Read Literature

To Read Poetry

Donald Hall

12APR84

class essay
eter
rhm
esis

10APR
p.131 "AFTER GREAT PAIN"
p.138 "I heard a fly ---"
p.135 "I can't live with--"
p.136 "Because I could - stop"

Holt, Rinehart and Winston

New York   Chicago   San Francisco   Philadelphia
Montreal   Toronto   London   Sydney   Tokyo   Mexico City
Rio de Janeiro   Madrid

To Ralph and Mary Lou

Acknowledgments of copyright ownership and permission to reproduce works included in this volume begin on page 378.

Library of Congress Cataloging in Publication Data
Hall, Donald, 1928–
 To read poetry.

 Includes index.

 1. Literature—History and criticism. 2. Literature
—Collections. I. Title.

PN524.H25   808.8   81–19971

ISBN 0–03–060549–0

CBS COLLEGE PUBLISHING
Holt, Rinehart and Winston
The Dryden Press
Saunders College Publishing

To the Student

Reasons for reading poems

This book introduces poetry—maybe the oldest, certainly the most intense of literature's genres.

When we learn to read poems, we acquire a pleasure and a resource we never lose. Although literary study is impractical in one sense—few people make their living reading poems—in another sense it is almost as practical as breathing. Literature records and embodies centuries of human thought and feeling, preserving for us the minds of people who lived before us, who were like us and unlike us, against whom we can measure our common humanity and our historical difference. And when we read our contemporaries they illuminate a world we share. Whatever we claim for literature in general we must especially claim for poetry, which concentrates the virtues we attribute to drama and fiction. If we learn to read poems first, we will begin the study of literature as literature itself began—with the most concentrated and intense of its utterances.

When we read great poetry, something changes in us that stays changed. Poetry remembered becomes material to think with, and no one who has absorbed Shakespeare or Keats is quite the same again. Reading poetry adds tools by which we observe, measure, and judge the people and the properties of our universe—inside and outside.

In the fable of the ant and the grasshopper, the wise ant builds his storehouse against winter and prospers; the foolish grasshopper saves nothing and perishes. Anyone who dismisses the study of poetry on the ground that it will not be useful—to a chemist or an engineer, to a foreman or an x-ray technician—imitates the grasshopper. When we shut from our lives everything except food and shelter, part of us starves to death. Food for this hunger is music, painting, film, plays, stories, novels—and poems. Reading poems in our language alone (there is more great poetry in the English language than in the literature of any other language) we take into ourselves the greatness of Chaucer and Shakespeare, of romantics like Blake, Keats, and Wordsworth, of the grandfathers and fathers of modern poetry—down to the contemporary poets who visit our colleges to read their poems. If there is a poetry reading at your school while you are studying poetry, do not miss it.

There is pleasure and understanding to take from the poetry of our language, but first anyone must learn how to read it. No one expects to walk up to a computer and be able to program it without first learning something about computers. We have needed to learn skills in order to ride a bicycle, drive a car, play a guitar, shoot baskets, or typewrite. For some reason—perhaps because we are familiar with words from childhood and take them for granted—we tend to think that a quick glance at a poem should reward us, and that if we do not find instant satisfaction the work is beyond us, or not worth it, or irrelevant, or boring.

There are other problems for the beginning student of poetry. The ideas we derive from literature can seem confusing. Equally great poems may contradict each other in the generalizations we derive from them. One poem may recommend solitude, another society. One may advise us to seize the moment, another to live a life of contemplation. For that matter, two good readers may disagree about the implication of any work and each argue convincingly, with detailed references to the poem, in support of different interpretations. A complex work of literature like a poem cannot be reduced to a simple, correct meaning. In an elementary arithmetic text the answers may be printed in the back of the book. There are no answers to be printed in the back of this book.

Such nebulousness or ambiguity disturbs some students. After an hour's class discussion of a poem, with varying interpretations offered, they want the teacher to supply the answer to "But what *does* it mean?" We must admit that literature is inexact, and that the truth of poetry is not easily verifiable. Probably the poem means several things *at once* and not one thing at all. This is not to say, of course, that it means anything that anybody finds in it. Although differing, equally defensible opinions are common, error is even more common.

When modern people speak of truth, they usually mean something scientific or tautological. Arithmetic contains the truth of tautology; two and two make four because our definitions of *two* and *four* say so. In laboratories we encounter the truth of statistics and the truth of observation. If we smoke cigarettes heavily, we have one chance in four to develop lung cancer. When we heat copper wire over a Bunsen burner, the flame turns blue.

But there is an older sense of truth in which statements apparently opposite can both be valid. In this older tradition, truth is dependent on the agreement of sensible men and women—like the "Guilty" or "Not guilty" verdict of a jury. A poem may be true when its characters behave according to probability within a context highly hypothetical. Because this literary (or philosophical, or legal, or historical) truth is inexact, changeable, and subject to argument, poetry can seem nebulous to minds accustomed to arithmetical certainty.

Let me argue this: If poetry is nebulous or inexact; if it is impossible to determine with scientific precision the value or the meaning of a work of art, this inexactness is the price literature pays for representing whole human beings and for embodying whole human feelings. Human beings themselves, in their feelings and in the wanderings of their short lives, are ambiguous and ambivalent, shifting mixtures of permanence and change, direction and disorder. Because literature is true to life, true to the complexities of human feeling, different people will read the same work with different responses. And literary art will sometimes affirm that opposite things are both true *because they are*. Such a condition is not tidy; it is perhaps regrettable—but it is human nature.

The definition of poetry

Before we attempt to define poetry we must admit that it is impossible. Some words are more definable than others. If we do not know what a grommet or an ampersand is, a dictionary will tell us. If we do not know what love is, a definition will not help. *Poetry* is almost as difficult to define as *love*. With words like these, a definition is useful as a starting point for discussion—but only when we have experienced what we discuss. Once we have experienced poetry firsthand, we can think about it by trying to define it. Here is a useful exercise while you study poetry: at the end of each week, write a one-sentence definition of poetry as you understand it now; keep your changing definitions as testimony to the range of poetry.

Many definitions of poetry center on the delight of reading it. "Poetry," says a contemporary poet, "is a pleasure, like making love." John Milton (1608–1674) compared poetry to philosophical discourse and found it "more simple, sensuous and passionate." Samuel Taylor Coleridge (1772–1834) said that poetry's "proper and immediate object" was "the communication of immediate pleasure." Defining poetry, instead, by naming its components, Coleridge also called the art "the best words in the best order." Matthew Arnold (1822–1888) made *best* more particular: "Poetry is simply the most beautiful, impressive and wisely effective mode of saying things. . . ." When he combined *beautiful* with *wisely effective,* Arnold sounded like Robert Frost (1874–1963), who claimed that poetry "begins in delight and ends in wisdom"—or for that matter the Roman poet Horace (65–8 B.C.), who declared that poetry instructs while it pleases.

William Wordsworth (1770–1850) defined poetry as "the spontaneous overflow of powerful feelings" and said that it "takes its origin from emotion recollected in tranquility." This definition derives from an idea of the poet's creative process. Probably most definitions, like the first quoted, describe the effect on the reader. John Keats (1795–1821): "Poetry should surprise by a fine excess, and not by singularity. It should strike the reader as a wording of his own highest thoughts, and appear almost as a remembrance." Or A. E. Housman (1859–1936): "Experience has taught me, when I am shaving of a morning, to keep watch over my thoughts, because, if a line of poetry strays into my memory, my skin bristles so that the razor ceases to act. . . ." If after this barrage of definitions any student feels confused, let me add one more confusion: Carl Sandburg (1878–1967) said "Poetry is a synthesis of hyacinths and biscuits."

Confusing, yes—but every one of these definitions makes its own sense when you have a broad experience of poems. Sandburg has fun with his definition—making a tongue-twister, among other things—but he is serious also: Poetry combines and reconciles within the same object things seemingly irreconcilable, like the flower with the Greek name and the simple product of the American kitchen. Metaphor brings together things that do not seem as if they could be brought together, as when Robert Frost says, "The petal of the rose / It was that stung. . . ," bringing together the soft rose petal and the bee's stinger. Metaphor is essential to poetry and a clue to its nature, for poetry juxtaposes things that really belong together but seem not to—like love and hate, like passion and indifference. Once again I must say: Poetry does this amalgamating because poetry is true to life, and in our lives we continually experience the simultaneous presence of opposing forces. We are not always aware of our ambivalence; poetry helps us understand the reality of our lives.

On the other hand: Poetry is words, and it is words arranged usually in lines, so that the right-hand side of the page is jagged. This definition is not so silly as it sounds: poems are not statements (the worst thing you can do to a poem is to reduce it to a rephrasing of its ideas) but objects, like paintings or sculptures, that include statements as *part* of their materials. The sound of a poem, controlled in large part by its lines, gives it an object's shapeliness and contributes to pleasure and wisdom both. The sound of a poem captures us—or perhaps we must surrender to it—and allows us access to its interior, which is perhaps why, in T. S. Eliot's words, "Genuine poetry can communicate before it is understood."

It can. But then, with close attention, it can be understood *as well*—and become an even greater pleasure.

The words themselves

Poetry is words. Mostly so far I have talked as if poetry were the feelings and thoughts we derive from reading poems, but feelings and thoughts are not poetry's medium. Whatever poetry accomplishes in us it accomplishes by words. As paint and canvas form the medium of painting; as sequences and combinations of sound different in pitch, duration, and quality form the medium of music, so the right words in the right order make poetry.

A Japanese named Basho wrote this haiku about three hundred years ago:

> The morning glory—
> another thing
> that will never be my friend.

Basho reminds us that the natural world is separate from us, that we may not shoulder our way into it, like invading troops of the imagination, and assume that we are intimate with everything. The American poet Robert Bly translated these lines. Here are three other versions:

> A. The morning glory
> is a separate being
> and I can never know it intimately.

> B. The morning glory
> is yet another object
> with which I will never become closely acquainted.

> C. The morning glory—
> something else
> that won't call me companion.

To understand and appreciate how these four versions differ from one another is to become sensitive to the words that make literature. In a general way, they all mean the same thing. After the identical first lines, the translations differ in diction, which is the kinds of words chosen, and in rhythm, which is the pace and tempo of the words. Versions A and B are dry, stiff, and unnatural. *Separate being* sounds pretentious compared to *another thing. Yet another object* is finicky with its *yet another,* and *object* is more scientific-sounding than the casual *thing.* "With which I will never become closely acquainted" is formal and distant, rhythmically slow. "And I can never know it intimately" lacks interest or surprise in its words. The simplicity of "that will never be my friend," coming to rest on the surprise of the last word, makes Bly's translation blossom in its final word. In version C, on the other hand, we have a translation nearly as pleasing as the original one. *Something else* has its own casual simplicity, and the little action of *call me companion*—where the morning glory is imagined capable of speech—has some of the surprise that the original translation found in *friend.*

The difference is the words and their order.

What's good, what's bad

The claims I make for poetry are large: that it alters and enlarges our minds, our connections with each other past and present, our understanding of our own feelings. These claims apply to excellent poems only. Some poems are better than others—and some verse is not poetry at all. Even if judgments are always subject to reversal, even if there is no way we can be certain of being correct, evaluation lives at the center of literary study. Of course it is never easy, even after a lifetime of literary study, to explain why one poem is better than another in words that will convince anyone who disagrees. Still, the struggle is worth it. The struggle to name reasons for value—to evaluate works of art—is lifelong, and although we may never arrive at satisfactory explanations, the struggle makes the mind more sensitive, more receptive to the next work of literature it encounters.

And as the mind becomes more sensitive and receptive to poetry, it may become more sensitive and receptive to all sorts of things.

The organization of this book

In reading a poem, we respond to poetry's elements: images and metaphors, for instance, tones of voice and allusions. For the sake of the ultimate pleasure of reading poems, most of the next chapters explore these elements, types, and forms of poetry. Then we collect many poems by four poets—John Keats, Emily Dickinson, Robert Frost, and Theodore Roethke—so that we can read a few poets in depth; and then we gather a few poems by many poets for further reading in the poetry of our language.

But before we take a separate look at poetry's elements, in the first chapter we will discuss two poems as a whole. Because eventually we wish to arrive at a sense of the poem as a whole, it makes sense to begin with models of such reading.

We will also take the time, right at the start, to learn from a little bad poetry.

. . and to the Instructor

In making selections and in writing the text for this collection, I have tried to serve one purpose: to help students read poetry with intelligence, gusto, and discrimination.

This book begins the study of poetry by examining whole poems, emphasizing that the goal of reading is not the analysis of parts but the understanding of wholes. For a fuller definition of poetry's elements, later chapters concentrate on parts.

Selections are frequently modern or contemporary; students best begin literary study without the distraction of an unfamiliar vocabulary, and without the handicap of historical ignorance. Of course it would be silly to let this principle cheat us of Shakespeare, of Wordsworth. . . . I feel that it is best to begin with contemporary examples, when the students are shyest, then gradually introduce them to examples from poetry's past.

I intend the text to be readable and entertaining while it remains serious. Because everyone is curious about the lives of authors (whether we ought to be or not) I have included biographical notes on all poets. My emphasis is obviously neither biographical nor historical but esthetic: I mean to examine the way poetry works.

Footnotes and glosses translate foreign-language material, provide essential identifications, and define words not available in many dictionaries or words used in an archaic sense. The Appendix, Writing about Poems, should provide guidance for students preparing papers.

I've taken advice from several hundred American teachers of literature. When this book was only a notion, several years back, many people answered a questionnaire about what it should include. I am grateful; I have followed many suggestions.

Other professors read portions of the manuscript and commented in detail. I should like especially to thank Christopher P. Baker, Walter L. Barker, Sylvan Barnet, Ronald Baughman, R. S. Beal, Gary Blake, John Boni, Larry Champion, Barbara J. Cicardo, Paul Davis, R. H. Deutsch, Richard Dietrich, Donald Drury, John L. Fell, Art Goldsher, Randolph Goodman, William J. Gracie, Jr., Barnett Guttenberg, Nancy J. Hazelton, Michael Hogan, Woodrow L. Holbein, John Huxhold, Henry E. Jacobs, Robert C. Johnson, John J. Keenan, Mike Keene, X. J. Kennedy, Hannah Laipson, Bette B. Lansdown, Robert Leggett, James MacKillop, James Moody, William W. Nolte II, Byron Petrakis, Anne Pidgeon, Doris Powers, William C. Pratt, Victoria Price, Jules Ryckebusch, Dennis Rygiel, H. Miller Solomon, Joe Sperry, William Stull, Cathy Turner, Ralph Voss, Martha Weathers, and James D. Welch.

Collaboration and help at Holt, Rinehart and Winston began with Harriett Prentiss and continued with Kenney Withers, Susan Katz, and Nedah Abbott, editors to whom I am especially grateful. Pamela Forcey was masterful at production and H. L. Kirk a superb copy editor. Anita Baskin and Terry Meade handled permissions and many other matters.

Finally, let me thank my own helpers in New Hampshire, in Ann Arbor, and in Santa Monica: Lois Fierro, Sharon Giannotta, Dorothy Foster, Pat Wykes, and Frank Barham—not to mention Jane Kenyon.

D.H.

Contents

Chapter 1 Good Poems and Bad

Robert Frost, "Stopping by Woods on a Snowy Evening"

Here is a detailed reading of a poem by Robert Frost, "Stopping by Woods on a Snowy Evening." A close reading is called an **explication**, which someone has defined as "an explanation with complications." A pure explanation might first paraphrase the poem, turning its lines into words of prose; an explication goes further, tries to account for the whole poem in its sounds, in its minute suggestions of meaning, in its shapeliness. No explication will equal the poem itself, but in a good explication we can feel that we have come close to noticing and naming everything in the poem that affects us.

Stopping by Woods on a Snowy Evening

Whose woods these are I think I know.
His house is in the village though;
He will not see me stopping here
To watch his woods fill up with snow.

My little horse must think it queer
To stop without a farmhouse near
Between the woods and frozen lake
The darkest evening of the year.

He gives his harness bells a shake
To ask if there is some mistake.
The only other sound's the sweep
Of easy wind and downy flake.

The woods are lovely, dark and deep,
But I have promises to keep,
And miles to go before I sleep,
And miles to go before I sleep.

10

Read this poem aloud, separating the lines with slight pauses but keeping your sense of whole sentences. The different lengths of pause between the lines affect a poem's rhythm. The pause you make at the end of the first line, where Frost ends the sentence with a period, should be longer than the pauses between lines in the second stanza, where there is no punctuation until the end. When we say or hear a poem, we encounter its body. Unless we feel a poem in our own bodies, we are apt to consider it merely an idea; we are apt to confuse a poem with its paraphrase.

But a good way to begin talking about a poem is to paraphrase or summarize it, to see if we are discussing the same poem. (A **paraphrase** finds different words for each of the poem's phrases. A **summary** is shorter, a simple report of the plot, the way *TV Guide* describes a television show.) Once we have paraphrased or summarized the poem, we can talk about its body and its soul. Here, summary is easy: *A man driving a horse pauses beside a forest to watch the snow falling on it; his horse seems to want to keep moving, and the man decides he ought to move on although the scene is pretty, and even inviting.*

Frost used to define poetry as what gets left out in a translation. You might as well say what gets left out in a summary; there's a gap the size of New Hampshire between Frost's sixteen lines and my forty-one words. But summary helps at the start of an explication. When you've read a poem two or three times—slowly and quickly, silently and out loud, and when you have arrived at a tentative paraphrase—you are ready to go back to the poem and look at it bit by bit, as if you were taking apart a machine in order to understand how it works.

Start with the title; sometimes it gives us information we need to understand a poem's wholeness. This title, "Stopping by Woods on a Snowy Evening," is a description or label; it tells us what we're going to see, and then we see it. This particular title requires little work on the reader's part.

In his first line—"Whose woods these are I think I know"—Frost turns normal word order around. Ordinary word order would have us say something like "I think I know whose woods these are." By moving *woods* to the start of the sentence, Frost gives it more prominence or power. We might say "What *nerve* you've got, heaven only knows!" for a similar emphasis.

In the second line, "His house is in the village though," the last word makes no logical sense; *though* or *although* should make some sort of contradiction or qualification to the statement that *I* know who owns this woodlot. But Frost writes as we usually speak—and the *though* qualifies something left out. To understand *though,* we might paraphrase the whole statement, bracketing what is implicit: "I know who owns this land [and I would feel self-conscious if the owner saw me standing and staring into space this way] but he doesn't live out here, and therefore he won't see me pausing to gaze idly." The word *though* implies more than its one syllable would seem able to contain.

At the same time *though* implies something, it rhymes with the word that ends the first line. A rhyme word must feel natural or the poet will seem to have chosen it for the sake of rhyming. Looking to the rest of the stanza, we see that Frost doesn't rhyme the next line with anything nearby but that the fourth line rhymes with the first and the second, tying the stanza together. Because we have the word *snowy* in the title, the idea of snow is important to this poem before we start reading it. Then the word *snow* ends a three-line sentence that makes snow the object of our attention. The last two lines of the stanza are a natural, inevitable journey to the culminating word *snow*. As soon as we get there, we realize that this is where we had to go, all the time. This inevitability is underlined by the rhyme, where *know* and *though* build up a sound-expectancy to culminate in *snow*.

Maybe the speaker's self-consciousness is the most important element in the first stanza. (I say "the speaker"—though it feels awkward—because I don't want to say "Robert Frost" and make the mistake of thinking that *I* in a poem necessarily means the poet.) To sense his embarrassment is to catch the tone of voice,* the way we all learn to catch the tone of people talking, when we understand by hundreds of small signals whether the person's tone is ironic or straightforward, conniving or sincere.

As the stanza ends we learn something besides the speaker's embarrassment; we learn his motive for stopping: "To watch his woods fill up with snow." Frost's language here is plain, but it could be plainer or flatter still; *I* could have said "to see it snow in his trees" or "to look at the snow falling on his forest." Saying *fill up* contributes to the image* or picture made by the poet; *his woods* becomes a container—empty or partly empty—which *snow* can fill.

As mentioned before, *here* doesn't rhyme with anything around it. If we hold the sound of the word in our ears, however, we are rewarded when we read the first line of the second stanza. We experience the pleasure of completing something begun earlier, like the moment in a piece of music that a theme (or a phrase or a chord) returns. Rhyme in this poem holds parts together, linking stanzas more firmly than many poems try to do. The third line of each stanza, unrhymed to the lines near it, rhymes with three of the lines in the stanza following. The four stanzas together are like four groups of four dancers doing the same dance, with one member of each foursome holding hands with the group beyond it.

If it's a dance, it must move to a tune. **Rhythm** is an approximate recurrence or repetition in the pacing of sound; rhythm is fast or slow, staccato or flowing. **Meter**, which is a measure or count of something, puts its own mark on certain rhythms. "Stopping by Woods" is written in meter, and this meter helps define the rhythm of the poem. Counting *evening* as two syllables, in every line the even-numbered syllables (two, four, six, and eight) are louder than the odd-numbered syllables. Not all the even syllables are loud, but they are louder; in *promises, prom-* is louder than the *have* before it, and *-ses* is louder than the *-i-* —just barely louder; you cannot say *prom–*IH*–ses*. This alternation of louder and softer syllables is the meter of the poem. Other matters besides meter contribute to differing lengths of pause at lines' ends. A poet can manipulate punctuation to speed or slow rhythm. In prose, if we said that we stopped between the woods and a frozen lake, the darkest evening of the year we would

---

*Tone and image as elements of poetry are subjects of later chapters.

put a comma after lake, as I do in this sentence. But Frost uses the line's pause and avoids a comma, which would slow the stanza down more than he wants it slowed. On the other hand, in prose he wouldn't need a comma if he were telling us that he had promises to keep and miles to go before he slept—but here the poet slows his rhythm at the measured ending of the poem, and he puts a comma after *keep*. Notice that Frost manipulates commas only where commas in prose would be optional.

The second stanza, picking up the *here* rhyme, tells us that the *little* horse (*little* sounds affectionate; this person seems to care about his horse's feelings) *must think it queer*. Consider the word *must* as we use it in speech. If we know that it's raining, we say "It's raining"; if we only think so—because of forecasts or the distant sound of falling water—we say "It *must* be raining." We only claim that something must be true if we don't know it for certain. When Frost writes "My little horse must think it queer," he uses the doubtful *must* because he knows a human cannot mindread his horse. The speaker in the poem attributes doubts to his horse because he himself believes it weird or eccentric to stop one's horse for no good reason out in the middle of nowhere to watch snow falling in the darkness. This man's uneasiness shows in his self-mockery: even his horse *must* think he's crazy.

As this stanza continues, ostensibly telling what the horse must think queer, the poet gives us more information, and he gives us information in images that carry feeling on their backs. The road, we learn, passes between *the woods*—which are like a container filling with snow—and the *frozen lake*. Sometimes an image informs us by what it omits. While *frozen* adds cold to the poem (an image records not just pictures but *any* experience of the senses, like cold), the line also increases the solitude of the scene: the lane runs between wood and lake only, no houses or factories here, no inns or filling stations, just these cold and natural things, on "The darkest evening of the year."

This last detail (if we read clearly enough, looking for the implications of words) is strange; it is strange if we take it literally, and when we read a poem we ought to try at first to take it literally. We cannot take it literally that this man has determined scientifically, using some instrument that measures light, that this clouded—moonless, starless—night contains fewer candlepower units than any other night in the preceding twelve months. We could take it, in a roundabout way, that tonight is December 22, the longest night of the year, and insist with some logic that the length of its darkness aggregates more darkness and that therefore this is indeed the "darkest evening in the year." But poetry usually works by common sense, not on riddles that ingenuity must solve. It's just too complicated to explain this line as telling us that tonight is the winter solstice. Probably we do best to take the line as an expressive exaggeration, the way people always talk about the weather: "There's enough snow out there to bury the barn." "It hasn't rained so much since Noah." "It's the darkest night of the whole damned year."

In the third stanza, the little horse does what horses do; he shudders or shakes, standing still in the cold night, and to the driver who still feels foolish pausing to gaze at snow in the woods, the horse's jingling harness bells seem like the horse's reproach. The jingling is another image—so far we've had images of sight (*to watch*), of touch (*frozen lake*), and of sound (*bells*)—and now the sound images multiply: "the sweep / Of easy wind and downy flake." Notice that images often appeal to more than one sense. If *frozen* is an image of cold in *frozen lake,* it is an image of sight also, because we know what a frozen lake looks like. And *the sweep* is a swooshing sound, but it's also (at least distantly) a visual broom moving.

The phrase *easy wind* is not an image at all. We could not draw (or play on an instrument, or hear) an easy wind as opposed to a difficult wind or an uneasy one. Does it mean anything at all to call the wind easy? First let us paraphrase, using alternative words. Perhaps this wind is light and gentle—*easy* as "full of ease," like the softness of *downy* that *easy* is parallel to. If this paraphrase is accurate, someone might ask why the poet doesn't call the wind "light and gentle" or, to keep line length the same, just "gentle." Because *gentle* is not the same as *easy* and *easy* does it better; the paraphrase is only intellectual, and *easy* says it better because of its sound. It is a long and luxuriant word. That long *e* stretches itself out like a big cat on a sofa, and then the *z*-sound (spelled with an *s*) slinks sensuously and stretches again into a shorter *e*, spelled *y* this time. These two syllables take longer to say than half a line elsewhere in the poem.

I would not argue that "sound imitates sense" in this word the way the sound of *drop* or *squish* is similar to the meanings of the words. (When sound imitates sense, we call it **onomatopoeia**.) I am not sure that a light wind speaks in long *es* and in *zs*. But I am sure that the grateful tongue delights in this word, picking up the long *e* of *sweep,* looking ahead to the long *e* that ends *downy,* and that these words, giving us in our minds qualities of the scene, at the same time give us a sound-pleasure. We have two pleasures at once, one in our minds as we assent to a description, the other in our mouths as the poet arranges vowels and consonants, much as a chef arranges flavors for our pleasure.

We have concentrated on *easy*. *Downy* gives pleasure also. The *y* picks up the *e* sound earlier in the line; the *ow* picks up a vowel from *sounds* in the line before. (This repetition of vowel sounds is called **assonance**.) If you don't know the word *downy,* look it up. Always look up words you are not certain of. *Down* means a good many things; among others it means goosefeathers, soft and white, and *downy* is an adjective made from the noun *down*. Because down is soft (touch) and white (vision), it gives us two kinds of image at once, and perhaps also distantly gives us an image of the snow as a great white bird. It is also a rural image, connected with barnyard and countryside. If Frost had tried comparing the whiteness of the snow to the whiteness of a sailboat's sails, his comparison would have gone far from the poem's world. Finally, the word *down* works its power on us for at least one more reason: it reminds us of the direction in which, relentlessly, snow must fall.

By the end of the third stanza the poem has erected a dramatic conflict, like a story or a play. The conflict lives in the mind of the speaker, who attributes one side of his feeling to his horse; of course, it is the speaker who thinks it queer to pause where he pauses; at the same time it is the speaker who stops to gaze into the lovely beauty of the wood, exercising the other side of his feeling. He is "of two minds about it," in the old expression. In the final stanza, mind 1 writes the first line and mind 2 answers with the second, third, and fourth; the mind with the most lines has the last word.

In our daily lives, we are often ambivalent—of two minds, sometimes of three or four—about what we do. Often simply two desires are in conflict; the woods are lovely, but I have duties; the scoop of ice cream will taste good, but I will get fat; I want to see this movie, but I want to pass that test. Human beings are ambivalent by nature: we often find ourselves headed in two directions at the same time. In our deepest selves we are never one-hundred percent *anything,* neither loving nor hating, and if we tell ourselves we are pure, we fool ourselves.

Poetry expresses human ambivalence. That's one reason poetry is complicated—because people are complicated, and because poetry is true to people. Bad poems are often bad—lying, distorted, phony, sentimental—exactly because they deny ambivalent feeling. This poem is excellent (here is one criterion for excellence in poetry) because it embodies with honest clarity true human ambivalence. This poem is almost *about* ambivalence and its conflicts; at least it acts out a particular ambivalence with so much clarity that the poem in the reader's mind can stand for other conflicts. What for Frost's speaker was a quarrel between woods and duties can translate, in our lives, into the quarrel between birdwatching or writing a letter. When one set of particulars can stand in for another set of relationships, we have a **symbol**.

Symbols raise another subject: in interpreting a poem, where does the reader stop? Many people find further complexities—"levels," "meanings"—in this poem. Some readers have found this poem suicidal and claimed that it contains a wish to die. People have often tended to look for a death wish in Frost because in his lifetime Frost spoke about suicidal feelings. But should we *therefore* consider that when Frost's speaker looks into the woods he takes the woods as a symbol for death and longs for the darkness of his own death? Not *therefore,* at any rate, for then we would be leaping from life to poem as if it were always possible to make equations between the facts of the life and the facts of the poem.

What can we say, finally, about the meaning of this poem—looking only at the poem itself? Meaning is not paraphrase, nor is it singling out words for their special effects, nor is it accounting for rhythm and form. It is all these things, and it is more. Meaning is what we try to explicate: the whole impression of a poem on our minds, our emotions, and our bodies. We can never wholly explicate a poem any more than we can explicate ourselves, or another person—but we can try to come close. The only way to stretch and exercise our ability to read a poem is to try to understand and to name our whole response.

Then how shall we understand this last stanza, and the implications of the whole poem? Implication is the word I want to use. Although I may understand what is said on the surface, another voice speaks from underneath the poem—not a "hidden meaning," implying that the poet is a riddler or an Easter-egg-hider, but a second language of the poem, which exists underneath the first language. This is the quiet voice of implication, the poet's psyche speaking to the reader's psyche in a language just underneath the commonsense words, a language only these words in this order could manage to imply.

A poem makes a contract with the reader: I agree to use words as thoroughly as I can; you agree to read them the same way. Because this is a poem, we shall do well to examine even the simplest words. First, we have the bald statement of attraction: "These woods are lovely, dark and deep." The word *lovely* has the word *love* in it, as *downy* included *down*. So the woods pertain somehow to love. *Dark* and *deep* go together, not just for their **alliteration** (the repetition of initial consonants). The woods are dark in this evening, filling up with snow that by definition is white; and they are deep, like a vessel with room for the filling. The woods are mysterious, perhaps a place suitable for hiding, and this sensation of mystery has an attraction like the attraction people feel for each other; so the woods are *lovely*. *Dark and deep* work together as a double adjective, explaining the *kind* of "lovely." How different the line would be if Frost had punctuated it differently and used a comma after *dark*. "The woods are lovely, dark, and deep"—pronounced as punctuated—makes a different sound, and even a different *meaning*: the extra comma makes the three adjectives enumerate separate qualities of the wood; in the line as Frost wrote it, instead of enumerated qualities we have a rush of feeling. Such difference a comma makes!

Apparently the feelings in this poem are universal, and all of us find in ourselves on occasion a desire to abandon the track of duty, the track of the everyday, and to embrace the peace of nothingness. But perhaps I go too far—in trying to name the unnameable—when in my paraphrase I say "the peace of nothingness." My naming is not so good as Frost's naming, and some readers will prefer their own different naming. "The peace of nothingness" attempts to paraphrase a feeling that for some people apparently sounds suicidal—and for others merely sleepy. My inadequate phrase attempts to bring together the two sides.

Different readings can be valid—but *not all readings*. There are limits to the validity of interpretations, limits set by the poem. One reader tells me that the poem indicates a desire to put a bullet through one's head. Another says the poem implies that Frost wants to move to Arizona and escape the winter. The suicidal reading is only a little askew. If all of us sometimes desire what we might call peace or oblivion, such feeling is not entirely alien to the desire to die. Perhaps sleep—"death's second self," as Shakespeare called it—will satisfy the desire. The speaker in this poem expresses a taste for darkness that resembles the wish to die but does not duplicate it; to find a death wish in this poem is only an exaggeration, like calling the pain of a stubbed toe "excruciating agony." On the other hand, the reader who finds Frost on his way to Arizona simply misreads; there is nothing like it in the poem. Presumably the cold of the poem made the reader think of a warm climate and then attribute the thought to Frost's poem. To avoid misinterpretation, always take care to distinguish the source of a notion: does Phoenix happen in the poem or in your own head?

After talking about one poem for so many pages, I think of Whitman's little poem about listening to the "Learn'd Astronomer," who spoke in scientific terms about astronomical data. Whitman's response is to go outside the lecture hall and look up "in perfect silence at the stars." Read again Robert Frost's simple, pleasurable, universal poem:

Stopping by Woods on a Snowy Evening

Whose woods these are I think I know.
His house is in the village though;
He will not see me stopping here
To watch his woods fill up with snow.

My little horse must think it queer
To stop without a farmhouse near
Between the woods and frozen lake
The darkest evening of the year.

He gives his harness bells a shake
To ask if there is some mistake.
The only other sound's the sweep
Of easy wind and downy flake.

The woods are lovely, dark and deep,
But I have promises to keep,
And miles to go before I sleep,
And miles to go before I sleep.

Questions and exercises

1. What happens when Frost repeats a line?

2. Whose feet these are I think I know.
   His head's beneath a T-shirt though.
   He will not mind an ice cube here . . .

   Complete a fourth line.

3. Rewrite the poem, staying as close to the original as you can, but change all the important words. Use a thesaurus or a dictionary of synonyms, if you like. Let *whose* and *I* and *his* remain; change *woods, know, horse,* and so forth. You could begin "Whose forest this is, I recognize . . ." Compare different versions in class, deciding which is closest to the original, and which most ingenious. Compare the class versions with Frost's original. (Sometimes it works best to concentrate on one stanza only or to divide the class into four sections, each doing one stanza.)

William Carlos Williams, "so much depends"

Robert Frost was a traditional poet, writing in rhyme and meter. During Frost's lifetime, the slightly younger William Carlos Williams made a different sort of poem. Williams was born in Rutherford, New Jersey, where he practiced medicine for more than forty years after education in Switzerland, at the University of Pennsylvania, and in Germany. He wrote **free verse**, lines of poetry strong in rhythm but free of the regular repetitions of meter. He is another good poet whose poems force us to acknowledge kinds of excellence foreign to Frost's excellence. Williams in his poems invents original shapes and forces us to become aware of the poem as a made object. He was a poet of images, of the *eye*; but as we will see, he wrote also for the *ear* and placed his words for our maximum pleasure in their sound.

> So much depends upon a red wheelbarrow, glazed with rainwater, beside the white chickens.

This sentence is unlikely to elicit much response. It seems nonsensical, unworthy of attention. In a way, attention is exactly the problem. This poem by William Carlos Williams is printed above not as a poem but as a one-sentence paragraph in which the words have not been *attended to. Attention,* which Williams brings to bear by his use of *lines,* is exactly what we miss.

When someone asks the difference between poetry and prose, I like to answer: "Poetry is jagged on the right-hand side of the page." Poetry is written in lines, and lines make a big difference. Lines act like a musician's notation, telling us how to say a poem aloud, or how to hear it. Yet most beginning readers of poetry either read as if lines didn't exist at all or as if the sense always stopped at the lines' ends.

Knowing that the wheelbarrow sentence is really a poem, let us try putting it into lines, starting with the most obvious arrangment:

> So much depends upon
> a red wheelbarrow
> glazed with rainwater
> beside the white chickens.

I call this arrangement obvious because the lines break where the phrases pause. If you were saying the prose sentence aloud and had to pause three times because you were out of breath, you would pause where these lines end. As it happens, these linebreaks are not the poet's—but if they were, let us see what we could find in them. Putting the sentence into these lines must affect the meaning of the sentence, if we take "meaning" to be the words' total impact on the reader. In search of meaning, let us first try paraphrase: "These things are really important: a small red cart with wheels on it, with water on it from a rainshower, next to the poultry." (I cannot paraphrase the simplicities of *red* and *white.*) When I asserted that meaning must be changed by the line arrangement, my claim was not grand; putting these clauses into lines slows down the sentence, adding pauses greater than the pauses we would make if we spoke the sentence as prose. The pauses isolate the clauses within white brackets of time, made visible on poetry's page by the white spaces around the poem. The result is focus, intensity, concentration, emphasis.

In the lines quoted, the last three make visual images, and the first line insists on the importance of what follows, therefore on the importance of the visual. To isolate these lines—by pauses and spaces—is to emphasize the singularity of each unit and to draw closer attention to the redness of the wheelbarrow, to the wetness of the rain, to the whiteness of the chickens. The greater emphasis of these lines *intensifies* meaning.

But not sufficiently for William Carlos Williams. Here is the poem as he actually wrote it:

> so much depends
> upon
>
> a red wheel
> barrow
>
> glazed with rain
> water
>
> beside the white
> chickens

By this arrangement meaning is further enhanced, sound released, and the poem made exact, fixed, permanent—like a carving. The prose sentence from page 9 is repeated exactly, but by breaking the words into these lines Williams makes an object; and his object enforces a meaning.

First, *look* at the poem William Carlos Williams wrote. Looking at shape on the page, without reading or understanding a word, the poem already begins to make a statement, saying "I am orderly; I am arranged on purpose; there is nothing sloppy or careless or inadvertent in me; I will reward careful reading." The visual statement of a poem on the page may be the least of poetry's sensuous qualities; but it exists.

The visual shape suggests an audible performance, behaving like musical notation. In its true form, the poem has more pauses than it had in the four-line version, and more variety in the pauses; generally, the pause between the lines of each two-line stanza is short—like the pause between *wheel* and *barrow*—while the pause that leaps the larger white space between stanzas is longer. But there are degrees of difference within this generalization. Syntax and sense require that the pause between *rain* and *water* be shorter than the pause between *white* and *chickens*. With seven places for pauses at line-ends, the poem calls for seven different degrees of pause.

More pause creates still more emphasis, focus. We see this most clearly in *wheelbarrow*: *wheel / barrow,* where a linebreak gives us two nouns for one, shows us the original parts of a compound word, and makes a statement about the importance of observing the physical world. This linebreak gives us twice as much *thingness,* making us recognize wheels as separate, barrow as separate, and wheelbarrow as a synthesis of the two, which is also a third thing. In *rainwater,* we see the same act repeated. The first line's *depend / upon* splits a verb phrase into its parts (like the later splitting of compound nouns) and hangs the preposition from a verb that originally meant "hang from." In the last stanza, splitting *white* from *chickens* gives us at least a little more attention to the quality of the color than we get if *white chickens* is printed on one line.

But the poem's arrangement does more than intensify meaning and more than make a pretty shape. It releases varied sounds, two assonances in particular, that grant the reader a pleasure equivalent to the eye's pleasure in seeing *red, rain,* and *white.* In the four-line arrangement, the third line was "glazed with rainwater." When the poet did it his way, the fifth line of the poem becomes "glazed with rain," and the long diphthong *āi* bursts twice into bloom. The flowering of the diphthong alters the pace of the line, for when the reader comes to *rain* and tastes the pleasure of the repeated sound, he or she stretches it a little; the *n* of "rain" allows the sound to be held on the tongue and savored.

And the next pair of lines gives the same pleasure to the mouth alerted to assonance. The long-*i* diphthong in the second syllable of *beside* finds itself mirrored and repeated in the vowel of *white,* buried midline in the earlier version. Both times the word stretched and exalted is a sensuous and meaningful word, *rain* describing the sources of *water, white* the color of chickens; insofar as sound specifies more attention given to a word, assonance impinges upon our understanding, and the coincidence of vowel sounds contributes to meaning.

This little poem by William Carlos Williams is not a vessel loaded with philosophical or intellectual content; it does not resemble the works of Plato or Thomas Jefferson. The poem does have meaning, but its statement belongs more to the area of sensation than to the area of thought.

Feelings and ideas happen at the same time, ideas carry feelings with them, and feelings imply ideas. If Williams's poem insists on the importance of the physical world, the *insistence* is an emotional value placed on a philosophical idea. And the poem makes its statement not by generalizing but by giving a particular example—something of the world, visible, stared at and held to. The visual details are perceived with passion and necessity, as if they were rails on a narrow bridge onto which we hold in order not to fall into the chasm below. The intensity of this experience, which makes the poem valuable, derives largely from the poet's skill in manipulating sounds. Here it is again:

so much depends
upon

a red wheel
barrow

glazed with rain
water

beside the white
chickens

Exercise

Using different words, imitate the shape and sound of Williams's poem.

A form is anything done a second time. The first time somebody wrote a sonnet, it was not a sonnet; the second time somebody wrote one, and the third—then we began to call them sonnets. So consider that you are writing a newly discovered form of poetry called a wheelbarrow. You can define a wheelbarrow as four two-line stanzas; each first line has three words, each second line has one word; each one-word second line has two syllables; each three-word first line has either three or four syllables.

Here's one student's wheelbarrow:

it is extremely
serious

to watch the
teacher

writing long words
in chalk

on blackboards
all morning

Which lines fit the form? Which don't?

Wallace Stevens, "Disillusionment of Ten O'Clock"

A third example of a good poem is one by Wallace Stevens, who was a friend of William Carlos Williams when they were both young and who met Robert Frost in Florida winters when both poets were old. After graduation from Harvard and the New York University Law School Stevens practiced law in New York City; he lived in Greenwich Village and spent much time with other writers who gathered there. In his late thirties he became associated with the Hartford Accident and Indemnity Company, serving as a vice-president for the last decade of his life.

Disillusionment of Ten O'Clock

The houses are haunted
By white night-gowns.
None are green,
Or purple with green rings,
Or green with yellow rings,
Or yellow with blue rings.
None of them are strange,
With socks of lace
And beaded ceintures.
10   People are not going
To dream of baboons and periwinkles.
Only, here and there, an old sailor,
Drunk and asleep in his boots,
Catches tigers
In red weather.

With this poem I will not provide an explication; instead, I will ask questions, hoping to suggest ways of arriving at an explication. Read the poem several times, slowly, before you begin to read the questions.

Questions

1. In the title, is *ten o'clock* A.M. or P.M.? What in the poem suggests one or the other?
2. Think of the word *disillusionment*. Take it apart. What might this word have to do with the hour of ten o'clock? Are there illusions or disillusions in the body of the poem?
3. Does *haunted* tell you anything about the title? How?
4. There is a ghost in the word *haunted*. Ordinarily there would be no ghost in the word *night-gown*. What word makes *haunted* go with *night-gown*?
5. Do you know whether there are bodies inside these nightgowns?
6. In lines 3 through 6 the poet presents images in the negative. Can we learn anything from being told that something does *not* exist? What do these negatives imply? What is missing from these houses?
7. In line 7 *strange* can be a vague and imprecise word; in this context, do other words define *strange* and make it less vague?
8. A ceinture is a belt, and the word was already unusual when Stevens published the poem in 1915. Why would a poet use a word most readers would have to look up? Can a poet mean something simply by using an outlandish word?
9. In line 10 we finally hear of people. Are these the people whose houses are haunted by white nightgowns? How can you tell?
10. Stevens could have broken his lines differently:

People are not
Going to dream of baboons . . .

or:

People are not going to dream
Of baboons . . .

Can you think of why it was a good idea to break the line where Stevens broke it?
11. In this poem, baboons and periwinkles are examples that are parallel to other examples. What words in this poem are they parallel to? Why?
12. What is the relationship of the last four lines of the poem to the lines that came earlier?
13. Why is the sailor drunk? What is he doing? How do these details contrast with the main scene of the poem?
14. Someone has said that in this poem Stevens was eating his cake and having it too. Comment.
15. Frost's poem was written in metrical four-line stanzas. Williams's poem was tightly structured free verse. Characterize sound and rhythm in this poem, pointing out particular effects. Can you find assonance? Alliteration?

To find other poems by these poets, check the index.

Some bad poems

Before undertaking chapters that investigate the elements of poetry, let us move from studying good poems to glancing at two bad ones. Bad poems outnumber good poems. Poems can fail for technical reasons—trite language, boring rhythms, dull sounds, clumsy metaphors, sloppy images—but most bad poetry fails when technical ineptness combines with emotional dishonesty or sentimentality. To be good, a poem must tell the truth of feeling, and it must tell the whole of a complex feeling, not just a part of it. In Robert Frost's "Stopping by Woods on a Snowy Evening," the poet acknowledged contrary emotions: he wants to stay, he feels foolish staying, he must go on. The sentimental poet, denying the ambivalence of his feelings and wishing to strike a grand pose, might have declared to us that he would remain sitting in his wagon staring into these woods forever and ever and ever.

In asserting badness, as in asserting goodness, the critic cannot prove himself right as he might in a laboratory, by measurement. There is an older sense of "proof" that operates outside laboratories, the proof of argument or discussion leading to the agreement of reasonable people. This sort of proof begins with premises and proceeds to demonstrate whether a poem fulfills these premises. We begin with a premise that poems should tell the complex truth of feeling. Then we add another premise; we demand also that the poem be shapely and whole—a formal premise all good poems satisfy, whether metrical or free. Earlier in this chapter, we emphasized the first premise in discussing Frost, the second in discussing Williams.

In every age since the invention of the printing press there have been popular poets who outsold the best poets of their day, and who a generation later have gone unread. Although the poet Alfred, Lord Tennyson was enormously popular in Victorian England, he was outsold in his own lifetime by a pious rhymester named Martin Tupper. Robert Frost, the most popular *good* poet in American history, won the Pulitzer Prize four times, and supported himself by his successful poetry readings, but the best-selling poet in the United States during most of Frost's lifetime was Edgar A. Guest, whose most famous poem begins "It takes a heap o' livin' in a house t' make it home."

Here is the kind of poem that made Edgar Guest the most popular of American poets a couple of generations back:

The Rough Little Rascal

A smudge on his nose and a smear on his cheek
And knees that might not have been washed in a week;
A bump on his forehead, a scar on his lip,
A relic of many a tumble and trip:
A rough little, tough little rascal, but sweet,
Is he that each evening I'm eager to meet.

A brow that is beady with jewels of sweat;
A face that's as black as a visage can get;
A suit that at noon was a garment of white,

10   Now one that his mother declares is a fright:
      A fun-loving, sun-loving rascal, and fine,
      Is he that comes placing his black fist in mine.

      A crop of brown hair that is tousled and tossed;
      A waist from which two of the buttons are lost;
      A smile that shines out through the dirt and the grime,
      And eyes that are flashing delight all the time:
      All these are the joys that I'm eager to meet
      And look for the moment I get to my street.

Rascal is a cuddly sort of word that sets off a chain of **stock responses** (substitute emotions, which *resemble* emotions but cause neither thought nor true feeling; they stand in for true responses the way plastic sometimes stands in for wood). Guest uses clichés to elicit stock responses. A rough little rascal, we could know before we read a line, would have a smudge on his nose. *Tumble* is a cuddly word for fall—the kind of fall that never ruptures a spleen. The notion of sweet is already contained in the connotation of *rascal*, at least when *little* is added. The combination is sentimental, and the poem never approaches an emotion—only the stock imitation of emotion, which is what some readers want: the naïve reader finds his tritest associations fulfilled by the poem.

Rod McKuen tomorrow will look like Edgar A. Guest today. In *Listen to the Warm,* a volume of poems, the title poem is a series of poems addressed to a lover. Here is the first of the series:

      This is the way it was
      while I was waiting for your eyes
                        to find me.
      I was drifting
              going no place.
      Hypnotized by sunshine
                  maybe,
      barking back at seals along the beach.
      Skipping flat stones on the water,
10   but much too wise for sand castles.
      My castles were across the sea
      or still within my mind.

      There were the beach bars
      and the other beach people
      sometimes little bedrooms were my beach,
                  but I was drifting.

      I must have thought the night could save me
      as I went down into pillows
                  looked up through dirty windows
20   smiled back from broken mattresses
      turned in Thunderbirds
                  and kissed in elevators.

I cried too sometimes.
> For me.

I loved every face I thought looked pretty
and every kindred eye I caught in crowds.
> But I was drifting,
> > before you.

The first line is a cliché, *the way it was,* commonplace enough to be the title of a television series. Then, "I was drifting," says the poet. This word, *drifting,* was once a useful metaphor; if something drifts, it is compared to a boat set loose without the direction of a rudder. In poems we use words efficiently, and if the poet mentions drifting, a good reader knows that the poet refers to a boat. But "I was drifting" has become another cliché. If somehow the poet was able to identify himself as a boat in his poem—fulfilling the metaphor, using other boat words to make *drift* come alive again—"Cut loose from my pier, I drifted / without oars or rudder . . ."—the poet would *establish* himself as a boat, and *continue* the metaphor. A good poet fulfills his metaphors so that the comparison flows with feeling, develops and grows. A bad poet, on the other hand, using a **cliché** or **dead metaphor** (a dead metaphor has lost its power to make a comparison because of triteness or overuse) like "I was drifting" without knowing what he is doing, quickly uses another dead metaphor that cancels out the first—the way McKuen uses *hypnotized.* This next metaphor requires two people: *I,* the subject of hypnosis, and the hypnotist, who is identified here as sunshine. If we read the whole of the word, we are treated to the spectacle of sunshine dressed up in a hypnotist suit, speaking in soothing tones to a rowboat. Then the rowboat barks at seals from the middle of its trance.

Because we cannot take the words seriously, we have less a mixed metaphor than mere slackness of language—the kind of language that will speak of being "haunted by a memory" without realizing that it has spoken of ghosts or "the key to the problem" without understanding that keys need keyholes and that keys lock doors.

McKuen's poem goes on to talk about skipping stones on water, which is plain enough, and waits for another line before it becomes poetical again. The poet is, he tells us, "much too wise for sand castles." We are meant to understand *much* as self-mockery, the poet gently chiding himself for believing that he is not a child. This mild self-mockery is self-love, the poet looking with affection at his small foibles. And *sand castles* is another cliché, a trite symbol for daydreams.

There are many failures in this poem that the attentive reader can notice: clichés, slack rhythms, confused or unresolved metaphors, words that do not go together, and emotional deceit. See what you can find.

Chapter 2 **Poems Are Made of Words**

A poem is single, whole, and seamless, but to discuss it we need to treat it as if we could take it apart and examine elements as we can examine elements of a machine: this is a carburetor, which mixes air and fuel; this is a spark plug. . . . The parts of an internal-combustion engine, however, are genuinely separate; in a poem, you cannot detach rhythm from imagery except by paying attention to the one element rather than to the other; within the poem, rhythm and imagery are properties of the same words.

But before we concentrate on the elements of poetry, let us look at the medium of poetry, which is words. Many people assume that poetry's medium is emotions and ideas. Emotions and ideas exist *in* poems or *through* poems, and we must account for them in paraphrase when we explicate, but they are not poetry's medium. If we argued that emotions and ideas are poetry's medium, we would have to claim that trees and mountains are the medium of landscape painting. Canvas and paint make the painter's medium, and poems are made of words.

Reading poetry, we read words used with the greatest *energy* and *fixity*.

Fixity is the unique correctness and immovability of a word in its place. If you change almost any word in a long novel, you change the novel very little; if you change a word in a good poem, you change the poem considerably: "His house is in the hamlet though" would change Frost's poem by substituting *hamlet* for *village*. This fixity is partly a function of size, but not entirely; it is a measure of relative exactness in use. Poetry does not acknowledge synonyms.

Roget's Thesaurus and any other dictionary of synonyms list words that resemble each other in their meaning, but a poet makes poems by manipulating the small differences in meaning between synonyms; think of the differences between *hamlet* and *village,* or the many differences among *hide, conceal, cover up, secrete, screen, obscure, suppress, veil, disguise, camouflage, shroud. . . .*

Energy comes from the efficiency with which the poet uses language, and to repeat: Poems are made of words used efficiently. When I write this sentence, I sound like an engineer—and I want to. An efficient machine turns energy received into a nearly equal amount of energy put out. Sloppy language wastes energy, often by failing to say what it means; at best it uses more words than are necessary, three vague words in place of the precise one; "glazed with rain / water" is better than "covered all over with dampness as a result of precipitation." *Good poetry is the perfect machine of language.*

To use words most efficiently, the writer must be aware of their wholeness, aware of the dictionary senses of words or **denotations**, and of **connotations**— the associations you do not usually get from a dictionary. The poet uses the history of a word, its family, its origins, its associations. *Snow* carries "whiteness" with it, a connotation. Other connotations for snow include cold and winter. Further associations can become less universal and more particular. For a Northerner *snow* may include "skiing"; for a Sun Belt resident, *snow* may include the notion of travel. If the associations of *snow* include not only travel but a three-day drive in a Plymouth that uses too much oil, we have passed connotation to make a private association. Much connotation is public enough for use not only by poets and not only for literature. Real estate agents do not sell houses; they sell *homes,* which denotes the same buildings *houses* denotes but connotes comfort, warmth, and a dog sleeping in front of the fireplace. A *sanitation engineer* may do the same work a plumber used to do, but the title sounds more impressive. If poets use connotations to tell us honest feelings, politicians and lobbyists can use connotations for deceit. *Honorarium* sounds better than *payment, payment* better than *bribe.* All three words are heavy with connotation.

Concepts of denotation and connotation are useful, but we need to understand that they don't tell us everything. The *con*notation of *wheelbarrow* does not include its compoundness, revealed only when a poet splits it back into two words: *wheel barrow.* And when a word has different *de*notations, different dictionary meanings, the peripheral definitions of the word in the poem hover around the central ones.

Poets do not always use every potential meaning of a word. By their context they can employ some connotations or unused denotations and shut off others. Thomas Hardy's poem "During Wind and Rain" includes the line

How the sick leaves reel down in throngs.

A dictionary may tell us that to reel is to be thrown off balance, to stagger, to move in a circle, to dance a reel, or to pull in a fishing line. In the context of the poem, not every meaning becomes active. When the word before *leaves* is *sick,* then *reel* as in "stagger"—like a sick person too weak to walk—becomes strengthened by context. Earlier in this poem, the poet speaks of music: "They sing their dearest songs . . . / Treble and tenor and bass / And one to play . . . ," and although the songs may be hymns or folk songs, the "dance" part of *reel* shows signs of life. (All of these meanings are related: *reel* started by meaning a kind of spool and evolved into all sorts of circular motions.) Connotations interweave, and peripheral denotations act like connotations. In this poem's context, the stagger-meaning is foremost, the dance-meaning acts like a strong connotation, and the fishing-meaning hovers unused in the distance. If a reader on first glancing at this line thought of *reel* as fishing reel, the line would remain obscure until the reader looked for another denotation of *reel.*

When leaves are compared to dancers, the poet has made a metaphor. And here we should mention one other matter connecting word and metaphor. Many readers leap to interpret a word as metaphor when the poet has used it literally. The insistence on the fanciful, at the expense of the plain, is a common source of misreading. Edwin Arlington Robinson begins a stanza about a dying man

Blind, with but a wandering hour to live . . .

Many readers see the word *blind* and think that Robinson means "obtuse" in the common metaphorical use of the word—as in "Egad, sir, are you *blind?*" But the rest of the stanza reveals that the man is sightless. Readers who hold onto the "obtuse" meaning find the poem highly obscure. It is wise to remember a rule of thumb: take poems literally until they make you take them figuratively. "Sightless" is the denotation of the word *blind. Blind* has meant "sightless" for a long time; the first citation in the *Oxford English Dictionary* (that wonderful, enormous dictionary that quotes words in contexts as they change over history) is dated A.D. 1000. And the first citation of *blind* as "obtuse" is also A.D. 1000, the metaphorical use as ancient as the literal.

Reading old poems, we need the *OED* to let us know how poets used words— efficiently, with energy and fixity—in their own times, for words change. When the eighteenth-century poet Alexander Pope spoke of *science* he did not mean physics or chemistry but knowledge in general; our word *science* comes from *scio,* Latin for "I know," which becomes a part of the participle *knowing* and then the noun *knowledge.*

Reading new poems, we can use the *OED* also, because many poets—seeking the energy that comes from using words in their wholeness—refer by their context to a word's history, its old or original meanings. Richard Wilbur is a contemporary American who likes to play with **etymology**, the study of word origins and history. In his poem "Lamarck Elaborated" he pretends to believe genetic theories which say that genes transmit acquired characteristics.* The theory is untrue, but with his imagination Wilbur tries out a world where the

---

*French naturalist Jean Baptiste Pierre Antoine de Monet, Chevalier de Lamarck (1744–1829). His flawed theory of evolution was nevertheless an important forerunner of the work of Charles Darwin.

things of the world created our bodies. The sun, for instance, made our eyes. Wilbur writes a stanza of complicated wordplay:

> The yielding water, the repugnant stone,
> The poisoned berry and the flaring rose
> Attired in sense the tactless finger-bone
> And set the taste-buds and inspired the nose.

Paraphrased, the stanza says that we acquired touch, taste, and smell by acts of touching, tasting, and smelling. Water, which gives to the touch, and stone, which doesn't—which pushes it back, which is what *repugnant* means—*attired* (clothed) *in sense* (in our senses) *the finger-bone,* which had formerly been clumsy or without tact; *tact* comes from the word for "touch," as in *tactile,* so *tactless* by etymology means "untouching": before it was clothed in sensation, the finger-bone was without touch. The *berry* that poisons us, which we distinguish by taste, *sets* our taste buds, the way a gardener sets out plants. The flaring rose (flared like a nostril to smell) *inspired* our noses. *Inspired* in one common usage means "invented"—"Monday Night Football was the inspiration of Roone Arledge"—but actually comes from a Latin word that means "to breathe in."

Here are a few poems—with questions intended to sharpen your sensitivity to the manipulation of words.

Hogwash

> The tongue that mothered such a metaphor
> Only the purest purist could despair of.
>
> Nobody ever called swill sweet but isn't
> Hogwash a daisy in a field of daisies?
>
> What beside sports and flowers could you find
> To praise better than the American language?
>
> Bruised by American foreign policy
> What shall I soothe me, what defend me with
>
> But a handful of clean unmistakable words—
> Daisies, daisies, in a field of daisies?
>   —*Robert Francis**

10

*See page 268 for a note about Robert Francis. Brief biographical notes on poets whose work is included in this book precede their poems in "A Gathering of Poems," which begins on page 165. For rapid location of dates and other information about any author represented in this volume, look for the italicized page number following the entry for his or her name in the index.

Questions

1. In the first line, what happens if you remove *mothered* and substitute "fathered?" "conjured"? "created"? "gathered"? "mounted"? "built up"? "constructed"? What are the associations of *mothered* and of the substitute words?
2. How does the word *swill* find its way into this poem? Would "junk" be just as good? "Garbage"?
3. Look up the word *daisy* to check on its ancestry. What are the insides of *daisy*? If you used "tulip," how would its different history match the rest of the poem? Is *daisy* better for this poem, or just different? If the word were "flower," would the poem be less than it is?
4. Does *defend,* in its associations, relate to other words in this poem?
5. In the last stanza, what sort of *handful* would you have if your hand were full of words? A handful of swill? What does the poet compare words to?

During Wind and Rain

They sing their dearest songs—
He, she, all of them—yea,
Treble and tenor and bass,
    And one to play;
With the candles mooning each face. . . .
    Ah, no; the years O!
How the sick leaves reel down in throngs!

They clear the creeping moss—
Elders and juniors—aye,
Making the pathway neat
    And the garden gay;
And they build a shady seat. . . .
    Ah, no; the years, the years;
See, the white storm-birds wing across!

They are blithely breakfasting all—
Men and maidens—yea,
Under the summer tree,
    With a glimpse of the bay,
While pet fowl come to the knee. . . .
    Ah, no; the years O!
And the rotten rose is ript from the wall.

They change to a high new house,
He, she, all of them—aye,
Clocks and carpets and chairs
    On the lawn all day,
And brightest things that are theirs. . . .
    Ah, no; the years, the years;
Down their carved names the rain-drop ploughs.
                     —*Thomas Hardy*

Questions

1. Consider the associations of *creeping*. Which are used? Which unused? Does the word make a comparison?
2. In line 21, Hardy uses the word *ript*. Substitute *pulled* and consider the differences. Substitute "descends" for *is ript*. Discuss the differing associations of the words. Discuss the differing grammar.
3. In line 22, try these substitutes for *high*: "tall," "white," "brand," "dark," and "low." Is difference in image a difference in value?
4. The last word of the poem is *ploughs*. How do its denotation, connotations, sound, and grammar—the whole word, family associations and all—contribute to this poem? Does the whole word *conclude* the poem?

Silence

My father used to say,
"Superior people never make long visits,
have to be shown Longfellow's grave
or the glass flowers at Harvard.
Self-reliant like the cat—
that takes its prey to privacy,
the mouse's limp tail hanging like a shoelace from its mouth—
they sometimes enjoy solitude,
and can be robbed of speech
10   by speech which has delighted them.
The deepest feeling always shows itself in silence;
not in silence, but restraint."
Nor was he insincere in saying, "Make my house your inn."
Inns are not residences.

—Marianne Moore

Questions

1. In the second line, the poet uses the word *superior*. Make a list of words that might be considered synonyms and that would make sense in this context. Discuss the difference each substitution would make to the poem.
2. Longfellow's grave is in Cambridge, Massachusetts, a city that also contains Harvard University, which shows in a museum some remarkably realistic glass reproductions of flowers—a favorite stop for tourists. What is the connection of the sentence containing these objects with the sentences that make the rest of this poem? In lines 3 and 4, what words provide the implicit connection?
3. In this poem, where does the idea of silence enter, after the title?
4. What do you make of this cat? Have you known cats who liked to show off their prey, who are not reticent at all? If you have, does the knowledge bother you in reading this poem? Do you feel that the cat somehow seems more important to the poem than its use as an illustrative simile could warrant? How?
5. How does the author show that although *Superior people* enjoy being by themselves, they are equipped to encounter others?

6. "Not in silence, but restraint." What is the difference? Why does the author say one thing and then correct it? What is the effect of using two words instead of one?
7. The last two lines make a distinction by means of definitions. How does this verbal contrast grow out of earlier lines of the poem?

When President John F. Kennedy was inaugurated in 1961, he invited Robert Frost to read a poem as part of the ceremony. Frost recited this poem, which he had written years before.

The Gift Outright

The land was ours before we were the land's.
She was our land more than a hundred years
Before we were her people. She was ours
In Massachusetts, in Virginia,
But we were England's, still colonials,
Possessing what we still were unpossessed by,
Possessed by what we now no more possessed.
Something we were withholding made us weak
Until we found out that it was ourselves
10   We were withholding from our land of living,
And forthwith found salvation in surrender.
Such as we were we gave ourselves outright
(The deed of gift was many deeds of war)
To the land vaguely realizing westward,
But still unstoried, artless, unenhanced,
Such as she was, such as she would become.

Questions

1. Or Frost almost recited it. For the next to last word he said *will* instead of *would*. How did this alter the meaning of the poem?
2. Distinguish different sorts of possession. Why does Frost use the same word when the reader must learn to distinguish different meanings for it? What allows you to find different meanings for one word in a single poem?
3. What sort of a phrase is *salvation in surrender*?
4. Does *realize* usually take an object? Does it here? How does the grammar help to define this use of the word?
5. Notice the many balances throughout the poem. List them.

Here's an old poem, written during Queen Elizabeth's reign, with its spelling modernized. Ben Jonson was a great playwright, a rival and friend of Shakespeare. He wrote on the death of his firstborn son.

On My First Son

Farewell, thou child of my right hand, and joy;
My sin was too much hope of thee, loved boy.
Seven years thou wert lent to me, and I thee pay,
Exacted by thy fate, on the just day.
O, could I lose all father now. For why
Will man lament the state he should envy?
To have so soon 'scaped° world's, and flesh's, rage,   escaped
And if no other misery, yet age?
Rest in soft peace, and, asked, say here doth lie
10   Ben Jonson, his° best piece of poetry.   Jonson's
For whose sake, henceforth, all his vows be such,
As what he loves may never like too much.

Questions

1. In the third line Jonson's word order puts *I* next to *thee*, which we would not do. *Thee* is the object of *pay*, and we would say "And I pay thee" or "And I pay you." In what sense is *pay* used?
2. How can Jonson call the day *just*? What other words—or what ideas carried by what words—support *just*?
3. How would you paraphrase *all father*?
4. Look up the word *poetry* in an etymological dictionary. How can Jonson use the word to stand in for his son?
5. The poem works by a series of contrasted words. What does *lament* contrast with? *rage*? *world's*?
6. Describe the contrast in the last line.

Chapter 3 **Images**

An **image** is language that speaks to our senses, recording a sensuous experience. Poetry abounds in visual images, directed to the sense of sight, like "white chickens" or ". . . woods fill up with snow." Poetry also includes images of touch, taste, smell, and hearing. Hot-and-cold is tactile, a form of touch; here is a poem made of images for heat:

Heat

O wind, rend open the heat,
cut apart the heat,
rend it to tatters.

Fruit cannot drop
through this thick air—
fruit cannot fall into heat
that presses up and blunts
the points of pears
and rounds the grapes.

10   Cut the heat—
plough through it,
turning it on either side
of your path.

               —H.D.

The American poet H.D. (Hilda Doolittle) was one of the Imagist poets, a group dedicated to writing vivid and precise natural description. When H.D. asks the wind to *rend open the heat*, she gives the invisible heat a bulk that can be *cut apart*, therefore making an image of heat as something thick, substantial. Then she tells us how bulky it is: "Fruit cannot drop / through this thick air." These lines imply a natural scene with fruit trees, and air so heavy that even a falling apple cannot penetrate it. H.D. communicates feeling through exaggeration; she does not merely render like a snapshot. She describes the heat not as an inert thing but as a pressure, antigravitational and upward, blunting the pears that would otherwise be sharp-angled; heat acts by its constant pressure to make grapes round. Then the poet ends her poem by returning implicitly to the wind for help—meteorological reality, because breezes blow away hot air—and when she asks the wind to become a plow, she again evokes the thickness, weight, and density of the heat, comparing it to earth a plow turns.

Images of touch like H.D.'s are not as common as visual images. Here's an old poem in which a male poet describes the appearance of a woman:

Upon Julia's Clothes

Whenas in silks my Julia goes,
Then, then, methinks, how sweetly flows
That liquefaction of her clothes.

Next, when I cast mine eyes, and see
That brave vibration, each way free,
O, how that glittering taketh me!
                    —*Robert Herrick*

Herrick describes something seen, and his images are visual. We are invited to *see* Julia in motion wearing a silk dress. We don't know the color of the silk, and we know nothing of Julia's appearance except for her dress. We have the watery image of *flows* and *liquefaction*, and later her sway from side to side and the silk's glitter. The poem gives us only a partial picture of Julia, but we feel Herrick's whole delight: the visual images embody Herrick's feeling.

Poets use images to embody feelings; they use images instead of abstract explanations. Here's a poem by Allen Ginsberg:

First Party at Ken Kesey's with Hell's Angels

Cool black night thru redwoods
cars parked outside in shade
behind the gate, stars dim above
the ravine, a fire burning by the side
porch and a few tired souls hunched over
in black leather jackets. In the huge
wooden house, a yellow chandelier
at 3 a.m. the blast of loudspeakers
hi-fi Rolling Stones Ray Charles Beatles

10   Jumping Joe Jackson and twenty youths
    dancing to the vibration thru the floor,
    a little weed in the bathroom, girls in scarlet
    tights, one muscular smooth skinned man
    sweating dancing for hours, beer cans
    bent littering the yard, a hanged man
    sculpture dangling from a high creek branch,
    children sleeping softly in bedroom bunks,
    And 4 police cars parked outside the painted
    gate, red lights revolving in the leaves.

The poem starts with a word of skin-feelings, *cool*, and ends with a compelling visual image. With the phrases *cool black*, *shade, stars dim*, and *fire burning*, Ginsberg sets a scene of contrasts. Then the poet speaks of *souls hunched over*, and we feel a tiredness. Next in the poem we have an image of sound, then dancing; the dancing comes as a visual image, but the word's associations contain muscular feeling as well. Then the poem leads us through everything seen, in a list of images—litter, a sculpture, children sleeping—with a cinematic effect, as if a camera panned slowly over a static scene, recording frame after frame of reality. Finally the camera settles on the ominous image of the police cars with lights revolving. The poem's effect comes entirely from its images; there is no commentary at all.

The reader is *shown*: he is not *told*. Modern poets usually avoid abstract language, using concrete details instead. At the end of this poem, Ginsberg might have written about fear or apprehensiveness or dread or ominousness. Using instead the images *police cars parked* and *red lights revolving*, he communicates feeling directly; abstractions would have communicated the *names* of feelings, or *ideas* about feelings, not the feelings themselves.

H.D.'s heat was tactile, using images of touch. Ginsberg's poem is mostly visual but also uses images of touch and hearing. When Robert Frost, in "Stopping by Woods on a Snowy Evening," wrote about "the sweep / Of easy wind . . ." he used an image of sound. Poets use images of smell more rarely—"the acrid odor of maple"—and also images of taste: when Keats longs for wine, he calls it "a draught of vintage that hath been / Cool'd a long time . . ."; he appeals to the touch-sense of the tongue, or taste.

All these images describe real things, and these poems come from the world we live in. Here are more poems of our world, with questions that mostly call attention to their images.

Nantucket

    Flowers through the window
    lavender and yellow

    changed by white curtains—
    Smell of cleanliness—

    Sunshine of late afternoon—
    On the glass tray

a glass pitcher, the tumbler
turned down, by which

a key is lying—And the
10   immaculate white bed
        —*William Carlos Williams*

Questions
1. Most of these images are visual. Is there an exception?
2. Is *changed* an image? Is it an idea?
3. Do these images carry feeling? Can you name the feeling?
4. Can you paraphrase this poem for its ideas?

Gary Soto is a young Chicano poet who grew up working in the fields of the San Joaquin Valley in California. He uses images from his experience as a farm worker. This poem comes from a sequence called "The Elements of San Joaquin":

Sun

In June the sun is a bonnet of light
Coming up,
Little by little,
From behind a skyline of pine.

The pastures sway with fiddle-neck
Tassels of foxtail.

At Piedra
A couple fish on the river's edge,
Their shadows deep against the water.
10   Above, in the stubbled slopes,
Cows climb down
As the heat rises
In a mist of blond locusts,
Returning to the valley.

Questions
1. Compare this poem with H.D.'s "Heat," p. 25.
2. Distinguish the different senses Soto's images appeal to.
3. What kind of action lies behind *sway* and connects it with *fiddle-neck*? What does the poet compare the foxtail to?

Denise Levertov is an American poet who takes great pleasure in observation of the world outside. Sight and sound, coolness and soot from chimneys.

The World Outside

i

On the kitchen wall a flash
of shadow:
                    swift pilgrimage
of pigeons, a spiral
celebration of air, of sky-deserts.
And on tenement windows
a blaze
            of lustred watermelon:
stain of the sun
10   westering somewhere back of Hoboken.

ii

The goatherd upstairs! Music
from his sweet flute
roves from summer to summer
in the dusty air of airshafts
and among the flakes
of soot that float
in a daze from chimney
to chimney—notes
remote, cool, speaking of slender
20   shadows under olive-leaves. A silence.

iii

Groans, sighs, in profusion,
with coughing, muttering, orchestrate
solitary grief; the crash of glass, a low voice
repeating over and over, 'No.
    No. I want my key. No you did not.
    No.'—a commonplace.
And in counterpoint, from other windows,
the effort to be merry—ay, maracas!
—sibilant, intricate—the voices wailing pleasure,
30   arriving perhaps at joy, late, after sets
have been switched off, and silences
are dark windows?

Questions

1. How many images can you find in this poem, appealing to how many senses?
2. When the poet says *pilgrimage*, what world does she enter? Is it figurative or literal? What other words go with *pilgrimage*?
3. Is there any sort of connection between "a blaze / of . . . watermelon" and "notes / remote, cool . . ."?

We have been reading poems that describe realities. Allen Ginsberg's dancers and police cars are really there—we accept his word for it. Herrick's Julia wears silk clothing. H.D.'s poem exaggerates, but it does not invent a bizarre world. William Carlos Williams, Gary Soto, and Denise Levertov describe an objective world in language that specifies the way they take it in.

But some poems use fantastic images to create worlds previously uncreated, as if the poet were recounting a dream. Here's a dreamy poem by Gregory Crr called "Washing My Face":

> Last night's dreams disappear.
> They are like the sink draining:
> a transparent rose swallowed by its stem.

The last image conjures up something imaginary—*a transparent rose*. Because we know what roses look like, and because we know what transparency means, we can assemble these words into an image of a transparent rose. Then we understand that the transparent rose resembles the water in the washstand, when we wash our faces at waking, making a swirling shape like petals as it disappears down the drain. The tenuousness of last night's dreams makes *transparent* feel right; the pleasant word *rose* implies that these disappearing dreams were happy ones.

Many contemporary Americans write poems that include realistic as well as fantastic images. These poems may move back and forth from one sort of concrete detail to another, from the seen to the dreamed and back again. James Wright wrote many poems that combined the two ways of seeing—looking out and looking in. Here is one:

Lying in a Hammock at William Duffy's Farm in Pine Island, Minnesota

> Over my head, I see the bronze butterfly,
> Asleep on the black trunk,
> Blowing like a leaf in green shadow.
> Down the ravine behind the empty house,
> The cowbells follow one another
> Into the distances of the afternoon.
> To my right,
> In a field of sunlight between two pines,
> The droppings of last year's horses
> 10 Blaze up into golden stones.
> I lean back, as the evening darkens and comes on.
> A chicken hawk floats over, looking for home.
> I have wasted my life.

The first time one reads the poem, the last line is a shock. Some people feel that the last line is not earned, that it comes out of nowhere, that the poem fails because of a trick ending. Other readers report that although they are shocked by the ending, it feels right. The issue is whether the last line grows naturally out of what goes before. Granted that it is a surprise, is it a cheap surprise or is it a surprise that leads to clear understanding?

Look back at what the poet sees, as he lies in the hammock at William Duffy's farm in Pine Island, Minnesota. Notice the lethargy and passivity, not only of lying in a hammock but also of the many enclosures of space—in a hammock, which is on a farm, which is in a town, which is named after an island, which is in a state. There are many layers to this cocoon.

First the poet sees a butterfly colored bronze. But bronze is not only a color; it is a metal, and if a butterfly were bronze it would be permanent and inorganic. One of the connotations of *butterfly*, on the other hand, is the fragility of a brief life. In the phrase *bronze butterfly*, fantastic when we think of the metal bronze, we find the paradox of evanescence and solidity, change and permanence. We also see the color of bronze in contrast to the tree trunk's color, and then we see the butterfly move, "Blowing like a leaf in green shadow," as if its fragility returned quickly and the vision of permanence were brief. In the dream world images can change quickly. The first three lines give us an extended image of clear contrasting colors—and contrasting senses of permanence and change. In the next three lines we cannot see the cows but, hearing the cowbells, we can visualize the ravine where they walk. Some of these words carry feeling without carrying images. "Into the distances of the afternoon" is not a visual image, nor is it addressed to any other sense, but the line takes the cows away from us, and the increasing distance—together with the emptiness of the house in the line before—introduces loneliness. The next four lines give us another scene and an absence of horses. We begin to realize that most things in this poem are gone. The horses have left behind only their manure.

In this poem, nothing goes down but what it must come up; nothing comes up but what it must go down. Any perception calls forth its opposite; if a butterfly is bronze it is also moving in the wind. Even when the poet talks of the cowbells (more frail and distant than cows) he has them *follow one another* (which is warm and companionable) *into the distances*, which is far, lonely, and separate. Now, like a playwright keeping our attention with dramatic contrast, the poet has built to something glorious—and shocks us with horse manure; then he shocks us again by making horse manure glorious: it blazes up "into golden stones," an image of fantasy. The more we look at these words, the more we realize the complications of feeling that control them. The poem is not intellectually complex; it is complex in feeling, an emotional density embodied in images.

In the next line, the poet at first departs from imaging the world around him, and says *I lean back* as if in passive withdrawal. Then he observes the world again, *as the evening darkens and comes on.* This is not the absence of light but the gathering of darkness, something coming close to him as everything else leaves. Loneliness slides toward something more desperate, and the poet writes the line that brings everything together. The next-to-last line is the climax of the poem and the skeleton key to the feelings of the poem: "A chicken hawk floats over, looking for home." In the mind of this lonely speaker, the bird is going home; even this predator, killer of the homely chicken, has a home to look for. By implication of the whole poem, and especially of the last line, the speaker does not have a home to go to. Instead, he lies in a hammock on somebody else's farm, and everything he looks at reminds him of his solitude and his unworthiness. We sense that wherever the poet looks in the landscape, he cannot help but see his own troubles.

Once you have understood the psychological state of the poem's speaker, its images make their melancholy point. At first sight, the butterfly was transformed into solidity and value—the speaker *wants* his life to change—then it becomes fragile and transitory again; but it remains beautiful in its sleep, as he does not in his passivity. The *empty house* is the home the speaker is exiled from, as he is exiled from cows' company. Wherever the cowbells move, we know that eventually in the afternoon the cows will go home to be milked; the bells remind us of a destination. While the speaker remains static, passive, unchanging, even horse droppings are glorified! All the speaker can think to do, under the ominous pressure of darkness, is give up.

Try reading another poem by James Wright and following the track of its different images.

A Blessing

Just off the highway to Rochester, Minnesota,
Twilight bounds softly forth on the grass.
And the eyes of those two Indian ponies
Darken with kindness.
They have come gladly out of the willows
To welcome my friend and me.
We step over the barbed wire into the pasture
Where they have been grazing all day, alone.
They ripple tensely, they can hardly contain their happiness
10   That we have come.
They bow shyly as wet swans. They love each other.
There is no loneliness like theirs.
At home once more,
They begin munching the young tufts of spring in the darkness.
I would like to hold the slenderer one in my arms,
For she has walked over to me
And nuzzled my left hand.
She is black and white,
Her mane falls wild on her forehead,
20   And the light breeze moves me to caress her long ear
That is delicate as the skin over a girl's wrist.
Suddenly I realize
That if I stepped out of my body I would break
Into blossom.

Questions

1. Which images describe a real world? Which are fantastic? Interpret the fantastic images.

2. Why is it appropriate that there be two ponies, instead of one or three?
3. In the second line, is the verb *bounds* an image? What sense does it bring you?
4. The poet puts together two sentences—"They love each other. There is no loneliness like theirs"—that would not normally seem to go together. Can you defend the juxtaposition?
5. Analyze the image *young tufts of spring*.

Other poetry goes further into fantasy than James Wright's. Sometimes a poet will use wholly bizarre images—without even the connection of rose to washbasin, or horse droppings to gold—to tell the truth of feeling. Chilean poet Pablo Neruda received the gift of a pair of socks hand-knitted by a peasant woman. He was pleased at this tribute, and wrote a poem that embodied his pleasure. Robert Bly translated it from the Spanish.

Ode to My Socks

Maru Mori brought me
a pair
of socks
which she knitted herself
with her sheep-herder's hands,
two socks as soft
as rabbits.
I slipped my feet
into them
10 as though into
two
cases
knitted
with threads of
twilight
and goatskin.
Violent socks,
my feet were
two fish made
20 of wool,
two long sharks
seablue, shot
through
by one golden thread,
two immense blackbirds,
two cannons,
my feet
were honored
in this way
30 by
these

heavenly
socks.
They were
so handsome
for the first time
my feet seemed to me
unacceptable
like two decrepit
40 firemen, firemen
unworthy
of that woven
fire,
of those glowing
socks.

Nevertheless
I resisted
the sharp temptation
to save them somewhere
50 as schoolboys
keep
fireflies,
as learned men
collect
sacred texts,
I resisted
the mad impulse
to put them
in a golden
60 cage
and each day give them
birdseed
and pieces of pink melon.
Like explorers
in the jungle who hand
over the very rare
green deer
to the spit
and eat it
70 with remorse,
I stretched out
my feet
and pulled on
the magnificent
socks
and then my shoes.

The moral
of my ode is this:
beauty is twice
80 beauty

and what is good is doubly
good
when it is a matter of two socks
made of wool
in winter.

Questions

1. When Neruda writes that he "resisted / the mad impulse / to put them / in a golden / cage . . . ," is he using an image to describe the socks? Did this help you know what they look like? If an image does not describe an object, what else can it describe?
2. In rapid succession, Neruda says that his feet were "two fish made / of wool," "two long sharks," "two immense blackbirds," and "two cannons." What does this do to advice about trying to take poems literally?
3. Find other examples of the fantastic image in this poem and interpret them.
4. Contrast:

Dear Maru Mori,
    Thank you ever so much for your kind gift of a pair of socks. They are very pretty. They are warm. They fit me perfectly. I will wear them all the time. Mrs. Neruda likes them too. Thank you again.

                                                Yours truly,
                                              Pablo Neruda

Chapter 4 **Figures of Speech, Especially Metaphors**

Figures of speech are extraordinary, original, nonliteral uses of language, common to lively speech and literature. It would be literal to say "She walked slowly across the field." To say "She walked across the field as slowly as a snail with a pulled muscle" uses a figure of speech; this figure is **simile**, which makes an explicit comparison using *like* or *as* or a verb like *seems* or *appears*. A **metaphor** resembles a simile by talking about one thing in terms of another, but a metaphor's comparison is implicit; it does not use *like* or *as, seems* or *appears:* "She snailed her painful way across the field." Poems abound in metaphors. This chapter deals mainly with metaphors and similes; at the end we will mention a few other figures of speech.

Here is another poem by Gregory Orr that uses simile:

All Morning

> All morning the dream lingers.
> I am like thick grass
> in a meadow, still
> soaked with dew at noon.

The poet compares himself to grass, declaring that he shares a quality with it. The simile works through a visual image—we *see* grass soaked with dew—but it is not the picture that does the comparing: a set of relationships makes the comparison work. This simile, like many, can be expressed as an equation: dew is to grass as dreams are to me. The comparison *states* that my dreams

36

remain with me for a while, the way dew clings to a blade of grass. Besides this statement there are two implications to the simile: eventually the dream/dew will vanish/evaporate; because dew brings nourishment to grass, dreaming has value for me.

If we omitted *like* from Orr's poem, we would have:

> All morning the dream lingers.
> I am thick grass
> in a meadow, still
> soaked with dew at noon.

The last three lines would make not a simile but a metaphor. The terms compared—*I* to *thick grass,* dreams to persistent dew—would remain the same, but the manner of the comparison would change. The reader is led by the simile: "I am *like* thick grass"; when the line becomes "I am thick grass," the guiding hand disappears and the reader may not know where to go.

Often metaphor is more powerful than simile. Apparently it is older and more primitive, and derives from "primary process thinking," as psychologists describe it, in which dissimilar things are perceived as identical. Metaphor is the poetic mode of thought, flying across barriers of logic to assert identities. When a small child speaks of the leg of a table or the hand of a clock, he or she perceives a flesh-and-blood leg and a hand; the table in his language has power to walk, the clock to gesture and to point. For the child, such metaphors are alive; for the adult they are dead. When the adult mind thinks in metaphor, it regains lost power misplaced in the pursuit of maturity.

All language began as metaphor, and in many of our words is buried an image that unites dissimilar things: a daisy was once a day's eye. In casual speech we use continual **personification** (a figure of speech by which we humanize the nonhuman): clouds frown, fires rage, distant mountains glower, meadows look cheerful, zippers prove recalcitrant, the sun smiles, and the horizon looks inviting.

Metaphors in poems often happen quickly; we are moved without knowing what has touched us; unless we are explicating, we do not even notice that the poet has used metaphor. One of Robert Frost's best poems, "To Earthward" (p. 145), begins by saying that when he was young feelings came easily; a tiny stimulus produced a strong response: "The petal of the rose," he says, "It was that stung." We understand *stung* as "gave pain" with the consciousness that this pain derives from pleasure too exquisite; the pang of beauty is overwhelming and therefore painful. If we think about it, *stung* is a metaphor, because a rose does not ordinarily sting anything. What stings us? A thorn pricks, but it does not sting. When Frost writes "The petal of the rose / It was that stung," he compares the soft petal of a flower to the harsh sting of a bee. Metaphors work by contrast as well as by comparison; things compared in a metaphor must be unlike, and the poet makes them alike. Usually difference affects us more than similarity; when a poet compares the seemingly incomparable he wins us with energy of resolved contrast.

It is easy to see how *sting* and *petal* contrast. But how do they come together? A bee—never named, yet part of the connotations of *sting*—belongs in a garden. A poem often finds its metaphors within an area, and Frost's poem moves among flowers and gardens for its images and metaphors. Bees work in gardens for pollen. If Frost had substituted for *stung* an image of a dentist's office— "The petal of the rose / It was that drilled"—we would not have been able to follow him in his feeling. Coherence of metaphor makes Frost's words operate upon us, even if we do not know that we are operated upon. Coherence of *rose* and *stung,* by way of an unstated bee, develops the metaphor.

Many metaphors in poetry work almost subliminally, like Frost's *stung,* but we also find extended metaphors. In the following poem, William Shakespeare starts by asking if he might make a comparison:

> Shall I compare thee to a summer's day?
> Thou art more lovely and more temperate:
> Rough winds do shake the darling buds of May,
> And summer's lease hath all too short a date.
> Sometime too hot the eye of heaven shines,
> And often is his gold complexion dimm'd;
> And every fair° from fair sometime declines,   beautiful thing
> By chance or nature's changing course untrimm'd.
> But thy eternal summer shall not fade
10 > Nor lose possession of that fair thou ow'st.   ownest: possess
> Nor shall Death brag thou wand'rest in his shade,
> When in eternal lines to time thou grow'st;
>> So long as men can breathe or eyes can see,
>> So long lives this and this gives life to thee.

This poem follows the common poetic form of the **sonnet,** fourteen lines of rhymed iambic pentameter (see pages 75, 88–90). In the course of his fourteen lines, Shakespeare compares relentlessly, always to the effect that A is greater than B. No, you are not like a summer's day, you are better. To prove his conclusion, he compares parts of wholes. He breaks a summer's day down into weather, temperature, and temperament. Weather is more changeable than you are; you remain the same as the weather does not. Even in May, when blossoms begin to show, the weather can be unpleasant—but not you. Summer is a tenant who has rented an estate for a short time only (Shakespeare's sonnets and plays are full of legal and financial metaphor) but your tenancy of beauty is longer than a mere summer. Notice that by the fourth line Shakespeare has established his comparison of *thee* and *summer* so thoroughly that he can introduce the further metaphor of tenancy without confusion.

If summer leases, summer resembles a human being. The fifth line introduces another personification, when we hear of *the eye of heaven,* and we identify the *eye* with the sun when we hear that this eye *shines.* Having established the sun, without speaking of it directly, Shakespeare describes *his gold complexion,* as if the yellow sun had skin, and makes a cloudy day the sun's loss. In contrast his love is never lessened or dimmed. Notice how the connotations of precious metal work to flatter the day, and thus flatter the love that is greater than the day.

The first eight lines of the poem—the **octave** of a sonnet—carry out its implications. The **sestet**—the sonnet's last six lines—expands upon the unchanging quality of the love and ends by praising itself. Death shall not brag of keeping this person-summer's day in shade, because these lines of poetry give eternal life. Shakespeare is able to bring Death into his metaphor, because shade treats sun as death treats life.

Shakespeare's poem extends a series of linked metaphors through fourteen lines. Here is another example of a single-word metaphor, like Frost's *stung,* which I use in order to move on to another subject. At the end of "During Wind and Rain" (page 21), Thomas Hardy writes:

> Down their carved names the rain-drop ploughs.

A plow is a natural object in the rural scene of this poem—and thus belongs in this poem's metaphorical area—but this is not a literal plow; metaphor turns a raindrop into an agricultural implement: raindrop is to gravestone as plow is to earth. The metaphor of *ploughs* has implications central to the poem: if raindrop acts on granite as plow on meadow, by implication many years have passed. If, however, we read the line lazily, taking *ploughs* as if it meant "moves vigorously forward"—as in a dead metaphor like "the fullback plows through the line" or "the tugboat plows through the waves"—nothing happens at all.

We constantly use figures of speech that once enjoyed freshness and vitality but that we no longer hear as figures of speech. Declaring we feel immovable, we say "I am glued to my chair." If we picture what we have said, we have a comical scene. But with dead metaphors, neither speaker nor hearer pictures anything at all. In a dead metaphor, the old comparison or assertion of identity is what is dead. If we did not say that we were glued to the chair, we might have said that we were anchored to the spot and no one would see the old schooner in the harbor, its anchor played out behind it, caught in the coral of the harbor bottom. For that matter, "dead metaphor" is a dead metaphor; and if I say that the old comparison is buried, I make the same morbid assertion. Once these metaphors were alive; now they are decayed corpses. The first time anyone used the metaphor of "dead metaphor," he implied that a hole had been dug—six feet deep, six feet long, three feet across—in the dirt of the phrase, and that somebody had placed the body of a comparison in this hole and heaped dirt over the body.

Live metaphors embody feelings. Dead metaphors embody stock responses, clichés, and lethargy. Bad poetry uses dead metaphors as commonly as we do in speech. Good poetry invents new metaphors, making vivid comparisons.

People often even mix their dead metaphors. "Then the hand of God stepped in . . . " makes a wonderful anatomical mixture. Of course *the hand of God* was used as if it meant "fortuitous circumstance," and *stepped in* as if it meant "happened next." When I first taught writing, one of my students wrote in a poem "The door yawned and beckoned." By *yawned* she meant that it opened, by *beckoned* that it looked inviting. But the two dead metaphors together made an impossible anatomy again, in which a door was an open mouth from which a hand suddenly extended. (Journalists as well as poets are experts at mixing dead metaphors. Take this example: "Mushrooming insurance and energy costs represent a double-barreled shotgun pointed at New England's ski areas." The writer of this sentence developed the ability *not* to see, or the writer could not have turned a soft vegetable into a steel weapon.)

Forming the habit of taking things literally, a reader becomes increasingly sensitive to language. Reading literally, we do not read the word *blind* automatically as if it meant "obtuse"—which is to use *blind* as a dead metaphor. When we read *blind*, we take it to mean "sightless" until we find out otherwise. Then we do not write a sentence like this one recently printed in a country weekly: " 'American optometrists are blind to the advantages of small town living,' said Dr. Harvey Bagnold to the Rotary Club last Tuesday."

Taking words as literally as possible—until the poem forces us to understand that we are reading a metaphor—we read the metaphor that is there. When Hamlet talks about his problems, he says that one possibility is to "take arms against a sea of troubles." The *Encyclopaedia Britannica*, in an otherwise sensible entry on "Metaphor," cites this figure as a mixed metaphor because people do not bear weapons against the ocean. It is not a mixed metaphor. It is visual metaphor embodying an idea and the emotions appropriate to that idea. Hamlet acknowledges that his problems are as soluble as the sea is vulnerable to his assault. The image expresses his feelings of futility. Shakespeare has Hamlet reveal his feelings by making a metaphor that provides an image of someone taking arms—in the context of the play, a sword or dagger—against an ocean.

Besides personification, a subdivision of metaphor mentioned on page 37, and **hyperbole**, or extreme exaggeration ("That room was two miles wide!"), we need mention only two other forms of figurative language, not quite so common as metaphor and simile. In **synechdoche** we speak of something by naming only a part of it. A poet might refer to a naval fleet as "two hundred keels," for instance, and his audience would understand that *keel* stood for boat. It is a way of referring to boats without using the word, which has perhaps lost freshness through overuse. We use synechdoche in everyday speech if we say that, during the summer, Gloria acquired wheels—she bought a used Oldsmobile. The part of the car stands in for the whole of the car.

In **metonomy** we speak of the object in terms of something closely connected with it, not a part of it as in synechdoche but a thing closely and legitimately associated with it. Thus we can refer to a stove as its heat, for heat is not a part of the stove but a quality of it, or an association. Charles Reznikoff writes:

> Holding the stem of the
> beauty she had
> as if it were still
> a rose.

The poet first uses *beauty* by metonomy, as a quality of flowers; then he makes the flower particular.

Here are some poems followed by questions about metaphor and other figures of speech.

> That time of year thou mayst in me behold
> When yellow leaves, or none, or few, do hang
> Upon those boughs which shake against the cold,
> Bare ruin'd choirs[1] where late the sweet birds sang.
> In me thou seest the twilight of such day
> As after sunset fadeth in the west,
> Which by and by black night doth take away,
> Death's second self, that seals up all in rest.
> In me thou seest the glowing of such fire
> That on the ashes of his youth doth lie,
> As the death-bed whereon it must expire,
> Consumed with that which it was nourish'd by.
>   This thou perceiv'st which makes thy love more strong,
>   To love that well which thou must leave ere long.
>   —*William Shakespeare*

10

[1]Choir lofts, the part of the church building where the choirboys sang during religious services.

Questions
1. Paraphrase the poem, summarize the content, and discern the structure.
2. Where do you find the first figure of speech? What sort of figure is it?
3. How are the three quatrains linked in idea? Is there metaphorical coherence? Imagistic coherence?
4. In the fourth line, are the birds literal or figurative or both?
5. In the eleventh and twelfth lines, does the analogy make a complex idea simpler? Or does it make a simple idea more difficult?
6. List and name all figures of speech in this sonnet.

Orchids
> They lean over the path,
> Adder-mouthed,
> Swaying close to the face,
> Coming out, soft and deceptive,
> Limp and damp, delicate as a young bird's tongue;
> Their fluttery fledgling lips
> Move slowly,
> Drawing in the warm air.
>
> And at night,
> The faint moon falling through whitewashed glass,
> The heat going down
> So their musky smell comes even stronger,

10

Drifting down from their mossy cradles:
So many devouring infants!
Soft luminescent fingers,
Lips neither dead nor alive,
Loose ghostly mouths
Breathing.

—Theodore Roethke

Questions

1. List the different things the orchids are compared to.
2. The poem moves from one metaphoric area to another. What are the areas? Does the poem cohere? What keeps its different parts together?

The Hill

It is sometime since I have been
to what it was had once turned me backwards,
and made my head into
a cruel instrument.

It is simple
to confess. Then done,
to walk away, walk away,
to come again.

But that form, I must answer,
10   is dead in me, completely,
and I will not allow it
to reappear—

Saith perversity, the willful,
the magnanimous cruelty,
which is in me
like a hill.

—Robert Creeley

Questions

1. What are the connotations of *instrument*? Is the word a metaphor?
2. Note all the metaphors in this poem. Is there a dead metaphor here? A personification?
3. Note other figures of speech.
4. Does the final figure of speech have impact on the earlier word *me*?

Chapter 5 **Tone, with a Note on Intentions**

A poem's **tone**, in common definition, reveals the writer's attitude toward subject, an attitude that could include sarcasm or irony or awe. In conversation we indicate tone by our manner of speaking or by our facial expression: "Great!" can be pronounced so that it is a compliment or an insult. When we discuss a poem's tone, we discuss the value we attribute to its statements. In Wallace Stevens's "Disillusionment of Ten O'Clock," he wrote:

> People are not going
> To dream of baboons and periwinkles.

In the context of this poem, which has already told us about "houses . . . haunted / By white night-gowns," we hear the speaker's tone as ironic. **Irony** is the perception of incongruity or discrepancy—between statement and meaning, for instance. Because we know that these unimaginative people will dream colorless dreams, it is ironic to name the exotic *baboons and periwinkles* as possible subjects of their dreams. Other poems are explosive and angry in tone, like John Donne's line beginning "The Canonization":

> For Godsake hold your tongue and let me love!

Other poems reveal sarcasm, as in E. E. Cummings's lines from "Poem, or Beauty Hurts Mr. Vinal":

take it from me kiddo
believe me
my country, 'tis of

you, land of the Cluett
Shirt Boston Garter and Spearmint
Girl With The Wrigley Eyes (of you
land of the Arrow Ide
and Earl &
Wilson
10   Collars) of you i
sing:land of Abraham Lincoln and Lydia E. Pinkham,
land above all of Just Add Hot Water and Serve—
from every B. V. D.

let freedom ring

These examples are relatively simple. As most poems are complex, many-sided, and ambivalent, so the tone of many poems is hard to name and easy to mistake.

When we speak of a poem's tone we make a metaphor, speaking of a poem as if it were a person and voiced its own words. It can help, studying tone in poetry, to try out the analogy of poems-as-people. If we sometimes misunderstand tone in poems, it is also true that we can misunderstand personal tones of voice, even when we have body and pitch, gesture and eyebrows to help us understand. In everyday life, we interpret people's tones every hour of the day, without noticing that we do it. When we are offended by someone, or when we are touched or pleased, it is often the tone that does the offending or the pleasing. Perhaps we live with someone, and after dinner one night someone says "I'll do the dishes." These four words, depending on their tone, could mean a great many things. They could mean "Of course I'm getting stuck with doing the dishes, you slob, the way I always do, and the way I get stuck with taking out the garbage and picking up the biology notes from Gerry and standing in line for the football tickets." Or they could mean "I want to do the dishes because you look so tired, and I'm always happy to take on a little work on your behalf, because you do so much for me, and I'm grateful for you getting that book from the library." Or they could mean "I'm about to ask a favor," or "I think you're mad at me," or "I'll get points this way," or "Here is something I can do in order to avoid doing homework," or "When you wash the dishes they never get clean."

Usually we can decode the tone of somebody's voice. For that matter, we decode the way someone crosses a room or closes a door or drinks a Coke. Decoding a roommate, we use a glossary of behavior that we have been learning since birth. Door slams mean anger, says this dictionary; deep sighs mean frustration. We receive signals through gestures and through words, and we respond in kind; we communicate by tones.

Readers of poetry learn a system of signals by which they understand the tone of a poem, just as everybody learns the tones of personal pitch and gesture. One of the contracts that poet makes with reader stipulates that tone shall be ascertainable: an assured tone is another criterion of excellence in poetry. Sometimes poems fail by not making tone clear enough. For instance, here is a portion of a poem by a talented student:

> . . . on sour air, the bells
> chimed season's greetings
> to the departed host
> of Christmas . . .

If you cannot decode the tone of this fragment, you are not alone. What is the author's attitude toward the subject? The poet intended *season's greetings* to be highly ironic, even sarcastic, but reading it one could not be certain; a potential irony floated, unanchored, two inches above the page. The poet might have anchored irony any number of ways, but it is worth saying that ironic clichés are difficult to control; sometimes a context that demands irony provides control, sometimes a structure that repeats and varies the same irony. This fragment fails to make the irony seem intentional.

A note on intentions

When most of us speak about poetry, we refer to an author's intentions without even noticing that we do it. Speaking of diction and idiom, metaphor and image, we couch our discoveries in terms of the poet's presumed wishes and endeavors. Interpreting meaning, we say "This is what the poet was trying to say." The last phrase is especially common—and it is unfortunate: it promotes a picture of the poet as a fumbling, inarticulate slob, unable to say what is meant. The expression suggests that we will help out the dolt standing there with mouth open; let us inform the grateful poet of what he or she was trying and failing to say.

Whenever we begin to speak of a poet's intentions, we ought to consider what we are *really* talking about. Surely no one is so presumptuous as to believe that he or she *really* knows what was in Milton's mind before he wrote *Paradise Lost*—or what was in Robert Frost's mind before he wrote "Stopping by Woods on a Snowy Evening," for that matter. Common sense reveals our ignorance; we need no degrees in psychology. Everything that ever happened to Robert Frost—every poem he ever read, every conversation he ever took part in, every winter he ever lived through, every horse he ever drove—entered his poem. Or so I am free to suppose.

We never know, with anything like certainty, why we make important decisions in our own lives. If ignorance prevails about our own intentions, how can we possibly presume to know someone else's? The formula What was he trying to do? How well did he accomplish his purposes? presupposes a sort of knowledge we cannot claim. It is true that some poets have revealed their intentions to us—in autobiography, in letters to editors or to friends, and in answer to questions. I suggest that we should not believe them. We should *listen* to what they say—if the poem is good, the poet's talk about it is bound to be interesting, even if only for what the poet leaves out. But we should listen skeptically, with our minds alert for falsity; we should not listen naively, as if we were getting the words from the horse's mouth. Often the most sophisticated people become naive when artists claim to explain their work. When politicians explain that their motives are noble and selfless, nobody believes them. When poets do the same, people nod their heads. Really, there is every reason for artists to lie to us when they tell us about their work—because they have every reason to lie to themselves. Good poems by their nature reveal many sides of a person, including sides poets may wish to conceal. Robert Frost, for instance, revealed a dark side in many poems—fears of madness, longings for oblivion, notions of evil, intimations of meaninglessness—which was not the self he chose to reveal on the lecture platform. In speaking about his poems, he denied their darkness.

Some poets have the illusion that they intend whatever takes place in their poems. They are like people who, in an argument, defend the rightness of everything they have ever said or done. Other poets admit that they wrote this phrase, or that whole poem, without knowing exactly what they were saying. T. S. Eliot, for instance, proclaimed his innocence of intention in much of "The Waste Land." Probably more often, a writer will consciously intend something on the surface—and write something else as well, underneath the surface, that the writer is not aware of until later, when somebody points it out, or that, sometimes, the writer denies even after it is pointed out. Some students and teachers talk in classrooms about "hidden meanings" in a poem, an unfortunate phrase that makes reading poems sound like detective work. If we must speak of "hidden meanings," we ought to acknowledge that poets frequently hide meanings from themselves, and not just from readers.

Maybe the word *intention* should be stricken from our critical vocabulary; for we begin to speak sometimes of "unconscious intentions," a phrase in which the noun contradicts the adjective. In our lives we tend to judge by actions or results rather than intentions; if someone breaks our jaw while "only trying to help," we are smarter to remember the broken jaw than to warm ourselves over the avowed intention. Thus with poems: we must pay no attention to intentions, or even to the idea of intentions, but to actions and results. We must attend to what is there, *really there on the page*, and to the impingements of those words upon us.

Tone is easy to miss or misinterpret. Many readers seize on one notion of tone, a quick reading, and ignore or cannot see alternative readings. Assuming one tone, we eliminate the possibility of others, or of tonal variation. Here is a short poem, alive with tone, requiring thoughtful reading.

Transformations

Portion of this yew
Is a man my grandsire knew,
Bosomed here at its foot:

This branch may be his wife,
A ruddy human life
Now turned to a green shoot.

These grasses must be made
Of her who often prayed,
Last century, for repose;
10 And the fair girl long ago
Whom I often tried to know
May be entering this rose.

So, they are not underground,
But as nerves and veins abound
In the growths of upper air,
And they feel the sun and rain,
And the energy again
That made them what they were!
            —*Thomas Hardy*

First, let us see if we can agree on a summary. A man walks among the graves of people he has heard about or has known in life. He observes that all these bodies endure, at least as particles in graveyard plants.

This summary is as pale as a government bulletin because I am trying to sanitize the tone of it. What, then, is the tone of Hardy's poem? Is he melancholy? Is he happy in the graveyard? Does he announce molecular immortality as a discovery of vast scientific and spiritual importance? At first glance, he may seem to do the last. One student writing about this poem said, at the end of a paper, "So after this depression about everybody dying Thos. Hardy shakes himself out of it. He decides to look on the bright side of things so he notices that everybody really lives and nobody really dies because the roses etcetera go on blooming year after year after year after year." These sentences run into trouble as a parphrase, and describe a poem which, if Hardy had written it, would have been dishonest; this student has Hardy turn himself away from sadness by lying to himself and to his readers. And this poem is *almost* the one Hardy wrote; I don't think that this student's interpretation is far off, but that it mistook Hardy's tone.

"Transformations" begins with a physical scene. An old man—many clues, like his acquaintance with someone "last century," hint that the speaker is getting on—walks musing in a graveyard. At the beginning, he thinks of deaths remote from him, and the tone is quiet and contemplative. As the old man moves forward in time, closer to his own end, the tone shifts.

Notice that Hardy begins by implying that he is certain, and modifies his tone of certainty as the poem develops. The change in the degree and in the type of assertion makes the change in tone. The first two lines are plain statement: "Portion of this yew / Is a man my grandsire knew. . . ." Obviously, the speaker knows the truth of what he says, and we believe him; the yew tree must be adjacent to the grave, and we can accept this assertion scientifically. If someone is buried next to a tree, after a number of years it must be true that some of the tree's molecules contain atoms that were earlier part of that person's body. When the speaker goes on "Bosomed here at its foot," he moves into metaphor. The metaphor has resonance and secondary implication, but it also carries information: the man my grandsire knew is buried (his burial compared to a baby snuggled up to a breast) at the base of the tree.

When the speaker continues, he has taken his certainty as a starting point and added fancy: "This branch *may be* his wife . . ." He plays straight with us: he *admits* that when he begins to think of a particular part of the tree as composed of a particular person, he is *playing* with the possibilities of his scientific commonplace. If the wife (as we can assume) is buried beside her husband "here at its foot," it is common sense to assume that she also participates in the tree's molecules, but it is fanciful to think of her as a special new branch. (That she's thought of as a *green shoot* implies that she died more recently than her husband.) The speaker modestly admits his lack of knowledge or certainty, admits his playful fancy, by using the verb form *may be*.

The first line of the second stanza appears at first glance to make a definite assertion: "These grasses must be made . . ." If *must be* in our usage meant "absolutely, incontrovertibly has to be," we would have a statement of certainty. But, with the typical oddity of our speech, *must be* encodes a lack of certainty. When Hardy writes "These grasses must be made," he uses *must be* the way we do when we say "It must be six o'clock." (Robert Frost, as we have seen, used the same idiom when he wrote "My little horse must think it queer . . .") In Hardy's poem, we are allowed to understand that a woman (who "prayed / Last century for repose") is buried hereabouts, so her remains may well be part of the grasses here; on the other hand, the lines say, possibly they are not (because of the length of time? because of possible error about the gravesite?). In the second part of this stanza Hardy reverts to the *may be* form of possibility, making the metaphor that is the high point of the poem: "the fair girl . . . / May be entering this rose." Her molecules promenade through the stem to the blossom. In the metaphor, the rose has doors or portals, like house or church, and the pretty young woman in the shape of her molecules walks through the door.

So far the tone has been simple. Hardy told us a certainty followed by fancies and probabilities. We walk beside an old man through a churchyard, where he ruminates on the persistence of matter translated from one organism to another. In the third stanza tone changes entirely. We can perceive the change in the poem's grammar. In his verb forms, Hardy reverts from *must be* and *may be* to direct assertion. "So," the poem tells us, as a result of what has just been said, "they [the dead] *are* not underground."

But they are. Yes, some molecules of decay may have escaped, but the dead are not *really* "as nerves or veins" abounding "In the growths of upper air." We know that the poem tells us false when it says that they *abound* and that "they *feel* the sun and rain / And the energy again / That made them what they were!" The *tone* of this assertion is made loud by the exclamation point, a triumphant, almost ecstatic assertion of the survival of the dead. It is the *tone* of the exclamation that must concern the reader. The poem seems to argue that it has proved survival after death by what it has observed of plant life. The poem began by winning our trust with its scrupulous use of verbs moving from *is* to *may be* and *must be*. Now it seems to violate that trust, by asserting *are* when we must be aware that the idea depends on speculation, on fantasy, and on a scientific notion that deals with particles of human flesh, not with whole human beings.

Because the leap to assertion is such a grand leap, because we have learned to trust the implicit reasonableness of the speaker, the leap to false assertion creates a tone of strong and urgent feeling, which speaks to us like unwritten lines of poetry, saying "I know this assertion to be false; I make it only because I must, because the mortality of bodies is unacceptable to me!" The poem, through its tone—tone accomplished mostly by variations in verbs—speaks to us eloquently of the dread and fear of death.

Hardy's intention, in writing the poem, is not known to the reader—not to me, not to you, not to Hardy's most devoted student or scholar. But his poem in its own words, in its slow and steady motion down the page, makes its shape inevitable—if we read with a steady care, with attention, and with the same sensitivity we use interpreting the gesture and pitch of a person we love.

Here are some poems to read for their tone.

Museum Piece

The good grey guardians of art
Patrol the halls on spongy shoes,
Impartially protective, though
Perhaps suspicious of Toulouse.[1]

Here dozes one against the wall,
Disposed upon a funeral chair.
A Degas[2] dancer pirouettes
Upon the parting of his hair.

See how she spins! The grace is there,
10   But strain as well is plain to see.
Degas loved the two together:
Beauty joined to energy.

Edgar Degas purchased once
A fine El Greco,[3] which he kept
Against the wall beside his bed
To hang his pants on while he slept.
                    —*Richard Wilbur*

[1]Henri de Toulouse-Lautrec Monfa (1864–1901) made notable paintings of Parisian life and characters but is best known for his posters of nightclubs and entertainers.
[2]Edgar Degas (1834–1917), one of the important French impressionists, is best known for his paintings and pastels of ballerinas.
[3]El Greco (1548?–1614? or 1625?), native of Crete and student of the Venetian master Titian, lived in Toledo from his late twenties and was the leading sixteenth-century mystical Spanish painter. His work often distorts the human form by elongating it.

Questions

1. In the first line, what is the tone of the word *good*?
2. Alliteration is the repetition of consonant sounds, as in *good gray guardians*. Does alliteration in the first line contribute to the tone of the line?
3. Notice the rhyme in the first stanza. Can a rhyme contribute to tone? Does this rhyme?
4. Does the first stanza introduce a tone that remains the same throughout the poem? Where does the poem's tone change? How do you know?
5. What is the tone of the last line of the poem? Does it resolve the differing tones earlier in the poem?

Hay for the Horses

He had driven half the night
From far down San Joaquin
Through Mariposa, up the
Dangerous mountain roads,
And pulled in at eight a.m.
With his big truckload of hay behind the barn.
With winch and ropes and hooks
We stacked the bales up clean
To splintery redwood rafters
10   High in the dark, flecks of alfalfa
Whirling through shingle-cracks of light,
Itch of haydust in the sweaty shirt and shoes.
At lunchtime under Black oak
Out in the hot corral,
—The old mare nosing lunchpails,
Grasshoppers crackling in the weeds—
'I'm sixty-eight,' he said,
'I first bucked hay when I was seventeen.
I thought, that day I started,
20   I sure would hate to do this all my life.
And dammit, that's just what
I've gone and done.'

—Gary Snyder

Questions

1. How would you characterize the tone of the first stanza of this poem? Do you trust it to be straightforward? Why?
2. In the poem's middle, does the tone change at all? Do you sense any change in the speaker's attitude toward the subject?
3. In the last part of the poem, the poet quotes another speaker. Does this new speaker have a characteristic tone? What do you know of him from his tone? What does the poet do to reveal his tone?

Ends

Loud talk in the overlighted house
That made us stumble past.
Oh, there had once been night the first,
But this was night the last.

Of all the things he might have said,
Sincere or insincere,
He never said she wasn't young,
And hadn't been his dear.

Oh, some as soon would throw it all
10   As throw a part away.
And some will say all sorts of things,
But some mean what they say.
              —*Robert Frost*

Questions

1. Who is *us*?
2. What is overheard?
3. Do any overheard words have a tone to them that you trust? distrust? What words give you your impressions?
4. What do you feel you know about the overheard people? Try to discover everything you can about them, and then decide how you know what you know.
5. What are these people arguing about? Do you know? Or do you only know the tone of the argument? Which is more important, the subject of an argument or its tone?

Chapter 6 **Symbols and Allusions**

We may begin by defining a symbol as a person, object, place, or event that comes to stand for something other than it is, usually something more than it is, and for a class of events or relationships. Reading poems, we must make distinctions among kinds of symbolism: the **conventional** (or **traditional**) **symbol**, the **natural symbol**, and the **literary symbol**. And we must speak as well about allusion and reference in poetry, devices that overlap when a poet refers or alludes to a traditional symbol and that resemble each other in the difficulty they cause for students.

It is easiest to speak first of *natural symbols,* which occur in literature but which tend toward cliché: night is a natural symbol of death, and so is autumn. Shakespeare and other geniuses have made great literature using natural symbols; remember "That time of year thou mayst in me behold . . ." (page 41), where both night and autumn are symbols of death. Because natural symbols tend to be trite, modern writers seldom use them, or use them in the negative, setting up the expectation of a stock response, and then disappointing it. The great modern poet T. S. Eliot began one of his first poems, "The Love Song of J. Alfred Prufrock," with

> Let us go then, you and I,
> When the evening is spread out against the sky . . .

appealing to stock responses, and to the natural symbolism of sunset as beauty or fulfillment. His audience, when he wrote the poem in 1911, might have expected him to go on:

> Like veils of painted gossamer on high . . .

Instead, he turned this expectation upside down with his actual third line:

> Like a patient etherized upon a table.

A natural symbol underwent a radical alteration.

The word *symbol* begins by meaning a simple sign, like a circle containing a cigarette, with a diagonal line crossing out the cigarette; everybody knows the sign of the symbol for NO SMOKING. We speak of *conventional symbols* like these signs and like national flags or the logos of sports teams. Another sort of conventional symbol (it would be better perhaps to speak of these as *traditional symbols*) are images or phrases that have acquired meaning over centuries of history or association, like the cross and the Star of David. When a poet uses an image of a cross, he can hardly avoid reference to Christ, Christianity, and to suffering. Therefore **reference** allies itself to traditional (and conventional) symbolism. We speak of conventional and traditional symbols together because the distinction between them is quantitative; "conventional" symbols are simple signs; "traditional" symbols are signs with long and complex associations.

Finally, there is the *literary symbol,* a use of symbolism peculiar to literature. Here is a poem by William Blake:

The Sick Rose

> O Rose, thou art sick!
> The invisible worm
> That flies in the night,
> In the howling storm,
>
> Has found out thy bed
> Of crimson joy,
> And his dark secret love
> Does thy life destroy.

Reading this poem, let us as always first try the literal. A sick rose could suffer from a plant bacterium. But the second line of the poem reveals that we cannot continue to read on a literal level, because invisible worms fly only in the imagination. Back to the first line, then. *Rose* is capitalized, which may give us the sense that this flower is more than a flower, or that a real flower is addressed as if it embodied something beyond itself. To connect this flower with the notion of sickness seems a violation of the natural, as if we said that a mountain squeaked like a mouse. The contrast between *rose* and *sick* occurs at the levels of both sound and idea, as the full *o*s of the first two syllables dwindle into the quick short *i*s of *sick* and *invisible*.

"The Sick Rose" makes a literary symbol. When we ask what it is a symbol *of*, we ask the wrong sort of question. A literary symbol is not a figure or a riddle to which there exists a simple answer, or a correct interpretation. Instead, it is a series of words—creating image or event or character or fantasy or plot or scene—that is irreducible, that in itself is a formula for a complex set of feelings and ideas never before rendered in the same way. *The literary symbol cannot be translated or identified.* We can talk about it and we can talk around it, but the symbol will always sit in the center of our words, smiling enigmatically, content to be itself. A great French symbolist poet, Stéphane Mallarmé, made a metaphor for the symbol: he said it was "the new word." We can find the metaphor useful to our thinking about the literary symbol, because it cannot be defined or named by anything except itself. It resembles, then, a "new word" as if the poet invented the word *chair* for the first time, and there were no other word for chair but *chair*.

William Blake makes a symbol for a new thing. *The invisible worm* is not described in terms of horns and claws; it is a general "worm," with the particular attribute of invisibility—and with other attributes as well that associate feelings with this *new word*. This is a worm gifted with flight like a dragon, and gifted especially to fly in a darkness (night as a natural symbol is frightening, possibly the place of evil) and through a storm (destruction, possibly divine wrath) that makes a noise like the cries of someone in pain. The sick rose and its worm live in a place of terror and fear, are themselves instruments and victims of terror and fear. Syntax of subject and object, predator and victim, locates a scene in the second stanza. The worm has found "thy bed / Of crimson joy . . ." The word *joy* seems unambivalent, but it is not: crimson is blood-color, one of sin's colors, and dangerous; at least violent and extreme. One would expect malice from such a worm, and one hears instead of *love*; but it is a *dark, secret* love, and it is a love that rhymes *joy* with *destroy*. When love is both dark and secret, adjectives like crimson complicate the wholeness of the noun; if they do not reverse love into hate, or joy into pain, or fondness into malice, they introduce elements of the negative into the positive; they make by their complexity a wholeness. It is a wholeness that is also a new, single thing: symbolist poem or "new word."

Many poems speak of roses, in many different ways—sometimes as traditional or literary symbols and sometimes not. Theodore Roethke's great contemporary poem, "The Rose" (page 160), makes a literary symbol, another new word like William Blake's. But in Charles Reznikoff's four-line poem,

> Holding the stem of the
> beauty she had
> as if it were still
> a rose.

rose is not a symbol but a type, "a thing of beauty." When Shakespeare says "A rose by any other name would smell as sweet," or when Gertrude Stein tells us "A rose is a rose is a rose," these writers do not make new words, but like Reznikoff use the rose as a type: a flower beautiful in its odor; a thing of this world.

The problem of allusion

Blake's "The Sick Rose" carries countless associations for the student of literature. If a contemporary poet wrote now about "the rose's worm"—he would make an **allusion** to "The Sick Rose," almost a quotation. Allusion works with ideas as well as with words. One critic reading Blake's "The Sick Rose" believed that he found an allusion to Shakespeare's line "Lilies that fester smell far worse than weeds." It is now time for us to focus on allusion. Poems can allude to other poems and to history, to ideas, to fact, and to myth. All poems retelling old stories are allusive; a new version of "Casey at the Bat" would be an allusion to the old ballad; a new poem that tells about Oedipus or Hamlet must be based on allusions to the old plays.

Allusion has become a problem for modern readers, because people no longer share the same backgrounds. A century ago, an allusion to the Bible supposed no special knowledge; a century ago, among literate people, it was not obscure to speak of Greek deities like Apollo or Aphrodite; a century ago, even scientific knowledge was commonly held, partly because there was relatively little of it. Now we not only specialize in fields; we find specialties within specialties. The high-energy physicist cannot understand the physicist who studies the behavior of particles at low temperatures.

Allusion is common in poetry, and acts as a barrier to understanding. Sensitivity to allusion in poetry can only grow with extended reading. It is not an element of poetry that can be studied by exercise and thought; it is an element of poetry that can be named and introduced—but then it must be learned and practiced by much reading. No short cut will solve the problem of allusion.

But one short cut, obvious enough, will *help* with certain poems. Here is an **epigram** (a short, pithy poem; see pages 95–96) by Louise Bogan:

To an Artist, to Take Heart

> Slipping in blood, by his own hand, through pride,
> Hamlet, Othello, Coriolanus fall.
> Upon his bed, however, Shakespeare died,
> Having endured them all.

Bogan alludes to three Shakespearean heroes. The names of Hamlet and Othello will be familiar to most American students, though not always the stories that their names allude to. The name of Coriolanus will be new to most.

Reading this poem, the student is forced to a dictionary or a reference book.* The problem of allusion is often a problem of vocabulary, especially when it is a matter of proper names. To know that Hamlet is the hero of a play by Shakespeare called *Hamlet*—as a dictionary might tell us—would not help, even with this brief poem. But if we know enough of the story to remember that Hamlet died young and by violence, we can begin to understand the allusion and the poem. We cannot understand the poem without understanding the allusions.

Checking allusions in Louise Bogan's four lines, we learn that Coriolanus's tragic flaw was pride; we add this fact to Othello's suicide and Hamlet's death in a duel. We notice that the three phrases of Bogan's first line follow the order of the three heroes' names in the second line. We understand that the playwright who conceived them lived longer than they did, even if he suffered (*endured* has the connotation of survival with difficulty) and ended by dying in bed—which is viewed as preferable to violent death.

Because of the difficulties of allusion, certain great and allusive poets are under-represented in this book, among them Milton, Dryden, and Pope. For the same reason, it is hard to choose poems that can give fair exercise in uncovering allusions. The poems that follow, and the questions that go with them, raise issues largely of symbolism. But not entirely.

Proust's Madeleine

Somebody has given my
Baby daughter a box of
Old poker chips to play with.
Today she hands me one while
I am sitting with my tired
Brain at my desk. It is red.
On it is a picture of
An elk's head and the letters
B.P.O.E.—a chip from
10   A small town Elks' Club. I flip
It idly in the air and
Catch it and do a coin trick
To amuse my little girl.

*Earlier this book urged the use of the *Oxford English Dictionary* (page 19). In the pursuit of allusions, the student can use the whole reference room. For help with the proper names in Bogan's poem, the *Oxford Companion to English Literature* would perhaps be the best resource, in which entries for these names summarize plots and tell the tragic flaws of heroes. Oxford also prints a *Companion to American Literature*, and *Companions* to the literatures of other languages. The *Oxford Classical Dictionary* is very good on mythology, and there are classical dictionaries and companions from other publishers. The *Readers' Encyclopedia* is a useful volume, as are more specialized volumes of reference: the *Encyclopedia of American Biography, Webster's Biographical Dictionary, An Encyclopedia of World History,* and of course the *Encyclopaedia Britannica.* The *New Columbia Encyclopedia* is an excellent resource in one volume. Reference librarians will often point you in the right direction. With certain poets, especially highly allusive poets of the eighteenth century who refer to their own contemporaries by name and by pseudonym, it is useful to consult the notes of a scholarly edition of the poet's work, where the research has been done for us.

Suddenly everything slips aside.
I see my father
Doing the very same thing,
Whistling "Beautiful Dreamer,"
His breath smelling richly
Of whiskey and cigars. I can
20   Hear him coming home drunk
From the Elks' Club in Elkhart
Indiana, bumping the
Chairs in the dark. I can see
Him dying of cirrhosis
Of the liver and stomach
Ulcers and pneumonia,
Or, as he said on his deathbed, of
Crooked cards and straight whiskey,
Slow horses and fast women.
                    —Kenneth Rexroth

Questions
1. Where does allusion begin in this poem? List and explain its allusions.
2. Does this poem use any sort of symbol?

Taking the hands of someone you love

Taking the hands of someone you love,
You see they are delicate cages . . .
Tiny birds are singing
In the secluded prairies
And in the deep valleys of the hand.
                    —Robert Bly

Question
Compare this poem with the poem above by Kenneth Rexroth. Does this one invite you to look for symbolism? What sort of symbolism? Why?

The Draft Horse

With a lantern that wouldn't burn
In too frail a buggy we drove
Behind too heavy a horse
Through a pitch-dark limitless grove.

And a man came out of the trees
And took our horse by the head
And reaching back to his ribs
Deliberately stabbed him dead.

The ponderous beast went down
10   With a crack of a broken shaft.

And the night drew through the trees
In one long invidious draft.

The most unquestioning pair
That ever accepted fate
And the least disposed to ascribe
Any more than we had to to hate,

We assumed that the man himself
Or someone he had to obey
Wanted us to get down
20 And walk the rest of the way.
                              —*Robert Frost*

Questions

1. Do you take this action literally?
2. Are there natural symbols here? Traditional or conventional symbols?
3. Does this poem make a "new word"? What in this poem gives you the suggestion that it might be symbolic?

The Monument

Now can you see the monument? It is of wood
built somewhat like a box. No. Built
like several boxes in descending sizes
one above the other.
Each is turned half-way round so that
its corners point toward the sides
of the one below and the angles alternate.
Then on the topmost cube is set
a sort of fleur-de-lys of weathered wood,
10 long petals of board, pierced with odd holes,
four-sided, stiff, ecclesiastical.
From it four thin, warped poles spring out,
(slanted like fishing-poles or flag-poles)
and from them jig-saw work hangs down,
four lines of vaguely whittled ornament
over the edges of the boxes
to the ground.
The monument is one-third set against
a sea; two-thirds against a sky.
20 The view is geared
(that is, the view's perspective)
so low there is no "far away,"
and we are far away within the view.
A sea of narrow, horizontal boards
lies out behind our lonely monument,
its long grains alternating right and left
like floor-boards—spotted, swarming-still,

and motionless. A sky runs parallel,
and it is palings, coarser than the sea's:
30   splintery sunlight and long-fibred clouds.
"Why does that strange sea make no sound?
Is it because we're far away?
Where are we? Are we in Asia Minor,
or in Mongolia?"
                    An ancient promontory,
an ancient principality whose artist-prince
might have wanted to build a monument
to mark a tomb or boundary, or make
a melancholy or romantic scene of it . . .
40   "But that queer sea looks made of wood,
half-shining, like a driftwood sea.
And the sky looks wooden, grained with cloud.
It's like a stage-set; it is all so flat!
Those clouds are full of glistening splinters!
What is that?"
                    It is the monument.
"It's piled-up boxes,
outlined with shoddy fret-work, half-fallen off,
cracked and unpainted. It looks old."
50   —The strong sunlight, the wind from the sea,
all the conditions of its existence,
may have flaked off the paint, if ever it was painted,
and made it homelier than it was.
"Why did you bring me here to see it?
A temple of crates in cramped and crated scenery,
what can it prove?
I am tired of breathing this eroded air,
this dryness in which the monument is cracking."

It is an artifact
60   of wood. Wood holds together better
than sea or cloud or sand could by itself,
much better than real sea or sand or cloud.
It chose that way to grow and not to move.
The monument's an object, yet those decorations,
carelessly nailed, looking like nothing at all,
give it away as having life, and wishing;
wanting to be a monument, to cherish something.
The crudest scroll-work says "commemorate,"
while once each day the light goes around it
70   like a prowling animal,
or the rain falls on it, or the wind blows into it.
It may be solid, may be hollow.
The bones of the artist-prince may be inside
or far away on even drier soil.
But roughly but adequately it can shelter

what is within (which after all
cannot have been intended to be seen).
It is the beginning of a painting,
a piece of sculpture, or poem, or monument,
80   and all of wood. Watch it closely.
                                   —*Elizabeth Bishop*

Questions

1. Is this a symbolist poem? What lines or words help you decide?
2. What sorts of symbol can you discover in this poem?

The Apparitions

Because there is safety in derision
I talked about an apparition,
I took no trouble to convince,
Or seem plausible to a man of sense,
Distrustful of that popular eye
Whether it be bold or sly.
Fifteen apparitions have I seen;
The worst a coat upon a coat-hanger.

I have found nothing half so good
10   As my long-planned half solitude,
Where I can sit up half the night
With some friend that has the wit
Not to allow his looks to tell
When I am unintelligible.
Fifteen apparitions have I seen;
The worst a coat upon a coat-hanger.

When a man grows old his joy
Grows more deep day after day,
His empty heart is full at length,
20   But he has need of all that strength
Because of the increasing Night
That opens her mystery and fright.
Fifteen apparitions have I seen;
The worst a coat upon a coat-hanger.
                                   —*William Butler Yeats*

Questions

1. Note any use of conventional or traditional symbols.
2. Does the image of *a coat upon a coat-hanger* change its implications as it is repeated?
3. Does the poem make a literary symbol?

The Return

See, they return; ah, see the tentative
      Movements, and the slow feet,
      The trouble in the pace and the uncertain
      Wavering!

See they return, one, and by one,
With fear, as half-awakened;
As if the snow should hesitate
And murmur in the wind,
          and half turn back;
10   These were the 'Wing'd-with-Awe,'
          Inviolable.

Gods of the wingèd shoe!
With them the silver hounds,
          sniffing the trace of air!

Haie! Haie!
          These were the swift to harry;
These the keen-scented;
These were the souls of blood.

Slow on the leash,
20   pallid the leash-men!
               —*Ezra Pound*

Questions

1. Can you find any allusions in this poem?
2. Can you identify *they* in this poem? If you cannot name a definite identity, can you name a kind of action that *they* embody?
3. If the poem is symbolic, what kind of a symbol does it make?

Chapter 7 **The Sound of Poems**

When we explicate a poem, we investigate its sound as well as its symbol, its shape and architecture as well as its paraphrase and implication. Talking about William Carlos Williams's wheelbarrow poem, we looked at the poem as artifact, as made object. This chapter concentrates on the pleasures poems make by their sound.

There are at least two distinct pleasures we derive from the sound of language in poetry. One is the pleasure of *rhythm*, of words in motion, uncoiling in sentences from poetic line to line. Here is the beginning of *Paradise Lost* by John Milton:

> Of man's first disobedience, and the fruit
> Of that forbidden tree, whose mortal taste
> Brought death into the world, and all our woe,
> With loss of Eden, till one greater Man
> Restore us, and regain the blissful seat,
> Sing, Heavenly Muse . . .

The pleasure of rhythm is like the pleasure of dancing, or of tapping our feet to keep time with music, and it recalls primitive origins of poetry where song and poem and dance happened together. This rhythm-pleasure of poetry's sound connects with our pleasure in bodily motion.

The other pleasure is the delight that we take in adjacent sounds rubbing together, vowels held and savored, consonants clicking together. Here are some lines from "To Autumn" by John Keats:

Then in a wailful choir the small gnats mourn
   Among the river sallows,° borne aloft   willows
      Or sinking as the light wind lives or dies; . . .

Rhythm and linebreak

First, let us look at rhythm. The lines of a poem are essential to its signature and its identity. Milton broke some of his lines where the meaning paused, as with

Brought death into the world, and all our woe . . .

When the sense pauses or stops at the end of a line we call it **end-stopped**. Most of the time, Milton broke his lines in the middle of a phrase, so that the sense of the sentence ran over into the line following, as with

With loss of Eden, till one greater Man
Restore us . . .

When the sense runs over the end of a line we call the line enjambed, and the practice **enjambment**.

Even when a line is enjambed, it retains its identity as a line of poetry, and reading it aloud we make a slight pause at the end. Or we show the line-end in another way, by raising our voice perhaps, or by holding onto the last syllable. We do not pause evenly—we pause longer when the line is end-stopped—but we find some means to show with our voices that we have come to the end of a line. If we do not, we might as well be reading prose. One eighteenth-century critic with no ear suggested that we print Milton as prose or that we re-break his lines according to phrases or sense, which could make the first lines of *Paradise Lost* look like this:

Of man's first disobedience
and the fruit
of that forbidden tree
whose mortal taste
brought death
into the world
and all our woe,
with loss of Eden,
till one greater Man
restore us,
and regain
the blissful seat,
sing
Heavenly Muse . . .

How boring and flat the lines become! There can be little attention to pauses within lines, because the critic would break the line wherever there might be a pause. There is no tension; music and sense become identical, which results in the disappearance of music.

We must develop a sense of the poetic line if we are to take pleasure in poetry. Here are lines by Louis Simpson:

> Caesar Augustus
> In his time lay
> Dying, and just as
> Cold as they,
> On the cold morning
> Of a cold day.

These lines lose their pleasure, as well as their dance and their power, if we space them according to the phrases of their sense:

> Caesar Augustus
> In his time lay dying
> And just as cold as they
> On the cold morning
> Of a cold day.

And as prose it disappears completely: "Caesar Augustus in his time lay dying and just as cold as they on the cold morning of a cold day."
(The complete poem is on pages 83–84.)

The examples we have looked at use rhyme and meter, subjects of the next chapter. With free verse, which lacks any regular beat, the line becomes the major way of organizing sound. Here is a stanza from a free-verse poem by John Haines, "And When the Green Man Comes," revised into phrase-unit lines:

> His eyes are blind with April,
> his breath distilled
> of butterflies and bees,
> and in his beard the maggot sings.

Here it is with the lines broken arbitrarily, *not* as the poet broke them in his finished poem:

> His eyes are
> blind with April, his
> breath
> distilled of
> butterflies and
> bees, and in
> his beard the
> maggot sings.

The first version is boring, the second jagged or nervous. Here is the stanza as Haines actually wrote it:

> His eyes are blind
> with April,
> his breath distilled
> of butterflies
> and bees, and in his beard
> the maggot sings.

Notice how the organized rhythm of the last version calls attention to sound; putting *eyes* and *blind* together in a short line, for instance, repeats the long *ai*s. Notice as well the repetition of *l*s, in the last syllable of each of the first four lines.

Sounds can exist for their own sakes—and because they can, sounds organize emphasis. *blind / with April* and *distilled / of butterflies* share a syntactic structure, but instead of ending at the same place, one of the two clauses continues *of butterflies / and bees*. Syntax and linebreak combine to isolate, in the last line of the stanza, the significant conclusion: *the maggot sings*. My earlier linebreaks, falsifying the poem, obscured or invalidated these possibilities.

Some free-verse poems use a long line in which the linebreak seldom interrupts the sense. They are all end-stopped. Take these lines by Walt Whitman, from "Song of Myself":

> I think I could turn and live with animals, they're so placid and self-contain'd,
> I stand and look at them long and long.
>
> They do not sweat and whine about their condition,
> They do not lie awake in the dark and weep for their sins,
> They do not make me sick discussing their duty to God,
> Not one is dissatisfied, not one is demented with the mania of owning things,
> Not one kneels to another, nor to his kind that lived thousands of years ago,
> Not one is respectable or unhappy over the whole earth.

If one printed these lines as prose, in paragraph form, one would lose the slow pace that the long lines give. On the other hand, one could slow the pace into absolute boredom by breaking the lines at the commas, making them shorter:

> I think I could turn and live
> with animals,
> they're so placid
> and self-contain'd.
> I stand and look at them
> long and long.
>
> They do not sweat and whine
> about their condition.

They do not lie awake in the dark
and weep for their sins.
They do not make me sick
discussing their duty to God.
Not one is dissatisfied.
Not one is demented
with the mania
of owning things.
Not one kneels to another
nor to his kind
that lived thousands of years ago.
Not one is respectable
or unhappy
over the whole earth.

In this mistreatment, I have reduced the various pauses—commas, shorter pauses between whole phrases, lone line-end pauses—into one sort of pause. We should be grateful for Whitman's generous line, which makes a satisfying rhythm within itself—and not only by its motion from line to line. A pause within the line is called a **caesura**, and is shown by a pair of vertical lines ‖. Whitman's lines include many pauses or caesuras. In a shorter line like Milton's we do not have so many, but we can often find an obvious place to pause, sometimes shown by punctuation:

Of man's first disobedience, ‖ and the fruit

and sometimes not, as in Keats's line:

Or sinking ‖ as the light wind lifts or dies . . .

Poets work with a variety of pauses, at the ends of lines and inside them, which contribute to the rhythm of the poetic line.

Here are some exercises possibly suited for out-loud performance in the class-room.

Exercises

1. Following is a passage from *Antony and Cleopatra*, done Shakespeare's way and as two actors with differing interpretations might have done it. Notice which lines are enjambed, which end-stopped, in the first passage. Discuss the difference the linebreaks make in the three versions.

   a. The barge she sat in, like a burnished throne,
   Burned on the water: the poop was beaten gold;
   Purple the sails, and so perfumèd that
   The winds were love-sick with them; the oars were silver,
   Which to the tune of flutes kept stroke, and made
   The water which they beat to follow faster.

b. The barge she sat in
   like a burnished throne
   burned on the water.
   The poop was beaten gold,
   purple the sails,
   and so perfumèd
   that the winds
   were love-sick with them.
   The oars were silver,
   which to the flutes kept stroke
   and made the water
   which they beat
   to follow faster.

c. The barge
   she sat in like
   a burnished throne burned on the
   water the poop was
   beaten
   gold purple the
   sails and so perfumèd that the winds
   were love-

   . . .

   sick
   with
   them
   the oars were silver which to the tune of flutes kept stroke and made the water
   which they beat to
   follow
   faster.

2. Here are three versions of a free-verse poem by William Carlos Williams. Which is the poet's? Which is the least pleasing lineation?

a. As the cat climbed
   over the top of

   the jamcloset first
   the right forefoot

   carefully then the
   hind stepped down

   into the pit of the
   empty flower pot

b. As the cat
   climbed over
   the top of

   the jamcloset
   first the right
   forefoot

   carefully
   then the hind
   stepped down

    into the pit of
    the empty
    flowerpot

c. As the cat climbed
    over the top
    of the jamcloset
    first the right
    forefoot carefully
    then the hind
    stepped down
    into the pit
    of the empty
    flower pot

Vowels and consonants

To enjoy the intimate sounds of poems, we take pleasure in savoring words and parts of words. This pleasure does not exclude meanings but it can exist for its own sake. Sometimes we enjoy tripping along with nonsense sounds, as when Yeats makes a line of "fol, de rol, de rolly o," or Shakespeare mixes words and sounds: "With a hey, ho, the wind and the rain."

Alliteration is the repetition of consonant sounds, especially at the beginning of words. When Wallace Stevens writes "In kitchen cups concupiscent curds," he keeps our tongues flicking at the roofs of our mouths.

Assonance is the repetition of vowel sounds—"beside the white"; "glazed with rain." We take pleasure in holding onto vowels which remind us of each other. The last line of Hardy's "During Wind and Rain" shows interlocking assonance and alliteration:

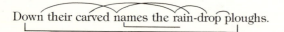

Down their carved names the rain-drop ploughs.

The two syllables at the beginning and end of the line contain the same *ow* vowel sound; in the middle of the line, there is the long *a* of *names* and the long *a* of *rain*. In addition, the lines repeat the *n* of *down*, *names*, and *rain*; the *r* of *carved*, *rain*, and *drop*; the *p* of *drop* and *ploughs*.

Poets typically ascend to assonance, holding long vowels, when their poems are most exalted, as when Hardy ends his lyric. When Keats wrote his odes—more than in his other poems—he especially delighted in repeating vowels and consonants. This stanza is from "Ode to a Nightingale":

I cannot see what flowers are at my feet,
    Nor what soft incense hangs upon the boughs,
But, in embalmèd darkness, guess each sweet
    Wherewith the seasonable month endows
The grass, the thicket, and the fruit-tree wild—

White hawthorn, and the pastoral eglantine;
　　Fast-fading violets covered up in leaves;
　　　　And mid-May's eldest child,
　　The coming musk-rose, full of dewy wine,
10　　　　　The murmurous haunt of flies on summer eves.

In the first line Keats mixes assonance and alliteration. The vowels of *see* and *feet* are identical, while *flowers* and *feet* begin with the same consonant. The consonant sound of *th* repeats softly through lines 4 to 6: *Wherewith, the* (four times), *month, thicket,* and *hawthorn.* Two of the sets of rhyme words have the same long *ai*: wild, eglantine, child, wine. The identical **diphthong** (a double vowel, this one composed of *ah* and *ee*) occurs elsewhere within the lines: *White, violets, flies.*

It is not a requirement of great poetry that sounds be so gorgeous. Frost is *never* so ornate, in his alliteration or his assonance, as Keats in the odes. Frost's attention dotes on rhythm, linebreak, on the happy and continuous tension between sentence and line. Here are poems for sound study.

New Year's Day

Again and then again . . . the year is born

To ice and death, and it will never do

To skulk behind storm-windows by the stove

To hear the postgirl sounding her French horn

When the thin tidal ice is wearing through.

Here is the understanding not to love

Each other, or tomorrow that will sieve

Our resolutions. While we live, we live

To snuff the smoke of victims. In the snow

10　The kitten heaved its hindlegs, as if fouled,

And died. We bent it in a Christmas box

And scattered blazing weeds to scare the crow

Until the snake-tailed sea-winds coughed and howled

For alms outside the church whose double locks

Wait for St. Peter, the distorted key.

Under St. Peter's bell the parish sea

Swells with its smelt into the burlap shack

Where Joseph plucks his hand-lines like a harp,

And hears the fearful *Puer natus est*[1]

20   Of Circumcision, and relives the wrack

And howls of Jesus whom he holds. How sharp

The burden of the Law before the beast:

Time and the grindstone and the knife of God.

The Child is born in blood, O child of blood.

—*Robert Lowell*

[1]The Child is born

Questions

1. At the end of each line, write either S (for end-stopped) or E (for enjambed).
2. What one consonant is most often repeated at the beginnings of words in this poem? Can you discover further alliteration?
3. In the next-to-last line, what vowel sound dominates?

I Wake and Feel the Fell of Dark

I wake and feel the fell of dark, not day.

What hours, O what black hours we have spent

This night! what sights you, heart, saw; ways you went!

And more must, in yet longer light's delay.

   With witness I speak this. But where I say

Hours I mean years, mean life. And my lament

Is cries countless, cries like dead letters sent

To dearest him that lives alas! away.

   I am gall, I am heartburn. God's most deep decree

10   Bitter would have me taste: my taste was me;

Bones built in me, flesh filled, blood brimmed the curse.

   Selfyeast of spirit a dull dough sours. I see

The lost are like this, and their scourge to be

As I am mine, their sweating selves; but worse.

—*Gerard Manley Hopkins*

Questions
1. Underline the alliteration in this poem.
2. Letter each line as end-stopped (S) or enjambed (E).

The Dalliance of the Eagles

Skirting the river road, (my forenoon walk, my rest,)

Skyward in air a sudden muffled sound, the dalliance of the eagles,

The rushing amorous contact high in space together,

The clinching interlocking claws, a living, fierce, gyrating wheel,

Four beating wings, two beaks, a swirling mass tight grappling,

In tumbling turning clustering loops, straight downward falling,

Till o'er the river pois'd, the twain yet one, a moment's lull,

A motionless still balance in the air, then parting, talons loosing,

Upward again on slow-firm pinions slanting, their separate diverse flight,

10   She hers, he his, pursuing.

—Walt Whitman

Questions
1. In this poem, mark the pauses within the line (caesuras) with a double line.
2. Note any alliteration or assonance.

To Autumn

I

Season of mists and mellow fruitfulness,

    Close bosom friend of the maturing sun,

Conspiring with him how to load and bless

    With fruit the vines that round the thatch-eaves run:

To bend with apples the mossed cottage-trees,

    And fill all fruit with ripeness to the core;

      To swell the gourd, and plump the hazel shells

    With a sweet kernel; to set budding more,

And still more, later flowers for the bees,

10   Until they think warm days will never cease,

      For summer has o'er-brimmed their clammy cells.

II

Who hath not seen thee oft amid thy store?

   Sometimes whoever seeks abroad may find

Thee sitting careless on a granary floor,

   Thy hair soft-lifted by the winnowing wind;

Or on a half-reaped furrow sound asleep,

   Drowsed with the fume of poppies, while thy hook

      Spares the next swath and all its twinèd flowers;

And sometimes like a gleaner thou dost keep

20   Steady thy laden head across a brook;

Or by a cider-press, with patient look,

      Thou watchest the last oozings, hours by hours.

III

Where are the songs of spring? Ay, where are they?

   Think not of them, thou hast thy music too—

While barrèd clouds bloom the soft-dying day,

   And touch the stubble-plains with rosy hue.

Then in a wailful choir the small gnats mourn

   Among the river sallows,° borne aloft   willows

      Or sinking as the light wind lives or dies;

30   And full-grown lambs loud bleat from hilly bourn;

   Hedge-crickets sing; and now with treble soft

   The redbreast whistles from a garden-croft;

   And gathering swallows twitter in the skies.

—John Keats

Question

Make curved marks over the lines showing the interconnections of alliteration; underneath the lines, make angular marks to connect assonances. (See the markings on a line by Thomas Hardy, page 68.)

Chapter 8 **Meter and Rhyme**

"Meter and Rhyme" is examined separately from "The Sound of Poetry" to make a point. From all poems we demand pleasing sound. All good poems are formal: the poem's words, and their order and arrangement, must seem inevitable and immovable. In some poems, meter and rhyme provide specialized means toward these ends. Now we must define meter, distinguishing it from rhythm, and exemplifying its use by poets in the English tradition. Because rhyme is a separate device, and because meter and rhyme can each occur without the other, we will treat rhyme separately later in the chapter.

Meter

English meter is a count of syllables, usually syllables in pairs of which one is louder than the other.

Meter is not the same as rhythm. Meter is numbers or counting; rhythm is a vaguer word, implying an approximate recurrence or repetition in the pacing of sound; rhythm is fast or slow, staccato or flowing. Words describing rhythm are imprecise, because rhythm cannot accept precise description. We compare rhythm to a liquid when we call it flowing, or to a broken solid when we call it jagged. The last chapter devoted space to rhythm in the poetic line, and contrasted the rhythm of Milton's metrical line with the rhythm of the same words broken into different lines; then it made the same contrast with free verse, using poems by John Haines and Walt Whitman (pages 64–66). In each example the poet's rhythms, deployed in lines, were pleasing to the ear. The same words, broken into other lines, made monotonous or unpleasing rhythms. When we read poems, we invariably perceive rhythm: in a good poem, the rhythm is pleasurable—and from time to time it is even expressive. In a bad poem, the rhythm tends to be weak, prosaic, boring, and without expressive function. Poems in free verse and poems in meter both have rhythm; in either metrical verse or free verse, rhythms may be good or bad.

Meter is numbers, or counting, as we have noted already. The word comes from a Greek word, *metron*, which means "measure"—like a yardstick or the metric system. Meter is a count of something we can hear.

Each language has its own genius, and in English the common meter (known by various names) counts relative loudness and softness of syllables.

Relative stress

In order to hear English meter, you must be able to distinguish relative loudness, which is also called *stress* or *accent*. Within a word that has more than one syllable, one syllable is louder than the rest. We speak of proNOUNcing a word, not of PROnouncing or of pronounCING it. In pronouncing the words of our own language, we have memorized a pattern of loudness. When we say conTENT our listeners know we are not speaking of CONtent, because we make two different words depending on which of the syllables we pronounce more loudly.

Practice your sense of relative loudness. Everyone knows how to pronounce the words that follow; everyone saying them aloud will put the **accent** at the right place. (Accent means prominence; in our language, accent is mostly achieved by relative volume. Sometimes greater length or pitch variation is *added* to volume for the sake of accentuation.) But not everyone, in his head, can name what it is he is doing when he pronounces correctly. Pronounce each of these words; then decide which of the two syllables is louder.

depict	necktie
hammer	destroy
cowbell	dispatch
rampart	debris
nugget	dental
neglect	

Try these words of three and more syllables:

memory	implement
rambunctious	implementation
amaryllis	compliment
reputation	comprehend
dangerous	

Three-syllable words which take their major accent on the first or the third syllable carry a minor accent on the syllable at the word's other end. In MEM-or-y, *mem* is the accentuated syllable, but the little -*y* at the end is louder, at least, than the -*or*- in the middle. The opposite arrangement works with compre-HEND. A word like ar-RANGE-ment, with the accent in the middle, shows no minor accent. (Minor accent is sometimes called secondary stress.) These habits of three-syllable words become important in metrical poems.

Iambic pentameter: the foot

For examples, let's start with the English ten-syllable line, arranged as **iambic pentameter**, the most common meter in great English poems. An **iambic foot** in English is a softer syllable followed by a louder one. *Pentameter* translates as "five-measure." Therefore, typical iambic pentameter is five groups of two syllables, the second syllable in each group louder than the first. When we scan—or put marks to indicate the meter of a line—we put bars to separate the feet of the line, making the typical line ⌣/ | ⌣/ | ⌣/ | ⌣/ | ⌣/ | : these bars erect a figurative barrier between the feet to emphasize that stress is relative (and relevant) *only within the foot.*

The ⌣/ | ⌣/ | ⌣/ | ⌣/ | ⌣/ | shows the counting which remains constant, which assures that the verse remains metrical. But while the counting, or **scansion**, stays the same, the rhythm can vary considerably. After all, ⌣/ | ⌣/ | ⌣/ | ⌣/ | ⌣/ | could contain ten monosyllables or two polysyllables; it could be fast, it could be slow; it could contain a period, the end of one sentence and the start of another; it could contain many commas, caesuras slowing the line, or it could contain no punctuation at all and move more quickly. The ⌣/ | ⌣/ | ⌣/ | ⌣/ | ⌣/ | tells us very little of what the line will sound like; it shows meter, not rhythm, five relative hills and five relative valleys. The hills at one point in the line may be lower in elevation than the valleys in another part of the line. "Bang *bang*, bang *bang*, bang *bang*, bang *bang*, bang *bang*" fulfills the pattern. (We can bang this out on the desk top, every even bang louder than every odd one.) But "The University of Michigan" also fulfills the pattern. Say it slowly, exaggerating a little, and you can hear it: "The U-ni-VER-sit-Y of MICH-i-GAN." If you try saying "THE u-NI-ver-SI-ty OF Mich-I-gan," you do not pronounce our language.

The scansion ⌣/ | ⌣/ | ⌣/ | ⌣/ | ⌣/ |, common to many lines different in rhythm, describes an expectation the mind develops from reading thousands of lines of poetry—iambic pentameter means, or translates, "the only thing which *all* these lines have in common."

Terms for feet and for length of line

In the examples we shall continue to concentrate on the iambic foot, most often in the pentameter line. Because we occasionally encounter other meters it is useful to know terms for the most common feet and lengths of lines.

Some types of feet:

Iambic: a softer syllable followed by a louder: *des*PAIR ⌣/
Trochaic: a louder syllable followed by a softer: HAPPy /⌣
Dactylic: a louder syllable followed by two softer ones: CHANGE*able* /⌣⌣
Anapestic: two softer syllables followed by a louder one: *in the* HOUSE ⌣⌣/

Some lengths of lines:

Monometer: one foot
Dimeter: two feet
Trimeter: three feet
Tetrameter: four feet
Pentameter: five feet
Hexameter (or the Alexandrine): six feet

Rhythmical variety within metrical regularity

Within absolute metrical regularity, every line scanning ⌣′ | ⌣′ | ⌣′ | ⌣′ | ⌣′ |, iambic pentameter can find all the variety it wants or needs. It need never depart from this scheme for variety's sake. Iambic pentameter finds most of its variety in playing upon the relativity of stress. Seldom in our literature do you find a line as evenly stressed as bang *bang,* or as "The man who stole the bread was making toast." "The University of Michigan," which has only two really loud noises, is more typical of iambic pentameter. Here is the beginning of Keats's "The Eve of St. Agnes":

St. Ăg | nĕs E′ve— | Ăh, bĭt | tĕr chĭll | ĭt wăs . . .

The first line scans exactly as our example does, ⌣′ | ⌣′ | ⌣′ | ⌣′ | ⌣′ |. There is a pause after the fourth syllable, a rhythmical fact the meter does not count. All the even-numbered syllables are louder than all the odd-numbered syllables in this line, and in this particular line, the "louder" sounds are almost equal to each other. The last syllable, *was,* is probably a little softer than the second, fourth, sixth, or eighth syllables—a fact that is part of the rhythm of the line but is irrelevant to its meter. The second line reads:

Thĕ owl, | fŏr all | hĭs feath | ĕrs, was | ă-cold;

which again scans like the pattern. Two caesuras after the second and the seventh syllables contribute rhythmical variation. Of the five relatively loud syllables, creating the five feet, three are *quite* loud; two are not so loud as the other three, but still louder than their proximate neighbors *all* and *was.* So the variations in true loudness, small as they are, make rhythmical variety, while the sameness of relative loudness makes metrical identity. In the third line,

Thĕ hare | lĭmp′d tremb | lĭng through | thĕ fro | zĕn grass,

we have another line that scans typically—but this line varies considerably in rhythm from the earlier two. For instance, *through* is louder than the *-ing* of *trembling,* and thus *-ing through* makes a regular foot of relative stress, but *through* is not truly loud at all; its softness—which remains louder than its neighbor—is *metrically* irrelevant, and *rhythmically* pleasing by providing variety. In the first half of this line, the second, third, and fourth syllables are all quite loud. Bang, bang, bang. I do not mean that they are *equally* loud; it would be absurd to suggest that they were each pronounced with an equal number of decibels. But they are all louder than the *through* that takes metrical stress later in the line.

But they cannot be louder than each other. English meter uses *relative* stress, and we can expect that the first loud syllable (the second syllable in the line) is louder than the first soft syllable; the line begins with a regular iamb. Then we have two loud syllables together, *limp'd tremb-*, and in English we would expect that one of the two—the second, if the poem appears iambic—can easily and naturally be spoken more loudly than the first. And so it can.

The order of these four syllables, as a reader says them, may climb four steps of increasing volume, each syllable a little louder than the one before it. If that is so, then *limp'd*—a softer syllable in the meter of the line—would in fact be louder than *hare*—a louder syllable in the meter of the whole line. *Because an invisible foot-separator comes between the two syllables, the relative loudness of* hare *and* limp'd *is metrically irrelevant.*

Keats's fourth line is more like his second line:

Ănd sí | lĕnt wás | thĕ flóck | ĭn wóol | lў fóld . . .

Was is not very loud, but it is relatively loud. Nowhere else in the line is there metrical ambiguity or a rhythmical variation.

Thus English meter, by shrewd use of relativity, can find rhythmical variation without changing the number of syllables in a line, and without changing the order of louder and softer syllables. Once we have read a few thousand lines with a typical swing of louder and softer, we have an expectation in our heads through which we perceive and sort out the syllables on the page. Meter is what lines have in common. If you were asked to scan the single line:

Rocks, caves, lakes, fens, bogs, dens, and shades of death

you would be right to refuse. But if you came upon this line deep in Milton's *Paradise Lost,* when you had learned to step to the tune of iambic pentameter, you would sort it by twos, giving a sharp beat like a foot tap to the even-numbered syllables:

Rocks, *caves,* lakes, *fens,* bogs, *dens,* and *shades* of *death* . . .

You would not sort it (as you could have done if the words had turned up in a prose paragraph) by threes, for instance:

Rocks, caves, *lakes,* bogs, fens, *dens,* and *shades* of *death* . . .

The reading dictated by meter allows large latitude—there can be different heights to these peaks and valleys—but meter imposes limits to its latitude: a peak remains peakish, relative to an adjacent valley.

The Miltonic line gives us an example of iambic pentameter which finds rhythmic variation by adding more volume. It has *more* loud noises in the line than we expect, though it retains only five relative stresses. More commonly, lines like "The University of Michigan" contain *fewer* loud noises than five. Scholars tell us that Shakespeare's pentameter averages about three loud noises a line—and, *not by average but always*, five relative stresses. In *Macbeth*

> Tomorrow and tomorrow and tomorrow . . .

makes a typical Shakespearean line. The three *-mor*-s, middles of three *tomor-rows*, make three loud noises, each louder than the syllable in front of it, the three *to*s. The two *and*s are not loud, but they are louder than the *-ows* which come before them, thus adding up to the five iambics of the pentameter.

Metrical variations

There are several common departures from the ˘′ | ˘′ | ˘′ | ˘′ | ˘′ | scheme, departures that are not irregularities; we call them metrical variations—they are variations *within* meter, not outside it—and we will talk about them in the order of their frequency. As they are used, they contribute to the variety of metrical verse.

Initial inversion   By far the most common metrical variation is reversal of the order of louder and softer syllables in one foot. This happens most frequently in the first foot in the line and is called **initial inversion.**

Suppose you have read a hundred lines that share ˘′ | ˘′ | ˘′ | ˘′ | ˘′ | . Then you come on a line beginning with a loud syllable—maybe a two-syllable word that can only be pronounced with the louder syllable first, like *studies*. The beginning of this line reverses for one second the order of louder and softer, only to return immediately to the old and expected order. This line with initial inversion scans ′˘ | ˘′ | ˘′ | ˘′ | ˘′ | . Look at this sample:

> The Ú | nivér | sity | of Mích | igán
> Stúdies | the pó | etry | of Keáts | and Fróst.

The little rhythmical turn at the beginning of the second line becomes a familiar dance step in the motion of metrical poetry in English: a little whirl, a sudden tipping-over and recovery, *bang* bang-bang *bang*. The movement can remind us of one of those large dolls children play with, weighted on the round bottom, which a child will push over and which will then immediately right itself. When Macbeth has said "Tomorrow and tomorrow and tomorrow," he continues,

> Creéps in | this pét | ty páce | from dáy | to dáy . . .

and it is clear that *in* is softer than *Creeps*. Although the remainder of this line scans like the pattern, the first foot is inverted—and the expectation that this foot *may* be inverted lurks in the head of the reader. Shakespeare, Milton, Keats, Frost—metrical poets use initial variation frequently. After Keats wrote

"And silent was the flock in woolly fold," his next line made the dance-step of initial inversion:

> Númb wĕre | thĕ beáds | măn's fíng | ĕrs, whíle | hĕ tóld . . .

and the next lines returned to regular motion:

> His rosary, and while his frosted breath
> Like pious incense from a censor old . . .

Medial inversion Less frequent than initial inversion is inversion elsewhere in the line, which is called **medial inversion** wherever it comes. Medial inversion makes its own pause, wherever it happens in the line; most medial inversions therefore take place after natural caesuras, often indicated by commas or other marks of punctuation:

> She said to me: open your book and read!

Open your book is that little dance-step of inversion again, now in the middle of the line. In "The Eve of St. Agnes," Keats makes this line:

> Frŏm húr | rў tó | ănd fró. | Sóon, ŭp | ălóft . . .

Soon is louder than its neighboring *up*. After the pause for the end of the preceding sentence, Keats has started a new thought with a medial inversion.

Even if the line lacks a natural caesura, medial inversion will make a pause. In Theodore Roethke's "My Papa's Waltz," the poet makes a sudden medial inversion (with an iambic trimeter line, three feet, not five):

> Yŏu béat | tíme ŏn | mў heád . . .

The slight awkwardness of the enforced pause between *beat* and *time* sounds just right for someone beating time on a small boy's head.

Feminine endings After inversion, the most common metrical variation is the extra syllable. Shakespeare's line

> Tomorrow and tomorrow and tomorrow . . .

is regular iambic. But it has eleven syllables, with an extra syllable at the end of the line, called a **feminine ending.** The extra syllable dangles into the pause at the end of the line. It does not feel like a variation, although it varies in fact from the basic scheme. We scan it ˘ / | ˘ / | ˘ / | ˘ / | ˘ / ˘ | . Robert Frost's blank verse has many feminine endings, as in "The Death of the Hired Man":

> Hĕ búnd | lĕs év | erў fórk | fŭl ín | tŏ pláce
> Ănd tágs | ănd númb | ĕrs it | fŏr fúr | thĕr réferĕnce
> Sŏ hé | căn fínd | ănd eás | ĭlў | dĭslódge ĭt.

The last two lines have feminine endings, providing you pronounce *reference* with two syllables, as Frost did.

Extra syllables   An extra syllable elsewhere in the line—or in the final foot *before* the last stress—is a palpable metrical variation. The extra syllable makes a second softer syllable, a foot of three syllables, which scans ◡◡/. Again in "The Death of the Hired Man," Frost writes:

> You never see him standing on the hay
> He's trying to lift, straining to lift himself.

Practice scanning these lines. In the second line, the meter begins easily enough with an iambic, *He's try-*; the line ends with three feet that start with a medial inversion: *straining | to lift | himself.* In between these two clumps we have the three syllables of an extra-syllabic foot: *-ing to lift.* You may notice that these three syllables are quick to say, occupying no more elapsed time than two syllables elsewhere in the line. Three-syllable feet in an iambic poem tend to be quick to say.

When metrical poetry sounds most conversational and speechlike (in later Shakespeare, in Robert Frost) we find most extra syllables and feminine endings.

Exercises

1. To mark the meter of a line, as we have done in the text, is to *scan*—the result called *scansion*, as we have seen. Scan the following poems, drawing vertical lines to separate the feet, and showing which syllables are louder, which softer.

from *Richard II*

> Let's talk of graves, of worms, and epitaphs,
>
> Make dust our paper, and with rainy eyes
>
> Write sorrow on the bosom of the earth . . .
>
> For God's sake, let us sit upon the ground,
>
> And tell sad stories of the death of kings:
>
> How some have been deposed; some slain in war;
>
> Some haunted by the ghosts they have deposed;
>
> Some poisoned by their wives; some sleeping killed;
>
> All murdered: for within the hollow crown
>
> 10 That rounds the mortal temples of a king
>
> Keeps Death his court; and there the antick sits,

Scoffing his state, and grinning at his pomp;

Allowing him a breath, a little scene,

To monarchize, be feared, and kill with looks;

Infusing him with self and vain conceit—

As if this flesh which walls about our life,

Were brass impregnable; and humoured thus,

Comes at the last, and with a little pin

Bores through his castle-wall, and—farewell king!

—William Shakespeare

To the Western World

A siren sang, and Europe turned away

From the high castle and the shepherd's crook.

Three caravels went sailing to Cathay

On the strange ocean, and the captains shook

Their banners out across the Mexique Bay.

And in our early days we did the same.

Remembering our fathers in their wreck

We crossed the sea from Palos where they came

And saw, enormous to the little deck,

10   A shore in silence waiting for a name.

The treasures of Cathay were never found.

In this America, this wilderness

Where the axe echoes with a lonely sound,

The generations labor to possess

And grave by grave we civilize the ground.

—Louis Simpson

2. The following examples, fabricated for this text, include metrical errors. Assume that they come from poems which have established themselves as iambic pentameter.

a. Ridiculous impoverishments of gold
   Adorn her throat, where jealousy was often told.

b. The dance of death, begun in August air,
   Regales the Autumn and the fair.

c. Harsh moments fail the resplendent flesh of
   Doorjambs heavy, gilt, worn, and repulsive.

Rhyme

Rhyme is a feature common to many metrical poems, not to all. **Blank verse** is iambic pentameter without rhyme; rhyme is what it is blank of. (Do not confuse blank verse with free verse. Free verse, which is free of meters, occasionally has rhyme.) The most common rhyme is the exact repetition, in two or more words, of the final vowel and consonants of a word. *Love*, as we all know, rhymes with *dove*. Here *-ove* is the unity, *l* and *d* the variety.

Direct rhyme

Look at a rhyming dictionary, and you may be astonished at the variety of rhymes available. Suppose I am writing a rhymed poem and am stuck for a rhyme with the word *decrease*. Probably I would find the right word in my head, but if I didn't I could look in *The Complete Rhyming Dictionary and Poet's Craft Book*, edited by Clement Wood, and find under the sound *ees* fifty-nine possible words, beginning: afterpiece/ambergris/battlepiece/Bereneice/Bernice/ cantatrice/caprice/cease/surrice/chimney-piece/Clarisse/coulease/crease . . . If I were rhyming on two or more syllables, **feminine rhyme**, I would find in another list: accretion/completion/concretion/deletion; for three-syllable rhyme, I would go to another list: credulous/sedulous. These examples are **direct rhyme**.

Indirect rhyme

Sometimes poets use **indirect rhyme** or **off-rhyme**, almost-but-not-quite directly rhyming. Rhyme/line, for instance, is indirect because the consonants though similar are not the same. In rhyme/spice, the vowels rhyme but the consonants differ; this example is also indirect rhyme, but the degree of indirectness is greater. Another poet might rhyme consonants and let the vowels fend for themselves: rhyme/lame/: goat/bleet. Emily Dickinson used indirect rhyme on many occasions, often rhyming open vowels together, vowels similar but not the same:

The Silence condescended—
Creation stopped—for Me—
But awed beyond my errand—
I worshipped—did not "pray"—

If you hold on to the vowel ending *pray*, its diphthong separates out into an *a* and an *e*. The *e* you end by holding rhymes with *Me*. Dickinson also rhymes consonants:

I cannot live with You—
It would be Life—
And Life is over there—
Behind the Shelf.

Cliché rhyme

When poets rhyme *love* with *dove*, they make a **cliché rhyme**. Other cliché rhymes include fire/desire, breath/death, and womb/tomb. Occasionally good poets get away with cliché rhyme, because their syntax or sense makes the second of the cliché rhymes somehow unexpected. Most times a cliché rhyme is a flaw in a poem. This is not an important tool in evaluating poems, but a way to look at what happens in rhyming. These rhymes are cliché not only because they have been used so often, but also because the words resemble each other: in the list above, each of the examples can be a noun, and all but one are monosyllables. Each belongs to the same level of diction. Most important, each recalls its mate by similarity or opposition of meaning. Fire is a symbol of desire. Breath is ended by death. What begins in the womb ends in the tomb. For all these reasons, the first word of each pair leads one to expect the second, and when expectation is exactly fulfilled, the result is boredom. A poem must balance the predictable with the unpredictable, expectation with surprise, unity with variety.

Original rhyme

In a rhyme, the unity is the repetition of sound; the variety is all the other differences two words can muster. For instance, words can differ in length, and we can rhyme a monosyllable with a polysyllable, like *tracks* with *haversacks*. We can rhyme words spelled differently, like *tracks* with *axe*. We can rhyme different parts of speech, a verb *hacks* with a noun *jacks*. We can rhyme words of different backgrounds, like *egomaniacs* with *humpbacks*,or *kleptomaniacs* with *packs*. We can rhyme combinations of alien words: Jack's/hypochondriacs/ kayaks/quacks. In feminine rhyme, we can pair two words with one, rhyming *pluck it* with *Nantucket*.

The further apart the words are, the more original the rhyme. At extremes, rhyme can be witty or comic. In one of his poems Ogden Nash uses a *boom-erang* for hunting in order to cook a *kangaroo meringue*. Witty rhyme would be inappropriate to many poems, in which neither poet nor reader would want rhyme to stand out and be noticeable apart from the poem's other qualities. Highly original rhyme is appropriate in this poem:

Early in the Morning

Early in the morning
The dark Queen said,
"The trumpets are warning
There's trouble ahead."
Spent with carousing,

With wine-soaked wits,
Antony drowsing
Whispered, "It's
Too cold a morning
10   To get out of bed."

The army's retreating,
The fleet has fled,
Caesar is beating
His drums through the dead.
"Antony, horses!
We'll get away,
Gather our forces
For another day . . ."
"It's a cold morning,"
20   Antony said.

Caesar Augustus
Cleared his phlegm.
"Corpses disgust us.
Cover them."
Caesar Augustus
In his time lay
Dying, and just as
Cold as they,
On the cold morning
30   Of a cold day.
                    —*Louis Simpson*

Line length contributes to the wit of rhyming here; with only two feet to a line, rhyming becomes a stunt. Who would have expected *drowsing* to rhyme with *carousing*, or *Augustus* with *just as* and *disgust us*?

Natural rhyme

On the other hand, here is a poem by Thomas Hardy in which rhyme is neither cliché nor witty, but through the skill of the poet appears natural in the poem while it adds its particular music.

The Oxen

Christmas Eve, and twelve of the clock.
    "Now they are all on their knees,"
An elder said as we sat in a flock
    By the embers in hearthside ease.

We pictured the meek mild creatures where
    They dwelt in their strawy pen,
Nor did it occur to one of us there
    To doubt they were kneeling then.

So fair a fancy few would weave
10   In these years! Yet, I feel,
If someone said on Christmas Eve,
    "Come; see the oxen kneel

"In the lonely barton° by yonder coomb°   farmyard; a hollow
    Our childhood used to know,"
I should go with him in the gloom,
    Hoping it might be so.
                              —*Thomas Hardy*

This rhyme helps fix the poem's form, click the lid of its box; it neither stands out as a stunt of wit nor bores us with the overly predictable.

Rhymed stanzas

"The Oxen" is written in **stanzas**; a stanza is an arrangement of metrical lines, sometimes different in length, with a repeated order of rhyme, a **rhyme-scheme**. Here, the first and third lines rhyme, and the second and fourth; we indicate rhyme-schemes by letters; this scheme is ABAB. (First and third lines are iambic tetrameter, second and fourth iambic trimeter.) Sometimes poets invent stanzas and rhyme schemes of great complexity, varying line length and the arrangements of rhyme.

Exercises

Look at the rhyming of these poems.

1. Mark the rhyme-schemes and stanza patterns in each poem.
2. Find three direct rhymes. Can you find indirect or off-rhymes of different sorts? Discuss the difference.
3. Can you find examples of cliché rhyme? Original rhyme? Natural rhyme?

Tywater

Death of Sir Nihil, book the *nth*,
Upon the charred and clotted sward,
Lacking the lily of our Lord,
Alases of the hyacinth.

Could flicker from behind his ear
A whistling silver throwing knife
And with a holler punch the life
Out of a swallow in the air.

Behind the lariat's butterfly
10   Shuttled his white and gritted grin,
And cuts of sky would roll within
The noose-hole, when he spun it high.

The violent, neat and practised skill
Was all he loved and all he learned;
When he was hit, his body turned
To clumsy dirt before it fell.

And what to say of him, God knows.
Such violence. And such repose.
                                    —*Richard Wilbur*

Samuel Sewall

Samuel Sewall, in a world of wigs,
Flouted opinion in his personal hair;
For foppery he gave not any figs,
But in his right and honor took the air.

Thus in his naked style, though well attired,
He went forth in the city, or paid court
To Madam Winthrop, whom he much admired,
Most godly, but yet liberal with the port.

And all the town admired for two full years
His excellent address, his gifts of fruit,
Her gracious ways and delicate white ears,
And held the course of nature absolute.

But yet she bade him suffer a peruke,
'That One be not distinguished from the All';
Delivered of herself this stern rebuke
Framed in the resonant language of St. Paul.

'Madam,' he answered her, 'I have a Friend
Furnishes me with hair out of His strength,
And He requires only I attend
Unto His charity and to its length.'

And all the town was witness to his trust:
On Monday he walked out with the Widow Gibbs,
A pious lady of charm and notable bust,
Whose heart beat tolerably beneath her ribs.

On Saturday he wrote proposing marriage,
And closed, imploring that she be not cruel,
'Your favorable answer will oblige,
Madam, your humble servant, Samuel Sewall.'
                                    —*Anthony Hecht*

Chapter 9 **Forms and Types of Poetry**

Poetic forms are traditional arrangements of line and rhyme-scheme, like the sonnet. (If we use the word *forms* for these arrangements, we are not calling other poetry—like free verse or blank verse—formless. *Form* is merely a traditional word for this sort of arrangement.)

By types of poetry we mean distinctions between narrative and dramatic poetry on the one hand and on the other subdivisions like the epigram and the prose poem.

Poetic forms

The limerick

Each form of poetry demands a particular number of lines, of certain length, rhyming in a certain way. In a *limerick*, for instance, two trimeter lines rhyme, followed by two dimeter lines which also rhyme, and then a fifth trimeter line which rhymes with the first two. The rhyme-scheme is AABBA, and the BB lines are often indented. A limerick's feet are usually three syllables long, each an **anapest**: softer, softer, louder, or ⌣⌣′. (Authors of limericks sometimes substitute iambs for anapests.) Here is an example by a modern master of the form, Edward Gorey (born 1925):

> Each night Father fills me with dread
> When he sits on the foot of my bed;
>   I'd not mind that he speaks
>   In gibbers and squeaks,
> But for seventeen years he's been dead.

These anonymous limericks can provide a refresher course in meter:

> There was a young man of Japan
> Whose verses would never scan.
> When he was asked why
> He would reply,
> Well, I simply try to get as many syllables into the last line as I possibly can.

> There was a young man of China
> Whose aesthetic was somewhat fina.
> It was his design
> To make the last line
> Short.

So much for limericks, which can serve as an example of many forms.*

The haiku

Many American students have written haikus in school. When the English haiku-writer follows the Japanese syllable count, he uses lines of five, seven, and five syllables. The **haiku** is an imagistic poem, usually including two images, of which the second is a surprise, a leap from the first; or at least the two images conflict. Here is a translation from a sixteenth-century Japanese poet named Moritaki:

> A falling petal
> drops upward, back to the branch;
> it's a butterfly.

Many poets writing haikus in English, aware of differences between English and Japanese, ignore syllable count and concentrate on images.

The sonnet

Important for us to know is a poetic form that has remained at the center of English poetry from the sixteenth century onward. English poets from Thomas Wyatt (1503–1542) to the present have found the sonnet a congenial form, mostly for emotional statement. In one of his own sonnets, Wordsworth spoke of the sonnet as the key with which Shakespeare unlocked his heart. Shakespeare wrote a sequence of sonnets, as did many other poets in the sixteenth and seventeenth centuries. Even when it is a part of a sequence, a sonnet is a whole and individual poem, a certain length with several possible internal structures whereby a poet can entertain and conclude a whole, small subject. Early sonnets and sonnet sequences were mostly concerned with love. John Donne's "Holy Sonnets" are religious, as are many of Milton's sonnets. More recently, sonnets have extended themselves to all sorts of feelings.

---

*Readers interested in the many poetic forms not mentioned here may consult Lewis Turco's *A Book of Forms*, which defines and exemplifies widely among special forms. Or look at the pages about poetic forms in Clement Wood's *Complete Rhyming Dictionary*.

The sonnet is fourteen lines long, and written in iambic pentameter. (We can find poems called sonnets that are exceptions to these rules; the word originally meant "little song" and some poets have interpreted the word broadly.) There are three main traditional structures and rhyme schemes. One is the **Italian** or **Petrarchan sonnet**, which is divided into two parts. The octave is the first eight lines, and it uses only two rhymes: ABBAABBA. The sestet in an Italian or Petrarchan sonnet can rhyme in several ways—CDECDE is common; so is CDCDCD—so long as it does not end in a couplet. Many English poets have practiced the Italian sonnet with success, notably Milton and Wordsworth.

The English language, however, is noted for the paucity of its rhyme, especially compared to the Italian richness in rhyme-words. Therefore the octave of the Italian sonnet can make trouble for the English poet because it uses only two rhyme-sounds for eight words. The **English sonnet**, more commonly called the **Shakespearean sonnet**, began a little earlier than Shakespeare—it was first used by Henry Howard, Earl of Surrey (1517–1547)—and uses a rhyme scheme more adapted to the English language: ABAB CDCD EFEF GG. Edmund Spenser, finding the Italian sonnet not suited to English but the English sonnet too loose, invented a third rhyme scheme that is a compromise between the two: ABAB BCBC CDCD EE. This arrangement makes the **Spenserian sonnet**.

Rhyme-schemes are probably less important to sonnets than structures of thought, but rhyme-schemes seem to suggest such structures. In the Italian sonnet, the octave and the sestet usually make a two-part structure not further subdivided. Frequently an octave will set forth a problem, or tell a story, to which the sestet may provide a solution, a counterdirection, a commentary, or a surprise. Of course there are exceptions; some Italian sonnets feature no division at all but make an indivisible fourteen-line poem.

On the other hand, the English or Shakespearean sonnet, which often breaks down into eight and six, may also break in other places. It may further subdivide into four and four, plus four and two, or it may break down into four, four, four, and two; or it may break down into eight, four, and two. If the Shakespearean sonnet is structurally more adaptable, it is for the same reason a less precise form.

Quoted throughout this text are sonnets by Shakespeare (see pages 38 and 41). Here is another:

Let me not to the marriage of true minds

Let me not to the marriage of true minds
Admit impediments. Love is not love
Which alters when it alteration finds,
Or bends with the remover to remove.
O no, it is an ever-fixèd mark
That looks on tempests and is never shaken;
It is the star to every wand'ring bark,
Whose worth's unknown, although his height be taken.

Love's not Time's fool, though rosy lips and cheeks
10   Within his bending sickle's compass come;
Love alters not with his brief hours and weeks,
But bears it out even to the edge of doom.
   If this be error and upon me proved,
   I never writ, nor no man ever loved.

Here is a sonnet by John Milton. Notice the rhyme scheme:

On the Late Massacre in Piedmont[1]

Avenge, O Lord, thy slaughtered saints, whose bones
Lie scattered on the Alpine mountains cold;
Ev'n them who kept thy truth so pure of old,
When all our fathers worshipped stocks and stones,
Forget not: in thy book record their groans
Who were thy sheep, and in their ancient fold
Slain by the bloody Piedmontese, that rolled
Mother with infant down the rocks. Their moans
The vales redoubled to the hills, and they
10   To heav'n. Their martyred blood and ashes sow
O'er all th' Italian fields, where still doth sway
The triple[2] Tyrant that from these may grow
A hundredfold, who, having learnt thy way,
Early may fly the Babylonian woe.[3]

[1]In 1655 the Protestant Waldenses of southern France were suppressed for refusing to adhere to Roman Catholicism.   [2]A reference to the papal crown.   [3]See Revelation 27:8.

Wordsworth, Keats, Tennyson, Frost—most great poets have turned to the sonnet during their lives. Examples of the sonnet may be found throughout this book. See, for instance, pages 70, 168, 171, 175, 176, 179, and 204.

Poetic types

Ballad

A ballad is almost a form; at least, there are typical stanzas, and even ballads we can call typical; but the word *ballad* does not represent a form as codified as sonnet. Although ballads tell stories, we separate them from the later category of narrative poetry because they form a great body of anonymous literature; and there is also the later, sophisticated imitation of the ballad. Here is an anonymous Scots ballad, with some old Scottish words footnoted.

Edward

"Why dois[1] your brand[2] sae[3] drap[4] wi bluid,[5]
    Edward, Edward,
Why dois your brand sae drap wi bluid,
    And why sae sad gang[6] yee O?"
"O I hae[7] killed my hauke[8] sae guid,[9]
    Mither, mither,
O I hae killed my hauke sae guid,
    And I had nae mair[10] but hee O."

"Your haukis bluid was nevir sae reid,[11]
10   Edward, Edward,
Your haukis bluid was nevir sae reid,
    My deir son I tell thee O."
"O I hae killed my reid roan steid,[12]
    Mither, mither,
O I hae killed my reid roan steid,
    That erst[13] was sae fair and free O."

"Your steid was auld,[14] and ye hae gat mair,
    Edward, Edward,
Your steid was auld, and ye hae gat mair,
20   Sum other dule[15] ye drie[16] O."
"O I hae killed my fadir[17] deir,
    Mither, mither,
O I hae killed my fadir deir,
    Alas, and wae[18] is mee O!"

"And whatten penance wul[19] ye drie for that,
    Edward, Edward?
And whatten penance wul ye drie for that?
    My deir son, now tell me O."
"Ile set my feet in yonder boat,
30   Mither, mither,
Ile set me feet in yonder boat,
    And Ile fare ovir the sea O."

"And what wul ye doe wi your towirs and your ha,[20]
    Edward, Edward?
And what wul ye doe wi your towirs and your ha,
    That were sae fair to see O?"
"Ile let thame stand tul they doun fa,
    Mither, mither,
Ile let thame stand tul they doun fa,
40   For here nevir mair maun[21] I bee O."

"And what wul ye leive to your bairns[22] and your wife,
    Edward, Edward?
And what wul ye leive to your bairns and your wife,
    Whan ye gang ovir the sea O?"
"The warldis[23] room, let them beg thrae[24] life,
    Mither, mither,

[1]does   [2]sword   [3]so   [4]drip   [5]blood   [6]go   [7]have   [8]hawk   [9]good   [10]more   [11]red
[12]steed   [13]formerly   [14]old   [15]grief   [16]suffer   [17]father   [18]woe   [19]will   [20]hall   [21]must
[22]children   [23]world's   [24]through

The warldis room, let them beg thrae life,
   For thame nevir mair wul I see O."

"And what wul ye leive to your ain[25] mither deir?
50   Edward, Edward?
And what wul ye leive to your ain mither deir?
   My deir son, now tell me O."
"The curse of hell frae[26] me sall[27] ye beir,[28]
   Mither, mither,
The curse of hell frae me sall ye beir,
   Sic[29] counseils ye gave to me O."
                   —*Anonymous*

[25]own   [26]from   [27]shall   [28]bear   [29]such

A ballad tells a story. In "Edward," the story is told in dialogue, as if the poem were a tiny play, the speeches organized into stanzas. In the tight and musical stanzas of this ballad, we hear a son reluctantly telling his mother that he has killed his father, and finally cursing his mother for having urged him to patricide. When a harrowing story is told in rhymed and delicate verses, the tension between form and content, story and music makes a dreadful energy.

See page 166 for another ballad.

Later poets imitated old ballad forms in writing narrative poems. One of the most famous literary ballads in English is by John Keats.

La Belle Dame sans Merci[1]

Oh, what can ail thee, knight-at-arms,
   Alone and palely loitering?
The sedge has withered from the lake,
   And no birds sing!

Oh, what can ail thee, knight-at-arms,
   So haggard and so woe-begone?
The squirrel's granary is full,
   And the harvest's done.

I see a lily on thy brow,
10   With anguish moist and fever-dew,
And on thy cheek a fading rose
   Fast withereth too.

I met a lady in the meads
   Full beautiful, a fairy's child.
Her hair was long, her foot was light,
   And her eyes were wild.

I made a garland for her head,
   And bracelets too, and fragrant zone;

[1]The beautiful, pitiless woman

She looked at me as she did love,
20   And made sweet moan.

I set her on my pacing steed,
    And nothing else saw all day long;
For sidelong would she bend, and sing
    A fairy's song.

She found me roots of relish sweet,
    And honey wild, and manna dew;
And sure in language strange she said,
    "I love thee true."

She took me to her elfin grot,
30   And there she wept, and sighed full sore,
And there I shut her wild wild eyes
    With kisses four.

And there she lullèd me asleep
    And there I dreamed—Ah! woe betide!—
The latest dream I ever dreamed
    On the cold hill side.

I saw pale kings and princes too,
    Pale warriors, death-pale were they all;
They cried—"La belle Dame sans merci
40   Hath thee in thrall!"

I saw their starved lips in the gloam
    With horrid warning gapèd wide,
And I awoke and found me here,
    On the cold hill side.

And this is why I sojourn here,
    Alone and palely loitering,
Though the sedge is withered from the lake,
    And no birds sing.

(On page 105 are examples of Keats's revisions of this poem.) The verse is smoother and more literary than the old ballads, and the language is closer to our own, but the poem makes its ancestry clear.

Narrative, epic, dramatic

Many poems, including ballads, tell stories, and are therefore narrative. The earliest surviving poetry is narrative, ancient epics originally chanted or sung to a form of musical accompaniment. *Gilgamesh* is the oldest surviving poem, composed in Sumeria about five thousand years ago; Homer's *Iliad* and *Odyssey* are a mere three thousand years old. These epics were composed orally, before the invention of writing; they were memorized, and changed ("revised") by generations of reciter-poets. (There was no single, innovative, sole-author Homer; though it is possible that one blind bard assembled and organized the *Iliad* and the *Odyssey* more thoroughly than any of his predecessors.)

Prehistoric Greeks remembered and celebrated their past by memorizing Homer. Epics are historical records of the heroes of the tribe, combining fact and legend. Centuries after these oral epics were composed, professional poets made sophisticated epics in imitation of the old collective style. The Roman Vergil, wishing to write a patriotic poem to flatter the emperor Augustus, followed the pattern of Homer when he composed *The Aeneid.*

In the Christian era, Dante's *Divine Comedy* is a sophisticated epic. Its embodiment of Christian theology makes it a vast departure from classical forms, but the ghost who guides Dante through hell to purgatory is Vergil himself. In English, the great epic is Milton's seventeenth-century account of creation, and the war between good and evil, in *Paradise Lost.*

Many poems are narrative tales, comic or tragic, without being epic. The great narrative poet in English is Geoffrey Chaucer. His language is archaic, and best saved for advanced study, but there is a sample of his poetry on page 165. *The Canterbury Tales* is a lengthy series of different stories told by and about ordinary people—not, like an epic, tales of gods and heroes making history.

After Chaucer, to the present time, many poets have written stories in rhyme and meter (less often in free verse). Sometimes the stories take dramatic form, most often as monologues by a speaker who reveals himself as he tells his story (see Robert Browning's "My Last Duchess," page 215). One example of modern narrative is a story poem by Robert Frost:

"Out, Out—"

The buzz saw snarled and rattled in the yard
And made dust and dropped stove-length sticks of wood.
Sweet-scented stuff when the breeze drew across it.
And from there those that lifted eyes could count
Five mountain ranges one behind the other
Under the sunset far into Vermont.
And the saw snarled and rattled, snarled and rattled,
As it ran light, or had to bear a load.
And nothing happened: day was all but done.
10   Call it a day, I wish they might have said
To please the boy by giving him the half hour
That a boy counts so much when saved from work.
His sister stood beside them in her apron
To tell them "Supper." At the word, the saw,
As if to prove saws knew what supper meant,
Leaped out at the boy's hand, or seemed to leap—
He must have given the hand. However it was,
Neither refused the meeting. But the hand!
The boy's first outcry was a rueful laugh,
20   As he swung toward them holding up the hand
Half in appeal, but half as if to keep
The life from spilling. Then the boy saw all—

Since he was old enough to know, big boy
Doing a man's work, though a child at heart—
He saw all spoiled. "Don't let him cut my hand off—
The doctor, when he comes. Don't let him, sister!"
So. But the hand was gone already.
The doctor put him in the dark of ether.
He lay and puffed his lips out with his breath.
30 And then—the watcher at his pulse took fright.
No one believed. They listened at his heart.
Little—less—nothing!—and that ended it.
No more to build on there. And they, since they
Were not the one dead, turned to their affairs.

Lyric and song

We have come to use **lyric** to mean a short poem, usually emotional or descriptive. The term is perhaps too general to be useful. Originally derived from the word for lyre (a musical instrument) the word indicated a poem composed for singing. Many old poems were originally written as songs. Here is one of Shakespeare's songs, from *Love's Labour's Lost*:

Winter

When icicles hang by the wall,
   And Dick the shepherd blows his nail,
And Tom bears logs into the hall,
   And milk comes frozen home in pail,
When blood is nipp'd, and ways be foul,
Then nightly sings the staring owl,
                  Tu-who;
Tu-whit, tu-who—a merry note,
While greasy Joan doth keel the pot.

10 When all aloud the wind doth blow,
   And coughing drowns the parson's saw,
And birds sit brooding in the snow,
   And Marian's nose looks red and raw,
When roasted crabs hiss in the bowl,
Then nightly sings the staring owl,
                  Tu-who;
Tu-whit, tu-who—a merry note,
While greasy Joan doth keel the pot.

Epigrams

An epigram is short, pithy, witty, and conclusive. Here is one by Thomas Hardy:

Epitaph on a Pessimist

I'm Smith of Stoke, aged sixty-odd,
 I've lived without a dame
From youth-time on; and would to God
 My Dad had done the same.

(An **epitaph** is an inscription for a gravestone; some epitaphs are also epigrams. Note that there is a third word sometimes confused with epigram and epitaph; an **epigraph** is a quotation an author places at the start of a work.) Walter Savage Landor wrote many epigrams, among them this one:

I strove with none, for none was worth my strife.
 Nature I loved and, next to Nature, Art:
I warmed both hands before the fire of life;
 It sinks, and I am ready to depart.

The modern American J. V. Cunningham has written most of his work in epigrammatic form, some of it very funny:

Naked I came, naked I leave the scene,
And naked was my pastime in between.

some not:

On a cold night I came through the cold rain
And false snow to the wind shrill on your pane
With no hope and no anger and no fear:
Who are you? and with whom do you sleep here?

Most epigrams rhyme. We call a short free-verse poem an epigram only when brevity combines with wit:

The Bath Tub

As a bathtub lined with white porcelain,
When the hot water gives out or goes tepid,
So is the slow cooling of our chivalrous passion,
O my much praised but-not-altogether-satisfactory lady.
       —Ezra Pound

Visual poetry

While most poetry appeals to the ear, some poetry arranges itself for the pleasure of the eye. Early in the seventeenth century, George Herbert wrote "Easter Wings."

Lord, who createdst man in wealth and store,
Though foolishly he lost the same,
Decaying more and more
Till he became
Most poor:
With thee
O let me rise
As larks, harmoniously,
And sing this day thy victories:
10   Then shall the fall further the flight in me.

My tender age in sorrow did begin;
And still with sicknesses and shame
Thou didst so punish sin,
That I became
Most thin.
With thee
Let me combine,
And feel this day thy victory;
For, if I imp my wing on thine,
20   Affliction shall advance the flight in me.

This poem is a pleasure both to ear and to eye. If you heard the poem read aloud, you would be aware of lines becoming shorter, then longer again—a closing in, an opening up—but you would not be aware that the poem created on the page the visual shape of an angel's wings. Reading and seeing the poem are separate pleasures. Herbert's "Easter Wings" is a concrete poem because a portion of its creation is visual.

Modern poems sometimes exist to the eye and not to the ear. When E. E. Cummings makes

l(a

le
af
fa

ll

s)
one
l

iness

there is no way to pronounce the poem except by spelling it and indicating marks of punctuation. (Even then the voicing will detract from the poem; the voice will have to decide whether the first character is *ell* or *one*. (It is *ell*, in terms of the words *loneliness* and *a leaf falls*, but the meaning of the poem is underscored by the visual pun on *ell* and *one*.) The poem exists, not to the eye and ear together, nor to both eye and ear separately, but to the eye alone.

Concrete poetry is a blend of poetry and painting, or visual art. Ian Hamilton Finlay is a contemporary leader among concretists. Here is his "Homage to Malevich"—the painter who tilted a white square on a white background in "White on White":

                lackblockblackb
                lockblackblockb
                lackblockblackb
                lockblackblockb
                lackblockblackb
                lockblackblockb
                lackblockblackb
                lockblackblockb

lackblockblackb   lackblockblackb   lackblockblackb
lockblackblockb   lockblackblockb   lockblackblockb
lackblockblackb   lackblockblackb   lackblockblackb
lockblackblockb   lockblackblockb   lockblackblockb
lackblockblackb   lackblockblackb   lackblockblackb
lockblackblockb   lockblackblockb   lockblackblockb
lackblockblackb   lackblockblackb   lackblockblackb
lockblackblockb   lockblackblockb   lockblackblockb

                lackblockblackb
                lockblackblockb
                lackblockblackb
                lockblackblockb
                lackblockblackb
                lockblackblockb
                lackblockblackb
                lockblackblockb

Some poems assembled as concrete are less like pictures and more like collections of letters for the mind to dwell on—like the French movement *lettrism*. Thus Aram Saroyan has composed poems of a single word like *oxygen*, or a single nonword like *blod* (immortalized by the *Guinness Book of Records* as the world's shortest poem). These poems are not so interesting in their own sensuous shape as they are in the thoughts they lead to. Thus they resemble conceptual sculpture, like Yoko Ono's row of empty flowerpots titled "Imagining Flowers."

Prose poems

Poems written in paragraphs have been a part of literature for more than a hundred years. Usually a prose poem shares most of the qualities we associate with poetry—images, metaphor, figures, controlled rhythm, and fantasy—except for lines and linebreaks. Most poets who make prose poems write lined poems also. Robert Bly's lined poems appear on pages 57 and 311.

The Dead Seal near McClure's Beach

1

Walking north toward the point, I came on a dead seal. From a few feet away, he looks like a brown log. The body is on its back, dead only a few hours. I stand and look at him. There's a quiver in the dead flesh. My God he is still alive. A shock goes through me, as if a wall of my room had fallen away.

His head is arched back, the small eyes closed, the whiskers sometimes rise and fall. He is dying. This is the oil. Here on its back is the oil that heats our houses so efficiently. Wind blows fine sand back toward the ocean. The flipper near me lies folded over the stomach, looking like an unfinished arm, lightly glazed with sand at the edges. The other flipper lies half underneath. The seal's skin looks like an old overcoat, scratched here and there, by sharp mussel-shells maybe. . . .

I reach out and touch him. Suddenly he rears up, turns over, gives three cries, Awaark! Awaark! Awaark!—like the cries from Christmas toys. He lunges toward me. I am terrified and leap back, although I know there can be no teeth in that jaw. He starts flopping toward the sea. But he falls over, on his face. He does not want to go back to the sea. He looks up at the sky, and he looks like an old lady who has lost her hair.

He puts his chin back on the sand, rearranges his flippers, and waits for me to go. I go.

2

Today I go back to say goodbye: he's dead now. But he's not—he's a quarter mile farther up the shore. Today he is thinner, squatting on his stomach, head out. The ribs show more—each vertebra on the back under the coat is now visible, shiny. He breathes in and out.

He raises himself up, and tucks his flippers under, as if to keep them warm. A wave comes in, touches his nose. He turns and looks at me—the eyes slanted, the crown of his head is like a black leather jacket. He is taking a long time to die. The whiskers white as porcupine quills, the forehead slopes . . . goodbye brother, die in the sound of waves, forgive us if we have killed you, long live your race, your inner-tube race, so uncomfortable on land, so comfortable in the ocean. Be comfortable in death then, where the sand will be out of your nostrils, and you can swim in long loops through the pure death, ducking under as assassinations break above you. You don't want to be touched by me. I climb the cliff and go home the other way.

Notice how in the form of prose Bly uses the details of the world and yet (as in a poem) leaps across spaces of thought to see inside things.

Russell Edson is another contemporary American who writes prose poems. He writes tiny narratives—which might be called fables, or novels to read through a microscope—that other people call prose poems. When it becomes difficult to decide whether a piece of writing is a story, a poem, a play, or an essay, then by and large the task is useless. Here is a prose poem—I'll call it—by Russell Edson:

Bringing a Dead Man Back into Life

The dead man is introduced back into life. They take him
to a country fair, to a French restaurant, a round of late
night parties . . .He's beginning to smell.

They give him a few days off in bed.

He's taken to a country fair again; a second engagement
at the French restaurant; another round of late night parties
. . . No response . . . They brush the maggots away . . .
That terrible smell! . . . No use . . .

What's wrong with you?

10   . . . No use . . .

They slap his face. His cheek comes off; bone under-
neath, jaws and teeth . . .

Another round of late night parties . . . Dropping his
fingers . . . An ear falls off . . . Loses a foot in a taxi . . .
No use . . . The smell . . . Maggots everywhere!

Another round of late night parties. His head comes off,
rolls on the floor. A woman stumbles on it, an eye rolls
out. She screams.

No use . . . Under his jacket nothing but maggots and

20   ribs . . . No use . . .

Chapter 10 **Versions of the Same**

This chapter gathers different versions of the same texts: poets' revisions of their own work, variant translations of one original, and a pedagogic paraphrase. Saying that different words express the same content, we beg questions; when two texts differ in their wording, by definition nothing is truly the same. Still, revisions and variant translations can give us multiple examples of phrases that resemble each other and are *not* the same, thus providing opportunity to examine differences of diction, rhythm, image, metaphor, sound, and (often) meter. By noticing these differences, we can review the study of poetry and sharpen our ability to tell better from good, best from better.

Poets' revisions

William Butler Yeats revised his poems many times. He published his first volume in 1885, and by 1895 he had revised some of these poems in a new collection of his work. When he was in his sixties he rewrote some poems he had written in his twenties. When people objected, he made an answer:

> The friends that have it I do wrong
> Whenever I remake a song,
> Should know what issue is at stake:
> It is myself that I remake.

With his early revisions, he remade style, not self. He changed:

> In three days' time he stood up with a moan
> And he went down to the long sands alone.

to:

> In three days' time, Cuchulain* with a moan
> Stood up, and came to the long sands alone.

In this revision a proper name replaces a pronoun, and a boring rhythm becomes varied and expressive: *Stood up*, with a pause after it, then eight syllables of walking, seems to imitate in its rhythm the action it describes.

In 1892, in the first version of a famous poem called "When You Are Old," Yeats wrote the couplet:

> Murmur, a little sad, "From us fled Love.
> He paced upon the mountains far above . . ."

The adjective *sad* goes strangely with the verb *murmur*, and the normal word order at the end of the first line would have been *Love fled from us*. Dissatisfied six years later, Yeats rewrote the lines to read:

> Murmur, a little sadly, how Love fled
> And paced upon the mountains overhead . . .

Now this line approaches natural speech, without affectation or awkwardness.

Four versions of the last stanza of "Cradle Song" show Yeats growing in simplicity and directness:

1889

> My darling I kiss you,
>   With arms round my own.
> Ah, how I shall miss you
>   When heavy and grown.

1892

> I kiss you and kiss you
>   With arms round my own.
> Ah, how I shall miss you
>   When, dear, you have grown.

1901

> I kiss you and kiss you
> My pigeon, my own.
> Ah, how I shall miss you,
> When you have grown.

Cuchulain is pronounced cuh-HULL-an.

1925

I sigh that kiss you
For I must own
That I shall miss you
When you have grown.

In the 1889 stanza, the first line lacks the energy it picked up later when Yeats packed the line with two verbs. In the last line, the word *heavy* is unfortunate—the kind of error any writer can make, where a word brings in an irrelevant association the writer is blind to; *heavy* for Yeats probably implied ponderous and slow-moving, an end to youth; unfortunately it is a euphemism for obesity. In 1892, he improved the first line and in the fourth line got rid of *heavy* but added the rhythmically awkward apostrophe to *dear*, chopping the line up with commas. In 1901 he repaired the fourth line—finally—but left behind the decorative *pigeon* and the decorative *Ah*. By 1925 he was all for spareness. In judging among these "versions of the same" there is room for difference of opinion, but I like the last version best. This 1925 change comes closer to remaking the self, like these two versions of "The Lamentation of the Old Pensioner" (original title "The Old Pensioner"):

1890

I had a chair at every hearth,
When no one turned to see
With "Look at that old fellow there;
And who may he be?"
And therefore do I wander on,
And the fret is on me.

The road-side trees keep murmuring—
Ah, wherefore murmur ye
As in the old days long gone by,
10   Green oak and poplar tree!
The well-known faces are all gone,
And the fret is on me.

1939

Although I shelter from the rain
Under a broken tree
My chair was nearest to the fire
In every company
That talked of love or politics,
Ere Time transfigured me.

Though lads are making pikes again
For some conspiracy,
And crazy rascals rage their fill
10   At human tyranny,
My contemplations are of Time
That has transfigured me.

There's not a woman turns her face
Upon a broken tree,
And yet the beauties that I loved
Are in my memory;
I spit into the face of Time
That has transfigured me.

Exercises

1. The two poems use a different sort of sound, for different effect. Pick out the characteristic sounds of each poem.
2. It is often said that Yeats's poems became more speechlike as he matured. Could you use these poems to support this assertion?

Here are more examples of Yeats's revisions. Those labeled A are the earlier versions, B the later. See if you can decide why Yeats changed the lines.

A

"My father," made he smiling answer then,
"Still treads the world amid his armed men."

B

"My father dwells among the sea-worn bands,
And breaks the ridge of battle with his hands."

A

The oldest hound with mournful din
   Lifts slow his wintery head:—
The servants bear the body in—
   The hounds keen for the dead.

B

The blind hound with a mournful din
   Lifts slow his wintery head;—
The servants bear the body in—
   The hounds wail for the dead.

Yeats was not the only great poet to revise his work. William Blake in "London" (page 196), originally wrote:

But most the midnight harlot's curse
From every dismal street I hear,
Weaves around the marriage hearse
And blasts the new born infant's tear.

A year later, he revised these lines into:

But most through midnight streets I hear
How the youthful harlot's curse
Blasts the new-born infant's tear
And blights with plagues the marriage hearse.

Notice that the elements of the first stanza—midnight, harlot's curse, street, infant, marriage hearse, blasts, tear—turn up again in the later stanza. We lose *dismal* and we gain another adjective, *youthful*, in exchange. We lose the pretty word *weave*—to weave is to create, to turn thread into cloth; in this context the pretty word is oddly used for destructive purpose—and we have in return the far more powerful *blights with plagues*, combining diseases of plants and animals. Although the first stanza was powerful, the revision increases the poem's power, the intensity, and the density, adding a new area of meaning in the metaphor of diseases. Before, death entered with *hearse*, but we lacked the cause of death. The order of things is changed in the second version, and the order itself makes the poetry more powerful. It moves from the innocent streets to the prostitute and her oath, to the damnation of the infant's weeping, and finally to the disease and death of the institution of marriage.

Exercise

In "La Belle Dame sans Merci," Keats originally wrote the stanza:

She took me to her elfin grot,
  And there she wept, and sighed full sore,
And there I shut her wild wild eyes
    With kisses four.

He changed these lines—three out of four—into:

She took me to her elfin grot,
  And there she gazed and sighèd deep,
And there I shut her wild sad eyes—
    So kissed to sleep.

Many critics feel that Keat's revision is inferior to the original. What do you think, and why?

Robert Frost kept most of his variant versions from the public. He liked to give the impression that he revised little. Still, he published a number of poems in an early version, tinkered with them, and published them in revised form. His most remarkable printed revision is that of "Design," one of his greatest poems. In 1912 he included in a letter this poem:

In White

A dented spider like a snowdrop white
On a white Heal-all,[1] holding up a moth
Like a white piece of lifeless satin cloth—
Saw ever curious eye so strange a sight?

[1] A flower, normally blue, reported to have healing qualities

Portent in little, assorted death and blight
Like the ingredients of a witches' broth?
The beady spider, the flower like a froth,
And the moth carried like a paper kite.

10   What had that flower to do with being white,
The blue Brunella,[2] every child's delight?
What brought the kindred spider to that height?
(Make we no thesis of the miller's° plight.)   moth
What but design of darkness and of night?
Design, design! Do I use the word aright?

[2]Another name for the healall

Not until 1922 did "In White" turn up again:

Design

I found a dimpled spider, fat and white,
On a white heal-all, holding up a moth
Like a white piece of rigid satin cloth—
Assorted characters of death and blight
Mixed ready to begin the morning right,
Like the ingredients of a witches' broth—
A snow-drop spider, a flower like a froth,
And dead wings carried like a paper kite.

10   What had that flower to do with being white,
The wayside blue and innocent heal-all?
What brought the kindred spider to that height,
Then steered the white moth thither in the night?
What but design of darkness to appall?—
If design govern in a thing so small.

It is useful with this poem, or these two poems, to compare them line by line. Here "In White" is in roman type, "Design" in italic.

1. A dented spider like a snowdrop white
   1. I found a dimpled spider, fat and white,
2. On a white Heal-all, holding up a moth
   2. On a white heal-all, holding up a moth
3. Like a white piece of lifeless satin cloth—
   3. Like a white piece of rigid satin cloth—
4. Saw ever curious eye so strange a sight?
   4. Assorted characters of death and blight
5. Portent in little, assorted death and blight
   5. Mixed ready to begin the morning right,
6. Like the ingredients of a witches' broth?
   6. Like the ingredients of a witches' broth—
7. The beady spider, the flower like a froth,
   7. A snow-drop spider, a flower like a froth,

8. And the moth carried like a paper kite.
   8. And dead wings carried like a paper kite.

9. What had that flower to do with being white,
   9. What had that flower to do with being white,
10. The blue Brunella every child's delight?
    10. The wayside blue and innocent heal-all?
11. What brought the kindred spider to that height?
    11. What brought the kindred spider to that height,
12. (Make we no thesis of the miller's plight.)
    12. Then steered the white moth thither in the night?
13. What the design of darkness and of night?
    13. What but design of darkness to appall?—
14. Design, design! Do I use the word aright?
    14. If design govern in a thing so small.

Exercises

1. In 1/1, compare *dented* with *dimpled*. What kind of object do you associate with *dented*? What kind with *dimpled*? Is either association preferable to the other in the context of the whole poem?
2. In 3/3, could you defend *lifeless* against *rigid*? Is either of these adjectives more specific than the other? More physical?
3. Paraphrase 3/4. How does the sentence work? Does 3/4 say something similar? Different? Does the grammar help the later poem?
4. In 7/7, compare *beady* and *snow-drop.*
5. In 8/8, compare the rhythms of the two lines at the beginning. What are the changes? Do you like the change? Can you say why?
6. The second stanzas or sestets of these two versions differ in a number of ways. List all the differences you can see. Decide whether you approve of the changes made. Imagine why Robert Frost might have wanted to make them. Look up the history of *appall* and decide how it is used in this poem. Which of the two poems is clearer? Which of the two poems is better? Why?

Different translations

Different translations of the same poem can offer us an opportunity to compare style, rhythm, and diction—even when we do not know the original. We can turn translations to our purposes by deciding which version we prefer, and why. We can sharpen our wits by defining our choices. Here is the Twenty-third Psalm, translated from the Hebrew of the Old Testament, in the seventeenth-century King James version:

> The Lord is my shepherd;
> I shall not want.
> He maketh me to lie down in green pastures: he leadeth me beside the still
>   waters.

He restoreth my soul: he leadeth me in the paths of righteousness for his
    name's sake.
Yea, though I walk through the valley of the shadow of death, I will fear
no evil: for thou art with me; thy rod and thy staff they comfort me.
    Thou preparest a table before me in the presence of mine enemies:
Thou annointest my head with oil; my cup runneth over.
    Surely goodness and mercy shall follow me all the days of my life:
10   And I will dwell in the house of the Lord forever.

Here is the Revised Standard Version, which came out first in 1952—very
close, but not the same:

The Lord is my shepherd, I shall not want;
    he makes me lie down in green pastures.
He leads me beside still waters;
    he restores my soul.
He leads me in paths of righteousness
    for his name's sake.

Even though I walk through the valley of the shadow of death,
    I fear no evil; for thou art with me;
    thy rod and thy staff,
10   they comfort me.

Thou preparest a table before me
in the presence of my enemies;
thou anointest my head with oil,
    my cup overflows.
Surely goodness and mercy shall follow me
    all the days of my life;
and I shall dwell in the house of the LORD
        for ever.

Here is the same Psalm in a version from *The Psalms for Modern Man,*
copyrighted by the American Bible Society in 1970:

The Lord is my shepherd;
    I have everything I need.
He lets me rest in fields of green grass
    and leads me to quiet pools of fresh water.
He gives me new strength.

He guides me in the right way,
    as he has promised.
Even if that way goes through deepest darkness,
    I will not be afraid, Lord,
10   because you are with me!
Your shepherd's rod and staff keep me safe.

You prepare a banquet for me,
    where all my enemies can see me;

You welcome me by pouring ointment on my head
    and filling my cup to the brim.
Certainly your goodness and love will be with me as long as I live;
    and your house will be my home forever.

Finally, here is a version by a young American poet named David Rosenberg who is translating "A Poet's Bible" book by book; this modern version is taken from *Blues of the Sky*, Rosenberg's selection from the Psalms:

The Lord is my shepherd
and keeps me from wanting
what I can't have

lush green grass is set
around me and crystal water
to graze by

there I revive with my soul
find the way that love makes
for his name

10   and though I pass through cities of pain, through death's living shadow
I'm not afraid to touch
to know what I am

your shepherd's staff is always there
to keep me calm
in my body

you set a table before me
in the presence of my enemies
you give me grace to speak

to quiet them
20   to be full with humanness
to be warm in my soul's lightness

to feel contact every day
in my hand and in my belly
love coming down to me

in the air of your name, Lord
in your house
in my life

Here is a poem in Pablo Neruda's Spanish, followed by four American translations:

Entierro en el Este

Yo trabajo de noche, rodeado de ciudad,
de pescadores, de alfareros, de difuntos quemados
con azafrán y frutas, envueltos en muselina escarlata:

bajo mi balcón esos muertos terribles
pasan sonando cadenas y flautas de cobre,
estridentes y finas y lúgubres silban
entre el color de las pesadas flores envenenadas
y el grito de los cenicientos danzarines
y el creciente monótono de los tamtam
10   y el humo de las maderas que arden y huelen.

Porque una vez doblado el camino, junto al turbio río,
sus corazones, detenidos o iniciando un mayor movimiento,
rodarán quemados, con la pierna y el pie hechos fuego,
y la trémula ceniza caerá sobre el agua,
flotará como ramo de flores calcinadas
o como extinto fuego dejado por tan poderosos viajeros
que hicieron arder algo sobre las negras aguas, y devoraron
un aliento desaparecido y un licor extremo.

Burial in the East

I work nights, in the ring of the city,
among fisherfolk, potters, cadavers, cremations
of saffron and fruits shrouded into red muslin.
Under my balcony pass the terrible dead
sounding their coppery flutes and their chains,
strident and mournful and delicate—they hiss
in a blazon of poisoned and ponderous flowers,
through the cries of the smoldering dancers,
the tom-tom's augmented monotony,
10   in the crackle and fume of the woodsmoke.

One turn in the road, by the ooze of the river,
and their hearts, clogging up or preparing some monstrous exertion,
will whirl away burning, their legs and their feet incandescent;
the tremulous ash will descend on the water
and float like a branching of carbonized flowers—
a bonfire put out by the might of some wayfarer
who lighted the black of the water and devoured some part
of a vanished subsistence, a consummate libation.

—Ben Bellitt

Burial in the East

I work at night, surrounded by city,
by fishermen, by potters, by the dead burned
with saffron and fruits, wrapped in red muslin:
under my balcony these terrible corpses
go past playing chains and copper flutes,
strident and thin and lugubrious they whistle
amidst the colour of the heavy poisoned flowers
and the cry of the holy fire-dancers

and the growing monotony of the tom-toms
10   and the smoke of the different woods burning and giving off odours.

Because once around the corner, by the muddy river,
their hearts, held in check or beginning a major motion,
will roll, burning, their legs and feet will be fire
and the tremulous ash will fall over the water,
will float like a branch of calcined flowers
or like an extinct fire left by such mighty voyagers
as forced to burn something over the black waters, and devoured
a vanished breath and an extreme liquor.

                                        —W. S. Merwin

Burial in the East

I work at night, surrounded by city,
by fishermen, by potters, by corpses burned
with saffron and fruit, wrapped in scarlet muslin:
underneath my balcony those terrible dead
go by, sounding their chains and copper flutes,
strident and clear and lugubrious they pipe
amid the colour of heavy poisoned flowers
and the cry of the ash-coloured dancers
and the mounting monotony of the drums
10   and smoke from logs that burn and smell.

For, once they reach the turn in the road, near the turbid river,
their hearts unmoving, or in greater movement,
they will roll burning, leg and foot made flame,
and the tremulous ashes will fall upon the water,
will float like a cluster of calcined flowers
or a quenched fire left by travelers so powerful
that they burned something over the black waters, and devoured
a vanished food, an utter liquor.

                                        —Angel Flores

Funeral in the East

I work at night, the city all around me,
fishermen, and potters, and corpses that are burned
with saffron and fruit, rolled in scarlet muslin:
those terrifying corpses go past under my balcony,
making their chains and copper flutes give off noise,
whistling sounds, harsh and pure and mournful,
among the brightness of the flowers heavy and poisoned,
and the cries of the dancers covered with ashes,
and the constantly rising monotony of the drum,
10   and the smoke from the logs scented and burning.

For once around the corner, near the muddy river,
their hearts, either stopping or starting off at a greater speed,

will roll over, burned, the leg and the foot turned to fire,
and the fluttering ashes will settle down on the water
and float like a branch of chalky flowers,
or like an extinct fire left by travellers with such great powers
they made something blaze up on the black waters, and bolted down
a food no longer found, and one finishing drink.

—Robert Bly

Shakespeare in paraphrase

Let us end with a gross example of paraphrase. Recently a publisher issued four Shakespearean tragedies with the original lines on the left-hand page and line-by-line paraphrases on the right. The editors—or translators—intended to provide pedagogical help for contemporary students, changing archaic words into modern synonyms. At the same time, they often turned Shakespeare's metaphors into plain speech. At the beginning of *Hamlet*, when the guards challenge each other, one of them says "Stand and unfold yourself." In the paraphrase the sentence reads "Stand still and tell me who you are."

When we remove metaphor in favor of plain speech, we remove images—and often we remove images that carry feelings on their backs. When Francisco asked Bernardo "Stand and unfold yourself," he thought of Bernardo physically opening up his body like a bird or like a butterfly expanding vulnerable wings or perhaps like a flag unfurling. But when Francisco asks Bernardo in the paraphrase "Stand still and tell me who you are," we have a mere request for identification. We have no picture, no image, no sense of something vulnerable, no sense of something formerly closed in on itself, now opening up.

Here is a well-known speech, with Shakespeare's text in roman type. Indented, in italic, after each Shakespearean line, is the modern paraphrase. You can read each speech as a whole or read one line at a time, first the original and then the paraphrase.

1. To be, or not to be: that is the question:
    1. To be, or not to be: that is what really matters.
2. Whether 'tis nobler in the mind to suffer
    2. Is it nobler to accept passively
3. The slings and arrows of outrageous fortune,
    3. the trials and tribulations that unjust fate sends,
4. Or to take arms against a sea of troubles,
    4. or to resist an ocean of troubles,
5. And by opposing end them. To die, to sleep—
    5. and, by our own effort, defeat them? To die, to fall asleep—
6. No more—and by a sleep to say we end
    6. perhaps that's all there is to it—and by that sleep suppose we put an end to
7. The heartache, and the thousand natural shocks
    7. the heartache and the thousands of pains and worries
8. That flesh is heir to! 'Tis a consummation

8. *that are a part of being human! That's an end*
9. Devoutly to be wished. To die, to sleep—
   9. we could all look forward to. To die, to sleep—
10. To sleep—perchance to dream: ay, there's the rub,
    10. to sleep—maybe to dream: yes, that's the catch.
11. For in that sleep of death what dreams may come
    11. For in that sleep of death the nightmares that may come
12. When we have shuffled off this mortal coil,
    12. when we have freed ourselves from the turmoil of this mortal life
13. Must give us pause. There's the respect
    13. must make us hesitate. There's the thought
14. That makes calamity of so long life:
    14. that makes a disaster out of living to a ripe old age.
15. For who would bear the whips and scorns of time,
    15. After all, who wants to put up with the lashes and insults of this world,
16. Th' oppressor's wrong, the proud man's contumely,
    16. the tyrant's injustice and contempt of arrogant men,
17. The pangs of despised love, the law's delay,
    17. the pains of rejected love, the law's frustrating slowness,
18. The insolence of office, and the spurns
    18. insults from our superiors, and the snubs
19. That patient merit of th' unworthy takes,
    19. that deserving and hopeful people have to take from powerful inferiors,
20. When he himself might his quietus make
    20. when he could end the whole process by killing himself
21. With a bare bodkin? . . .
    21. with a bare dagger? . . .

In Shakespeare's first line he speaks of *the question*, which as Hamlet thinks out loud becomes a true, unanswerable question—not a question in the abstracted sense of problem, like "the Middle East question." Instead of using *question*, the paraphraser speaks of *what really matters*, which is empty language. The difference is small, because Shakespeare's *question* is not a word of great importance in Hamlet's speech. Yet the difference in the two words is typical: *question* is concrete, in the form of a real question; *what really matters* has neither "reality" nor "matter" in its syllabic bones.

When the paraphraser substitutes *to accept passively* for *in the mind to suffer*, one wants to argue. Shakespeare distinguishes between inaction, which includes mental suffering, and external action against huge forces. The paraphraser includes the notion of passivity but excludes mental suffering; Shakespeare seems mistranslated. In *trials and tribulations* we find a cliché to substitute for an image of weapons. Although the *slings and arrows* may be abstracted into *trials and tribulations* in our minds—almost like calling them "nuisances and annoyances"—the cliché is pale; we lose the implication of pain and death carried in *slings and arrows*. Paraphrasing *outrageous* as *unjust* is another diminishment. *Outrageous* retains in modern speech most of its old character, especially when we denounce something with the noun an *outrage*. *Unjust* is less emotional, more intellectual. We begin to see that the paraphrase, by draining the language of particularity in metaphor and image, drains the poetry of feeling.

So much for the first five lines. The rest of this speech, and another famous one, can bear more attention.

Exercises

1. In 7/7 discuss the removal of *natural*. Is anything missing that Shakespeare may have felt essential?
2. In 8/8, what is the first metaphor removed? Does the missing metaphor have any general relevance to this play?
3. In 9/9, is *devoutly* paraphrased?
4. 12/12. Using a large dictionary (the *Oxford English Dictionary*, usually in a college library, would be the best) consider the metaphor of *shuffle . . . coil*. Does *the turmoil of this mortal life* paraphrase parts of Shakespeare's line? Does it paraphrase the whole?
5. In 14/14, find a new metaphor added by the paraphraser. Is it good poetry?
6. 15/15, are the substitute words examples of the occasional usefulness of paraphrases in reading older authors? Do you find other good examples of paraphrase in this passage from *Hamlet*?

A paraphrase from *Macbeth*

22. Tomorrow, and tomorrow, and tomorrow
    22. *Tomorrow follows tomorrow and is followed by tomorrow,*
23. Creeps in this petty pace from day to day,
    23. *feebly creeping from day to day*
24. To the last syllable of recorded time;
    24. *to the last syllable of written history,*
25. And all our yesterdays have lighted fools
    25. *and our entire past has lighted the way for fools*
26. The way to dusty death. Out, out, brief candle!
    26. *down the path to dusty death. Burn out, burn out, you short candle of life.*
27. Life's but a walking shadow, a poor player
    27. *A man's life is only a walking shadow, a poor actor*
28. That struts and frets his hour upon the stage
    28. *who swaggers and paces about the stage for an hour*
29. And then is heard no more. It is a tale
    29. *and then is never heard from again. Life is a tale*
30. Told by an idiot, full of sound and fury
    30. *told by an idiot, full of noise and rage,*
31. Signifying nothing . . .
    31. *but meaning nothing . . .*

Exercises

1. In 22–23/22–23, notice the change in grammatical mood and syntactic structure. Does Shakespeare's syntax enforce Shakespeare's meaning? Is the paraphrased syntax equal in energy?

2. In 25/25, discuss the difference between *all our yesterdays* and *our entire past*. Is it accurate paraphrase? Is it equal in forcefulness? Why?

3. In 25–26, readers have noticed that Macbeth's image of a candle derived from his earlier notion of *yesterday* that *lighted* people on a path or *way*. When *candle* becomes *candle of life*, what happens to the notion of the passage?

4. No one expects paraphrase to equal the sound and rhythm of the original; however, one may *use* a paraphrase's relative deficiency in sound as a way to notice the sound of the poet's original language. Analyze the rhythmic distinction between lines 27–31 and *27–31*.

Four Poets

After studying elements of poetry, where examples are as brief as a line and as long as a single poem, it will be useful to concentrate next on a group of poems by a single poet. Here are selections from the work of one English and three American poets, each represented by characteristic poems. The Englishman was born in 1795; when he died at the age of twenty-five, he had written several of the best poems of the language. The Americans are one woman and two men born in 1830, 1874, and 1908: an Easterner who lived most of her life in one town, a Californian who became the great poet of New England, and a Midwesterner who ended his life as a poet of the Pacific Northwest.

John Keats

John Keats (1795–1821) trained to become a physician, then gave up his medical studies to devote himself to poetry. Among his friends were the critic William Hazlitt and the older poet Leigh Hunt. Keats published his first book of poems in 1817. In the nineteenth century, literary criticism was frequently affected by political beliefs or associations, and Keats's poems were attacked viciously because of his associations with the liberal thinkers of his day. He developed tuberculosis early. In the space of a few months he wrote his best work, his poems on a Grecian Urn, to a Nightingale, to Autumn. He went to Italy for his health in September 1820 but died on February 23 of the next year. Carved on his tomb at his request were the words "Here lies one whose name was writ in water." Keats's letters contain superb speculations on the nature of poetry. See also pages 71, 72.

On First Looking into Chapman's Homer

Much have I travelled in the realms of gold,
   And many goodly states and kingdoms seen;
   Round many western islands have I been
Which bards in fealty to Apollo hold.
Oft of one wide expanse had I been told
   That deep-browed Homer ruled as his demesne;

Yet did I never breathe its pure serene
Till I heard Chapman speak out loud and bold.
Then felt I like some watcher of the skies
10   When a new planet swims into his ken;
Or like stout Cortez when with eagle eyes
    He stared at the Pacific, and all his men
Looked at each other with a wild surmise—
    Silent, upon a peak in Darien.

When I have fears
that I may cease to be

When I have fears that I may cease to be
    Before my pen has gleaned my teeming brain,
Before high-pilèd books, in charactery,
    Hold like rich garners the full ripened grain;
When I behold, upon the night's starred face,
    Huge cloudy symbols of a high romance,
And think that I may never live to trace
    Their shadows with the magic hand of chance;
And when I feel, fair creature of an hour,
10   That I shall never look upon thee more,
Never have relish in the fairy power
    Of unreflecting love; then on the shore
Of the wide world I stand alone and think
Till love and fame to nothingness do sink.

The Eve of St. Agnes

I

St. Agnes' Eve—ah, bitter chill it was!
The owl, for all his feathers, was a-cold;
The hare limped trembling through the frozen grass,
And silent was the flock in woolly fold.
Numb were the Beadsman's fingers, while he told
His rosary, and while his frosted breath,
Like pious incense from a censer old,
Seemed taking flight for heaven, without a death,
Past the sweet Virgin's picture, while his prayer he saith.

II

10   His prayer he saith, this patient, holy man;
Then takes his lamp, and riseth from his knees,
And back returneth, meagre, barefoot, wan,
Along the chapel aisle by slow degrees.
The sculptured dead, on each side, seem to freeze,
Emprisoned in black, purgatorial rails.
Knights, ladies, praying in dumb orat'ries,
He passeth by; and his weak spirit fails
To think how they may ache in icy hoods and mails.

III

Northward he turneth through a little door,
20 And scarce three steps, ere music's golden tongue
Flattered to tears this agèd man and poor;
But no—already had his deathbell rung,
The joys of all his life were said and sung;
His was harsh penance on St. Agnes' Eve.
Another way he went, and soon among
Rough ashes sat he for his soul's reprieve,
And all night kept awake for sinners' sake to grieve.

IV

That ancient Beadsman heard the prelude soft,
And so it chanced for many a door was wide
30 From hurry to and fro. Soon, up aloft,
The silver, snarling trumpets 'gan to chide;
The level chambers, ready with their pride,
Were glowing to receive a thousand guests;
The carvèd angels, ever eager-eyed,
Stared, where upon their heads the cornice rests,
With hair blown back, and wings put cross-wise on their
    breasts.

V

At length burst in the argent revelry,
With plume, tiara, and all rich array,
Numerous as shadows haunting fairily
40 The brain, new-stuffed in youth, with triumphs gay
Of old romance. These let us wish away,
And turn, sole-thoughted, to one Lady there,
Whose heart had brooded, all that wintry day,
On love, and winged St. Agnes' saintly care,
As she had heard old dames full many times declare.

VI

They told her how, upon St. Agnes' Eve,
Young virgins might have visions of delight,
And soft adorings from their loves receive
Upon the honeyed middle of the night,
50 If ceremonies due they did aright;
As, supperless to bed they must retire,
And couch supine their beauties, lily white,
Nor look behind, nor sideways, but require
Of Heaven with upward eyes for all that they desire.

VII

Full of this whim was thoughtful Madeline.
The music, yearning like a God in pain,
She scarcely heard; her maiden eyes divine,
Fixed on the floor, saw many a sweeping train

Pass by—she heeded not at all; in vain
60   Came many a tiptoe, amorous cavalier,
And back retired—not cooled by high disdain,
But she saw not; her heart was otherwhere.
She sighed for Agnes' dreams, the sweetest of the year.

VIII

She danced along with vague, regardless eyes,
Anxious her lips, her breathing quick and short.
The hallowed hour was near at hand. She sighs
Amid the timbrels and the thronged resort
Of whisperers in anger, or in sport;
'Mid looks of love, defiance, hate, and scorn,
70   Hookwinked with fairy fancy—all amort,
Save to St. Agnes and her lambs unshorn,
And all the bliss to be before to-morrow morn.

IX

So, purposing each moment to retire,
She lingered still. Meantime, across the moors,
Had come young Porphyro, with heart on fire
For Madeline. Beside the portal doors,
Buttressed from moonlight, stands he and implores
All saints to give him sight of Madeline
But for one moment in the tedious hours,
80   That he might gaze and worship all unseen;
Perchance speak, kneel, touch, kiss—in sooth such things
       have been.

X

He ventures in—let no buzzed whisper tell,
All eyes be muffled, or a hundred swords
Will storm his heart, love's feverous citadel.
For him, those chambers held barbarian hordes,
Hyena foemen, and hot-blooded lords,
Whose very dogs would execrations howl
Against his lineage; not one breast affords
Him any mercy, in that mansion foul,
90   Save one old beldame, weak in body and in soul.

XI

Ah, happy chance! The agèd creature came,
Shuffling along with ivory-headed wand,
To where he stood, hid from the torch's flame,
Behind a broad hall-pillar, far beyond
The sound of merriment and chorus bland.
He startled her; but soon she knew his face,
And grasped his fingers in her palsied hand,
Saying, 'Mercy, Porphyro! Hie thee from this place;
They are all here to-night, the whole blood-thirsty race!

XII

100   'Get hence! get hence! there's dwarfish Hildebrand—
    He had a fever late, and in the fit
    He cursèd thee and thine, both house and land;
    Then there's that old Lord Maurice, not a whit
    More tame for his gray hairs. Alas me! Flit,
    Flit like a ghost away!' 'Ah, Gossip dear,
    We're safe enough; here in this arm-chair sit,
    And tell me how—' 'Good saints! Not here, not here;
Follow me, child, or else these stones will be thy bier.'

XIII

    He followed through a lowly archèd way,
110   Brushing the cobwebs with his lofty plume,
    And as she muttered 'Well-a—well-a-day!'
    He found him in a little moonlight room,
    Pale, latticed, chill, and silent as a tomb.
    'Now tell me where is Madeline,' said he,
    'Oh, tell me, Angela, by the holy loom
    Which none but secret sisterhood may see,
When they St. Agnes' wool are weaving piously.'

XIV

    'St. Agnes? Ah! It is St. Agnes' Eve—
    Yet men will murder upon holy days:
120   Thou must hold water in a witch's sieve,
    And be liege-lord of all the elves and fays,
    To venture so; it fills me with amaze
    To see thee, Porphyro!—St. Agnes' Eve!
    God's help! My lady fair the conjuror plays
    This very night. Good angels her deceive!
But let me laugh awhile, I've mickle time to grieve.'

XV

    Feebly she laugheth in the languid moon,
    While Porphyro upon her face doth look,
    Like puzzled urchin on an agèd crone
130   Who keepeth closed a wondrous riddle-book,
    As spectacled she sits in chimney nook.
    But soon his eyes grew brilliant, when she told
    His lady's purpose, and he scarce could brook
    Tears at the thought of those enchantments cold,
And Madeline asleep in lap of legends old.

XVI

    Sudden a thought came like a full-blown rose,
    Flushing his brow, and in his painèd heart
    Made purple riot; then doth he propose
    A stratagem that makes the beldame start:
140   'A cruel man and impious thou art—

Sweet lady, let her pray, and sleep, and dream
Alone with her good angels, far apart
From wicked men like thee. Go, go! I deem
Thou canst not surely be the same that thou didst seem.'

XVII

'I will not harm her, by all saints I swear,'
Quoth Porphyro: 'Oh, may I ne'er find grace
When my weak voice shall whisper its last prayer,
If one of her soft ringlets I displace,
Or look with ruffian passion in her face—
150   Good Angela, believe me by these tears,
Or I will, even in a moment's space,
Awake with horrid shout my foemen's ears,
And beard them, though they be more fanged than
    wolves and bears.'

XVIII

'Ah! why wilt thou affright a feeble soul?
A poor, weak, palsy-stricken, churchyard thing,
Whose passing-bell may ere the midnight toll!
Whose prayers for thee, each morn and evening,
Were never missed.' Thus plaining doth she bring
A gentler speech from burning Porphyro,
160   So woeful, and of such deep sorrowing,
That Angela gives promise she will do
Whatever he shall wish, betide her weal or woe.

XIX

Which was, to lead him, in close secrecy,
Even to Madeline's chamber, and there hide
Him in a closet, of such privacy
That he might see her beauty unespied,
And win perhaps that night a peerless bride,
While legioned fairies paced the coverlet
And pale enchantment held her sleepy-eyed.
170   Never on such a night have lovers met
Since Merlin paid his Demon all the monstrous debt.

XX

'It shall be as thou wishest,' said the Dame,
'All cates and dainties shall be storèd there
Quickly on this feast-night; by the tambour frame
Her own lute thou wilt see. No time to spare,
For I am slow and feeble, and scarce dare
On such a catering trust my dizzy head.
Wait here, my child, with patience; kneel in prayer
The while. Ah! Thou must needs the lady wed,
180   Or may I never leave my grave among the dead.'

XXI

So saying she hobbled off with busy fear.
The lover's endless minutes slowly passed;
The dame returned, and whispered in his ear
To follow her; with agèd eyes aghast
From fright of dim espial. Safe at last,
Through many a dusky gallery, they gain
The maiden's chamber, silken, hushed, and chaste,
Where Porphyro took covert, pleased amain.
His poor guide hurried back with agues in her brain.

XXII

190   Her faltering hand upon the balustrade,
Old Angela was feeling for the stair,
When Madeline, St. Agnes' charmèd maid,
Rose, like a missioned spirit, unaware.
With silver taper's light, and pious care,
She turned and down the agèd gossip led
To a safe level matting. Now prepare,
Young Porphyro, for gazing on that bed—
She comes, she comes again, like ring-dove frayed and
    fled.

XXIII

Out went the taper as she hurried in;
200   Its little smoke, in pallid moonshine, died.
She closed the door, she panted, all akin
To spirits of the air, and visions wide—
No uttered syllable, or woe betide!
But to her heart, her heart was voluble,
Paining with eloquence her balmy side,
As though a tongueless nightingale should swell
Her throat in vain, and die, heart-stifled, in her dell.

XXIV

A casement high and triple-arched there was,
All garlanded with carven imageries,
210   Of fruits, and flowers, and bunches of knot-grass,
And diamonded with panes of quaint device
Innumerable of stains and splendid dyes,
As are the tiger-moth's deep-damasked wings;
And in the midst, 'mong thousand heraldries,
And twilight saints, and dim emblazonings,
A shielded scutcheon blushed with blood of queens and
    kings.

XXV

Full on this casement shone the wintry moon,
And threw warm gules on Madeline's fair breast
As down she knelt for Heaven's grace and boon;
220   Rose-bloom fell on her hands, together pressed,

And on her silver cross soft amethyst,
And on her hair a glory, like a saint.
She seemed a splendid angel, newly dressed,
Save wings, for heaven. Porphyro grew faint;
She knelt, so pure a thing, so free from mortal taint.

XXVI

Anon his heart revives; her vespers done,
Of all its wreathèd pearls her hair she frees;
Unclasps her warmèd jewels one by one;
Loosens her fragrant bodice; by degrees
230   Her rich attire creeps rustling to her knees.
Half-hidden, like a mermaid in sea-weed,
Pensive awhile she dreams awake, and sees,
In fancy, fair St. Agnes in her bed,
But dares not look behind, or all the charm is fled.

XXVII

Soon, trembling in her soft and chilly nest,
In sort of wakeful swoon, perplexed she lay,
Until the poppied warmth of sleep oppressed
Her soothèd limbs, and soul fatigued—away
Flown, like a thought, until the morrow-day;
240   Blissfully havened both from joy and pain;
Clasped like a missal where swart Paynims pray;
Blinded alike from sunshine and from rain,
As though a rose should shut, and be a bud again.

XXVIII

Stol'n to this paradise, and so entranced,
Porphyro gazed upon her empty dress,
And listened to her breathing, if it chanced
To wake into a slumbrous tenderness;
Which when he heard, that minute did he bless,
And breathed himself, then from the closet crept,
250   Noiseless as fear in a wide wilderness—
And over the hushed carpet, silent, stepped,
And 'tween the curtains peeped, where, lo!—how fast
    she slept.

XXIX

Then by the bed-side, where the faded moon
Made a dim, silver twilight, soft he set
A table and, half anguished, threw thereon
A cloth of woven crimson, gold, and jet.
Oh, for some drowsy Morphean amulet!
The boisterous, midnight, festive clarion,
The kettle-drum, and far-heard clarionet,
260   Affray his ears, though but in dying tone;
The hall door shuts again, and all the noise is gone.

XXX

And still she slept an azure-lidded sleep,
In blanchèd linen, smooth, and lavendered,
While he from forth the closet brought a heap
Of candied apple, quince, and plum, and gourd,
With jellies soother than the creamy curd,
And lucent syrops, tinct with cinnamon;
Manna and dates, in argosy transferred
From Fez; and spicèd dainties, every one,
270   From silken Samarcand to cedared Lebanon.

XXXI

These delicates he heaped with glowing hand
On golden dishes and in baskets bright
Of wreathèd silver; sumptuous they stand
In the retired quiet of the night,
Filling the chilly room with perfume light.
'And now, my love, my seraph fair, awake!
Thou art my heaven, and I thine eremite.
Open thine eyes, for meek St. Agnes' sake,
Or I shall drowse beside thee, so my soul doth ache.'

XXXII

280   Thus whispering, his warm, unnervèd arm
Sank in her pillow. Shaded was her dream
By the dusk curtains: 'twas a midnight charm
Impossible to melt as icèd stream.
The lustrous salvers in the moonlight gleam,
Broad golden fringe upon the carpet lies.
It seemed he never, never could redeem
From such a steadfast spell his lady's eyes;
So mused awhile, entoiled in woofèd phantasies.

XXXIII

Awakening up, he took her hollow lute,
290   Tumultuous, and, in chords that tenderest be,
He played an ancient ditty, long since mute,
In Provence called, 'La belle dame sans mercy,'
Close to her ear touching the melody—
Wherewith disturbed, she uttered a soft moan.
He ceased—she panted quick—and suddenly
Her blue affrayèd eyes wide open shone;
Upon his knees he sank, pale as smooth-sculptured stone.

XXXIV

Her eyes were open, but she still beheld,
Now wide awake, the vision of her sleep—
300   There was a painful change, that nigh expelled
The blisses of her dream so pure and deep.

At which fair Madeline began to weep,
And moan forth witless words with many a sigh,
While still her gaze on Porphyro would keep;
Who knelt, with joinèd hands and piteous eye,
Fearing to move or speak, she looked so dreamingly.

XXXV

'Ah, Porphyro!' said she, 'but even now
Thy voice was at sweet tremble in mine ear,
Made tuneable with every sweetest vow,
310   And those sad eyes were spiritual and clear.
How changed thou art! How pallid, chill, and drear!
Give me that voice again, my Porphyro,
Those looks immortal, those complainings dear!
Oh, leave me not in this eternal woe,
For if thou diest, my love, I know not where to go.'

XXXVI

Beyond a mortal man impassioned far
At these voluptuous accents, he arose,
Ethereal, flushed, and like a throbbing star
Seen mid the sapphire heaven's deep repose;
320   Into her dream he melted, as the rose
Blendeth its odour with the violet,
Solution sweet—meantime the frost-wind blows
Like Love's alarum, pattering the sharp sleet
Against the window-panes; St. Agnes' moon hath set.

XXXVII

'Tis dark: quick pattereth the flaw-blown sleet.
'This is no dream, my bride, my Madeline!'
'Tis dark; the icèd gusts still rave and beat.
'No dream, alas! alas! and woe is mine!
Porphyro will leave me here to fade and pine.
330   Cruel! What traitor could thee hither bring?
I curse not, for my heart is lost in thine,
Though thou forsakest a deceivèd thing—
A dove forlorn and lost with sick, unprunèd wing.'

XXXVIII

'My Madeline! Sweet dreamer! Lovely bride!
Say, may I be for ay thy vassal blest?
Thy beauty's shield, heart-shaped and vermeil dyed?
Ah, silver shrine, here will I take my rest
After so many hours of toil and quest,
A famished pilgrim—saved by miracle.
340   Though I have found, I will not rob thy nest
Saving of thy sweet self; if thou think'st well
To trust, fair Madeline, to no rude infidel.

XXXIX

'Hark! 'Tis an elfin-storm from fairy land,
Of haggard seeming, but a boon indeed.
Arise—arise! The morning is at hand;
The bloated wassaillers will never heed.
Let us away, my love, with happy speed—
There are no ears to hear, or eyes to see,
Drowned all in Rhenish and the sleepy mead.
350 Awake! Arise, my love, and fearless be!
For o'er the southern moors I have a home for thee.'

XL

She hurried at his words, beset with fears,
For there were sleeping dragons all around,
At glaring watch, perhaps, with ready spears;
Down the wide stairs a darkling way they found.
In all the house was heard no human sound;
A chain-drooped lamp was flickering by each door;
The arras, rich with horseman, hawk, and hound,
Fluttered in the besieging wind's uproar;
360 And the long carpets rose along the gusty floor.

XLI

They glide, like phantoms, into the wide hall;
Like phantoms, to the iron porch they glide;
Where lay the Porter, in uneasy sprawl,
With a huge empty flagon by his side.
The wakeful bloodhound rose and shook his hide,
But his sagacious eye an inmate owns.
By one, and one, the bolts full easy slide;
The chains lie silent on the footworn stones;
The key turns, and the door upon its hinges groans.

XLII

370 And they are gone—aye, ages long ago
These lovers fled away into the storm.
That night the Baron dreamt of many a woe,
And all his warrior-guests, with shade and form
Of witch, and demon, and large coffin-worm,
Were long be-nightmared. Angela the old
Died palsy-twitched, with meagre face deform;
The Beadsman, after thousand aves told,
For ay unsought for slept among his ashes cold.

Ode to a Nightingale

I

My heart aches, and a drowsy numbness pains
   My sense, as though of hemlock[1] I had drunk,

---

[1]Poison hemlock, a lethally poisonous herb of the carrot family, was used in ancient Greece to execute criminals.

Or emptied some dull opiate to the drains
  One minute past, and Lethe-wards[2] had sunk.
'Tis not through envy of thy happy lot,
  But being too happy in thine happiness,—
    That thou, light-wingèd Dryad° of the trees,   *nymph*
      In some melodious plot
  Of beechen green, and shadows numberless,
10   Singest of summer in full-throated ease.

II

O for a draught of vintage that hath been
  Cooled a long age in the deep-delvèd earth,
Tasting of Flora[3] and the country green,
  Dance, and Provençal song,[4] and sunburnt mirth!
O for a beaker full of the warm South,
  Full of the true, the blushful Hippocrene,[5]
    With beaded bubbles winking at the brim,
      And purple-stainèd mouth,
That I might drink, and leave the world unseen,
20 And with thee fade away into the forest dim.

III

Fade far away, dissolve, and quite forget
  What thou among the leaves hast never known,
The weariness, the fever, and the fret
  Here, where men sit and hear each other groan;
Where palsy shakes a few, sad, last gray hairs,
  Where youth grows pale, and spectre-thin, and dies;
    Where but to think is to be full of sorrow
      And leaden-eyed despairs;
Where Beauty cannot keep her lustrous eyes,
30 Or new Love pine at them beyond to-morrow.

IV

Away! away! for I will fly to thee,
  Not charioted by Bacchus and his pards,[6]
But on the viewless° wings of Poesy,   *invisible*
  Though the dull brain perplexes and retards.
Already with thee! tender is the night,
  And haply the Queen-Moon is on her throne,
    Clustered around by all her starry fays;°   *fairies*
      But here there is no light,
Save what from heaven is with the breezes blown
40 Through verdurous glooms and winding mossy ways.

[2]In Greek mythology, Lethe was the river in the underworld from which the shades of the dead drank to obtain forgetfulness of the past. [3]Roman goddess of flowers and spring. [4]Provence, the South of France, was famous for the songs of love and adventure constructed or repeated by its medieval troubadors. [5]The "Fountain of the Horse" on Mount Helicon, sacred to the Muses. [6]Bacchus, the Roman god of wine, was sometimes portrayed riding in a chariot drawn by leopards.

V

I cannot see what flowers are at my feet,
    Nor what soft incense hangs upon the boughs,
But, in embalmèd° darkness, guess each sweet   fragrant
    Wherewith the seasonable month endows
The grass, the thicket, and the fruit-tree wild—
    White hawthorn, and the pastoral eglantine;
        Fast-fading violets covered up in leaves;
           And mid-May's eldest child,
    The coming musk-rose, full of dewy wine,
50   The murmurous haunt of flies on summer eves.

VI

Darkling° I listen, and for many a time   In darkness
    I have been half in love with easeful Death,
Called him soft names in many a musèd rhyme,
    To take into the air my quiet breath;
Now more than ever seems it rich to die,
    To cease upon the midnight with no pain,
        While thou art pouring forth thy soul abroad
           In such an ecstasy.
    Still wouldst thou sing, and I have ears in vain—
60   To thy high requiem become a sod.

VII

Thou wast not born for death, immortal bird!
    No hungry generations tread thee down;
The voice I hear this passing night was heard
    In ancient days by emperor and clown:
Perhaps the self-same song that found a path
    Through the sad heart of Ruth,[7] when, sick for home,
        She stood in tears amid the alien corn;°   wheat
           The same that oft-times hath
    Charmed magic casements, opening on the foam
70   Of perilous seas, in faery lands forlorn.

VIII

Forlorn! the very word is like a bell
    To toll me back from thee to my sole self!
Adieu! the fancy cannot cheat so well
    As she is famed to do, deceiving elf.
Adieu! adieu! thy plaintive anthem fades
    Past the near meadows, over the still stream,
        Up the hill-side; and now 'tis buried deep
           In the next valley-glades:
    Was it a vision, or a waking dream?
80   Fled is that music . . . Do I wake or sleep?

[7]A reference to the Moabite widow whose story is told in the Old Testament book of Ruth

Ode on a Grecian Urn

I

Thou still unravished bride of quietness,
    Thou foster-child of silence and slow time,
Sylvan historian, who canst thus express
    A flowery tale more sweetly than our rhyme!
What leaf-fringed legend haunts about thy shape
    Of deities or mortals, or of both,
        In Tempe or the dales of Arcady?[1]
    What men or gods are these? What maidens loth?
What mad pursuit? What struggle to escape?
10   What pipes and timbrels? What wild ecstasy?

II

Heard melodies are sweet, but those unheard
    Are sweeter; therefore, ye soft pipes, play on;
Not to the sensual° ear, but, more endeared,   *sensuous*
    Pipe to the spirit ditties of no tone.
Fair youth beneath the trees, thou canst not leave
    Thy song, nor ever can those trees be bare;
        Bold lover, never, never canst thou kiss,
Though winning near the goal—yet do not grieve:
    She cannot fade, though thou hast not thy bliss,
20   For ever wilt thou love, and she be fair!

III

Ah, happy, happy boughs, that cannot shed
    Your leaves, nor ever bid the spring adieu;
And, happy melodist, unwearièd,
    For ever piping songs for ever new!
More happy love, more happy, happy love!
    For ever warm and still to be enjoyed,
        For ever panting, and for ever young—
All breathing human passion far above,
    That leaves a heart high-sorrowful and cloyed,
30   A burning forehead, and a parching tongue.

IV

Who are these coming to the sacrifice?
    To what green altar, O mysterious priest,
Lead'st thou that heifer lowing at the skies,
    And all her silken flanks with garlands drest?
What little town by river or sea shore,
    Or mountain built with peaceful citadel,
        Is emptied of this folk, this pious morn?
And, little town, thy streets for evermore
    Will silent be; and not a soul to tell
40   Why thou art desolate can e'er return.

[1]Tempe and the glens of Arcady are landscapes of legendary beauty.

V

O Attic[2] shape! Fair attitude! With brede°   pattern, design
  Of marble men and maidens overwrought,
With forest branches and the trodden weed—
  Thou, silent form, dost tease us out of thought
As doth eternity. Cold pastoral!
    When old age shall this generation waste,
      Thou shalt remain, in midst of other woe
Than ours, a friend to man, to whom thou say'st,
    "Beauty is truth, truth beauty"—that is all
50   Ye know on earth, and all ye need to know.

This Living Hand

This living hand, now warm and capable
Of earnest grasping, would, if it were cold
And in the icy silence of the tomb,
So haunt thy days and chill thy dreaming nights
That thou would wish thine own heart dry of blood
So in my veins red life might stream again,
And thou be conscience-calmed. See here it is—
I hold it towards you.

[2]Attic equals Athenian and therefore classic grace and simplicity.

Emily Dickinson

Emily Dickinson (1830–1886) grew up in Amherst, Massachusetts, where her family was associated with Amherst College. She attended school with other young women, but as she grew older became reclusive, until she rarely left her own room. Her eccentricities of punctuation, not to mention the strangeness of her metaphors and rhymes, may derive from her sense that she was her own and only audience. Yet power and insight accumulated in her isolation. She is probably the greatest female poet of our language, and every year her audience grows wider.

He put the Belt around my life—

He put the Belt around my life—
I heard the Buckle snap—
And turned away, imperial,
My Lifetime folding up—

Deliberate, as a Duke would do
A Kingdom's Title Deed—
Henceforth, a Dedicated sort—
A Member of the Cloud.

Yet not too far to come at call—
10 And do the little Toils
That make the Circuit of the Rest—
And deal occasional smiles
To lives that stoop to notice mine—
And kindly ask it in—
Whose invitation, know you not
For Whom I must decline?

He fumbles at your Soul

He fumbles at your Soul
As Players at the Keys
Before they drop full Music on—
He stuns you by degrees—
Prepares your brittle Nature
For the Ethereal Blow
By fainter Hammers—further heard—
Then nearer—Then so slow
Your Breath has time to straighten—
10 Your Brain—to bubble Cool—
Deals—One—imperial—Thunderbolt—
That scalps your naked Soul—

When Winds take Forests in their Paws—
The Universe—is still—

After great pain, a formal feeling comes—

After great pain, a formal feeling comes—
The Nerves sit ceremonious, like Tombs—
The stiff Heart questions was it He, that bore,
And Yesterday, or Centuries before?

The Feet, mechanical, go round—
Of Ground, or Air, or Ought—
A Wooden way
Regardless grown,
A Quartz contentment, like a stone—

10 This is the Hour of Lead—
Remembered, if outlived,
As Freezing persons, recollect the Snow—
First—Chill—then Stupor—then the letting go—

The first Day's Night had come—

The first Day's Night had come—
And grateful that a thing

So terrible—had been endured—
I told my Soul to sing—

She said her Strings were snapt—
Her Bow—to Atoms blown—
And so to mend her—gave me work
Until another Morn—

And then—a Day as huge
10   As Yesterdays in pairs,
Unrolled its horror in my face—
Until it blocked my eyes—

My Brain—begun to laugh—
I mumbled—like a fool—
And tho' 'tis Years ago—that Day—
My Brain keeps giggling—still.

And Something's odd—within—
That person that I was—
And this One—do not feel the same—
20   Could it be Madness—this?

Much Madness is divinest Sense—

Much Madness is divinest Sense—
To a discerning Eye—
Much Sense—the starkest Madness—
'Tis the Majority
In this, as All, prevail—
Assent—and you are sane—
Demur—you're straightway dangerous—
And handled with a Chain—

I heard a Fly buzz—when I died—

I heard a Fly buzz—when I died—
The Stillness in the Room
Was like the Stillness in the Air—
Between the Heaves of Storm—

The Eyes around—had wrung them dry—
And Breaths were gathering firm
For that last Onset—when the King
Be witnessed—in the Room—

I willed my Keepsakes—Signed away
10   What portion of me be
Assignable—and then it was
There interposed a Fly—

With Blue—uncertain stumbling Buzz—
Between the light—and me—
And then the Windows failed—and then
I could not see to see—

I would not paint—a picture—

I would not paint—a picture—
I'd rather be the One
Its bright impossibility
To dwell—delicious—on—
And wonder how the fingers feel
Whose rare—celestial—stir—
Evokes so sweet a Torment—
Such sumptuous—Despair—

I would not talk, like Cornets—
10   I'd rather be the One
Raised softly to the Ceilings—
And out, and easy on—
Through Villages of Ether—
Myself endued Balloon
By but a lip of Metal—
The pier to my Pontoon—

Nor would I be a Poet—
It's finer—own the Ear—
Enamored—impotent—content—
20   The License to revere,
A privilege so awful
What would the Dower be,
Had I the Art to stun myself
With Bolts of Melody!

I'm ceded—I've stopped being Theirs—

I'm ceded—I've stopped being Theirs—
The name They dropped upon my face
With water, in the country church
Is finished using, now,
And They can put it with my Dolls,
My childhood, and the string of spools,
I've finished threading—too—

Baptized, before, without the choice,
But this time, consciously, of Grace—
10   Unto supremest name—
Called to my Full—The Crescent dropped—
Existence's whole Arc, filled up,
With one small Diadem.

My second Rank—too small the first—
Crowned—Crowing—on my Father's breast—
A half unconscious Queen—
But this time—Adequate—Erect,
With Will to choose, or to reject,
And I choose, just a Crown—

The Soul has Bandaged moments—

The Soul has Bandaged moments—
When too appalled to stir—
She feels some ghastly Fright come up
And stop to look at her—

Salute her—with long fingers—
Caress her freezing hair—
Sip, Goblin, from the very lips
The Lover—hovered—o'er—
Unworthy, that a thought so mean
10   Accost a Theme—so—fair—

The soul has moments of Escape—
When bursting all the doors—
She dances like a Bomb, abroad,
And swings upon the Hours,

As do the Bee—delirious borne—
Long Dungeoned from his Rose—
Touch Liberty—then know no more,
But Noon, and Paradise—

The Soul's retaken moments—
20   When, Felon led along,
With shackles on the plumed feet,
And staples, in the Song,

The Horror welcomes her, again,
These, are not brayed of Tongue—

The Province of the Saved

The Province of the Saved
Should be the Art—To save—
Through Skill obtained in Themselves—
The Science of the Grave

No Man can understand
But He that hath endured
The Dissolution—in Himself—
That Man—be qualified

To qualify Despair
10   To Those who failing new—
Mistake Defeat for Death—Each time—
Till acclimated—to—

A still—Volcano—Life—

A still—Volcano—Life—
That flickered in the night—

When it was dark enough to do
Without erasing sight—

A quiet—Earthquake Style—
Too subtle to suspect
By natures this side Naples—
The North cannot detect

The Solemn—Torrid—Symbol—
10   The lips that never lie—
Whose hissing Corals part—and shut—
And Cities—ooze away—

I cannot live with You—

I cannot live with You—
It would be Life—
And Life is over there—
Behind the Shelf

The Sexton keeps the Key to—
Putting up
Our Life—His Porcelain—
Like a Cup—

Discarded of the Housewife—
10   Quaint—or Broke—
A newer Sevres pleases—
Old Ones crack—

I could not die—with You—
For One must wait
To shut the Other's Gaze down—
You—could not—

And I—Could I stand by
And see You—freeze—
Without my Right of Frost—
20   Death's privilege?

Nor could I rise—with You—
Because Your Face
Would put out Jesus'—
That New Grace

Glow plain—and foreign
On my homesick Eye—
Except that You than He
Shone closer by—

They'd judge Us—How—
30   For You—served Heaven—You know,
Or sought to—
I could not—

Because You saturated Sight—
And I had no more Eyes
For sordid excellence
As Paradise

And were You lost, I would be—
Though My Name
Rang loudest
40   On the Heavenly fame—

And were You—saved—
And I—condemned to be
Where You were not—
That self—were Hell to Me—

So We must meet apart—
You there—I—here—
With just the Door ajar
That Oceans are—and Prayer—
And that White Sustenance—
50   Despair—

Me from Myself—to banish—

Me from Myself—to banish—
Had I Art—
Impregnable my Fortress
Unto All Heart—

But since Myself—assault Me—
How have I peace
Except by subjugating
Consciousness?

And since We're mutual Monarch
10   How this be
Except by Abdication—
Me—of Me?

Because I could not stop for Death—

Because I could not stop for Death—
He kindly stopped for me—
The Carriage held but just Ourselves—
And Immortality.

We slowly drove—He knew no haste
And I had put away
My labor and my leisure too,
For His Civility—

      We passed the School, where Children strove
10   At Recess—in the Ring—
      We passed the Fields of Gazing Grain—
      We passed the Setting Sun—

      Or rather—He passed Us—
      The Dews drew quivering and chill—
      For only Gossamer, my Gown—
      My Tippet—only Tulle—

      We paused before a House that seemed
      A Swelling of the Ground—
      The Roof was scarcely visible—
20   The Cornice—in the Ground—

      Since then—'tis Centuries—and yet
      Feels shorter than the Day
      I first surmised the Horses' Heads
      Were toward Eternity—

My Life had stood—a Loaded Gun—

      My Life had stood—a Loaded Gun—
      In Corners—till a Day
      The Owner passed—identified—
      And carried Me away—

      And now We roam in Sovereign Woods—
      And now We hunt the Doe—
      And every time I speak for Him—
      The Mountains straight reply—

      And do I smile, such cordial light
10   Upon the Valley glow—
      It is as a Vesuvian face
      Had let its pleasure through—

      And when at Night—Our good Day done—
      I guard My Master's Head—
      'Tis better than the Eider-Duck's
      Deep Pillow—to have shared—

      To foe of His—I'm deadly foe—
      None stir the second time—
      On whom I lay a Yellow Eye—
20   Or an emphatic Thumb—

      Though I than He—may longer live
      He longer must—than I—

      For I have but the power to kill,
      Without—the power to die—

Severer Service of myself

Severer Service of myself
I—hastened to demand
To fill the awful Vacuum
Your life had left behind—

I worried Nature with my Wheels
When Hers had ceased to run—
When she had put away Her Work
My own had just begun.

I strove to weary Brain and Bone—
10   To harass to fatigue
The glittering Retinue of nerves—
Vitality to clog

To some dull comfort Those obtain
Who put a Head away
They knew the Hair to—
And forget the color of the Day—

Affliction would not be appeased—
The Darkness braced as firm
As all my stratagem had been
20   The Midnight to confirm—

No Drug for Consciousness—can be—
Alternative to die
Is Nature's only Pharmacy
For Being's Malady—

I felt a Cleaving in my Mind—

I felt a Cleaving in my Mind—
As if my Brain had split—
I tried to match it—Seam by Seam—
But could not make them fit.

The thought behind, I strove to join
Unto the thought before—
But Sequence ravelled out of Sound
Like Balls—upon a Floor.

A narrow Fellow in the Grass

A narrow Fellow in the Grass
Occasionally rides—
You may have met Him—did you not
His notice sudden is—

The Grass divides as with a Comb—
A spotted shaft is seen—

And then it closes at your feet
And opens further on—

He likes a Boggy Acre
10   A Floor too cool for Corn—
Yet when a Boy, and Barefoot—
I more than once at Noon
Have passed, I thought, a Whip lash
Unbraiding in the Sun
When stooping to secure it
It wrinkled, and was gone—

Several of Nature's People
I know, and they know me—
I feel for them a transport
20   Of cordiality—

But never met this Fellow
Attended, or alone
Without a tighter breathing
And Zero at the Bone—

Robert Frost

Robert Frost (1874–1963) was born in California and died in New England at the age of eighty-eight. The New England countryside, its people, and their speech take center stage in his poems. Frost's father died when he was ten, and his mother took him back East. He attended high school in Massachusetts, went to Dartmouth briefly, worked in mills, and after marriage spent two years at Harvard without taking a degree. He tried his hand at farming while he wrote poems, but his poems did not win acceptance from American editors. In 1912 he took his family to England, where a London publisher recognized the quality of the work; *A Boy's Will* appeared in 1913. When Frost returned to the United States in 1915, he found America ready for him. He won the Pulitzer Prize four times, and two years before he died read a poem at the inauguration of President John F. Kennedy.

The Pasture

I'm going out to clean the pasture spring;
I'll only stop to rake the leaves away
(And wait to watch the water clear, I may)
I sha'n't be gone long.—You come too.

I'm going out to fetch the little calf
That's standing by the mother. It's so young
It totters when she licks it with her tongue.
I sha'n't be gone long.—You come too.

Mowing

There was never a sound beside the wood but one,
And that was my long scythe whispering to the ground.
What was it it whispered? I knew not well myself;
Perhaps it was something about the heat of the sun,
Something, perhaps, about the lack of sound—
And that was why it whispered and did not speak.
It was no dream of the gift of idle hours,
Or easy gold at the hand of fay or elf:
Anything more than the truth would have seemed too weak
10   To the earnest love that laid the swale in rows,
Not without feeble-pointed spikes of flowers
(Pale orchises), and scared a bright green snake.
The fact is the sweetest dream that labor knows.
My long scythe whispered and left the hay to make.

Home Burial

He saw her from the bottom of the stairs
Before she saw him. She was starting down,
Looking back over her shoulder at some fear.
She took a doubtful step and then undid it
To raise herself and look again. He spoke
Advancing toward her: 'What is it you see
From up there always—for I want to know.'
She turned and sank upon her skirts at that,
And her face changed from terrified to dull.
10   He said to gain time: 'What is it you see,'
Mounting until she cowered under him.
'I will find out now—you must tell me, dear.'
She, in her place, refused him any help
With the least stiffening of her neck and silence.
She let him look, sure that he wouldn't see,
Blind creature; and awhile he didn't see.
But at last he murmured, 'Oh,' and again, 'Oh.'

'What is it—what?' she said.

                              'Just that I see.'

20 'You don't,' she challenged. 'Tell me what it is.'

'The wonder is I didn't see at once.
I never noticed it from here before.
I must be wonted to it—that's the reason.
The little graveyard where my people are!
So small the window frames the whole of it.
Not so much larger than a bedroom, is it?
There are three stones of slate and one of marble,
Broad-shouldered little slabs there in the sunlight
On the sidehill. We haven't to mind *those*.
30 But I understand: it is not the stones,
But the child's mound—'

             'Don't, don't, don't, don't,' she cried.

She withdrew shrinking from beneath his arm
That rested on the bannister, and slid downstairs;
And turned on him with such a daunting look,
He said twice over before he knew himself:
'Can't a man speak of his own child he's lost?'

'Not you! Oh, where's my hat? Oh, I don't need it!
I must get out of here. I must get air.
40 I don't know rightly whether any man can.'

'Amy! Don't go to someone else this time.
Listen to me. I won't come down the stairs.'
He sat and fixed his chin between his fists.
'There's something I should like to ask you, dear.'

'You don't know how to ask it.'

             'Help me, then.'

Her fingers moved the latch for all reply.

'My words are nearly always an offense.
I don't know how to speak of anything
50 So as to please you. But I might be taught
I should suppose. I can't say I see how.
A man must partly give up being a man
With women-folk. We could have some arrangement
By which I'd bind myself to keep hands off
Anything special you're a-mind to name.
Though I don't like such things 'twixt those that love
Two that don't love can't live together without them.
But two that do can't live together with them.'
She moved the latch a little. 'Don't—don't go.
60 Don't carry it to someone else this time.
Tell me about it if it's something human.
Let me into your grief. I'm not so much
Unlike other folks as your standing there
Apart would make me out. Give me my chance.

I do think, though, you overdo it a little.
What was it brought you up to think it the thing
To take your mother-loss of a first child
So inconsolably—in the face of love.
You'd think his memory might be satisfied—'

70   'There you go sneering now!'

                                    'I'm not, I'm not!
You make me angry. I'll come down to you.
God, what a woman! And it's come to this,
A man can't speak of his own child that's dead.'

'You can't because you don't know how to speak.
If you had any feelings, you that dug
With your own hand—how could you?—his little grave;
I saw you from that very window there,
Making the gravel leap and leap in air,
80   Leap up, like that, like that, and land so lightly
And roll back down the mound beside the hole.
I thought, Who is that man? I didn't know you.
And I crept down the stairs and up the stairs
To look again, and still your spade kept lifting.
Then you came in. I heard your rumbling voice
Out in the kitchen, and I don't know why,
But I went near to see with my own eyes.
You could sit there with the stains on your shoes
Of the fresh earth from your own baby's grave
90   And talk about your everyday concerns.
You had stood the spade up against the wall
Outside there in the entry, for I saw it.'

'I shall laugh the worst laugh I ever laughed.
I'm cursed. God, if I don't believe I'm cursed.'

'I can repeat the very words you were saying.
"Three foggy mornings and one rainy day
Will rot the best birch fence a man can build."
Think of it, talk like that at such a time!
What had how long it takes a birch to rot
100   To do with what was in the darkened parlor.
You *couldn't* care! The nearest friends can go
With anyone to death, comes so far short
They might as well not try to go at all.
No, from the time when one is sick to death,
One is alone, and he dies more alone.
Friends make pretense of following to the grave,
But before one is in it, their minds are turned
And making the best of their way back to life
And living people, and things they understand.
110   But the world's evil. I won't have grief so
If I can change it. Oh, I won't, I won't!'

'There, you have said it all and you feel better.
You won't go now. You're crying. Close the door.

The heart's gone out of it: why keep it up.
Amy! There's someone coming down the road!'

'*You*—oh, you think the talk is all. I must go—
Somewhere out of this house. How can I make you—'

'If—you—do!' She was opening the door wider.
'Where do you mean to go? First tell me that.
120   I'll follow and bring you back by force. I *will!*—'

After Apple-Picking

My long two-pointed ladder's sticking through a tree
Toward heaven still,
And there's a barrel that I didn't fill
Beside it, and there may be two or three
Apples I didn't pick upon some bough.
But I am done with apple-picking now.
Essence of winter sleep is on the night,
The scent of apples: I am drowsing off.
I cannot rub the strangeness from my sight
10   I got from looking through a pane of glass
I skimmed this morning from the drinking trough
And held against the world of hoary grass.
It melted, and I let it fall and break.
But I was well
Upon my way to sleep before it fell,
And I could tell
What form my dreaming was about to take.
Magnified apples appear and disappear,
Stem end and blossom end,
20   And every fleck of russet showing clear.
My instep arch not only keeps the ache,
It keeps the pressure of a ladder round.
I feel the ladder sway as the boughs bend.
And I keep hearing from the cellar bin
The rumbling sound
Of load on load of apples coming in.
For I have had too much
Of apple-picking: I am overtired
Of the great harvest I myself desired.
30   There were ten thousand thousand fruit to touch,
Cherish in hand, lift down, and not let fall.
For all
That struck the earth,
No matter if not bruised or spiked with stubble,
Went surely to the cider-apple heap
As of no worth.

One can see what will trouble
This sleep of mine, whatever sleep it is.
Were he not gone,
40   The woodchuck could say whether it's like his
Long sleep, as I describe its coming on,
Or just some human sleep.

The Road Not Taken

Two roads diverged in a yellow wood,
And sorry I could not travel both
And be one traveler, long I stood
And looked down one as far as I could
To where it bent in the undergrowth;

Then took the other, as just as fair,
And having perhaps the better claim,
Because it was grassy and wanted wear;
Though as for that the passing there
10   Had worn them really about the same,

And both that morning equally lay
In leaves no step had trodden black.
Oh, I kept the first for another day!
Yet knowing how way leads on to way,
I doubted if I should ever come back.

I shall be telling this with a sigh
Somewhere ages and ages hence:
Two roads diverged in a wood, and I—
I took the one less traveled by,
20   And that has made all the difference.

Birches

When I see birches bend to left and right
Across the lines of straighter darker trees,
I like to think some boy's been swinging them.
But swinging doesn't bend them down to stay
As ice-storms do. Often you must have seen them
Loaded with ice a sunny winter morning
After a rain. They click upon themselves
As the breeze rises, and turn many-colored
As the stir cracks and crazes their enamel.
10   Soon the sun's warmth makes them shed crystal shells
Shattering and avalanching on the snow-crust—
Such heaps of broken glass to sweep away
You'd think the inner dome of heaven had fallen.
They are dragged to the withered bracken by the load,
And they seem not to break; though once they are bowed
So low for long, they never right themselves:

You may see their trunks arching in the woods
Years afterwards, trailing their leaves on the ground
Like girls on hands and knees that throw their hair
20   Before them over their heads to dry in the sun.
But I was going to say when Truth broke in
With all her matter-of-fact about the ice-storm
I should prefer to have some boy bend them
As he went out and in to fetch the cows—
Some boy too far from town to learn baseball,
Whose only play was what he found himself,
Summer or winter, and could play alone.
One by one he subdued his father's trees
By riding them down over and over again
30   Until he took the stiffness out of them,
And not one but hung limp, not one was left
For him to conquer. He learned all there was
To learn about not launching out too soon
And so not carrying the tree away
Clear to the ground. He always kept his poise
To the top branches, climbing carefully
With the same pains you use to fill a cup
Up to the brim, and even above the brim.
Then he flung outward, feet first, with a swish,
40   Kicking his way down through the air to the ground.
So was I once myself a swinger of birches.
And so I dream of going back to be.
It's when I'm weary of considerations,
And life is too much like a pathless wood
Where your face burns and tickles with the cobwebs
Broken across it, and one eye is weeping
From a twig's having lashed across it open.
I'd like to get away from earth awhile
And then come back to it and begin over.
50   May no fate willfully misunderstand me
And half grant what I wish and snatch me away
Not to return. Earth's the right place for love:
I don't know where it's likely to go better.
I'd like to go by climbing a birch tree,
And climb black branches up a snow-white trunk
Toward heaven, till the tree could bear no more,
But dipped its top and set me down again.
That would be good both going and coming back.
One could do worse than be a swinger of birches.

To Earthward

Love at the lips was touch
As sweet as I could bear;
And once that seemed too much;
I lived on air

That crossed me from sweet things
The flow of—was it musk
From hidden grapevine springs
Down hill at dusk?

I had the swirl and ache
10   From sprays of honeysuckle
That when they're gathered shake
Dew on the knuckle.

I craved strong sweets, but those
Seemed strong when I was young;
The petal of the rose
It was that stung.

Now no joy but lacks salt
That is not dashed with pain
And weariness and fault;
20   I crave the stain

Of tears, the aftermark
Of almost too much love,
The sweet of bitter bark
And burning clove.

When stiff and sore and scarred
I take away my hand
From leaning on it hard
In grass and sand,

The hurt is not enough:
30   I long for weight and strength
To feel the earth as rough
To all my length.

.

The Need of Being Versed in Country Things

The house had gone to bring again
To the midnight sky a sunset glow.
Now the chimney was all of the house that stood,
Like a pistil after the petals go.

The barn opposed across the way,
That would have joined the house in flame
Had it been the will of the wind, was left
To bear forsaken the place's name.

No more it opened with all one end
10   For teams that came by the stony road
To drum on the floor with scurrying hoofs
And brush the mow with the summer load.

The birds that came to it through the air
At broken windows flew out and in,
Their murmur more like the sigh we sigh
From too much dwelling on what has been.

Yet for them the lilac renewed its leaf,
And the aged elm, though touched with fire;
And the dry pump flung up an awkward arm;
20   And the fence post carried a strand of wire.

For them there was really nothing sad.
But though they rejoiced in the nest they kept,
One had to be versed in country things
Not to believe the phoebes wept.

Once by the Pacific

The shattered water made a misty din.
Great waves looked over others coming in,
And thought of doing something to the shore
That water never did to land before.
The clouds were low and hairy in the skies,
Like locks blown forward in the gleam of eyes.
You could not tell, and yet it looked as if
The shore was lucky in being backed by cliff,
The cliff in being backed by continent;
10   It looked as if a night of dark intent
Was coming, and not only a night, an age.
Someone had better be prepared for rage.
There would be more than ocean-water broken
Before God's last *Put out the Light* was spoken.

Acquainted with the Night

I have been one acquainted with the night.
I have walked out in rain—and back in rain.
I have outwalked the furthest city light.

I have looked down the saddest city lane.
I have passed by the watchman on his beat
And dropped my eyes, unwilling to explain.

I have stood still and stopped the sound of feet
When far away an interrupted cry
Came over houses from another street,

10   But not to call me back or say good-by;
And further still at an unearthly height,
One luminary clock against the sky

Proclaimed the time was neither wrong nor right.
I have been one acquainted with the night.

Desert Places

Snow falling and night falling fast, oh, fast
In a field I looked into going past,
And the ground almost covered smooth in snow,
But a few weeds and stubble showing last.

The woods around it have it—it is theirs.
All animals are smothered in their lairs.
I am too absent-spirited to count;
The loneliness includes me unawares.

And lonely as it is that loneliness
10 Will be more lonely ere it will be less—
A blanker whiteness of benighted snow
With no expression, nothing to express.

They cannot scare me with their empty spaces
Between stars—on stars where no human race is.
I have it in me so much nearer home
To scare myself with my own desert places.

Neither Out Far Nor In Deep

The people along the sand
All turn and look one way.
They turn their back on the land.
They look at the sea all day.

As long as it takes to pass
A ship keeps raising its hull;
The wetter ground like glass
Reflects a standing gull.

The land may vary more;
10 But wherever the truth may be—
The water comes ashore,
And the people look at the sea.

They cannot look out far.
They cannot look in deep.
But when was that ever a bar
To any watch they keep?

The Silken Tent

She is as in a field a silken tent
At midday when a sunny summer breeze
Has dried the dew and all its ropes relent,
So that in guys it gently sways at ease,
And its supporting central cedar pole,

That is its pinnacle to heavenward
And signifies the sureness of the soul,
Seems to owe naught to any single cord,
But strictly held by none, is loosely bound
10   By countless silken ties of love and thought
To everything on earth the compass round,
And only by one's going slightly taut
In the capriciousness of summer air
Is of the slightest bondage made aware.

Come In

As I came to the edge of the woods,
Thrush music—hark!
Now if it was dusk outside,
Inside it was dark.

Too dark in the woods for a bird
By sleight of wing
To better its perch for the night,
Though it still could sing.

The last of the light of the sun
10   That had died in the west
Still lived for one song more
In a thrush's breast.

Far in the pillared dark
Thrush music went—
Almost like a call to come in
To the dark and lament.

But no, I was out for stars:
I would not come in.
I meant not even if asked,
20   And I hadn't been.

The Most of It

He thought he kept the universe alone;
For all the voice in answer he could wake
Was but the mocking echo of his own
From some tree-hidden cliff across the lake.
Some morning from the boulder-broken beach
He would cry out on life, that what it wants
Is not its own love back in copy speech,
But counter-love, original response.
And nothing ever came of what he cried

10   Unless it was the embodiment that crashed
In the cliff's talus on the other side,
And then in the far distant water splashed.
But after a time allowed for it to swim,
Instead of proving human when it neared
And someone else additional to him,
As a great buck it powerfully appeared,
Pushing the crumpled water up ahead,
And landed pouring like a waterfall,
And stumbled through the rocks with horny tread,
20   And forced the underbrush—and that was all.

Other poems by Robert Frost will be found on pages 1, 23, 51, 57, 94, and 105–106.

Theodore Roethke

Theodore Roethke (1908–1963) was born in Saginaw, Michigan, where his father kept the greenhouse that figures so prominently in his poems. He attended the University of Michigan and spent his last sixteen years in Seattle, where he was a professor at the University of Washington. He began by writing tight, formal stanzas and later broadened his repertoire to include a wide variety of tones and manners. Possibly no other major poet has traveled so widely in the realms of style. When he died he had recently written his best work, notably "The Rose."

Cuttings

(later)

This urge, wrestle, resurrection of dry sticks,
Cut stems struggling to put down feet,
What saint strained so much,
Rose on such lopped limbs to a new life?

I can hear, underground, that sucking and sobbing,
In my veins, in my bones I feel it,—
The small waters seeping upward,

The tight grains parting at last.
When sprouts break out,
10   Slippery as fish,
I quail, lean to beginnings, sheath-wet.

Big Wind

Where were the greenhouses going,
Lunging into the lashing
Wind driving water
So far down the river
All the faucets stopped?—
So we drained the manure-machine
For the steam plant,
Pumping the stale mixture
Into the rusty boilers,
10   Watching the pressure gauge
Waver over to red,
As the seams hissed
And the live steam
Drove to the far
End of the rose-house,
Where the worst wind was,
Creaking the cypress window-frames,
Cracking so much thin glass
We stayed all night,
20   Stuffing the holes with burlap;
But she rode it out,
That old rose-house,
She hove into the teeth of it,
The core and pith of that ugly storm,
Ploughing with her stiff prow,
Bucking into the wind-waves
That broke over the whole of her,
Flailing her sides with spray,
Flinging long strings of wet across the roof-top,
30   Finally veering, wearing themselves out, merely
Whistling thinly under the wind-vents;
She sailed until the calm morning,
Carrying her full cargo of roses.

Dolor

I have known the inexorable sadness of pencils,
Neat in their boxes, dolor of pad and paper-weight,
All the misery of manilla folders and mucilage,
Desolation in immaculate public places,
Lonely reception room, lavatory, switchboard,
The unalterable pathos of basin and pitcher,

Ritual of multigraph, paper-clip, comma,
Endless duplication of lives and objects.
And I have seen dust from the walls of institutions,
10   Finer than flour, alive, more dangerous than silica,
Sift, almost invisible, through long afternoons of tedium,
Dropping a fine film on nails and delicate eyebrows,
Glazing the pale hair, the duplicate grey standard faces.

My Papa's Waltz

The whiskey on your breath
Could make a small boy dizzy;
But I hung on like death:
Such waltzing was not easy.

We romped until the pans
Slid from the kitchen shelf;
My mother's countenance
Could not unfrown itself.

The hand that held my wrist
10   Was battered on one knuckle;
At every step you missed
My right ear scraped a buckle.

You beat time on my head
With a palm caked hard by dirt,
Then waltzed me off to bed
Still clinging to your shirt.

The Lost Son

1. The Flight

At Woodlawn I heard the dead cry:
I was lulled by the slamming of iron,
A slow drip over stones,
Toads brooding wells.
All the leaves stuck out their tongues;
I shook the softening chalk of my bones,
Saying,
Snail, snail, glister me forward,
Bird, soft-sigh me home,
10   Worm, be with me.
This is my hard time.

Fished in an old wound,
The soft pond of repose;
Nothing nibbled my line,
Not even the minnows came.

Sat in an empty house
Watching shadows crawl,

Scratching.
There was one fly.

20   Voice, come out of the silence.
Say something.
Appear in the form of a spider
Or a moth beating the curtain.

Tell me:
Which is the way I take;
Out of what door do I go,
Where and to whom?

      Dark hollows said, lee to the wind,
      The moon said, back of an eel,
30   The salt said, look by the sea,
      Your tears are not enough praise,
      You will find no comfort here,
      In the kingdom of bang and blab.

      Running lightly over spongy ground,
      Past the pasture of flat stones,
      The three elms,
      The sheep strewn on a field,
      Over a rickety bridge
      Toward the quick-water, wrinkling and rippling.

40   Hunting along the river,
      Down among the rubbish, the bug-riddled foliage,
      By the muddy pond-edge, by the bog-holes,
      By the shrunken lake, hunting, in the heat of summer.

The shape of a rat?
      It's bigger than that.
      It's less than a leg
      And more than a nose,
      Just under the water
      It usually goes.

50   Is it soft like a mouse?
Can it wrinkle its nose?
Could it come in the house
On the tips of its toes?

      Take the skin of a cat
      And the back of an eel,
      Then roll them in grease,—
      That's the way it would feel.

      It's sleek as an otter
      With wide webby toes
60   Just under the water
      It usually goes.

2. The Pit

Where do the roots go?
  Look down under the leaves.
Who put the moss there?
  These stones have been here too long.
Who stunned the dirt into noise?
  Ask the mole, he knows.
I feel the slime of a wet nest.
  Beware Mother Mildew.
70 Nibble again, fish nerves.

3. The Gibber

At the wood's mouth,
By the cave's door,
I listened to something
I had heard before.

Dogs of the groin
Barked and howled,
The sun was against me,
The moon would not have me.

The weeds whined,
80 The snakes cried,
The cows and briars
Said to me: Die.

What a small song. What slow clouds. What dark water.
Hath the rain a father? All the caves are ice. Only the snow's here.
I'm cold. I'm cold all over. Rub me in father and mother.
Fear was my father, Father Fear.
His look drained the stones.

    What gliding shape
    Beckoning through halls,
90   Stood poised on the stair,
    Fell dreamily down?

    From the mouths of jugs
    Perched on many shelves,
    I saw substance flowing
    That cold morning.

    Like a slither of eels
    That watery cheek
    As my own tongue kissed
    My lips awake.

100 Is this the storm's heart? The ground is unstilling itself.
My veins are running nowhere. Do the bones cast out their fire?
Is the seed leaving the old bed? These buds are live as birds.
Where, where are the tears of the world?
Let the kisses resound, flat like a butcher's palm;

Let the gestures freeze; our doom is already decided.
All the windows are burning! What's left of my life?
I want the old rage, the lash of primordial milk!
Goodbye, goodbye, old stones, the time-order is going,
I have married my hands to perpetual agitation,
110   I run, I run to the whistle of money.

    Money money money
    Water water water

    How cool the grass is.
    Has the bird left?
    The stalk still sways.
    Has the worm a shadow?
    What do the clouds say?

These sweeps of light undo me.
Look, look, the ditch is running white!
120   I've more veins than a tree!
Kiss me, ashes, I'm falling through a dark swirl.

4. The Return

    The way to the boiler was dark,
    Dark all the way,
    Over slippery cinders
    Through the long greenhouse.

    The roses kept breathing in the dark.
    They had many mouths to breathe with.
    My knees made little winds underneath
    Where the weeds slept.

130   There was always a single light
    Swinging by the fire-pit,
    Where the fireman pulled out roses,
    The big roses, the big bloody clinkers.

    Once I stayed all night.
    The light in the morning came slowly over the white
    Snow.
    There were many kinds of cool
    Air.
    Then came steam.

140   Pipe-knock.

Scurry of warm over small plants.
Ordnung! ordnung!
Papa is coming!

    A fine haze moved off the leaves;
    Frost melted on far panes;
    The rose, the chrysanthemum turned toward the light.
    Even the hushed forms, the bent yellowy weeds
    Moved in a slow up-sway.

5. "It was beginning winter"

It was beginning winter,
150   An in-between time,
The landscape still partly brown:
The bones of weeds kept swinging in the wind,
Above the blue snow.

It was beginning winter,
The light moved slowly over the frozen field,
Over the dry seed-crowns,
The beautiful surviving bones
Swinging in the wind.

Light traveled over the wide field;
160   Stayed.
The weeds stopped swinging.
The mind moved, not alone,
Through the clear air, in the silence.

    Was it light?
    Was it light within?
    Was it light within light?
    Stillness becoming alive,
    Yet still?

A lively understandable spirit
170   Once entertained you.
It will come again.
Be still.
Wait.

Elegy for Jane

My Student, Thrown by a Horse

I remember the neckcurls, limp and damp as tendrils;
And her quick look, a sidelong pickerel smile;
And how, once startled into talk, the light syllables leaped for her,
And she balanced in the delight of her thought,
A wren, happy, tail into the wind,
Her song trembling the twigs and small branches.
The shade sang with her;
The leaves, their whispers turned to kissing;
And the mold sang in the bleached valleys under the rose.

10   Oh, when she was sad, she cast herself down into such a pure depth,
Even a father could not find her:
Scraping her cheek against straw;
Stirring the clearest water.

My sparrow, you are not here,
Waiting like a fern, making a spiny shadow.

The sides of wet stones cannot console me,
Nor the moss, wound with the last light.

If only I could nudge you from this sleep,
My maimed darling, my skittery pigeon.
20   Over this damp grave I speak the words of my love:
I, with no rights in this matter,
Neither father nor lover.

The Sloth

In moving-slow he has no Peer.
You ask him something in his Ear,
He thinks about it for a Year;

And, then, before he says a Word
There, upside down (unlike a Bird),
He will assume that you have Heard—

A most Ex-as-per-at-ing Lug.
But should you call his manner Smug,
He'll sigh and give his Branch a Hug;

10   Then off again to Sleep he goes,
Still swaying gently by his Toes,
And you just *know* he knows he knows.

I Knew a Woman

I knew a woman, lovely in her bones,
When small birds sighed, she would sigh back at them;
Ah, when she moved, she moved more ways than one:
The shapes a bright container can contain!
Of her choice virtues only gods should speak,
Or English poets who grew up on Greek
(I'd have them sing in chorus, cheek to cheek).

How well her wishes went! She stroked my chin,
She taught me Turn, and Counter-turn, and Stand;
10   She taught me Touch, that undulant white skin;
I nibbled meekly from her proffered hand;
She was the sickle; I, poor I, the rake,
Coming behind her for her pretty sake
(But what prodigious mowing we did make).

Love likes a gander, and adores a goose:
Her full lips pursed, the errant note to seize;
She played it quick, she played it light and loose;
My eyes, they dazzled at her flowing knees;
Her several parts could keep a pure repose,
20   Or one hip quiver with a mobile nose
(She moved in circles, and those circles moved).

Let seed be grass, and grass turn into hay:
I'm martyr to a motion not my own;
What's freedom for? To know eternity.
I swear she cast a shadow white as stone.
But who would count eternity in days?
These old bones live to learn her wanton ways:
(I measure time by how a body sways).

The Visitant

1

A cloud moved close. The bulk of the wind shifted.
A tree swayed over water.
A voice said:
Stay. Stay by the slip-ooze. Stay.

Dearest tree, I said, may I rest here?
A ripple made a soft reply.
I waited, alert as a dog.
The leech clinging to a stone waited;
And the crab, the quiet breather.

2

10 Slow, slow as a fish she came,
Slow as a fish coming forward,
Swaying in a long wave;
Her skirts not touching a leaf,
Her white arms reaching towards me.

She came without sound,
Without brushing the wet stones;

In the soft dark of early evening,
She came,
The wind in her hair,
20 The moon beginning.

3

I woke in the first of morning.
Staring at a tree, I felt the pulse of a stone.
Where's she now, I kept saying.
Where's she now, the mountain's downy girl?
But the bright day had no answer.
A wind stirred in a web of appleworms;
The tree, the close willow, swayed.

Journey to the Interior

1

In the long journey out of the self,
There are many detours, washed-out interrupted raw places

Where the shale slides dangerously
And the back wheels hang almost over the edge
At the sudden veering, the moment of turning.
Better to hug close, wary of rubble and falling stones.
The arroyo cracking the road, the wind-bitten buttes, the canyons,
Creeks swollen in midsummer from the flash-flood roaring into the narrow
    valley.
Reeds beaten flat by wind and rain,
10   Grey from the long winter, burnt at the base in late summer.
—Or the path narrowing,
Winding upward toward the stream with its sharp stones,
The upland of alder and birchtrees,
Through the swamp alive with quicksand,
The way blocked at last by a fallen fir-tree,
The thickets darkening,
The ravines ugly.

2

I remember how it was to drive in gravel,
Watching for dangerous down-hill places, where the wheels whined beyond
    eighty—
20   When you hit the deep pit at the bottom of the swale,
The trick was to throw the car sideways and charge over the hill, full of the
    throttle.
Grinding up and over the narrow road, spitting and roaring.
A chance? Perhaps. But the road was part of me, and its ditches,
And the dust lay thick on my eyelids,—Who ever wore goggles?—
Always a sharp turn to the left past a barn close to the roadside,
To a scurry of small dogs and a shriek of children,
The highway ribboning out in a straight thrust to the North,
To the sand dunes and fish flies, hanging, thicker than moths,
Dying brightly under the street lights sunk in coarse concrete,
30   The towns with their high pitted road-crowns and deep gutters,
Their wooden stores of silvery pine and weather-beaten red courthouses,
An old bridge below with a buckled iron railing, broken by some idiot plunger;
Underneath, the sluggish water running between weeds, broken wheels, tires,
    stones.
And all flows past—
The cemetery with two scrubby trees in the middle of the prairie,
The dead snakes and muskrats, the turtles gasping in the rubble,
The spikey purple bushes in the winding dry creek bed—
The floating hawks, the jackrabbits, the grazing cattle—
I am not moving but they are,
40   And the sun comes out of a blue cloud over the Tetons,
While, farther away, the heat-lightning flashes.
I rise and fall in the slow sea of a grassy plain,
The wind veering the car slightly to the right,
Whipping the line of white laundry, bending the cottonwoods apart,
The scraggly wind-break of a dusty ranch-house.

I rise and fall, and time folds
Into a long moment;
And I hear the lichen speak,
And the ivy advance with its white lizard feet—
50   On the shimmering road,
On the dusty detour.

3

I see the flower of all water, above and below me, the never receding,
Moving, unmoving in a parched land, white in the moonlight:
The soul at a still-stand,
At ease after rocking the flesh to sleep,
Petals and reflections of petals mixed on the surface of a glassy pool,
And the waves flattening out when the fishermen drag their nets over the
stones.

In the moment of time when the small drop forms, but does not fall,
I have known the heart of the sun,—
60   In the dark and light of a dry place,
In a flicker of fire brisked by a dusty wind.
I have heard, in a drip of leaves,
A slight song,
After the midnight cries.
I rehearse myself for this:
The stand at the stretch in the face of death,
Delighting in surface change, the glitter of light on waves,
And I roam elsewhere, my body thinking,
Turning toward the other side of light,
70   In a tower of wind, a tree idling in air,
Beyond my own echo,
Neither forward nor backward,
Unperplexed, in a place leading nowhere.

As a blind man, lifting a curtain, knows it is morning,
I know this change:
On one side of silence there is no smile;
But when I breathe with the birds,
The spirit of wrath becomes the spirit of blessing,
And the dead begin from their dark to sing in my sleep.

The Rose

1

There are those to whom place is unimportant,
But this place, where sea and fresh water meet,
Is important—
Where the hawks sway out into the wind,
Without a single wingbeat,
And the eagles sail low over the fir trees,
And the gulls cry against the crows

In the curved harbors,
And the tide rises up against the grass
10   Nibbled by sheep and rabbits.

A time for watching the tide,
For the heron's hieratic fishing,
For the sleepy cries of the towhee,
The morning birds gone, the twittering finches,
But still the flash of the kingfisher, the wingbeat of the scoter,
The sun a ball of fire coming down over the water,
The last geese crossing against the reflected afterlight,
The moon retreating into a vague cloud-shape
To the cries of the owl, the eerie whooper.
20   The old log subsides with the lessening waves,
And there is silence.

I sway outside myself
Into the darkening currents,
Into the small spillage of driftwood,
The waters swirling past the tiny headlands.
Was it here I wore a crown of birds for a moment
While on a far point of the rocks
The light heightened,
And below, in a mist out of nowhere,
30   The first rain gathered?

2

As when a ship sails with a light wind—
The waves less than the ripples made by rising fish,
The lacelike wrinkles of the wake widening, thinning out,
Sliding away from the traveler's eye,
The prow pitching easily up and down,
The whole ship rolling slightly sideways,
The stern high, dipping like a child's boat in a pond—
Our motion continues.

But this rose, this rose in the sea-wind,
40   Stays,
Stays in its true place,
Flowering out of the dark,
Widening at high noon, face upward,
A single wild rose, struggling out of the white embrace of the morning-glory,
Out of the briary hedge, the tangle of matted underbrush,
Beyond the clover, the ragged hay,
Beyond the sea pine, the oak, the wind-tipped madrona,
Moving with the waves, the undulating driftwood,
Where the slow creek winds down to the black sand of the shore
50   With its thick grassy scum and crabs scuttling back into their glistening craters.

And I think of roses, roses,
White and red, in the wide six-hundred-foot greenhouses,
And my father standing astride the cement benches,

Lifting me high over the four-foot stems, the Mrs. Russells, and his own
    elaborate hybrids.
And how those flowerheads seemed to flow toward me, to beckon me, only a
    child, out of myself.

What need for heaven, then,
With that man, and those roses?

3

What do they tell us, sound and silence?
I think of American sounds in this silence:
On the banks of the Tombstone, the wind-harps having their say,
The thrush singing alone, that easy bird,
The killdeer whistling away from me,
The mimetic chortling of the catbird
Down in the corner of the garden, among the raggedy lilacs,
The bobolink skirring from a broken fencepost,
The bluebird, lover of holes in old wood, lilting its light song,
And that thin cry, like a needle piercing the ear, the insistent cicada,
And the ticking of snow around oil drums in the Dakotas,
The thin whine of telephone wires in the wind of a Michigan winter,
The shriek of nails as old shingles are ripped from the top of a roof,
The bulldozer backing away, the hiss of the sandblaster,
And the deep chorus of horns coming up from the streets in early morning.
I return to the twittering of swallows above water,
And that sound, that single sound,
When the mind remembers all,
And gently the light enters the sleeping soul,
A sound so thin it could not woo a bird,

Beautiful my desire, and the place of my desire.

I think of the rock singing, and light making its own silence,
At the edge of a ripening meadow, in early summer,
The moon lolling in the close elm, a shimmer of silver,
Or that lonely time before the breaking of morning
When the slow freight winds along the edge of the ravaged hillside,
And the wind tries the shape of a tree,
While the moon lingers,
And a drop of rain water hangs at the tip of a leaf
Shifting in the wakening sunlight
Like the eye of a new-caught fish.

4

I live with the rocks, their weeds,
Their filmy fringes of green, their harsh
Edges, their holes
Cut by the sea-slime, far from the crash
Of the long swell,
The oily, tar-laden walls
Of the toppling waves,

Where the salmon ease their way into the kelp beds,
And the sea rearranges itself among the small islands.

Near this rose, in this grove of sun-parched, wind-warped madronas,
Among the half-dead trees, I came upon the true ease of myself,
100 As if another man appeared out of the depths of my being,
And I stood outside myself,
Beyond becoming and perishing,
A something wholly other,
As if I swayed out on the wildest wave alive,
And yet was still.
And I rejoiced in being what I was:
In the lilac change, the white reptilian calm,
In the bird beyond the bough, the single one
With all the air to greet him as he flies,
110 The dolphin rising from the darkening waves;

And in this rose, this rose in the sea-wind,
Rooted in stone, keeping the whole of light,
Gathering to itself sound and silence—
Mine and the sea-wind's.

The Meadow Mouse

1

In a shoe box stuffed in an old nylon stocking
Sleeps the baby mouse I found in the meadow,
Where he trembled and shook beneath a stick
Till I caught him up by the tail and brought him in,
Cradled in my hand,
A little quaker, the whole body of him trembling,
His absurd whiskers sticking out like a cartoon-mouse,
His feet like small leaves,
Little lizard-feet,
10 Whitish and spread wide when he tried to struggle away,
Wriggling like a miniscule puppy.

Now he's eaten his three kinds of cheese and drunk from his bottle-cap
       watering-trough—
So much he just lies in one corner,
His tail curled under him, his belly big
As his head: his bat-like ears
Twitching, tilting toward the least sound.

Do I imagine he no longer trembles
When I come close to him?
He seems no longer to tremble.

2

20 But this morning the shoe-box house on the back porch is empty.
Where has he gone, my meadow mouse,

My thumb of a child that nuzzled in my palm?—
To run under the hawk's wing,
Under the eye of the great owl watching from the elm-tree,
To live by courtesy of the shrike, the snake, the tom-cat.

I think of the nestling fallen into the deep grass,
The turtle gasping in the dusty rubble of the highway,
The paralytic stunned in the tub, and the water rising,—
All things innocent, hapless, forsaken.

Another poem by Theodore Roethke may be found on page 41.

A Gathering of Poems

Geoffrey Chaucer

Geoffrey Chaucer (1340?–1400) grew up in London, son of a man who made wine. He fought for England in France, and later worked for his king as a diplomat on foreign service. During his busy public life, he wrote poems, most notably *The Canterbury Tales*, a loose assemblage of stories told by pilgrims traveling to the shrine in Kent. He is the first great poet of England, and remains the funniest. Because the Middle English that was his language requires special study, this selection is small—only a hint of the sound that Chaucer makes.

from the Prologue to *The Canterbury Tales*

Whan that Aprill with his shoures soote[1]
The droghte[2] of March hath perced[3] to the roote,
And bathed every veyne[4] in swich licour,[5]
Of which vertu[6] engendred is the flour;[7]
Whan Zephyrus eek[8] with his sweete breeth
Inspired hath in every holt and heeth
The tendre croppes,[9] and the yonge sonne
Hath in the Ram his halfe cours yronne,
And smale foweles[10] maken melodye
10 That slepen al the nyght with open yë[11]—
So priketh hem Nature in hir corages[12]—
Thanne longen folk to goon on pilgrimages,

[1]sweet showers [2]drought [3]pierced [4]vein [5]such liquid [6]power [7]flower [8]also
[9]shoots [10]birds [11]eye [12]hearts

And palmeres for to seken straunge strondes[13]
To ferne halwes,[14] kouthe[15] in sondry londes;
And specially from every shires ende
Of Engelond to Caunterbury[16] they wende,
The holy blisful martir for to seke
That hem[17] hath holpen[18] whan that they were seeke.[19]

[13]shores   [14]distant shrines   [15]known   [16]shrine of Thomas à Becket (1118?–1170), English martyr   [17]them   [18]helped   [19]sick

Anonymous ballads and songs

For a few words about ballads, see pages 62–63. Anonymous songs made up the best poetry between Chaucer's time and the great explosion of poetry that happened under the Tudor monarchs.

Anonymous
Lord Randal

"O where hae° ye been, Lord Randal, my son?   have
O where hae ye been, my handsome young man?"
"I hae been to the wild wood; mother, make my bed soon,
For I'm weary wi hunting, and fain wald° lie down."   would

"Where gat ye your dinner, Lord Randal, my son?
Where gat ye your dinner, my handsome young man?"
"I din'd wi my true-love; mother, make my bed soon,
For I'm weary wi hunting, and fain wald lie down."

"What gat ye to your dinner, Lord Randal, my son?
10   What gat ye to your dinner, my handsome young man?"
"I gat eels boiled in broo,° mother, make my bed soon,   broth
For I'm weary wi hunting, and fain wald lie down."

"What became of your bloodhounds, Lord Randal, my son?
What became of your bloodhounds, my handsome young man?"
"O they swelld and they died; mother, make my bed soon,
For I'm weary wi hunting, and fain wald lie down."

"O I fear ye are poisond, Lord Randal, my son!
O I fear ye are poisond, my handsome young man!"
"O yes! I am poisond; mother, make my bed soon,
20   For I'm sick at the heart, and I fain wald lie down."

Adam Lay I-Bowndyn

Adam lay i-bowndyn,
   Bowndyn in a bond—
Fowre thousand wynter
   Thoght he not too long;

And al was for an appil,
　　An appil that he tok,
As clerkes° fynden,　　　　　　　　　　　　　　　scholars
　　Writen in here° book.　　　　　　　　　　　　　their

　　Ne hadde the appil takë ben,[1]
10　　The appil taken ben,
Ne haddë never our lady
　　A ben° hevenë quene.　　　　　　　　　　　　have been
Blyssid be the tyme
　　That appil takë was,
Ther fore we mown° syngyn　　　　　　　　　　　must
　　Deo Gracias.[2]

[1]If the apple had not been taken　　　[2]Thanks be to God

Thomas Wyatt

Sir Thomas Wyatt (1503–1542) was ambassador for Henry VIII—and several
times imprisoned by him in the Tower of London for alleged offenses. Wyatt
brought the sonnet to England, imitating the form used by Italian poets. When
the music of English verse had vanished for a hundred years after Chaucer's
death, Wyatt's lyrics and sonnets began its restoration.

They Flee from Me

They flee from me, that sometime did me seek,
With naked foot, stalking in my chamber.
I have seen them, gentle, tame, and meek,
That now are wild, and do not remember
That sometime they put themselves in danger
To take bread at my hand, and now they range,
Busily seeking with a continual change.

Thankèd be fortune, it hath been otherwise
Twenty times better; but once, in special,
10　In thin array, after a pleasant guise,
When her loose gown from her shoulders did fall,
And she me caught in her arms long and small,
Therewithal sweetly did me kiss,
And softly said, "Dear heart, how like you this?"

It was no dream; I lay broad waking.
But all is turned, thorough my gentleness,
Into a strange fashion of forsaking;
And I have leave to go, of her goodness,
And she also to use new-fangledness.
20　But since that I so kindely° am served,　　　　　naturally
I would fain know what she hath deserved.

Sir Walter Ralegh

Sir Walter Ralegh (1552?–1618) is the same man who was alleged to have spread his cloak over a puddle that his queen might walk dry-shod. More reliably, we know of Ralegh as adventurer, explorer, and prisoner. He was a man of action who fought in France and who led several voyages to the New World. Three times, on various charges, he was committed to the Tower, where he probably wrote most of his poetry. After a failed expedition to the Orinoco, during which a Spanish colony was raised, Ralegh was executed (a major cause of death among Elizabethan poets).

Verses Written the Night Before His Execution

Even such is time, that takes in trust
Our youth, our joys, our all we have,
And pays us but with age and dust;
Who in the dark and silent grave,
When we have wandered all our ways,
Shuts up the story of our days:
But from this earth, this grave, this dust,
My God shall raise me up, I trust.

Sir Philip Sidney

Sir Philip Sidney (1554–1586) died fighting for England against Spain, and none of his considerable work appeared until after his death. In his generation he was widely admired and became the subject of several elegies, most notably Spenser's. He was loved not only for his talent and his intelligence but also for the nobility of his character. According to legend, while he was dying he refused a cup of water, sending it to the wounded man beside him, claiming "Thy necessity is greater than mine."

from Astrophel and Stella

With how sad steps, O Moon! thou climb'st the skies!
How silently, and with how wan a face!
What! may it be, that even in heavenly place
That busy archer° his sharp arrows tries?   Cupid
Sure, if that long-with-love-acquainted eyes
Can judge of love, thou feel'st a lover's case;
I read it in thy looks; thy languish'd grace,
To me that feel the like, thy state descries.
Then, even of fellowship, O Moon, tell me,
10 Is constant love deem'd there but want of wit?
Are beauties there as proud as here they be?
Do they above love to be loved, and yet
   Those lovers scorn whom that love doth possess?
   Do they call virtue there ungratefulness?

Robert Southwell

Robert Southwell (1561?–1595), a Catholic, wrote most of his devotional poetry in prison, where he was tortured and finally executed.

The Burning Babe

As I in hoary winter's night stood shivering in the snow,
Surprised I was with sudden heat, which made my heart to glow;
And lifting up a fearful eye to view what fire was near,
A pretty Babe all burning bright, did in the air appear,
Who scorched with excessive heat, such floods of tears did shed,
As though His floods should quench His flames which with His tears were fed;
Alas! quoth He, but newly born, in fiery heats I fry,
Yet none approach to warm their hearts or feel my fire but I!
My faultless breast the furnace is, the fuel wounding thorns,
10   Love is the fire, and sighs the smoke, the ashes shame and scorns;
The fuel Justice layeth on, and Mercy blows the coals,
The metal in this furnace wrought are men's defilèd souls,
For which, as now on fire I am to work them to their good,
So will I melt into a bath to wash them in My blood:
With this He vanished out of sight, and swiftly shrank away,
And straight I callèd unto mind that it was Christmas-day.

Christopher Marlowe

Christopher Marlowe (1564–1593) was a great playwright, slightly younger than Shakespeare, who helped establish English poetry upon the stage. Two of his best plays were his *Tragedy of Doctor Faustus* and *Edward II*. He was murdered in a tavern at Deptford by a man named Ingram Frisar.

The Passionate Shepherd to His Love

Come live with me and be my love,
And we will all the pleasures prove
That hills and valleys, dale and field,
And all the craggy mountains yield!

There will we sit upon the rocks
And see the shepherds feed their flocks,
By shallow rivers, to whose falls
Melodious birds sing madrigals.

There will I make thee beds of roses
10   With a thousand fragrant posies;
A cap of flowers, and a kirtle
Embroider'd all with leaves of myrtle;

A gown made of the finest wool
Which from our pretty lambs we pull;
Fair lined slippers for the cold,
With buckles of the purest gold;

A belt of straw and ivy buds,
With coral clasps and amber studs:
And if these pleasures may thee move,
20   Come live with me and be my love!

Thy silver dishes, for thy meat
As precious as the gods do eat,
Shall on an ivory table be
Prepared each day for thee and me.

The shepherd swains shall dance and sing
For thy delight each May morning.
If these delights thy mind may move,
Then live with me and be my love!

Sir Walter Ralegh wrote an answer for the Nymph to address to the Shepherd:

The Nymph's Reply to the Shepherd

If all the world and love were young,
And truth in every shepherd's tongue,
These pretty pleasures might me move
To live with thee and be thy love.

Time drives the flocks from field to fold
When rivers rage and rocks grow cold,
And Philomel° becometh dumb;   the nightingale
The rest complains of care to come.

The flowers do fade, and wanton fields
10   To wayward winter reckoning yields;
A honey tongue, a heart of gall,
Is fancy's spring, but sorrow's fall.

Thy gowns, thy shoes, thy beds of roses,
Thy cap, thy kirtle,° and thy posies   underdress
Soon break, soon wither, soon forgotten—
In folly ripe, in reason rotten.

Thy belt of straw and ivy buds,
Thy coral clasps and amber studs,
All these in me no means can move
20   To come to thee and be thy love.

But could youth last and love still breed,
Had joys no date nor age no need,
Then these delights my mind might move
To live with thee and be thy love.

William Shakespeare

William Shakespeare (1564–1616) left Stratford in 1585, three years after he married, and arrived a year later in London, where he became an actor. He was in the original cast of two of Ben Jonson's plays. He began writing for the stage in about 1591, and his last finished work was *The Tempest*, 1611–1612. He spent the last years of his life largely in retirement at New Place, which he built in Stratford with his London earnings. His sonnets appeared during his lifetime (1609); scholars conjecture that they were written earlier, most of them between 1593 and 1596. He also wrote three long poems, but the best of his poetry is spoken by characters in his plays; his finest lyrics are sung by the same characters.

When, in disgrace with fortune and men's eyes

When, in disgrace with fortune and men's eyes,
I all alone beweep my outcast state
And trouble deaf heaven with my bootless° cries   useless
And look upon myself and curse my fate,
Wishing me like to one more rich in hope,
Featured like him, like him with friends possess'd,
Desiring this man's art and that man's scope,
With what I most enjoy contented least;
Yet in these thoughts myself almost despising
10 Haply I think on thee, and then my state,
Like to the lark at break of day arising
From sullen earth, sings hymns at heaven's gate;
    For thy sweet love remember'd such wealth brings
    That then I scorn to change my state with kings.

They that have power to hurt and will do none

They that have power to hurt and will do none,
That do not do the thing they most do show,
Who, moving others, are themselves as stone,
Unmovèd, cold, and to temptation slow,—
They rightly do inherit heaven's graces
And husband nature's riches from expense;
They are the lords and owners of their faces,
Others but stewards of their excellence.
The summer's flower is to the summer sweet,
10 Though to itself it only live and die:
But if that flower with base infection meet,
The basest weed outbraves his dignity:
    For sweetest things turn sourest by their deeds;
    Lilies that fester smell far worse than weeds.

Not mine own fears, nor the prophetic soul

Not mine own fears, nor the prophetic soul
Of the wide world dreaming on things to come,
Can yet the lease of my true love control,
Supposed as forfeit to a confined doom.

The mortal moon hath her eclipse endured,
And the sad augurs mock their own presage;
Incertainties now crown themselves assured,
And peace proclaims olives of endless age.
Now with the drops of this most balmy time
10   My love looks fresh, and Death to me subscribes,
Since, spite of him, I'll live in this poor rhyme,
While he insults o'er dull and speechless tribes.
  And thou in this shalt find thy monument,
  When tyrants' crests and tombs of brass are spent.

from *Twelfth Night*

When that I was and a little tiny boy,
  With hey, ho, the wind and the rain,
A foolish thing was but a toy,
  For the rain it raineth every day.

But when I came to man's estate
  With hey, ho, the wind and the rain,
'Gainst knaves and thieves men shut their gate,
  For the rain it raineth every day.

But when I came, alas! to wive,
10   With hey, ho, the wind and the rain,
By swaggering could I never thrive,
  For the rain it raineth every day.

But when I came unto my beds,
  With hey, ho, the wind and the rain,
With toss-pots still had drunken heads,
  For the rain it raineth every day.

A great while ago the world begun,
  With hey, ho, the wind and the rain,
But that's all one, our play is done,
20   And we'll strive to please you every day.

Thomas Campion

Thomas Campion (1567–1620) composed music for his lyrics, one of the few artists to become master of two arts. Although he could rhyme well enough when he wanted to, he despised English rhyming as vulgar, and argued for the establishment of Greek and Roman meters in English verse.

Rose-Cheeked Laura

Rose-cheeked Laura, come,
Sing thou smoothly with thy beauty's
Silent music, either other
  Sweetly gracing.

Lovely forms do flow
From concent° divinely framèd;   sounds in harmony
Heaven is music, and thy beauty's
    Birth is heavenly.

These dull notes we sing
10 Discords need for helps to grace them;
Only beauty purely loving
    Knows no discord,

But still moves delight,
Like clear springs renewed by flowing,
Ever perfect, ever in them-
    Selves eternal.

Thomas Nashe

Thomas Nashe (1567–1601) was a literary jack-of-all-trades—pamphleteer,
playwright, poet, and author of the first adventure novel in English. Ever
contentious, he wrote a comedy called "The Isle of Dogs" which attacked the
government so thoroughly that Nashe spent some months in jail. This poem is
said to have been written during the Plague that afflicted London from 1592
to 1594.

Adieu! Farewell Earth's Bliss!

Adieu! farewell earth's bliss!
This world uncertain is:
Fond are life's lustful joys,
Death proves them all but toys,
None from his darts can fly:
I am sick, I must die.
    Lord, have mercy on us!

Rich men, trust not in wealth!
Gold cannot buy you health;
10 Physic himself must fade,
All things to end are made,
The plague full swift goes by:
I am sick, I must die.
    Lord, have mercy on us!

Beauty is but a flower
Which wrinkles will devour;
Brightness falls from the air,
Queens have died young and fair,
Dust hath closed Helen's eye:
20 I am sick, I must die.
    Lord, have mercy on us!

Strength stoops unto the grave:
Worms feed on Hector brave;
Swords may not fight with fate;

Earth still holds ope her gate;
'Come! come!' the bells do cry.
I am sick, I must die.
   Lord, have mercy on us!

Wit with his wantonness
30   Tasteth death's bitterness;
Hell's executioner
Hath no ears for to hear
What vain art can reply:
I am sick, I must die.
   Lord, have mercy on us!

Haste, therefore, each degree,
To welcome destiny:
Heaven is our heritage,
Earth but a player's stage,
40   Mount we unto the sky:
I am sick, I must die.
   Lord, have mercy on us!

John Donne

John Donne (1572–1631) was chief of the "Metaphysical Poets." It was his wit,
and that of other metaphysicals, to speak of one thing in terms of another far
removed, as when the parting of husband and wife is compared to the two feet
of a geometric compass. In youth he wrote playful and complex erotic poetry;
after he became an Anglican priest in 1615, his poetry became increasingly
religious, thus providing literary observers with a division into two poets, Jack
Donne and Dr. Donne. His devotional prose, including his sermons, ranks
among the best English prose of the seventeenth century. From 1621 until he
died, he was Dean of St. Paul's in London, and he preached his final sermon
wearing a shroud.

The Canonization

For Godsake hold your tongue, and let me love,
   Or chide my palsy, or my gout,
My five grey hairs, or ruined fortune flout;
   With wealth your state, your mind with arts improve,
      Take you a course, get you a place,
      Observe his Honor, or his Grace;
Or the king's real, or his stampèd face[1]
   Contemplate; what you will, approve,
So you will let me love.

10   Alas, alas, who's injured by my love?
   What merchant's ships have my sighs drowned?
Who says my tears have overflowed his ground?
   When did my colds a forward spring remove?

[1]On coins

When did the heats which my veins fill
    Add one more to the plaguy bill?[2]
Soldiers find wars, and lawyers find out still
    Litigious men, which quarrels move,
    Though she and I do love.

Call us what you will, we are made such by love;
20   Call her one, me another fly,
We're tapers too, and at our own cost die,
    And we in us find the eagle and the dove.
      The phoenix riddle hath more wit
      By us; we two being one are it.
So to one neutral thing both sexes fit,
    We die and rise the same, and prove
    Mysterious by this love.

We can die by it, if not live by love,
    And if unfit for tombs and hearse
30   Our legend be, it will be fit for verse;
    And if no piece of chronicle we prove,
      We'll build in sonnets pretty rooms;
      As well a well-wrought urn becomes
The greatest ashes, as half-acre tombs,
    And by these hymns all shall approve
    Us canonized for love:

And thus invoke us; You, whom reverend love
    Made one another's hermitage;
You, to whom love was peace, that now is rage;
40   Who did the whole world's soul contract, and drove
      Into the glasses of your eyes—
      So made such mirrors, and such spies,
That they did all to you epitomize,
    Countries, towns, courts: beg from above
    A pattern of your love!

[2]List of those dead of plague

Death, Be Not Proud

Death, be not proud, though some have callèd thee
Mighty and dreadful, for thou are not so;
For those whom thou think'st thou dost overthrow
Die not, poor Death; nor yet canst thou kill me.
From rest and sleep, which but thy pictures be,
Much pleasure; then from thee much more must flow;
And soonest our best men with thee do go—
Rest of their bones and souls' delivery!
Thou'rt slave to fate, chance, kings, and desperate men,
10   And dost with poison, war, and sickness dwell;
And poppy or charms can make us sleep as well

And better than thy stroke. Why swell'st thou then?
One short sleep past, we wake eternally,
And Death shall be no more: Death, thou shalt die.

Batter My Heart

Batter my heart, three-personed God; for you
As yet but knock, breathe, shine, and seek to mend.
That I may rise and stand, o'erthrow me and bend
Your force to break, blow, burn, and make me new.
I, like an usurped town, to another due,
Labor to admit you, but, oh, to no end;
Reason, your viceroy in me, me should defend,
But is captived and proves weak or untrue.
Yet dearly I love you and would be lovèd fain,
10   But am betrothed unto your enemy:
Divorce me, untie or break that knot again,
Take me to you, imprison me, for I,
Except you enthrall me, never shall be free,
Nor ever chaste, except you ravish me.

Ben Jonson

Ben Jonson (1572–1637) was actor as well as playwright, and his great plays rank second only to Shakespeare's. In 1598 he killed another actor in a duel but avoided execution by pleading benefit of clergy—at least he spoke Latin. Although his plays remain at the center of his work, he mastered the art of poetry in all forms, and his works are voluminous and superb in range and in accomplishment.

To Heaven

Good and great God! can I not think of Thee,
    But it must straight my melancholy be?
Is it interpreted in me disease,
    That, laden with my sins, I seek for ease?
O be Thou witness, that the reins dost know
    And hearts of all, if I be sad for show;
And judge me after, if I dare pretend
    To aught but grace, or aim at other end.
As Thou art all, so be Thou all to me,
10   First, midst, and last, converted One and Three!
My faith, my hope, my love; and, in this state,
    My judge, my witness, and my advocate!
Where have I been this while exiled from Thee,
    And whither rapt, now Thou but stoop'st to me?
Dwell, dwell here still! O, being everywhere,
    How can I doubt to find Thee ever here?
I know my state, both full of shame and scorn,
    Conceived in sin, and unto labor born,

Standing with fear, and must with horror fall,
20   And destined unto judgment, after all.
I feel my griefs too, and there scarce is ground
      Upon my flesh t'inflict another wound;
Yet dare I not complain or wish for death
      With holy Paul, lest it be thought the breath
Of discontent; or that these prayers be
      For weariness of life, not love of Thee.

Robert Herrick

Robert Herrick (1591–1674) is among the most playful of English poets. An admirer of Ben Jonson, he wrote short poems, sacred and profane, in a variety of forms.

Delight in Disorder

A sweet disorder in the dress	
Kindles in clothes a wantonness:	
A lawn° about the shoulders thrown	a thin fabric
Into a fine distraction;	
An erring lace, which here and there	
Enthralls the crimson stomacher;°	decorative garment,
A cuff neglectful, and thereby	often embroidered
Ribands to flow confusedly;	
A winning wave, deserving note,	

10   In the tempestuous petticoat;
A careless shoe-string, in whose tie
I see a wild civility,—
Do more bewitch me, than when art
Is too precise in every part.

George Herbert

George Herbert (1593–1633) was a priest and author of great religious poetry. He attended Cambridge University and died as a country parson.

The Pulley

When God at first made Man,
Having a glass of blessings standing by;
Let us (said He) pour on him all we can:
Let the world's riches, which dispersèd lie,
      Contract into a span.

So strength first made a way;
Then beauty flow'd, then wisdom, honour, pleasure:
When almost all was out, God made a stay,
Perceiving that alone, of all His treasure,
10   Rest in the bottom lay.

       For if I should (said He)
   Bestow this jewel also on My creature,
   He would adore My gifts instead of Me,
   And rest in Nature, not the God of Nature:
       So both should losers be.

       Yet let him keep the rest,
   But keep them with repining restlessness:
   Let him be rich and weary, that at least,
   If goodness lead him not, yet weariness
20   May toss him to My breast.

Church Monuments

   While that my soul repairs to her devotion,
   Here I intomb my flesh, that it betimes
   May take acquaintance of this heap of dust;
   To which the blast of death's incessant motion,
   Fed with the exhalation of our crimes,
   Drives all at last. Therefore I gladly trust

   My body to this school, that it may learn
   To spell his elements, and find his birth
   Written in dusty heraldry and lines;
10   Which dissolution sure doth best discern,
   Comparing dust with dust, and earth with earth.
   These laugh at jet and marble, put for signs,

   To sever the good fellowship of dust,
   And spoil the meeting. What shall point out them
   When they shall bow, and kneel, and fall down flat
   To kiss those heaps, which now they have in trust?
   Dear flesh, while I do pray, learn here thy stem
   And true descent, that when thou shalt grow fat,

   And wanton in thy cravings, thou mayst know,
20   That flesh is but the glass which holds the dust
   That measures all our time; which also shall
   Be crumbled into dust. Mark here below
   How tame these ashes are, how free from lust—
   That thou mayst fit thyself against thy fall.

John Milton

John Milton (1608–1674) was a precocious poet. He prepared himself assiduously for his poetic vocation, and in 1637 wrote the remarkable elegy "Lycidas" for a young man he had known at Cambridge. During the next twenty years he wrote a few sonnets—excellent poems—but largely he substituted politics and political action for poetry, working as Cromwell's Latin secretary. His first marriage was tempestuous, and he wrote prose works advocating divorce, which earned him considerable denunciation. He became blind while he was still Cromwell's secretary, and was assisted by several helpers, notably Andrew Marvell. After Cromwell's death and the restoration of the monarchy, he was imprisoned, released, and lived in poverty. He had begun his great work, the religious epic *Paradise Lost*, while he was chiefly engaged in politics, but he completed it in blindness and poverty. Afterward he wrote "Paradise Regained" and "Samson Agonistes." In prose, his "Areopagitica" (on freedom of the press) is his most celebrated work.

On His Blindness

When I consider how my light is spent
Ere half my days in this dark world and wide,
And that one talent which is death to hide
Lodged with me useless, though my soul more bent
To serve therewith my Maker, and present
My true account, lest He returning chide,
"Doth God exact day-labor, light denied?"
I fondly ask. But Patience, to prevent
That murmur, soon replies, "God doth not need
10   Either man's work or his own gifts. Who best
Bear His mild yoke, they serve Him best. His state
Is kingly: thousands at His bidding speed,
And post o'er land and ocean without rest;
They also serve who only stand and wait."

Andrew Marvell

Andrew Marvell (1621–1678) was a poet in youth who, as he grew older, became increasingly more political than poetical. A defender of Cromwell and Milton, after the restoration of the monarchy he joined Parliament and represented his birthplace, Hull, attacking the king and his ministers with considerable vigor.

The Garden

How vainly men themselves amaze
To win the palm, the oak, or bays;[1]
And their incessant labours see
Crowned from some single herb or tree,
Whose short and narrow-vergèd shade
Does prudently their toils upbraid;
While all flowers and all trees do close
To weave the garlands of repose.

[1]Laurel wreaths, symbolizing achievement in sport, politics, and poetry

Fair Quiet, have I found thee here,
10 And Innocence, thy sister dear!
Mistaken long, I sought you then
In busy companies of men.
Your sacred plants, if here below,
Only among the plants will grow:
Society is all but rude
To this delicious solitude.

No white nor red was ever seen
So amorous as this lovely green.
Fond lovers, cruel as their flame,
20 Cut in these trees their mistress' name:
Little, alas, they know or heed,
How far these beauties hers exceed!
Fair trees! wheres'e'er your barks I wound,
No name shall but your own be found.

When we have run our passion's heat,
Love hither makes his best retreat.
The gods, that mortal beauty chase,
Still in a tree did end their race.
Apollo hunted Daphne so,
30 Only that she might laurel grow;
And Pan did after Syrinx speed,
Not as a nymph, but for a reed.

What wondrous life in this I lead!
Ripe apples drop about my head;
The luscious clusters of the vine
Upon my mouth do crush their wine;
The nectarine, and curious peach,
Into my hands themselves do reach;
Stumbling on melons, as I pass,
40 Ensnared with flowers, I fall on grass.

Meanwhile the mind, from pleasure less,
Withdraws into its happiness:
The mind, that ocean where each kind
Does straight its own resemblance find;
Yet it creates, transcending these,
Far other worlds, and other seas;
Annihilating all that's made
To a green thought in a green shade.

Here at the fountain's sliding foot,
50 Or at some fruit-tree's mossy root,
Casting the body's vest aside,
My soul into the boughs does glide:
There like a bird it sits and sings,
Then whets, and combs its silver wings;
And, till prepared for longer flight,
Waves in its plumes the various light.

Such was that happy garden-state,
While man there walked without a mate:
After a place so pure and sweet,
60   What other help could yet be meet?
But 'twas beyond a mortal's share
To wander solitary there:
Two Paradises 'twere in one,
To live in Paradise alone.

How well the skilful gardener drew
Of flowers and herbs this dial new!
Where, from above, the milder sun
Does through a fragrant zodiac run;
And, as it works, the industrious bee
70   Computes its time as well as we
How could such sweet and wholesome hours
Be reckoned but with herbs and flowers?

To His Coy Mistress

Had we but world enough, and time,
This coyness, Lady, were no crime.
We would sit down, and think which way
To walk, and pass our long love's day.
Thou by the Indian Ganges' side
Shouldst rubies find; I by the tide
Of Humber would complain. I would
Love you ten years before the Flood;
And you should, if you please, refuse
10   Till the conversion of the Jews.
My vegetable° love should grow   vegetative
Vaster than empires, and more slow.
An hundred years should go to praise
Thine eyes, and on thy forehead gaze;
Two hundred to adore each breast;
But thirty thousand to the rest:
An age, at least, to every part,
And the last age should show your heart.
For, Lady, you deserve this state,
20   Nor would I love at lower rate.
But, at my back, I always hear
Time's wingèd chariot hurrying near:
And yonder, all before us lie
Deserts of vast eternity.
Thy beauty shall no more be found;
Nor, in thy marble vault, shall sound
My echoing song. Then worms shall try
That long preserved virginity:
And your quaint honour turn to dust;
30   And into ashes all my lust.
The grave's a fine and private place,
But none, I think, do there embrace.

Now, therefore, while the youthful hue
Sits on thy skin like morning dew,
And while thy willing soul transpires
At every pore with instant fires,
Now let us sport us while we may;
And now, like amorous birds of prey,
Rather at once our time devour,
40   Than languish in his slow-chapt° power.   slow-jawed
Let us roll all our strength, and all
Our sweetness, up into one ball;
And tear our pleasures, with rough strife,
Thorough° the iron gates of life.   through
    Thus, though we cannot make our sun
Stand still, yet we will make him run.

Henry Vaughan

Henry Vaughan (1622–1695), a great religious poet, was an admirer of George
Herbert.

The World

I saw Eternity the other night,
Like a great ring of pure and endless light,
    All calm, as it was bright;
And round beneath it, Time in hours, days, years,
    Driven by the spheres
Like a vast shadow moved; in which the world
    And all her train were hurled.
The doting lover in his quaintest strain
    Did there complain;
10   Near him, his lute, his fancy, and his flights,
    Wit's sour delights;
With gloves, and knots, the silly snares of pleasure,
    Yet his dear treasure,
All scattered lay, while he his eyes did pour
    Upon a flower.

The darksome statesman, hung with weights and woe,
Like a thick midnight-fog, moved there so slow,
    He did not stay, nor go;
Condemning thoughts—like sad eclipses—scowl
20   Upon his soul,
And clouds of crying witnesses without
    Pursued him with one shout.
Yet digged the mole, and lest his ways be found,
    Worked underground,
Where he did clutch his prey; but one did see
    That policy.
Churches and altars fed him; perjuries
    Were gnats and flies;

It rained about him blood and tears, but he
Drank them as free.

The fearful miser on a heap of rust
Sat pining all his life there, did scarce trust
His own hands with the dust,
Yet would not place one piece above, but lives
In fear of thieves.
Thousands there were as frantic as himself
And hugged each one his pelf;
The downright epicure placed heav'n in sense,
And scorned pretence;
While others, slipped into a wide excess,
Said little less;
The weaker sort slight, trivial wares enslave,
Who think them brave;
And poor, despisèd Truth sat counting by
Their victory.

Yet some, who all this while did weep and sing,
And sing and weep, soared up into the ring;
But most would use no wing.
Oh, fools—said I—thus to prefer dark night
Before true light!
To live in grots and caves, and hate the day
Because it shows the way;
The way, which from this dead and dark abode
Leads up to God;
A way where you might tread the sun, and be
More bright than he!
But as I did their madness so discuss,
One whispered thus,
'This ring the Bridegroom did for none provide,
But for His bride.'

John Dryden

John Dryden (1631–1700) was a prolific writer, a great literary man, Milton's successor and Pope's predecessor—without being quite so great a poet as either of them. He wrote many of his plays in rhymed couplets. The heroic couplet is Dryden's particular measure: pairs of end-stopped pentameter lines, rhymed directly, usually forming a complete two-line unit of thought or narrative; Dryden codified the form. Chaucer had written in couplets, as had Ben Jonson. Dryden made the form more rigid while retaining great vigor and force. Pope, with unprecedented dexterity and skill, carried it even further, and some feel that Dryden's verse is more vigorous than Pope's. Most of his best work is in long poems, philosophical or satirical, allusive, difficult to read without study of the age. This short poem shows Dryden's finish and his energy.

To the Memory of Mr. Oldham

Farewell, too little and too lately known,
Whom I began to think and call my own;

For sure our souls were near allied, and thine
Cast in the same poetic mold with mine.
One common note on either lyre did strike,
And knaves and fools we both abhorred alike.
To the same goal did both our studies drive:
The last set out the soonest did arrive.
Thus Nisus[1] fell upon the slippery place,
10　Whilst his young friend performed and won the race.
O early ripe! to thy abundant store
What could advancing age have added more?
It might (what nature never gives the young)
Have taught the numbers° of thy native tongue.　　　poetic meters
But satire needs not those, and wit will shine
Through the harsh cadence of a rugged line.
A noble error, and but seldom made,
When poets are by too much force betrayed.
Thy gen'rous fruits, though gathered ere their prime,
20　Still shewed a quickness; and maturing time
But mellows what we write to the dull sweets of rhyme.
Once more, hail, and farewell! farewell, thou young,
But ah! too short, Marcellus[2] of our tongue!
Thy brows with ivy and with laurels bound;
But fate and gloomy night encompass thee around.

[1]In Vergil's *Aeneid* Nisus is beaten in a race by a younger friend.　　[2]Marcus Claudius Marcellus, nephew and adopted son of Augustus Caesar, died at twenty and is lamented by Vergil in the sixth book of the *Aeneid*.

Alexander Pope

Alexander Pope (1688–1744), crippled by a childhood disease, was unusually small. He was precocious, beginning to write with considerable excellence at sixteen. The "Essay on Criticism," from which this poem is excerpted, appeared when he was only twenty-three. Much of the later and greater work is highly allusive. Although the poetry becomes more subtle and wise, the wit-work of the young Pope was never surpassed. Pope was so proficient at the couplet that he was able to translate the entire *Iliad* and *Odyssey* into these twenty-syllable units.

Part II *of* An Essay on Criticism

Of all the Causes which conspire to blind
Man's erring judgment, and misguide the mind,
What the weak head with strongest bias rules,
Is *Pride*, the never-failing vice of fools.
Whatever Nature has in worth denied,
She gives in large recruits of needful Pride:
For as in bodies, thus in souls, we find
What wants in blood and spirits, swelled with wind:
Pride, where Wit fails, steps in to our defence,
10　And fills up all the mighty Void of sense.

If once right reason drives that cloud away,
Truth breaks upon us with resistless day.
Trust not yourself; but your defects to know,
Make use of every friend—and every foe.
    A *little learning* is a dangerous thing;
Drink deep, or taste not the Pierian spring:[1]
There shallow draughts intoxicate the brain,
And drinking largely sobers us again.
Fired at first sight with what the Muse imparts,
20   In fearless youth we tempt the heights of Arts,
While from the bounded level of our mind,
Short views we take, nor see the lengths behind;
But more advanced, behold with strange surprise
New distant scenes of endless science° rise!   knowledge
So pleased at first the towering Alps we try,
Mount o'er the vales, and seem to tread the sky,
Th' eternal snows appear already past,
And the first clouds and mountains seem the last:
But, those attained, we tremble to survey
30   The growing labours of the lengthened way;
Th' increasing prospect tires our wandering eyes,
Hills peep o'er hills, and Alps on Alps arise!
    A perfect Judge will read each work of Wit
With the same spirit that its author writ:
Survey the WHOLE, nor seek slight faults to find
Where nature moves, and rapture warms the mind;
Nor lose, for that malignant dull delight,
The generous pleasure to be charmed with wit.
But in such lays as neither ebb, nor flow,
40   Correctly cold, and regularly low,
That shunning faults, one quiet tenour keep;
We cannot blame indeed——but we may sleep.
In Wit, as Nature, what affects our hearts
Is not th' exactness of peculiar parts;
'Tis not a lip, or eye, we beauty call,
But the joint force and full result of all.
Thus when we view some well-proportioned dome,
(The world's just wonder, and even thine, O Rome!)
No single parts unequally surprise,
50   All comes united to th' admiring eyes;
No monstrous height, or breadth, or length appear;
The Whole at once is bold, and regular.
    Whoever thinks a faultless piece to see,
Thinks what ne'er was, nor is, nor e'er shall be.
In every work regard the writer's End,
Since none can compass more than they intend;
And if the means be just, the conduct true,
Applause, in spite of trivial faults, is due.

[1]In Greek mythology, a spring sacred to the Muses

As men of breeding, sometimes men of wit,
60   T' avoid great errors, must the less commit:
Neglect the rules each verbal Critic lays,
For not to know some trifles is a praise.
Most Critics, fond of some subservient art,
Still make the Whole depend upon a Part:
They talk of principles, but notions prize,
And all to one loved Folly sacrifice.
    Once on a time, La Mancha's Knight,° they say,   Don Quixote
A certain Bard encountering on the way,
Discoursed in tems as just, with looks as sage,
70   As e'er could Dennis[2] of the Grecian stage;
Concluding all were desperate sots and fools,
Who durst depart from Aristotle's rules.
Our Author, happy in a judge so nice,
Produced his Play, and begged the Knight's advice;
Made him observe the subject, and the plot,
The manners, passions, unities; what not?
All which, exact to rule, were brought about,
Were but a Combat in the lists left out.
"What! leave the Combat out?" exclaims the Knight;
80   "Yes, or we must renounce the Stagirite."°   Aristotle
"Not so by Heaven!" (he answers in a rage)
"Knights, squires, and steeds, must enter on the stage."
"So vast a throng the stage can ne'er contain."
"Then build a new, or act it in a plain."
    Thus Critics, of less judgment than caprice,
Curious not knowing, not exact but nice,
Form short Ideas; and offend in arts
(As most in manners) by a love to parts.
    Some to *Conceit* alone their taste confine,
90   And glittering thoughts struck out at every line;
Pleased with a work where nothing's just or fit;
One glaring Chaos and wild heap of wit.
Poets like painters, thus, unskilled to trace
The naked nature and the living grace,
With gold and jewels cover every part,
And hide with ornaments their want of art.
True Wit is Nature to advantage dressed,
What oft was thought, but ne'er so well expressed;
Something, whose truth convinced at sight we find,
100   That gives us back the image of our mind.
As shades more sweetly recommend the light,
So modest plainness sets off sprightly wit.
For works may have more wit than does 'em good,
As bodies perish through excess of blood.
    Others for *Language* all their care express,
And value books, as women men, for Dress:

[2]John Dennis (1657–1734), an author Pope satirizes

Their praise is still,—the Style is excellent:
The Sense, they humbly take upon content.
Words are like leaves; and where they most abound,
110   Much fruit of sense beneath is rarely found.
False Eloquence, like the prismatic glass,
Its gaudy colours spreads on every place;
The face of Nature we no more survey,
All glares alike, without distinction gay:
But true Expression, like th' unchanging Sun,
Clears, and improves whate'er it shines upon,
It gilds all objects, but it alters none.
Expression is the dress of thought, and still
Appears more decent, as more suitable;
120   A vile conceit in pompous words expressed,
Is like a clown in regal purple dressed:
For different styles with different subjects sort,
As several garbs with country, town, and court.
Some by old words to fame have made pretence,
Ancients in phrase, mere moderns in their sense;
Such laboured nothings, in so strange a style,
Amaze th' unlearned, and make the learnèd smile.
Unlucky, as Fungoso in the Play,[3]
These sparks with awkward vanity display
130   What the fine gentleman wore yesterday;
And but so mimic ancient wits at best,
As apes our grandsires, in their doublets drest.
In words, as fashions, the same rule will hold;
Alike fantastic, if too new, or old:
Be not the first by whom the new are tried,
Nor yet the last to lay the old aside.
      But most by Numbers° judge a Poet's song;   poetic meters
And smooth or rough, with them is right or wrong:
In the bright Muse though thousand charms conspire,
140   Her Voice is all these tuneful fools admire;
Who haunt Parnassus[4] but to please their ear,
Not mend their minds; as some to Church repair,
Not for the doctrine, but the music there.
These equal syllables alone require,
Though oft the ear the open vowels tire;
While expletives their feeble aid do join;
And ten low words oft creep in one dull line:
While they ring round the same unvaried chimes,
With sure returns of still expected rhymes;
150   Where'er you find "the cooling western breeze,"
In the next line, it "whispers through the trees:"
If crystal streams "with pleasing murmurs creep,"
The reader's threatened (not in vain) with "sleep:"
Then, at the last and only couplet, fraught

[3]Ben Jonson's *Every Man Out of His Humour*   [4]Mountain home of the Muses

With some unmeaning thing they call a thought,
A needless Alexandrine ends the song,
That, like a wounded snake, drags its slow length along.
Leave such to tune their own dull rhymes, and know
What's roundly smooth, or languishingly slow;
160   And praise the easy vigour of a line,
Where Denham's strength, and Waller's[5] sweetness join.
True ease in writing comes from art, not chance,
As those move easiest who have learned to dance.
'Tis not enough no harshness gives offence,
The sound must seem an Echo to the sense:
Soft is the strain when Zephyr[6] gently blows,
And the smooth stream in smoother numbers flows;
But when loud surges lash the sounding shore,
The hoarse, rough verse should like the torrent roar:
170   When Ajax[7] strives some rock's vast weight to throw,
The line too labours, and the words move slow;
Not so, when swift Camilla[8] scours the plain,
Flies o'er th' unbending corn, and skims along the main.
Hear how Timotheus'[9] varied lays surprise,
And bid alternate passions fall and rise!
While, at each change, the son of Libyan Jove[10]
Now burns with glory, and then melts with love;
Now his fierce eyes with sparkling fury glow,
Now sighs steal out, and tears begin to flow:
180   Persians and Greeks like turns of nature found,
And the World's victor stood subdued by Sound!
The power of Music all our hearts allow,
And what Timotheus was, is DRYDEN now.
      Avoid Extremes; and shun the fault of such,
Who still are pleased too little or too much.
At every trifle scorn to take offence,
That always shows great pride, or little sense;
Those heads, as stomachs, are not sure the best,
Which nauseate all, and nothing can digest.
190   Yet let not each gay Turn thy rapture move;
For fools admire,° but men of sense approve: wonder at
As things seem large which we through mists descry,
Dulness is ever apt to magnify.
      Some foreign writers, some our own despise;
The Ancients only, or the Moderns prize.
Thus Wit, like Faith, by each man is applied
To one small sect, and all are damned beside.
Meanly they seek the blessing to confine,
And force that sun but on a part to shine,
200   Which not alone the southern wit sublimes,

[5]Sir John Denham (1615–1669) and Edmund Waller (1606–1687) were poets Pope admired.   [6]The West Wind   [7]A strong warrior in Homer's *Iliad*   [8]A maiden warrior in Vergil's *Aeneid*   [9]A Greek musician   [10]A reference to Dryden's poem in praise of music, "Alexander's Feast"

But ripens spirits in cold northern climes;
Which from the first has shone on ages past,
Enlights the present, and shall warm the last;
Though each may feel increases and decays,
And see now clearer and now darker days.
Regard not then if Wit be old or new,
But blame the false, and value still the true.
    Some ne'er advance a Judgment of their own,
But catch the spreading notion of the Town;
210 They reason and conclude by precedent,
And own stale nonsense which they ne'er invent.
Some judge of authors' names, not works, and then
Nor praise nor blame the writings, but the men.
Of all this servile herd, the worst is he
That in proud dulness joins with Quality.
A constant Critic at the great man's board,
To fetch and carry nonsense for my Lord.
What woeful stuff this madrigal would be,
In some starved hackney sonneteer, or me?
220 But let a Lord once own the happy lines,
How the wit brightens! how the style refines!
Before his sacred name flies every fault,
And each exalted stanza teems with thought!
    The Vulgar thus through Imitation err;
As oft the Learned by being singular;
So much they scorn the crowd, that if the throng
By chance go right, they purposely go wrong:
So Schismatics the plain believers quit,
And are but damned for having too much wit.
230 Some praise at morning what they blame at night;
But always think the last opinion right.
A Muse by these is like a mistress used,
This hour she's idolized, the next abused;
While their weak heads like towns unfortified,
Twixt sense and nonsense daily change their side.
Ask them the cause; they're wiser still, they say;
And still tomorrow's wiser than today.
We think our fathers fools, so wise we grow;
Our wiser sons, no doubt, will think us so.
240 Once School divines this zealous isle o'erspread;
Who knew most Sentences, was deepest read;
Faith, Gospel, all, seemed made to be disputed,
And none had sense enough to be confuted:
Scotists and Thomists,[11] now, in peace remain,
Amidst their kindred cobwebs in Duck Lane.[12]
If Faith itself has different dresses worn,
What wonder modes in Wit should take their turn?

[11]Followers of the differing theologians Duns Scotus (1265?–1308) and Thomas Aquinas (1225?–1274) [12]A London street known for dealers in old books

Oft, leaving what is natural and fit,
The current folly proves the ready wit;
250   And authors think their reputation safe,
Which lives as long as fools are pleased to laugh.
    Some valuing those of their own side or mind,
Still make themselves the measure of mankind:
Fondly we think we honour merit then,
When we but praise ourselves in other men.
Parties in Wit attend on those of State,
And public faction doubles private hate.
Pride, Malice, Folly, against Dryden rose,
In various shapes of Parsons, Critics, Beaus;
260   But sense survived, when merry jests were past;
For rising merit will buoy up at last.
Might he return, and bless once more our eyes,
New Blackmores and new Milbourns[13] must arise:
Nay should great Homer lift his awful head,
Zoilus[14] again would start up from the dead.
Envy will merit, as its shade, pursue;
But like a shadow, proves the substance true;
For envied Wit, like Sol eclipsed, makes known
Th' opposing body's grossness, not its own.
270   When first that sun too powerful beams displays,
It draws up vapours which obscure its rays;
But even those clouds at last adorn its way,
Reflect new glories, and augment the day.
    Be thou the first true merit to befriend;
His praise is lost, who stays till all commend.
Short is the date, alas, of modern rhymes,
And 'tis but just to let them live betimes.
No longer now that golden age appears,
When Patriarch wits survived a thousand years:
280   Now length of Fame (our second life) is lost,
And bare threescore is all even that can boast;
Our sons their fathers' failing language see,
And such as Chaucer is, shall Dryden be.
So when the faithful pencil has designed
Some bright Idea of the master's mind,
Where a new world leaps out at his command,
And ready Nature waits upon his hand;
When the ripe colours soften and unite,
And sweetly melt into just shade and light;
290   When mellowing years their full perfection give,
And each bold figure just begins to live,
The treacherous colours the fair art betray,
And all the bright creation fades away!
    Unhappy Wit, like most mistaken things,

---

[13]Richard Blackmore (1652–1729) and Luke Milbourn (1649–1720) attacked Dryden.   [14]Critic
of Homer, fourth century B.C.

Atones not for that envy which it brings.
In youth alone its empty praise we boast,
But soon the short-lived vanity is lost:
Like some fair flower the early spring supplies,
That gaily blooms, but even in blooming dies.
300 What is this Wit, which must our cares employ?
The owner's wife, that other men enjoy;
Then most our trouble still when most admired,
And still the more we give, the more required;
Whose fame with pains we guard, but lose with ease,
Sure some to vex, but never all to please;
'Tis what the vicious fear, the virtuous shun,
By fools 'tis hated, and by knaves undone!
   If Wit so much from Ignorance undergo,
Ah let not Learning too commence its foe!
310 Of old, those met rewards who could excel,
And such were praised who but endeavoured well:
Though triumphs were to generals only due,
Crowns were reserved to grace the soldiers too.
Now, they who reach Parnassus' lofty crown,
Employ their pains to spurn some others down;
And while self-love each jealous writer rules,
Contending wits become the sport of fools:
But still the worst with most regret commend,
For each ill Author is as bad a Friend.
320 To what base ends, and by what abject ways,
Are mortals urged through sacred lust of praise!
Ah ne'er so dire a thirst of glory boast,
Nor in the Critic let the Man be lost.
Good nature and good sense must ever join;
To err is human, to forgive, divine.
   But if in noble minds some dregs remain
Not yet purged off, of spleen and sour disdain;
Discharge that rage on more provoking crimes,
Nor fear a dearth in these flagitious° times.   vicious
330 No pardon vile Obscenity should find,
Though wit and art conspire to move your mind;
But Dulness with Obscenity must prove
As shameful sure as Impotence in love.
In the fat age of pleasure, wealth and ease,
Sprung the rank weed, and thrived with large increase:
When love was all an easy Monarch's care;
Seldom at council, never in a war:
Jilts ruled the state, and statesmen farces writ;
Nay wits had pensions, and young Lords had wit:
340 The Fair sat panting at a Courtier's play,
And not a Mask went unimproved away:
The modest fan was lifted up no more,
And Virgins smiled at what they blushed before.
The following license of a Foreign reign

Did all the dregs of bold Socinus[15] drain;
Then unbelieving Priests reformed the nation,
And taught more pleasant methods of salvation;
Where Heaven's free subjects might their rights dispute,
Lest God himself should seem too absolute:
350   Pulpits their sacred satire learned to spare,
And Vice admired to find a flatterer there!
Encouraged thus, Wit's Titans braved the skies,
And the press groaned with licensed blasphemies.
These monsters, Critics! with your darts engage,
Here point your thunder, and exhaust your rage!
Yet shun their fault, who, scandalously nice,
Will needs mistake an author into vice;
All seems infected that th' infected spy,
As all looks yellow to the jaundiced eye.

[15]Author of the Socinian heresy condemned by the Inquisition

Christopher Smart

Christopher Smart (1722–1771) wrote the long poem excerpted below when he
was insane. It was his habit, in his madness, to go down on his knees in a
crowded street and ask other people to pray with him. Samuel Johnson,
apprised of Smart's eccentricities, avowed that he would as soon pray with Kit
Smart as with any man.

from Jubilate Agno[1]

For I will consider my Cat Jeoffry.
For he is the servant of the Living God, duly and daily serving him.
For at the first glance of the glory of God in the East he worships in his way.
For is this done by wreathing his body seven times round with elegant
        quickness.
For then he leaps up to catch the musk,° which is the blessing of   catnip (?)
        God upon his prayer.
For he rolls upon prank to work it in.
For having done duty and received blessing he begins to consider himself.
For this he performs in ten degrees.
For first he looks upon his fore-paws to see if they are clean.
10   For secondly he kicks up behind to clear away there.
For thirdly he works it upon stretch with the fore-paws extended.
For fourthly he sharpens his paws by wood.
For fifthly he washes himself.
For sixthly he rolls upon wash.
For seventhly he fleas himself, that he may not be interrupted upon the beat.
For eighthly he rubs himself against a post.
For ninthly he looks up for his instructions.
For tenthly he goes in quest of food.

[1]Rejoice in the Lamb

For having considered God and himself he will consider his neighbor.
20 For if he meets another cat he will kiss her in kindness.
For when he takes his prey he plays with it to give it chance.
For one mouse in seven escapes by his dallying.
For when his day's work is done his business more properly begins.
For he keeps the Lord's watch in the night against the adversary.
For he counteracts the powers of darkness by his electrical skin and glaring
   eyes.
For he counteracts the Devil, who is death, by brisking about the life.
For in his morning orisons he loves the sun and the sun loves him.
For he is of the tribe of Tiger.
For the Cherub Cat is a term of the Angel Tiger.
For he has the subtlety and hissing of a serpent, which in goodness he
30   suppresses.
For he will not do destruction if he is well-fed, neither will he spit without
   provocation.
For he purrs in thankfulness, when God tells him he's a good Cat.
For he is an instrument for the children to learn benevolence upon.
For every house is incomplete without him and a blessing is lacking in the
   spirit.
For the Lord commanded Moses concerning the cats at the departure of the
   Children of Israel from Egypt.
For every family had one cat at least in the bag.
For the English Cats are the best in Europe.

William Cowper

William Cowper (1731–1800) suffered from fits of depression and was suicidal.
His temporary insanity was influenced, in its particular shape, by his
Calvinism, whereby he was convinced that he was one of the damned. His
metaphor for damnation is "The Castaway." If Elizabethan poets suffered from
a malady of executions, many eighteenth-century poets seem to have
specialized in insanity.

The Castaway

Obscurest night involved the sky,
   The Atlantic billows roared,
When such a destined wretch as I,
   Washed headlong from on board,
Of friends, of hope, of all bereft,
His floating home forever left.

No braver chief could Albion° boast   England
   Than he with whom he went,[1]
Nor ever ship left Albion's coast,
10   With warmer wishes sent.
He loved them both, but both in vain,
Nor him beheld, nor her again.

[1]"He" is George, Lord Anson (1697–1762), from whose *Voyage Round the World* Cowper took
this story.

Not long beneath the whelming brine,
   Expert to swim, he lay;
Nor soon he felt his strength decline,
   Or courage die away;
But waged with death a lasting strife,
Supported by despair of life.

He shouted; nor his friends had failed
20   To check the vessel's course,
But so the furious blast prevailed,
   That, pitiless perforce,
They left their outcast mate behind,
And scudded still before the wind.

Some succor yet they could afford;
   And, such as storms allow,
The cask, the coop, the floated cord,
   Delayed not to bestow.
But he (they knew) nor ship, nor shore,
30 Whate'er they gave, should visit more.

Nor, cruel as it seemed, could he
   Their haste himself condemn,
Aware that flight, in such a sea,
   Alone could rescue them;
Yet bitter felt it still to die
Deserted, and his friends so nigh.

He long survives, who lives an hour
   In ocean, self-upheld;
And so long he, with unspent power,
40   His destiny repelled;
And ever, as the minutes flew,
Entreated help, or cried, "Adieu!"

At length, his transient respite past,
   His comrades, who before
Had heard his voice in every blast,
   Could catch the sound no more.
For then, by toil subdued, he drank
The stifling wave, and then he sank.

No poet wept him; but the page
50   Of narrative sincere,
That tells his name, his worth, his age,
   Is wet with Anson's tear.
And tears by bards or heroes shed
Alike immortalize the dead.

I therefore purpose not, or dream,
   Descanting on his fate,
To give the melancholy theme
   A more enduring date:

But misery still delights to trace
60   Its semblance in another's case.

No voice divine the storm allayed,
   No light propitious shone,
When, snatched from all effectual aid,
   We perished, each alone;
But I beneath a rougher sea,
And whelmed in deeper gulfs than he.

William Blake

William Blake (1757–1827) called his first major work *Songs of Innocence and Experience*. This sequence included many pairings of poems, the one viewed under the aspect of innocence and the other under the aspect of experience. So we have paired poems which follow under the same names; and we have on the one hand the lamb, and on the other the tiger. His later work is obscure, difficult—and superbly rewarding. He was an engraver by trade, and executed his own etchings and engravings. Like Campion, Blake was master of two arts. He was a mystic, and told how some of his poems were dictated to him by voices.

The Lamb

   Little Lamb, who made thee?
   Dost thou know who made thee;
Gave thee life and bid thee feed
By the stream and o'er the mead;
Gave thee clothing of delight,
Softest clothing, woolly, bright;
Gave thee such a tender voice
Making all the vales rejoice?
   Little Lamb, who made thee?
10   Dost thou know who made thee?

   Little Lamb, I'll tell thee,
   Little Lamb, I'll tell thee:
He is callèd by thy name,
For He calls Himself a Lamb.
He is meek and He is mild:
He became a little child.
I a child and thou a lamb,
We are callèd by His name.
   Little Lamb, God bless thee.
20   Little Lamb, God bless thee.

The Tyger

   Tyger! Tyger! burning bright
In the forests of the night,
What immortal hand or eye
Could frame thy fearful symmetry?

In what distant deeps or skies
Burnt the fire of thine eyes?
On what wings dare he aspire?
What the hand dare seize the fire?

10
And what shoulder, and what art,
Could twist the sinews of thy heart?
And when thy heart began to beat,
What dread hand? and what dread feet?

What the hammer? what the chain?
In what furnace was thy brain?
What the anvil? what dread grasp
Dare its deadly terrors clasp?

When the stars threw down their spears
And watered heaven with their tears,
Did he smile his work to see?
20
Did he who made the Lamb make thee?

Tyger! Tyger! burning bright
In the forests of the night,
What immortal hand or eye
Dare frame thy fearful symmetry?

The Garden of Love

I went to the Garden of Love,
And saw what I never had seen:
A Chapel was built in the midst,
Where I used to play on the green.

And the gates of this Chapel were shut,
And "Thou shalt not" writ over the door;
So I turned to the Garden of Love
That so many sweet flowers bore;

And I saw it was filled with graves,
10
And tomb-stones where flowers should be,
And Priests in black gowns were walking their rounds,
And binding with briars my joys and desires.

London

I wander thro' each chartered street,
Near where the chartered Thames does flow,
And mark in every face I meet
Marks of weakness, marks of woe.

In every cry of every Man,
In every Infant's cry of fear,

In every voice, in every ban,
The mind-forged manacles I hear.

How the Chimney-sweeper's cry
10   Every black'ning Church appalls;
And the hapless Soldier's sigh
Runs in blood down Palace walls.

But most thro' midnight streets I hear
How the youthful Harlot's curse
Blasts the new-born Infant's tear,
And blights with plagues the Marriage hearse.

Mock On, Mock On, Voltaire, Rousseau

Mock on, mock on, Voltaire, Rousseau,
    Mock on, mock on, 'tis all in vain;
You throw the sand against the wind
    And the wind blows it back again.

And every sand becomes a gem
    Reflected in the beams divine;
Blown back, they blind the mocking eye,
    But still in Israel's paths they shine.

The atoms of Democritus
10   And Newton's particles of light
Are sands upon the Red Sea shore,
    Where Israel's tents do shine so bright.

from Milton

And did those feet in ancient time
Walk upon England's mountains green?
And was the Holy Lamb of God
On England's pleasant pastures seen?

And did the countenance divine
Shine forth upon our clouded hills?
And was Jerusalem builded here
Among these dark satanic mills?

Bring me my bow of burning gold!
10   Bring me my arrows of desire!
Bring me my spear! O clouds, unfold!
Bring me my chariot of fire!

I will not cease from mental fight,
Nor shall my sword sleep in my hand,
Till we have built Jerusalem
In England's green and pleasant land.

Robert Burns

Robert Burns (1759–1796), after the medieval poets, is the great poet of Scotland. He is one of the few British poets to arise from the working classes, having begun life as a farm laborer. Much of his work derives from a folk tradition and from anonymous Scots songs.

Green Grow the Rashes, O

Chorus

Green grow the rashes, O;
  Green grow the rashes, O;
The sweetest hours that e'er I spend,
  Are spent among the lasses, O!

There's nought but care on ev'ry han',
  In ev'ry hour that passes, O:
What signifies the life o' man,
  An' 'twere na for the lasses, O.

The war'ly° race may riches chase,   worldly
10   An' riches still may fly them, O;
An' tho' at last they catch them fast,
  Their hearts can ne'er enjoy them, O.

But gie me a canny° hour at e'en   quiet
  My arms about my dearie, O,
An' war'ly cares, an' war'ly men
  May a' gae tapsalteerie,° O!   topsy-turvy

For you sae douce,° ye sneer at this;   sedate
  Ye're nought but senseless asses, O;
The wisest man the warl' e'er saw,
20   He dearly lov'd the lasses, O.

Auld Nature swears, the lovely dears
  Her noblest work she classes, O:
Her prentice han' she try'd on man,
  An' then she made the lasses, O.

John Anderson My Jo

John Anderson my jo,° John,   darling
  When we were first acquent,
Your locks were like the raven,
  Your bonnie brow was brent;°   straight, steep
But now your brow is beld,° John,   bald
  Your locks are like the snaw,
But blessings on your frosty pow,°   head
  John Anderson, my jo.

John Anderson my jo, John,
10   We clamb° the hill thegither,   climbed
And monie a cantie° day, John,   merry

198

We've had wi' ane anither
Now we maun° totter down, John,   must
   And hand in hand we'll go,
And sleep thegither at the foot,
   John Anderson my jo.

William Wordsworth

William Wordsworth (1770–1850) attended Cambridge, afterward touring
Europe on foot and living for a year in France when the revolutionary society
was at its most exciting. Back in England, he continued to write poems, and in
1795 began his long and close friendship with Samuel Taylor Coleridge. The
two poets, with Wordsworth's sister Dorothy and with Coleridge's wife, lived
near each other for a time, and Wordsworth and Coleridge published *Lyrical
Ballads* in 1798, a collection of poetry by both of them, including Coleridge's
"Rime of the Ancient Mariner" and Wordsworth's "Lines Written Above Tintern
Abbey." The year of publication provides as good a date as any for the
beginning of the romantic movement in English literature. Two years later,
reprinting the volume, Wordsworth added prose "observations" in which he
defended his own theory of poetry, deriving his language from rustic life. His
imagery also derived from rustic life, and his poems were at first denounced as
obscure and meaningless. Later, he became one of the most popular poets of
the English tradition. In his long life he wrote prolifically; most of his best work
is early.

Ode: Intimations of Immortality
from Recollections of Early Childhood

       The Child is father of the Man;
       And I could wish my days to be
       Bound each to each by natural piety.

I

There was a time when meadow, grove, and stream,
The earth, and every common sight,
      To me did seem
      Apparelled in celestial light,
The glory and the freshness of a dream.
It is not now as it hath been of yore;—
      Turn whereso'er I may,
        By night or day,
The things which I have seen I now can see no more.

II

10   The Rainbow comes and goes,
       And lovely is the Rose,
       The Moon doth with delight
Look round her when the heavens are bare,
      Waters on a starry night
      Are beautiful and fair;
   The sunshine is a glorious birth;
   But yet I know, where'er I go,
That there hath past away a glory from the earth.

III

Now, while the birds thus sing a joyous song,
20   And while the young lambs bound
              As to the tabor's sound.
To me alone there came a thought of grief:
A timely utterance gave that thought relief,
              And I again am strong:
The cataracts blow their trumpets from the steep;
No more shall grief of mine the season wrong;
I hear the Echoes through the mountains throng,
The Winds come to me from the fields of sleep,
              And all the earth is gay;
30   Land and sea
          Give themselves up to jollity,
              And with the heart of May
          Doth every Beast keep holiday;—
              Thou Child of Joy,
Shout round me, let me hear thy shouts, thou happy
              Shepherd-boy!

IV

Ye blessèd Creatures, I have heard the call
          Ye to each other make; I see
The heavens laugh with you in your jubilee;
40   My heart is at your festival,
              My head hath its coronal,
The fulness of your bliss, I feel—I feel it all.
              Oh evil day! if I were sullen
              While Earth herself is adorning,
                  This sweet May-morning,
              And the Children are culling
                  On every side,
              In a thousand valleys far and wide,
              Fresh flowers; while the sun shines warm,
50 And the Babe leaps up on his Mother's arm:—
              I hear, I hear, with joy I hear!
              —But there's a Tree, of many, one,
A single Field which I have looked upon,
Both of them speak of something that is gone:
              The Pansy at my feet
              Doth the same tale repeat:
Whither is fled the visionary gleam?
Where is it now, the glory and the dream?

V

Our birth is but a sleep and a forgetting:
60 The Soul that rises with us, our life's Star,
              Hath had elsewhere its setting,
                  And cometh from afar:

Not in entire forgetfulness,
And not in utter nakedness,
But trailing clouds of glory do we come
From God, who is our home:
Heaven lies about us in our infancy!
Shades of the prison-house begin to close
Upon the growing Boy,
70 But He beholds the light, and whence it flows,
He sees it in his joy;
The Youth, who daily farther from the east
Must travel, still is Nature's Priest,
And by the vision splendid
Is on his way attended;
At length the Man perceives it die away,
And fade into the light of common day.

VI

Earth fills her lap with pleasures of her own;
Yearnings she hath in her own natural kind,
80 And, even with something of a Mother's mind,
And no unworthy aim,
The homely Nurse doth all she can
To make her Foster-child, her Inmate Man,
Forget the glories he hath known,
And that imperial palace whence he came.

VII

Behold the Child among his new-born blisses,
A six years' Darling of a pigmy size!
See, where 'mid work of his own hand he lies,
Fretted by sallies of his mother's kisses,
90 With light upon him from his father's eyes!
See, at his feet, some little plan or chart,
Some fragment from his dream of human life,
Shaped by himself with newly-learned art;
A wedding or a festival,
A mourning or a funeral;
And this hath now his heart,
And unto this he frames his song.
Then will he fit his tongue
To dialogues of business, love, or strife;
100 But it will not be long
Ere this be thrown aside,
And with new joy and pride
The little Actor cons another part;
Filling from time to time his "humorous stage"
With all the Persons, down to palsied Age,
That Life brings with her in her equipage;
As if his whole vocation
Were endless imitation.

VIII

Thou, whose exterior semblance doth belie
110 Thy Soul's immensity;
Thou best Philosopher, who yet dost keep
Thy heritage, thou Eye among the blind,
That, deaf and silent, read'st the eternal deep,
Haunted for ever by the eternal mind,—
  Mighty Prophet! Seer blest!
  On whom those truths do rest,
Which we are toiling all our lives to find,
In darkness lost, the darkness of the grave,
Thou, over whom thy Immortality
120 Broods like the Day, a Master o'er a Slave,
A Presence which is not to be put by;
Thou little Child, yet glorious in the might
Of heaven-born freedom on thy being's height,
Why with such earnest pains dost thou provoke
The years to bring the inevitable yoke,
Thus blindly with thy blessedness at strife?
Full soon thy Soul shall have her earthly freight,
And custom lie upon thee with a weight,
Heavy as frost, and deep almost as life!

IX

130 O joy! that in our embers
  Is something that doth live,
  That nature yet remembers
  What was so fugitive!
The thought of our past years in me doth breed
Perpetual benediction: not indeed
For that which is most worthy to be blest;
Delight and liberty, the simple creed
Of Childhood, whether busy or at rest,
With new-fledged hope still fluttering in his breast:—
140 Not for these I raise
  The song of thanks and praise;
  But for those obstinate questionings
  Of sense and outward things,
  Fallings from us, vanishings;
  Blank misgivings of a Creature
Moving about in worlds not realised,
High instincts before which our mortal Nature
Did tremble like a guilty Thing surprised:
  But for those first affections,
150 Those shadowy recollections,
  Which, be they what they may,
Are yet the fountain-light of all our day,
Are yet a master-light of all our seeing;
  Uphold us, cherish, and have power to make
Our noisy years seem moments in the being

Of the eternal Silence: truths that wake,
      To perish never:
Which neither listlessness, nor mad endeavour,
      Nor Man nor Boy,
160   Nor all that is at enmity with joy,
Can utterly abolish or destroy!
        Hence in a season of calm weather
        Though inland far we be,
Our Souls have sight of that immortal sea
        Which brought us hither,
      Can in a moment travel thither,
And see the Children sport upon the shore,
And hear the mighty waters rolling evermore.

X

Then sing, ye Birds, sing, sing a joyous song!
170   And let the young Lambs bound
        As to the tabor's sound!
We in thought will join your throng,
      Ye that pipe and ye that play,
      Ye that through your hearts today
      Feel the gladness of the May!
What though the radiance which was once so bright
Be now for ever taken from my sight,
      Though nothing can bring back the hour
Of splendour in the grass, of glory in the flower;
180   We will grieve not, rather find
        Strength in what remains behind;
        In the primal sympathy
        Which having been must ever be;
        In the soothing thoughts that spring
        Out of human suffering;
        In the faith that looks through death,
In years that bring the philosophic mind.

XI

And O, ye Fountains, Meadows, Hills, and Groves,
Forebode not any severing of our loves!
190   Yet in my heart of hearts I feel your might;
I only have relinquished one delight
To live beneath your more habitual sway.
I love the Brooks which down their channels fret,
Even more than when I tripped lightly as they;
The innocent brightness of a new-born Day
        Is lovely yet;
The Clouds that gather round the setting sun
Do take a sober colouring from an eye
That hath kept watch o'er man's mortality;
200   Another race hath been, and other palms are won.
Thanks to the human heart by which we live,

Thanks to its tenderness, its joys, and fears,
To me the meanest flower that blows can give
Thoughts that do often lie too deep for tears.

The World Is Too Much with Us

The world is too much with us; late and soon,
Getting and spending, we lay waste our powers:
Little we see in Nature that is ours;
We have given our hearts away, a sordid boon!
The sea that bares her bosom to the moon;
The winds that will be howling at all hours,
And are up-gathered now like sleeping flowers;
For this, for everything, we are out of tune;
It moves us not.—Great God! I'd rather be
10 A pagan suckled in a creed outworn;
So might I, standing on this pleasant lea,
Have glimpses that would make me less forlorn;
Have sight of Proteus rising from the sea;
Or hear old Triton blow his wreathèd horn.

It Is a Beauteous Evening

It is a beauteous evening, calm and free;
The holy time is quiet as a nun
Breathless with adoration; the broad sun
Is sinking down in its tranquillity;
The gentleness of heaven broods o'er the sea:
Listen! the mighty Being is awake,
And doth with his eternal motion make
A sound like thunder—everlastingly.
Dear child! dear girl! that walkest with me here,
10 If thou appear untouched by solemn thought,
Thy nature is not therefore less divine:
Thou liest in Abraham's bosom all the year,
And worship'st at the Temple's inner shrine,
God being with thee when we know it not.

Samuel Taylor Coleridge

Samuel Taylor Coleridge (1772–1834), thinker, talker, and preacher as well as poet, was a man of enormous promise. His failure to live up to the extent of his promise has obscured his real accomplishment. After he collaborated with Wordsworth on *Lyrical Ballads*, the volume of his poetry declined considerably, though the quality of an occasional poem remained high. His literary autobiography, called *Biographia Literaria*, adds to the valuable critical work English poets have contributed to the language.

Kubla Khan

In Xanadu did Kubla Khan
A stately pleasure-dome decree:
Where Alph, the sacred river, ran
Through caverns measureless to man
   Down to a sunless sea.
So twice five miles of fertile ground
With walls and towers were girdled round:
And there were gardens bright with sinuous rills,
Where blossomed many an incense-bearing tree;
10   And here were forests ancient as the hills,
Enfolding sunny spots of greenery.

But oh! that deep romantic chasm which slanted
Down the green hill athwart a cedarn cover!
A savage place! as holy and enchanted
As e'er beneath a waning moon was haunted
By woman wailing for her demon-lover!
And from this chasm, with ceaseless turmoil seething,
As if this earth in fast thick pants were breathing,
A mighty fountain momently was forced:
20   Amid whose swift half-intermitted burst
Huge fragments vaulted like rebounding hail,
Or chaffy grain beneath the thresher's flail:
And 'mid these dancing rocks at once and ever
It flung up momently the sacred river
Five miles meandering with a mazy motion
Through wood and dale the sacred river ran,
Then reached the caverns measureless to man,
And sank in tumult to a lifeless ocean:
And 'mid this tumult Kubla heard from far
30   Ancestral voices prophesying war!
     The shadow of the dome of pleasure
     Floated midway on the waves;
     Where was heard the mingled measure
     From the fountain and the caves.
It was a miracle of rare device,
A sunny pleasure-dome with caves of ice!

     A damsel with a dulcimer
     In a vision once I saw:
     It was an Abyssinian maid,
40   And on her dulcimer she played,
     Singing of Mount Abora.
     Could I revive within me
     Her symphony and song,
     To such a deep delight 'twould win me,
That with music loud and long,
I would build that dome in air,

That sunny dome! those caves of ice!
And all who heard should see them there,
And all should cry, Beware! Beware!
His flashing eyes, his floating hair!
Weave a circle round him thrice,
And close your eyes with holy dread,
For he on honey-dew hath fed,
And drunk the milk of Paradise.

50

Walter Savage Landor

Walter Savage Landor (1775–1864) wrote short poems over a long life. He was
famous for his violent temper; according to one often-repeated anecdote, he took out
his anger on a servant by throwing her through a window onto a garden. He was best
at the epigram and short, pointed verse. See also page 96.

I Strove with None

I strove with none, for none was worth my strife.
    Nature I loved and, next to Nature, Art:
I warmed both hands before the fire of life;
    It sinks, and I am ready to depart.

George Gordon, Lord Byron

George Gordon, Lord Byron (1788–1824) in his life was the stereotype of the
romantic poet—handsome, promiscuous, daring. His most romantic poems,
valuing emotion above all things, were not his best work, which was satirical
and comic and shared attitudes, though not form or diction, with the poets of
the eighteenth century. In 1823 Byron joined a Greek revolutionary movement
striving to establish freedom for the Greek people; he died of a fever at
Missolonghi in April 1824.

So We'll Go No More A-Roving

So we'll go no more a-roving
    So late into the night,
Though the heart be still as loving,
    And the moon be still as bright.

For the sword outwears its sheath,
    And the soul wears out the breast,
And the heart must pause to breathe,
    And Love itself have rest.

Though the night was made for loving,
    And the day returns too soon,
Yet we'll go no more a-roving
    By the light of the moon.

10

Stanzas
(When a man hath no freedom to fight for at home)

When a man hath no freedom to fight for at home,
    Let him combat for that of his neighbors;
Let him think of the glories of Greece and of Rome,
    And get knocked on the head for his labors.

To do good to mankind is the chivalrous plan,
    And is always as nobly requited;
Then battle for freedom wherever you can,
    And, if not shot or hanged, you'll get knighted.

Percy Bysshe Shelley

Percy Bysshe Shelley (1792–1822) was expelled from Oxford in 1811 for writing a pamphlet in defense of atheism. That year he married his first wife, who was sixteen, from whom he separated three years later. She killed herself. He married Mary Wollstonecraft—author of *Frankenstein*—in 1814 and spent much of the rest of his life in Italy. He was friendly with Byron and acquainted with Keats. In Italy, in the last three years of his life, he wrote his best poems, including "Ode to the West Wind." On July 8, 1822, he was shipwrecked in a storm while sailing off the Italian coast and drowned.

Ode to the West Wind

1

O wild West Wind, thou breath of Autumn's being,
Thou, from whose unseen presence the leaves dead
Are driven, like ghosts from an enchanter fleeing,

Yellow, and black, and pale, and hectic red,
Pestilence-stricken multitudes: O thou,
Who chariotest to their dark wintry bed

The wingéd seeds, where they lie cold and low,
Each like a corpse within its grave, until
Thine azure sister of the Spring shall blow

10 Her clarion o'er the dreaming earth, and fill
(Driving sweet buds like flocks to feed in air)
With living hues and odours plain and hill:

Wild Spirit, which art moving everywhere;
Destroyer and preserver; hear, oh, hear!

2

Thou on whose stream, 'mid the steep sky's commotion,
Loose clouds like earth's decaying leaves are shed,
Shook from the tangled boughs of Heaven and Ocean,

Angels of rain and lightning: there are spread
On the blue surface of thine airy surge,
20 Like the bright hair uplifted from the head

Of some fierce Mænad, even from the dim verge
Of the horizon to the zenith's height,
The locks of the approaching storm. Thou dirge

Of the dying year, to which this closing night
Will be the dome of a vast sepulchre,
Vaulted with all thy congregated might

Of vapours, from whose solid atmosphere
Black rain, and fire, and hail will burst: oh, hear!

3

Thou who didst waken from his summer dreams
The blue Mediterranean, where he lay,   *30*
Lulled by the coil of his crystálline streams,

Beside a pumice isle in Baiæ's bay,
And saw in sleep old palaces and towers
Quivering within the wave's intenser day,

All overgrown with azure moss and flowers
So sweet, the sense faints picturing them! Thou
For whose path the Atlantic's level powers

Cleave themselves into chasms, while far below
The sea-blooms and the oozy woods which wear
The sapless foliage of the ocean, know   *40*

Thy voice, and suddenly grow gray with fear,
And tremble and despoil themselves: oh, hear!

4

If I were a dead leaf thou mightest bear;
If I were a swift cloud to fly with thee;
A wave to pant beneath thy power, and share

The impulse of thy strength, only less free
Than thou, O uncontrollable! If even
I were as in my boyhood, and could be

The comrade of thy wanderings over Heaven,
As then, when to outstrip thy skyey speed   *50*
Scarce seemed a vision; I would ne'er have striven

As thus with thee in prayer in my sore need.
Oh, lift me as a wave, a leaf, a cloud!
I fall upon the thorns of life! I bleed!

A heavy weight of hours has chained and bowed
One too like thee: tameless, and swift, and proud.

5

Make me thy lyre, even as the forest is:
What if my leaves are falling like its own!
The tumult of thy mighty harmonies

60   Will take from both a deep, autumnal tone,
Sweet though in sadness. Be thou, Spirit fierce,
My spirit! Be thou me, impetuous one!

Drive my dead thoughts over the universe
Like withered leaves to quicken a new birth!
And, by the incantation of this verse,

Scatter, as from an unextinguished hearth
Ashes and sparks, my words among mankind!
Be through my lips to unawakened earth

The trumpet of a prophecy! O, wind,
70   If Winter comes, can Spring be far behind?

John Clare

John Clare (1793–1864) was an agricultural laborer who went insane in 1837 but continued to write poems in the asylum.

I Am

I am: yet what I am none cares or knows,
    My friends forsake me like a memory lost;
I am the self-consumer of my woes,
    They rise and vanish in oblivious host,
Like shades in love and death's oblivion lost;
And yet I am, and live with shadows tost

Into the nothingness of scorn and noise,
    Into the living sea of waking dreams,
Where there is neither sense of life nor joys,
10   But the vast shipwreck of my life's esteems;
And e'en the dearest—that I loved the best—
Are strange—nay, rather stranger than the rest.

I long for scenes where man has never trod,
    A place where woman never smiled or wept;
There to abide with my Creator, God,
    And sleep as I in childhood sweetly slept:
Untroubling and untroubled where I lie,
The grass below—above the vaulted sky.

Edward Fitzgerald

Edward Fitzgerald (1809–1883) first translated the *Rubáiyát* of Omar Khayyám in 1859 and continued to revise it the rest of his life. His other poems and translations have attracted little attention, but this translation—more adaptation than translation—has endured like no other foreign poem done into English.

from The Rubáiyát of Omar Khayyám

1

Wake! for the Sun, who scattered into flight
The Stars before him from the Field of Night,
    Drives Night along with them from Heav'n, and strikes
The Sultán's Turret with a Shaft of Light.

7

Come, fill the Cup, and in the fire of Spring
Your Winter-garment of Repentance fling:
    The Bird of Time has but a little way
To flutter—and the Bird is on the Wing.

12

A Book of Verses underneath the Bough,
A jug of Wine, a Loaf of Bread—and Thou
    Beside me singing in the Wilderness—
Oh, Wilderness were Paradise enow!

13

Some for the Glories of This World; and some
Sigh for the Prophet's Paradise to come;
    Ah, take the Cash, and let the Credit go,
Nor heed the rumble of a distant Drum!

19

I sometimes think that never blows so red
The Rose as where some buried Cæsar bled;
    That every Hyacinth the Garden wears
Dropt in her Lap from some once lovely Head.

22

For some we loved, the loveliest and the best
That from his Vintage rolling Time hath prest,
    Have drunk their Cup a Round or two before,
And one by one crept silently to rest.

27

Myself when young did eagerly frequent
Doctor and Saint, and heard great argument
    About it and about: but evermore
Came out by the same door where in I went.

71

The Moving Finger writes; and, having writ,
30 Moves on: nor all your Piety nor Wit
    Shall lure it back to cancel half a Line,
Nor all your Tears wash out a Word of it.

100

Yon rising Moon that looks for us again—
How oft hereafter will she wax and wane;
    How oft hereafter rising look for us
Through this same Garden—and for *one* in vain!

101

And when like her, oh Sákí, you shall pass
Among the Guests Star-scatter'd on the Grass,
    And in your joyous errand reach the spot
40 Where I made One—turn down an empty Glass!

Edgar Allan Poe

Edgar Allan Poe (1809–1849) may be the strangest of all major American authors—in a literature whose greatest artists often seem to specialize in eccentricity. He attended West Point briefly, the University of Virginia inconclusively, and began early to explore the exotic, necrophiliac geography of his stories and poems. He died in Baltimore on election day, apparently victim of alcohol passed out to potential voters.

The City in the Sea

Lo! Death has reared himself a throne
In a strange city lying alone
Far down within the dim West,
Where the good and the bad and the worst and the best
Have gone to their eternal rest.
There shrines and palaces and towers
(Time-eaten towers that tremble not!)
Resemble nothing that is ours.
Around, by lifting winds forgot,
10 Resignedly beneath the sky
The melancholy waters lie.

No rays from the holy heaven come down
On the long night-time of that town;
But light from out the lurid sea
Streams up the turrets silently—
Gleams up the pinnacles far and free—
Up domes—up spires—up kingly halls—
Up fanes—up Babylon-like walls—
Up shadowy long-forgotten bowers
20 Of sculptured ivy and stone flowers—

Up many and many a marvellous shrine
Whose wreathéd friezes intertwine
The viol, the violet, and the vine.

Resignedly beneath the sky
The melancholy waters lie.
So blend the turrets and shadows there
That all seem pendulous in air,
While from a proud tower in the town
Death looks gigantically down.

30 There open fanes and gaping graves
Yawn level with the luminous waves;
But not the riches there that lie
In each idol's diamond eye—
Not the gaily-jewelled dead
Tempt the waters from their bed;
For no ripples curl, alas!
Along that wilderness of glass—
No swellings tell that winds may be
Upon some far-off happier sea—
40 No heavings hint that winds have been
On seas less hideously serene.

But lo, a stir is in the air!
The wave—there is a movement there!
As if the towers had thrust aside,
In slightly sinking, the dull tide—
As if their tops had feebly given
A void within the filmy Heaven.
The waves have now a redder glow—
The hours are breathing faint and low—
50 And when, amid no earthly moans,
Down, down that town shall settle hence,
Hell, rising from a thousand thrones,
Shall do it reverence.

Alfred, Lord Tennyson

Alfred, Lord Tennyson (1809–1892), who began to publish poems before he was twenty, matured in technical accomplishment early. After his great friend Arthur Hallam died in 1833, Tennyson matured in other ways, beginning his long, elegiac "In Memoriam." In Tennyson's character there was a quarrel between a personal predilection for melancholy and the Victorian duty to be optimistic and progressive. For much of his life, Victorian optimism won out; he is the poet of his age. When he speaks the philosophy of imperialism, as in "Ulysses," he speaks it with eloquence and vigor. In his more private poems, sweetness and fire remain as public gusto vanishes.

Ulysses

It little profits that an idle king,
By this still hearth, among these barren crags,
Matched with an agèd wife, I mete and dole
Unequal laws unto a savage race,
That hoard, and sleep, and feed, and know not me.
I cannot rest from travel: I will drink
Life to the lees: all times I have enjoyed
Greatly, have suffered greatly, both with those
That loved me, and alone; on shore, and when
10   Through scudding drifts the rainy Hyades
Vext the dim sea: I am become a name;
For always roaming with a hungry heart
Much have I seen and known; cities of men
And manners, climates, councils, governments,
Myself not least, but honored of them all;
And drunk delight of battle with my peers,
Far on the ringing plains of windy Troy.
I am a part of all that I have met;
Yet all experience is an arch wherethro'
20   Gleams that untraveled world, whose margin fades
For ever and for ever when I move.
How dull it is to pause, to make an end,
To rust unburnished, not to shine in use!
As though to breathe were life. Life piled on life
Were all too little, and of one to me
Little remains: but every hour is saved
From that eternal silence, something more,
A bringer of new things; and vile it were
For some three suns to store and hoard myself,
30   And this gray spirit yearning in desire
To follow knowledge like a sinking star,
Beyond the utmost bound of human thought.

This is my son, mine own Telemachus,
To whom I leave the scepter and the isle—
Well-loved of me, discerning to fulfill
This labor, by slow prudence to make mild
A rugged people, and through soft degrees

Subdue them to the useful and the good.
Most blameless is he, centered in the sphere
40 Of common duties, decent not to fail
In offices of tenderness, and pay
Meet adoration to my household gods,
When I am gone. He works his work, I mine.

There lies the port; the vessel puffs her sail:
There gloom the dark broad seas. My mariners,
Souls that have toiled, and wrought, and thought with me—
That ever with a frolic welcome took
The thunder and the sunshine, and opposed
Free hearts, free foreheads—you and I are old;
50 Old age hath yet his honor and his toil;
Death closes all: but something ere the end,
Some work of noble note, may yet be done,
Not unbecoming men that strove with Gods.
The lights begin to twinkle from the rocks:
The long day wanes: the slow moon climbs: the deep
Moans round with many voices. Come, my friends,
'Tis not too late to seek a newer world.
Push off, and sitting well in order smite
The sounding furrows; for my purpose holds
60 To sail beyond the sunset, and the baths
Of all the western stars, until I die.
It may be that the gulfs will wash us down:
It may be we shall touch the Happy Isles,
And see the great Achilles, whom we knew.
Though much is taken, much abides; and though
We are not now that strength which in old days
Moved earth and heaven; that which we are, we are;
One equal temper of heroic hearts,
Made weak by time and fate, but strong in will
70 To strive, to seek, to find, and not to yield.

Tears, Idle Tears

Tears, idle tears, I know not what they mean,
Tears from the depth of some divine despair
Rise in the heart, and gather to the eyes,
In looking on the happy Autumn-fields,
And thinking of the days that are no more.

Fresh as the first beam glittering on a sail,
That brings our friends up from the underworld,
Sad as the last which reddens over one
That sinks with all we love below the verge;
10 So sad, so fresh, the days that are no more.

Ah, sad and strange as in dark summer dawns
The earliest pipe of half-awakened birds

To dying ears, when unto dying eyes
The casement slowly grows a glimmering square;
So sad, so strange, the days that are no more.

Dear as remembered kisses after death,
And sweet as those by hopeless fancy feigned
On lips that are for others; deep as love,
Deep as first love, and wild with all regret;
20   O Death in Life, the days that are no more.

The Eagle

He clasps the crag with crooked hands;
Close to the sun in lonely lands,
Ringed with the azure world, he stands.

The wrinkled sea beneath him crawls;
He watches from his mountain walls,
And like a thunderbolt he falls.

Robert Browning

Robert Browning (1812–1889) was three years younger than Tennyson and
shared with him first rank among Victorian poets. In 1846 he and Elizabeth
Barrett were married and wrote poems together for fifteen years, until she died
in 1861. He is most celebrated for his dramatic monologues. He is buried in
Westminster Abbey.

My Last Duchess

FERRARA

That's my last Duchess painted on the wall,
Looking as if she were alive. I call
That piece a wonder, now: Frà Pandolf's hands
Worked busily a day, and there she stands.
Will't please you sit and look at her? I said
"Frà Pandolf" by design, for never read
Strangers like you that pictured countenance,
The depth and passion of its earnest glance,
But to myself they turned (since none puts by
10   The curtain I have drawn for you, but I)
And seemed as they would ask me, if they durst,
How such a glance came there; so, not the first
Are you to turn and ask thus. Sir, 'twas not
Her husband's presence only, called that spot
Of joy into the Duchess' cheek: perhaps
Frà Pandolf chanced to say, "Her mantle laps
Over my lady's wrist too much," or "Paint
Must never hope to reproduce the faint
Half-flush that dies along her throat." Such stuff
20   Was courtesy, she thought, and cause enough

For calling up that spot of joy. She had
A heart—how shall I say?—too soon made glad,
Too easily impressed; she liked whate'er
She looked on, and her looks went everywhere.
Sir, 'twas all one! My favour at her breast,
The dropping of the daylight in the West,
The bough of cherries some officious fool
Broke in the orchard for her, the white mule
She rode with round the terrace—all and each
30   Would draw from her alike the approving speech,
Or blush, at least. She thanked men,—good! but thanked
Somehow—I know not how—as if she ranked
My gift of a nine-hundred-years-old name
With anybody's gift. Who'd stoop to blame
This sort of trifling? Even had you skill
In speech—(which I have not)—to make your will
Quite clear to such an one, and say, "Just this
"Or that in you disgusts me; here you miss,
"Or there exceed the mark"—and if she let
40   Herself be lessoned so, nor plainly set
Her wits to yours, forsooth, and made excuse,
—E'en then would be some stooping; and I choose
Never to stoop. Oh sir, she smiled, no doubt,
Whene'er I passed her; but who passed without
Much the same smile? This grew; I gave commands;
Then all smiles stopped together. There she stands
As if alive. Will't please you rise? We'll meet
The company below, then. I repeat,
The Count your master's known munificence
50   Is ample warrant that no just pretense
Of mine for dowry will be disallowed;
Though his fair daughter's self, as I avowed
At starting, is my object. Nay, we'll go
Together down, sir. Notice Neptune, though,
Taming a sea-horse, thought a rarity,
Which Claus of Innsbruck cast in bronze for me!

Emily Brontë

Emily Brontë (1818–1848) was sister of Charlotte and Anne; all novelists, all
poets in their youths. Emily wrote *Wuthering Heights*.

No Coward Soul Is Mine

No coward soul is mine,
No trembler in the world's storm-troubled sphere:
    I see Heaven's glories shine,
And faith shines equal, arming me from fear.

O God within my breast,
Almighty, ever-present Deity!
   Life, that in me hast rest
As I, undying life, have power in Thee!

   Vain are the thousand creeds
10 That move men's hearts: unutterably vain;
   Worthless as withered weeds,
Or idlest froth amid the boundless main,

   To waken doubt in one
Holding so fast by Thy infinity,
   So surely anchored on
The steadfast rock of immortality.

   With wide embracing love
Thy spirit animates eternal years,
   Pervades and broods above,
20 Changes, sustains, dissolves, creates, and rears.

   Though earth and moon were gone,
And suns and universes cease to be,
   And Thou wert left alone,
Every existence would exist in Thee.

   There is not room for death,
Nor atom that his might could render void:
   Since Thou art Being and Breath
And what Thou art may never be destroyed.

Walt Whitman

Walt Whitman (1819–1892) is the first great American poet. He is also one
of the greatest innovators in the history of the art. His long, loose rhythms
derive in part from the King James version of the Bible and in part from the
expansive gestures of nineteenth-century political oratory. But largely they
seem Whitman's own creation.
   Born on Long Island, son of a carpenter who was also a farmer, Whitman was
sporadically educated, became a newspaper editor, and created himself as a
poet. The first edition of *Leaves of Grass*, which through subsequent editions
became a collection of his life's work, appeared in 1855. Emerson praised him,
but few other early readers had the imagination to understand that his writing
was poetry at all. Not only was his work innovative; in its broad sensuality and
in its hints at homoeroticism, it was shocking. Emily Dickinson's comment,
in a letter to Thomas Wentworth Higginson, tells the tale: "You speak of Mr.
Whitman—I never read his Book—but was told that he was disgraceful—"

Out of the Cradle Endlessly Rocking

   Out of the cradle endlessly rocking,
   Out of the mocking-bird's throat, the musical shuttle,
   Out of the Ninth-month midnight,
   Over the sterile sands and the fields beyond, where the child leaving his bed
        wandered alone, bareheaded, barefoot,

Down from the showered halo,
Up from the mystic play of shadows twining and twisting as if they were alive,
Out from the patches of briers and blackberries,
From the memories of the bird that chanted to me,
From your memories sad brother, from the fitful risings and fallings I heard,
10   From under that yellow half-moon late-risen and swollen as if with tears,
From those beginning notes of yearning and love there in the mist,
From the thousand responses of my heart never to cease,
From the myriad thence-aroused words,
From the word stronger and more delicious than any,
From such as now they start the scene revisiting,
As a flock, twittering, rising, or overhead passing,
Borne hither, ere all eludes me, hurriedly,
A man, yet by these tears a little boy again,
Throwing myself on the sand, confronting the waves,
20   I, chanter of pains and joys, uniter of here and hereafter,
Taking all hints to use them, but swiftly leaping beyond them,
A reminiscence sing.

Once Paumanok,
When the lilac-scent was in the air and Fifth-month grass was growing,
Up this seashore in some briers,
Two feathered guests from Alabama, two together,
And their nest, and four light-green eggs spotted with brown,
And every day the he-bird to and fro near at hand,
And every day the she-bird crouched on her nest, silent, with bright eyes,
30   And every day I, a curious boy, never too close, never disturbing them,
Cautiously peering, absorbing, translating.

Shine! shine! shine!
Pour down your warmth, great sun!
While we bask, we two together.

Two together!
Winds blow south, or winds blow north,
Day come white, or night come black,
Home, or rivers and mountains from home,
Singing all time, minding no time,
40   *While we two keep together.*

Till of a sudden,
May-be killed, unknown to her mate,
One forenoon the she-bird crouched not on the nest,
Nor returned that afternoon, nor the next,
Nor ever appeared again.

And thenceforward all summer in the sound of the sea,
And at night under the full of the moon in calmer weather,
Over the hoarse surging of the sea,
Or flitting from brier to brier by day,
50   I saw, I heard at intervals the remaining one, the he-bird,
The solitary guest from Alabama.

Blow! blow! blow!
Blow up sea-winds along Paumanok's shore;
I wait and I wait till you blow my mate to me.

Yes, when the stars glistened,
All night long on the prong of a moss-scalloped stake,
Down almost amid the slapping waves,
Sat the lone singer wonderful causing tears.

He called on his mate,
60 He poured forth the meanings which I of all men know.

Yes my brother I know,
The rest might not, but I have treasured every note,
For more than once dimly down to the beach gliding,
Silent, avoiding the moonbeams, blending myself with the shadows,
Recalling now the obscure shapes, the echoes, the sounds and sights after their
      sorts,
The white arms out in the breakers tirelessly tossing,
I, with bare feet, a child, the wind wafting my hair,
Listened long and long.

Listened to keep, to sing, now translating the notes,
70 Following you my brother.

Soothe! soothe! soothe!
Close on its wave soothes the wave behind,
And again another behind embracing and lapping, every one close,
But my love soothes not me, not me.

Low hangs the moon, it rose late,
It is lagging—O I think it is heavy with love, with love.

O madly the sea pushes upon the land,
With love, with love.

O night! do I not see my love fluttering out among the breakers?
80 *What is that little black thing I see there in the white?*

Loud! loud! loud!
Loud I call to you, my love!

High and clear I shoot my voice over the waves,
Surely you must know who is here, is here,
You must know who I am, my love.

Low-hanging moon!
What is that dusky spot in your brown yellow?
O it is the shape, the shape of my mate!
O moon do not keep her from me any longer.

90 *Land! land! O land!*
Whichever way I turn, O I think you could give me my mate back again if you
      only would,
For I am almost sure I see her dimly whichever way I look.

O rising stars!
Perhaps the one I want so much will rise, will rise with some of you.

O throat! O trembling throat!
Sound clearer through the atmosphere!
Pierce the woods, the earth,
Somewhere listening to catch you must be the one I want.

Shake out carols!
100   *Solitary here, the night's carols!*
Carols of lonesome love! death's carols!
Carols under that lagging, yellow, waning moon!
O under that moon where she droops almost down into the sea!
O reckless despairing carols.

But soft! sink low!
Soft! let me just murmur,
And do you wait a moment you husky-noised sea,
For somewhere I believe I heard my mate responding to me,
So faint, I must be still, be still to listen,
110   *But not altogether still, for then she might not come immediately to me.*

Hither my love!
Here I am! Here!
With this just-sustained note I announce myself to you,
This gentle call is for you my love, for you.

Do not be decoyed elsewhere,
That is the whistle of the wind, it is not my voice,
That is the fluttering, the fluttering of the spray,
Those are the shadows of leaves.

O darkness! O in vain!
120   *O I am very sick and sorrowful.*

O brown halo in the sky near the moon, drooping upon the sea!
O troubled reflection in the sea!
O throat! O throbbing heart!
And I singing uselessly, uselessly all the night.

O past! O happy life! O songs of joy!
In the air, in the woods, over fields,
Loved! loved! loved! loved! loved!
But my mate no more, no more with me!
We two together no more.

130   The aria sinking,
All else continuing, the stars shining,
The winds blowing, the notes of the bird continuous echoing,
With angry moans the fierce old mother incessantly moaning,
On the sands of Paumanok's shore gray and rustling,
The yellow half-moon enlarged, sagging down, drooping, the face of the sea
        almost touching,

The boy ecstatic, with his bare feet the waves, with his hair the atmosphere
   dallying,
The love in the heart long pent, now loose, now at last tumultuously bursting,
The aria's meaning, the ears, the soul, swiftly depositing,
The strange tears down the cheeks coursing,
140   The colloquy there, the trio, each uttering,
The undertone, the savage old mother incessantly crying,
To the boy's soul's questions sullenly timing, some drowned secret hissing,
To the outsetting bard.

Demon or bird! (said the boy's soul,)
Is it indeed toward your mate you sing? or is it really to me?
For I, that was a child, my tongue's use sleeping, now I have heard you,
Now in a moment I know what I am for, I awake,
And already a thousand singers, a thousand songs, clearer, louder and more
   sorrowful than yours,
A thousand warbling echoes have started to life within me, never to die.

150   O you singer solitary, singing by yourself, projecting me,
O solitary me listening, never more shall I cease perpetuating you,
Never more shall I escape, never more the reverberations,
Never more the cries of unsatisfied love be absent from me,
Never again leave me to be the peaceful child I was before what there in the
   night,
By the sea under the yellow and sagging moon,
The messenger there aroused, the fire, the sweet hell within,
The unknown want, the destiny of me.

O give me the clue! (it lurks in the night here somewhere,)
O if I am to have so much, let me have more!

160   A word then, (for I will conquer it,)
The word final, superior to all,
Subtle, sent up—what is it?—I listen;
Are you whispering it, and have been all the time, you sea-waves?
Is that it from your liquid rims and wet sands?

Whereto answering, the sea,
Delaying not, hurrying not,
Whispered me through the night, and very plainly before daybreak,
Lisped to me the low and delicious word death,
And again death, death, death, death,
170   Hissing melodious, neither like the bird nor like my aroused child's heart,
But edging near as privately for me rustling at my feet,
Creeping thence steadily up to my ears and laving me softly all over,
Death, death, death, death, death.

Which I do not forget,
But fuse the song of my dusky demon and brother,
That he sang to me in the moonlight on Paumanok's gray beach,
With the thousand responsive songs at random,
My own songs awaked from that hour,

And with them the key, the word up from the waves,
180   The word of the sweetest song and all songs,
That strong and delicious word which, creeping to my feet,
(Or like some old crone rocking the cradle, swathed in sweet garments, bending
    aside,)
The sea whispered me.

A Farm Picture

Through the ample open door of the peaceful country barn,
A sunlit pasture field with cattle and horses feeding,
And haze and vista, and the far horizon fading away.

Cavalry Crossing a Ford

A line in long array where they wind betwixt green islands,
They take a serpentine course, their arms flash in the sun—hark to the musical
    clank,
Behold the silvery river, in it the splashing horses loitering stop to drink,
Behold the brown-faced men, each group, each person a picture, the negligent
    rest on the saddles,
Some emerge on the opposite bank, others are just entering the ford—while,
Scarlet and blue and snowy white,
The guidon flags flutter gayly in the wind.

Matthew Arnold

Matthew Arnold (1822–1888) comes after Tennyson and Browning as a poet of
the Victorian age, but as a man of letters he comes after no one. His father was
headmaster of Rugby, and Arnold was educated at Rugby, at Winchester, and
at Oxford, where he won the Newdigate Prize for Poetry. For many years he
inspected schools for the government. He lectured on poetry at Oxford. He
wrote his poems mostly in early life; as he grew older, he concentrated on the
essay.

Dover Beach

The sea is calm tonight,
The tide is full, the moon lies fair
Upon the straits;—on the French coast the light
Gleams and is gone; the cliffs of England stand,
Glimmering and vast, out in the tranquil bay.
Come to the window, sweet is the night-air!
Only, from the long line of spray
Where the sea meets the moon-blanched land,
Listen! you hear the grating roar
10   Of pebbles which the waves draw back, and fling,
At their return, up the high strand,
Begin and cease, and then again begin,
With tremulous cadence slow, and bring
The eternal note of sadness in.

Sophocles long ago
Heard it on the Aegean, and it brought
Into his mind the turbid ebb and flow
Of human misery; we
Find also in the sound a thought,
20   Hearing it by this distant northern sea.

The Sea of Faith
Was once, too, at the full, and round earth's shore
Lay like the folds of a bright girdle furled.
But now I only hear
Its melancholy, long, withdrawing roar,
Retreating, to the breath
Of the night-wind, down the vast edges drear
And naked shingles of the world.

Ah, love, let us be true
30   To one another! for the world, which seems
To lie before us like a land of dreams,
So various, so beautiful, so new,
Hath really neither joy, nor love, nor light,
Nor certitude, nor peace, nor help for pain;
And we are here as on a darkling plain
Swept with confused alarms of struggle and flight,
Where ignorant armies clash by night.

(See also "The Dover Bitch," page 305.)

Emily Dickinson (1830–1886)

See pages 130–137.

Lewis Carroll

Lewis Carroll was the pen name of Charles Lutwidge Dodgson (1832–1898), a distinguished mathematician, when he wrote *Alice's Adventures in Wonderland* and other works of fantasy and nonsense. On the faculty at Oxford, amateur photographer as well as writer, Carroll made up numerous words when he composed "Jabberwocky"; some of them have taken their place in language.

Jabberwocky

'Twas brillig, and the slithy toves
    Did gyre and gimble in the wabe:
All mimsy were the borogoves,
    And the mome raths outgrabe.

"Beware the Jabberwock, my son!
    The jaws that bite, the claws that catch!
Beware the Jubjub bird, and shun
    The frumious Bandersnatch!"

He took his vorpal sword in hand;
10   Long time the manxome foe he sought—
So rested he by the Tumtum tree,
      And stood awhile in thought.

And, as in uffish thought he stood,
      The Jabberwock, with eyes of flame,
Came whiffling through the tulgey wood,
      And burbled as it came!

One, two! One, two! And through and through
      The vorpal blade went snicker-snack!
He left it dead, and with its head
20   He went galumphing back.

"And hast thou slain the Jabberwock?
      Come to my arms, my beamish boy!
O frabjous day! Callooh, Callay!"
      He chortled in his joy.

'Twas brillig, and the slithy toves
      Did gyre and gimble in the wabe:
All mimsy were the borogoves,
      And the mome raths outgrabe.

Thomas Hardy

Thomas Hardy (1840–1928) is better known as a novelist than as a poet, but many devoted readers find the poetry even better than the fiction. He began life as an architect and published his first novel when he was thirty-two. For many years Hardy wrote few poems and concentrated on novels, of which the best-known are *The Return of the Native, The Mayor of Casterbridge, Tess of the D'Urbervilles,* and *Jude the Obscure. Jude* appeared in 1896, and was denounced as obscene. Perhaps using that denunciation as an excuse, Hardy renounced fiction, and—now freed by the success of his fiction from the necessity to make money—devoted himself to poetry, as he had always wanted to do. He was almost sixty when his first book of poems appeared. Between 1898 and his death at eighty-eight in 1928 he published the fifteen hundred poems that appear in his *Collected Poems.* He is a poet admired by other poets.

The Man He Killed

"Had he and I but met
      By some old ancient inn,
We should have sat us down to wet
      Right many a nipperkin!°   half-pint cup

"But ranged as infantry,
      And staring face to face,
I shot at him as he at me,
      And killed him in his place.

"I shot him dead because—
10   Because he was my foe,
      Just so: my foe of course he was;
        That's clear enough; although

      "He thought he'd 'list,° perhaps,   *enlist*
      Off-hand like—just as I—
    Was out of work—had sold his traps°—   *possessions*
        No other reason why.

      "Yes; quaint and curious war is!
      You shoot a fellow down
    You'd treat if met where any bar is,
20   Or help to half-a-crown."°   *two and a half shillings*

The Ruined Maid

"O'Melia, my dear, this does everything crown!
Who could have supposed I should meet you in Town?
And whence such fair garments, such prosperi-ty?"—
"O didn't you know I'd been ruined?" said she.

—"You left us in tatters, without shoes or socks,
Tired of digging potatoes, and spudding up docks;°   *digging weeds*
And now you've gay bracelets and bright feathers three!"—
"Yes: that's how we dress when we're ruined," said she.

—"At home in the barton° you said 'thee' and 'thou,'   *farmyard*
10 And 'thik oon,' and 'theäs oon,' and 't'other'; but now
Your talking quite fits 'ee for high compa-ny!"—
"Some polish is gained with one's ruin," said she.

—"Your hands were like paws then, your face blue and bleak
But now I'm bewitched by your delicate cheek,
And your little gloves fit as on any la-dy!"—
"We never do work when we're ruined," said she.

—"You used to call home-life a hag-ridden dream,
And you'd sigh, and you'd sock; but at present you seem
To know not of megrims° or melancho-ly!"—   *depressions*
20 "True. One's pretty lively when ruined," said she.

—"I wish I had feathers, a fine sweeping gown,
And a delicate face, and could strut about Town!"—
"My dear—a raw country girl, such as you be,
Cannot quite expect that. You ain't ruined," said she.

Gerard Manley Hopkins

Gerard Manley Hopkins (1844–1889) attended Oxford, and in his early twenties converted to Roman Catholicism, becoming a Jesuit in 1868. He corresponded with Robert Bridges and Coventry Patmore and devoted himself considerably to his poetry insofar as such devotion was consistent with his calling. But he did not publish, and he was not known until Robert Bridges collected his poems after Hopkins's death and edited and published them. He has been a major influence on modern poets.

Spring and Fall
To a Young Child

Márgarét, are you gríeving
Over Goldengrove unleaving?
Leáves, líke the things of man, you
With your fresh thoughts care for, can you?
Áh! ás the heart grows older
It will come to such sights colder
By and by, nor spare a sigh
Though worlds of wanwood leafmeal lie;
And yet you wíll weep and know why.
10   Now no matter, child, the name:
Sórrow's spríngs áre the same.
Nor mouth had, no nor mind, expressed
What heart heard of, ghost guessed:
It ís the blight man was born for,
It is Margaret you mourn for.

The Windhover
To Christ Our Lord

I caught this morning morning's minion, king-
   dom of daylight's dauphin, dapple-dawn-drawn Falcon, in his riding
     Of the rolling level underneath him steady air, and striding
High there, how he rung upon the rein of a wimpling wing
In his ecstasy! then off, off forth on swing,
   As a skate's heel sweeps smooth on a bow-bend; the hurl and gliding
     Rebuffed the big wind. My heart in hiding
Stirred for a bird,—the achieve of, the mastery of the thing!

Brute beauty and valor and act, oh, air, pride, plume, here
10   Buckle! AND the fire that breaks from thee then, a billion
Times told lovelier, more dangerous, O my chevalier!

   No wonder of it: shéer plód makes plough down sillion
Shine, and blue-bleak embers, ah my dear,
   Fall, gall themselves, and gash gold-vermilion.

Carrion Comfort

Not, I'll not, carrion comfort, Despair, not feast on thee;
Not untwist—slack they may be—these last strands of man
In me ór, most weary, cry *I can no more.* I can;
Can something, hope, wish day come, not choose not to be.
But ah, but O thou terrible, why wouldst thou rude on me
Thy wring-world right foot rock? lay a lionlimb against me? scan
With darksome devouring eyes my bruisèd bones? and fan,
O in turns of tempest, me heaped there; me frantic to avoid thee and flee?

Why? That my chaff might fly; my grain lie, sheer and clear.
10   Nay in all that toil, that coil, since (seems) I kissed the rod,
Hand rather, my heart lo! lapped strength, stole joy, would laugh, chéer.
Cheer whom though? the hero whose heaven-handling flung me, fóot tród
Me? or me that fought him? O which one? is it each one? That night, that year
Of now done darkness I wretch lay wrestling with (my God!) my God.

A. E. Housman

Alfred Edward Housman (1859–1936) was a classical scholar and professor of
Latin at Cambridge University. He wrote little poetry, notably *A Shropshire Lad*
in 1896 and *Last Poems* in 1922, but what he wrote was extraordinarily fine
and finished, if lacking in range and depth.

Eight O'Clock

He stood, and heard the steeple
    Sprinkle the quarters on the morning town.
One, two, three, four, to market-place and people
    It tossed them down.

Strapped, noosed, nighing his hour,
    He stood and counted them and cursed his luck;
And then the clock collected in the tower
    Its strength, and struck.

To an Athlete Dying Young

The time you won your town the race
We chaired you through the market-place;
Man and boy stood cheering by,
And home we brought you shoulder-high.

To-day, the road all runners come,
Shoulder-high we bring you home,
And set you at your threshold down,
Townsman of a stiller town.

Smart lad, to slip betimes away
10 From fields where glory does not stay
And early though the laurel grows
It withers quicker than the rose.

Eyes the shady night has shut
Cannot see the record cut,
And silence sounds no worse than cheers
After earth has stopped the ears:

Now you will not swell the rout
Of lads that wore their honors out,
Runners whom renown outran
20 And the name died before the man.

So set, before its echoes fade,
The fleet foot on the sill of shade,
And hold to the low lintel up
The still-defended challenge-cup.

And round that early-laurelled head
Will flock to gaze the strengthless dead,
And find unwithered on its curls
The garland briefer than a girl's.

William Butler Yeats

William Butler Yeats (1865–1939), born in Dublin, grew up largely in Ireland in an Anglo-Irish family. Both his father and his brother were well-known artists. Yeats published his first collection of poetry when he was twenty-four and wrote continually until his death fifty years later. Considered by many the greatest of modern poets, Yeats was a leader in the Irish renaissance, playwright and a founder of the Abbey Theatre, an Irish patriot and a denouncer of nationalism, mystic and skeptic—a man of passion and conflict whose poetry derived from passionate conflict. He married in 1917, and his wife's automatic writing helped him explore mystical theories, which culminated in a prose work called *A Vision*, published in 1925. In 1919 he acquired Thoor Ballylee, an ancient Norman tower in the west of Ireland that became a feature and a fixture in his poetry. He became a senator of independent Ireland and was awarded the Nobel Prize for literature in 1923. He made his best books of poems after receiving the prize: *The Tower* in 1928 and the posthumous *Last Poems* in 1940.

Who Goes with Fergus?

Who will go drive with Fergus[1] now,
And pierce the deep wood's woven shade,
And dance upon the level shore?
Young man, lift up your russet brow,
And lift your tender eyelids, maid,
And brood on hopes and fear no more.

[1]Legendary king who renounced his throne to become an itinerant poet

And no more turn aside and brood
Upon love's bitter mystery;
For Fergus rules the brazen cars,
10   And rules the shadows of the wood,
And the white breast of the dim sea
And all dishevelled wandering stars.

The Magi

Now as at all times I can see in the mind's eye,
In their stiff, painted clothes, the pale unsatisfied ones
Appear and disappear in the blue depth of the sky
With all their ancient faces like rain-beaten stones,
And all their helms of silver hovering side by side,
And all their eyes still fixed, hoping to find once more,
Being by Calvary's turbulence unsatisfied,
The uncontrollable mystery on the bestial floor.

The Second Coming

Turning and turning in the widening gyre°   spiral
The falcon cannot hear the falconer;
Things fall apart; the centre cannot hold;
Mere anarchy is loosed upon the world,
The blood-dimmed tide is loosed, and everywhere
The ceremony of innocence is drowned;
The best lack all conviction, while the worst
Are full of passionate intensity.

Surely some revelation is at hand;
10   Surely the Second Coming is at hand.
The Second Coming! Hardly are those words out
When a vast image out of *Spiritus Mundi*°   soul of the world
Troubles my sight: somewhere in sands of the desert
A shape with lion body and the head of a man,
A gaze blank and pitiless as the sun,
Is moving its slow thighs, while all about it
Reel shadows of the indignant desert birds.
The darkness drops again; but now I know
That twenty centuries of stony sleep
20   Were vexed to nightmare by a rocking cradle,
And what rough beast, its hour come round at last,
Slouches towards Bethlehem to be born?

Sailing to Byzantium

I

That is no country for old men. The young
In one another's arms, birds in the trees
—Those dying generations—at their song,

The salmon-falls, the mackerel-crowded seas,
Fish, flesh, or fowl, commend all summer long
Whatever is begotten, born, and dies.
Caught in that sensual music all neglect
Monuments of unageing intellect.

II

An aged man is but a paltry thing,
10   A tattered coat upon a stick, unless
Soul clap its hands and sing, and louder sing
For every tatter in its mortal dress,
Nor is there singing school but studying
Monuments of its own magnificence;
And therefore I have sailed the seas and come
To the holy city of Byzantium.

III

O sages standing in God's holy fire
As in the gold mosaic of a wall,
Come from the holy fire, perne° in a gyre,   *wind or unwind*
20   And be the singing-masters of my soul.
Consume my heart away; sick with desire
And fastened to a dying animal
It knows not what it is; and gather me
Into the artifice of eternity.

IV

Once out of nature I shall never take
My bodily form from any natural thing,
But such a form as Grecian goldsmiths make
Of hammered gold and gold enamelling
To keep a drowsy Emperor awake;
30   Or set upon a golden bough to sing
To lords and ladies of Byzantium
Of what is past, or passing, or to come.

Leda and the Swan

A sudden blow: the great wings beating still
Above the staggering girl, her thighs caressed
By the dark webs, her nape caught in his bill,
He holds her helpless breast upon his breast.

How can those terrified vague fingers push
The feathered glory from her loosening thighs?
And how can body, laid in that white rush,
But feel the strange heart beating where it lies?

A shudder in the loins engenders there
10   The broken wall, the burning roof and tower

And Agamemnon dead.
                    Being so caught up,
So mastered by the brute blood of the air,
Did she put on his knowledge with his power
Before the indifferent beak could let her drop?

Among School Children

I

I walk through the long schoolroom questioning;
A kind old nun in a white hood replies;
The children learn to cipher and to sing,
To study reading-books and history,
To cut and sew, be neat in everything
In the best modern way—the children's eyes
In momentary wonder stare upon
A sixty-year-old smiling public man.

II

I dream of a Ledaean body, bent
10 Above a sinking fire, a tale that she
Told of a harsh reproof, or trivial event
That changed some childish day to tragedy—
Told, and it seemed that our two natures blent
Into a sphere from youthful sympathy,
Or else, to alter Plato's parable,
Into the yolk and white of the one shell.

III

And thinking of that fit of grief or rage
I look upon one child or t'other there
And wonder if she stood so at that age—
20 For even daughters of the swan can share
Something of every paddler's heritage—
And had that color upon cheek or hair,
And thereupon my heart is driven wild:
She stands before me as a living child.

IV

Her present image floats into the mind—
Did Quattrocento finger fashion it
Hollow of cheek as though it drank the wind
And took a mess of shadows for its meat?
And I though never of Ledaean kind
30 Had pretty plumage once—enough of that,
Better to smile on all that smile, and show
There is a comfortable kind of old scarecrow.

V

What youthful mother, a shape upon her lap
Honey of generation had betrayed,
And that must sleep, shriek, struggle to escape
As recollection or the drug decide,
Would think her son, did she but see that shape
With sixty or more winters on its head,
A compensation for the pang of his birth,
40   Or the uncertainty of his setting forth?

VI

Plato thought nature but a spume that plays
Upon a ghostly paradigm of things;
Solider Aristotle played the taws
Upon the bottom of a king of kings;[1]
World-famous golden-thighed Pythagoras
Fingered upon a fiddle-stick or strings
What a star sang and careless Muses heard:
Old clothes upon old sticks to scare a bird.

VII

Both nuns and mothers worship images,
50   But those the candles light are not as those
That animate a mother's reveries,
But keep a marble or a bronze repose.
And yet they too break hearts—O Presences
That passion, piety or affection knows,
And that all heavenly glory symbolize—
O self-born mockers of man's enterprise;

VIII

Labor is blossoming or dancing where
The body is not bruised to pleasure soul,
Nor beauty born out of its own despair,
60   Nor blear-eyed wisdom out of midnight oil.
O chestnut-tree, great-rooted blossomer,
Are you the leaf, the blossom or the bole?
O body swayed to music, O brightening glance,
How can we know the dancer from the dance?

[1]Aristotle tutored Alexander the Great.

Crazy Jane Talks with the Bishop

I met the Bishop on the road
And much said he and I.
'Those breasts are flat and fallen now,
Those veins must soon be dry;
Live in a heavenly mansion,
Not in some foul sty.'

'Fair and foul are near of kin,
And fair needs foul,' I cried.
'My friends are gone, but that's a truth
10   Nor grave nor bed denied,
Learned in bodily lowliness
And in the heart's pride.

'A woman can be proud and stiff
When on love intent;
But Love has pitched his mansion in
The place of excrement;
For nothing can be sole or whole
That has not been rent.'

Edwin Arlington Robinson

Edwin Arlington Robinson (1869–1935) was born in Maine, and many of his poems use the background of small towns in New England. Most of his adult life, he spent the summers in New Hampshire at the MacDowell Colony and the rest of the year in a New York apartment. He wrote many book-length poems, some of them on subjects like *Merlin* and *Lancelot*. For most readers, the best of his work is the shorter poems of character and narrative.

Eros Turannos[1]

She fears him, and will always ask
   What fated her to choose him;
She meets in his engaging mask
   All reasons to refuse him;
But what she meets and what she fears
Are less than are the downward years,
Drawn slowly to the foamless weirs
   Of age, were she to lose him.

Between a blurred sagacity
10   That once had power to sound him,
And Love, that will not let him be
   The Judas that she found him,
Her pride assuages her almost,
As if it were alone the cost.—
He sees that he will not be lost,
   And waits and looks around him.

A sense of ocean and old trees
   Envelops and allures him;
Tradition, touching all he sees,
20   Beguiles and reassures him;
And all her doubts of what he says
Are dimmed with what she knows of days—
Till even prejudice delays
   And fades, and she secures him.

[1]Love, the Tyrant

The falling leaf inaugurates
   The reign of her confusion:
The pounding wave reverberates
   The dirge of her illusion;
And home, where passion lived and died,
30   Becomes a place where she can hide,
While all the town and harbor side
   Vibrate with her seclusion.

We tell you, tapping on our brows,
   The story as it should be,—
As if the story of a house
   Were told, or ever could be;
We'll have no kindly veil between
Her visions and those we have seen,—
As if we guessed what hers have been,
40   Or what they are or would be.

Meanwhile we do no harm; for they
   That with a god have striven,
Not hearing much of what we say,
   Take what the god has given;
Though like waves breaking it may be,
Or like a changed familiar tree,
Or like a stairway to the sea
   Where down the blind are driven.

Mr. Flood's Party

Old Eben Flood, climbing alone one night
Over the hill between the town below
And the forsaken upland hermitage
That held as much as he should ever know
On earth again of home, paused warily.
The road was his with not a native near;
And Eben, having leisure, said aloud,
For no man else in Tilbury Town to hear:

"Well, Mr. Flood, we have the harvest moon
10   Again, and we may not have many more;
The bird is on the wing, the poet says,
And you and I have said it here before.
Drink to the bird." He raised up to the light
The jug that he had gone so far to fill,
And answered huskily: "Well, Mr. Flood,
Since you propose it, I believe I will."

Alone, as if enduring to the end
A valiant armor of scarred hopes outworn,
He stood there in the middle of the road
20   Like Roland's[1] ghost winding a silent horn.

[1]A hero of French medieval romances who died, ambushed by Saracens, after summoning help by blowing his famous horn

Below him, in the town among the trees,
Where friends of other days had honored him,
A phantom salutation of the dead
Rang thinly till old Eben's eyes were dim.

Then, as a mother lays her sleeping child
Down tenderly, fearing it may awake,
He set the jug down slowly at his feet
With trembling care, knowing that most things break;
And only when assured that on firm earth
30   It stood, as the uncertain lives of men
Assuredly did not, he paced away,
And with his hand extended paused again:

"Well, Mr. Flood, we have not met like this
In a long time; and many a change has come
To both of us, I fear, since last it was
We had a drop together. Welcome home!"
Convivially returning with himself,
Again he raised the jug up to the light;
And with an acquiescent quaver said:
40   "Well, Mr. Flood, if you insist, I might.

"Only a very little, Mr. Flood—
For auld lang syne. No more, sir; that will do."
So, for the time, apparently it did,
And Eben evidently thought so too;
For soon amid the silver loneliness
Of night he lifted up his voice and sang,
Secure, with only two moons listening,
Until the whole harmonious landscape rang—

"For auld lang syne." The weary throat gave out,
50   The last word wavered, and the song was done.
He raised again the jug regretfully
And shook his head, and was again alone.
There was not much that was ahead of him,
And there was nothing in the town below—
Where strangers would have shut the many doors
That many friends had opened long ago.

Hillcrest

(To Mrs. Edward MacDowell)[1]

No sound of any storm that shakes
Old island walls with older seas
Comes here where now September makes
An island in a sea of trees.

---

[1]Marian Nevins MacDowell, widow of the important American composer Edward MacDowell (1861–1908), founded the MacDowell Colony in Peterborough, New Hampshire, and was its moving force until her death in 1956 at ninety-nine.

Between the sunlight and the shade
A man may learn till he forgets
The roaring of a world remade,
And all his ruins and regrets;

And if he still remembers here
10   Poor fights he may have won or lost,—
If he be ridden with the fear
Of what some other fight may cost,—

If, eager to confuse too soon,
What he has known with what may be,
He reads a planet out of tune
For cause of his jarred harmony,—

If here he venture to unroll
His index of adagios,
And he be given to console
20   Humanity with what he knows,—

He may by contemplation learn
A little more than what he knew,
And even see great oaks return
To acorns out of which they grew.

He may, if he but listen well,
Through twilight and the silence here,
Be told what there are none may tell
To vanity's impatient ear;

And he may never dare again
30   Say what awaits him, or be sure
What sunlit labyrinth of pain
He may not enter and endure.

Who knows to-day from yesterday
May learn to count no thing too strange:
Love builds of what Time takes away,
Till Death itself is less than Change.

Who sees enough in his duress
May go as far as dreams have gone;
Who sees a little may do less
40   Than many who are blind have done;

Who sees unchastened here the soul
Triumphant has no other sight
Than has a child who sees the whole
World radiant with his own delight.

Far journeys and hard wandering
Await him in whose crude surmise
Peace, like a mask, hides everything
That is and has been from his eyes;

And all his wisdom is unfound,
50   Or like a web that error weaves
On airy looms that have a sound
No louder now than falling leaves.

Robert Frost (1874–1963)

See pages 139–149.

Carl Sandburg

Carl Sandburg (1878–1967) became known as a poet in 1914, when *Poetry* published "Chicago," later reprinted in *Chicago Poems*. Deriving from Whitman, populist, a celebrator of the commonplace, Sandburg was a popular poet who became the biographer of Abraham Lincoln (six volumes, awarded a Pulitzer Prize in 1939) and toward the end of his life the author of a long novel called *Remembrance Rock*.

Chicago

Hog Butcher for the World,
Tool Maker, Stacker of Wheat,
Player with Railroads and the Nation's Freight Handler;
Stormy, husky, brawling,
City of the Big Shoulders:
They tell me you are wicked and I believe them, for I have seen your painted
women under the gas lamps luring the farm boys.
And they tell me you are crooked and I answer: Yes, it is true I have seen the
gunman kill and go free to kill again.
And they tell me you are brutal and my reply is: On the faces of women and
children I have seen the marks of wanton hunger.
And having answered so I turn once more to those who sneer at this my city,
and I give them back the sneer and say to them:
10   Come and show me another city with lifted head singing so proud to be alive
and coarse and strong and cunning.
Flinging magnetic curses amid the toil of piling job on job, here is a tall bold
slugger set vivid against the little soft cities;
Fierce as a dog with tongue lapping for action, cunning as a savage pitted
against the wilderness,
Bareheaded,
Shoveling,
Wrecking,
Planning,
Building, breaking, rebuilding,
Under the smoke, dust all over his mouth, laughing with white teeth,
Under the terrible burden of destiny laughing as a young man laughs,
20   Laughing even as an ignorant fighter laughs who has never lost a battle,

Bragging and laughing that under his wrist is the pulse, and under his ribs the
   heart of the people,
                              Laughing!
Laughing the stormy, husky, brawling laughter of Youth, half-naked, sweating,
   proud to be Hog Butcher, Tool Maker, Stacker of Wheat, Player with
   Railroads and Freight Handler to the Nation.

Edward Thomas

Edward Thomas (1878 –1917) was Robert Frost's great English friend, a
freelance writer of prose whom Frost teased and encouraged into poetry.
Thomas came to poetry late, wrote furiously in his brief poetic life, and was
killed in World War I.

The Owl

Downhill I came, hungry, and yet not starved;
Cold, yet had heat within me that was proof
Against the North wind; tired, yet so that rest
Had seemed the sweetest thing under a roof.

Then at the inn I had food, fire, and rest,
Knowing how hungry, cold, and tired was I.
All of the night was quite barred out except
An owl's cry, a most melancholy cry

Shaken out long and clear upon the hill,
10   No merry note, nor cause of merriment,
But one telling me plain what I escaped
And others could not, that night, as in I went.

And salted was my food, and my repose,
Salted and sobered, too, by the bird's voice
Speaking for all who lay under the stars,
Soldiers and poor, unable to rejoice.

Vachel Lindsay

Vachel Lindsay (1879–1931) is best known for the long poems—like "General
William Booth Enters into Heaven" and "The Congo"—which he recited on
platforms with energy, showmanship, and pizzaz. His readings were popular,
his poetry successful for many years. Toward the end of his life, during the
Great Depression, he found it difficult to make a living. He had perhaps
published too much, too uncritically.

The Flower-Fed Buffaloes

The flower-fed buffaloes of the spring
In the days of long ago,
Ranged where the locomotives sing
And the prairie flowers lie low:—

The tossing, blooming, perfumed grass
Is swept away by the wheat,
Wheels and wheels and wheels spin by
In the spring that still is sweet.
But the flower-fed buffaloes of the spring
10   Left us, long ago.
They gore no more, they bellow no more,
They trundle around the hills no more:—
With the Blackfeet, lying low,
With the Pawnees, lying low,
Lying low.

Wallace Stevens

Wallace Stevens (1879–1955) is one of the finest of American poets. He
attended Harvard, tried his luck as a journalist, and went to New York
University Law School. After practicing some years in New York City, he took a
job with the legal department of Hartford Accident and Indemnity, an
insurance company, and eventually moved to Hartford, thus becoming known
as "the insurance man who is a poet." His poetry has a delicacy, a Frenchified
elegance, and a nice concern for matters epistemological. There seemed to
be a clear and sustained break between the poetry he wrote and the life he
lived. Perhaps they came together in Florida, which like many Connecticut
businessmen he visited every winter and which entered his poems as a place of
unsurpassable bright lushness.

The Emperor of Ice-Cream

Call the roller of big cigars,
The muscular one, and bid him whip
In kitchen cups concupiscent curds.
Let the wenches dawdle in such dress
As they are used to wear, and let the boys
Bring flowers in last month's newspapers.
Let be be finale of seem.
The only emperor is the emperor of ice-cream.

Take from the dresser of deal,
10   Lacking the three glass knobs, that sheet
On which she embroidered fantails once
And spread it so as to cover her face.
If her horny feet protrude, they come
To show how cold she is, and dumb.
Let the lamp affix its beam.
The only emperor is the emperor of ice-cream.

The Snow Man

One must have a mind of winter
To regard the frost and the boughs
Of the pine-trees crusted with snow;

And have been cold a long time
To behold the junipers shagged with ice,
The spruces rough in the distant glitter

Of the January sun; and not to think
Of any misery in the sound of the wind,
In the sound of a few leaves,

10 Which is the sound of the land
Full of the same wind
That is blowing in the same bare place

For the listener, who listens in the snow,
And, nothing himself, beholds
Nothing that is not there and the nothing that is.

Sunday Morning

I

Complacencies of the peignoir, and late
Coffee and oranges in a sunny chair,
And the green freedom of a cockatoo
Upon a rug mingle to dissipate
The holy hush of ancient sacrifice.
She dreams a little, and she feels the dark
Encroachment of that old catastrophe,
As a calm darkens among water-lights.
The pungent oranges and bright, green wings
10 Seem things in some procession of the dead,
Winding across wide water, without sound.
The day is like wide water, without sound,
Stilled for the passing of her dreaming feet
Over the seas, to silent Palestine,
Dominion of the blood and sepulchre.

II

Why should she give her bounty to the dead?
What is divinity if it can come
Only in silent shadows and in dreams?
Shall she not find in comforts of the sun,
20 In pungent fruit and bright, green wings, or else
In any balm or beauty of the earth,
Things to be cherished like the thought of heaven?
Divinity must live within herself:
Passions of rain, or moods in falling snow;
Grievings in loneliness, or unsubdued
Elations when the forest blooms; gusty
Emotions on wet roads on autumn nights;
All pleasures and all pains, remembering
The bough of summer and the winter branch.
30 These are the measures destined for her soul.

III

Jove in the clouds had his inhuman birth.
No mother suckled him, no sweet land gave
Large-mannered motions to his mythy mind
He moved among us, as a muttering king,
Magnificent, would move among his hinds,
Until our blood, commingling, virginal,
With heaven, brought such requital to desire
The very hinds discerned it, in a star.
Shall our blood fail? Or shall it come to be
40 The blood of paradise? And shall the earth
Seem all of paradise that we shall know?
The sky will be much friendlier then than now,
A part of labor and a part of pain,
And next in glory to enduring love,
Not this dividing and indifferent blue.

IV

She says, "I am content when wakened birds,
Before they fly, test the reality
Of misty fields, by their sweet questionings;
But when the birds are gone, and their warm fields
50 Return no more, where, then, is paradise?"
There is not any haunt of prophecy,
Nor any old chimera of the grave,
Neither the golden underground, nor isle
Melodious, where spirits gat them home,
Nor visionary south, nor cloudy palm
Remote on heaven's hill, that has endured
As April's green endures; or will endure
Like her remembrance of awakened birds,
Or her desire for June and evening, tipped
60 By the consummation of the swallow's wings.

V

She says, "But in contentment I still feel
The need of some imperishable bliss."
Death is the mother of beauty; hence from her,
Alone, shall come fulfilment to our dreams
And our desires. Although she strews the leaves
Of sure obliteration on our paths,
The path sick sorrow took, the many paths
Where triumph rang its brassy phrase, or love
Whispered a little out of tenderness,
70 She makes the willow shiver in the sun
For maidens who were wont to sit and gaze
Upon the grass, relinquished to their feet.
She causes boys to pile new plums and pears
On disregarded plate. The maidens taste
And stray impassioned in the littering leaves.

VI

Is there no change of death in paradise?
Does ripe fruit never fall? Or do the boughs
Hang always heavy in that perfect sky,
Unchanging, yet so like our perishing earth,
80   With rivers like our own that seek for seas
They never find, the same receding shores
That never touch with inarticulate pang?
Why set the pear upon those river-banks
Or spice the shores with odors of the plum?
Alas, that they should wear our colors there,
The silken weavings of our afternoons,
And pick the strings of our insipid lutes!
Death is the mother of beauty, mystical,
Within whose burning bosom we devise
90   Our earthly mothers waiting, sleeplessly.

VII

Supple and turbulent, a ring of men
Shall chant in orgy on a summer morn
Their boisterous devotion to the sun,
Not as a god, but as a god might be,
Naked among them, like a savage source
Their chant shall be a chant of paradise,
Out of their blood, returning to the sky;
And in their chant shall enter, voice by voice,
The windy lake wherein their lord delights,
100   The trees, like serafin, and echoing hills,
That choir among themselves long afterward.
They shall know well the heavenly fellowship
Of men that perish and of summer morn.
And whence they came and whither they shall go
The dew upon their feet shall manifest.

VIII

She hears, upon that water without sound,
A voice that cries, "The tomb in Palestine
Is not the porch of spirits lingering.
It is the grave of Jesus, where he lay."
110   We live in an old chaos of the sun,
Or old dependency of day and night,
Or island solitude, unsponsored, free,
Of that wide water, inescapable.
Deer walk upon our mountains, and the quail
Whistle about us their spontaneous cries;
Sweet berries ripen in the wilderness;
And, in the isolation of the sky,
At evening, casual flocks of pigeons make
Ambiguous undulations as they sink,
120   Downward to darkness, on extended wings.

William Carlos Williams

William Carlos Williams (1883–1963) knew Ezra Pound at the University of Pennsylvania when they were students. Williams went on to become a medical doctor, living most of his life in suburban Rutherford, New Jersey, where he practiced medicine, specializing in obstetrics. His poetry was resolute in its use of the American idiom. Followers have turned his theory and his practice into one of the main schools of contemporary American poetry.

This Is Just to Say

I have eaten
the plums
that were in
the icebox

and which
you were probably
saving
for breakfast

Forgive me
10   they were delicious
so sweet
and so cold

Spring and All

By the road to the contagious hospital
under the surge of the blue
mottled clouds driven from the
northeast—a cold wind. Beyond, the
waste of broad, muddy fields
brown with dried weeds, standing and fallen

patches of standing water
the scattering of tall trees

All along the road the reddish
10   purplish, forked, upstanding, twiggy
stuff of bushes and small trees
with dead, brown leaves under them
leafless vines—

Lifeless in appearance, sluggish
dazed spring approaches—

They enter the new world naked,
cold, uncertain of all
save that they enter. All about them
the cold, familiar wind—

20   Now the grass, tomorrow
the stiff curl of wildcarrot leaf

One by one objects are defined—
It quickens: clarity, outline of leaf

But now the stark dignity of
entrance—Still, the profound change
has come upon them: rooted they
grip down and begin to awaken

D. H. Lawrence

David Herbert Lawrence (1885–1930) was the son of a coalminer, born in a
working-class district of England. He wrote from an early age, and with the aid
of scholarships wrested himself away from his background to become a writer.
Best known as a novelist, especially for *The Rainbow, Women in Love,* and *Lady
Chatterley's Lover,* he was a great essayist, literary critic, writer of travel books,
letter-writer—and to some critics best of all as a poet. He died of tuberculosis,
having accomplished an enormous volume of work, before he turned forty-five.

The Song of a Man Who Has Come Through

Not I, not I, but the wind that blows through me!
A fine wind is blowing the new direction of Time.
If only I let it bear me, carry me, if only it carry me!
If only I am sensitive, subtle, oh, delicate, a winged gift!
If only, most lovely of all, I yield myself and am borrowed
By the fine, fine wind that takes its course through the chaos of the world
Like a fine, an exquisite chisel, a wedge-blade inserted;
If only I am keen and hard like the sheer tip of a wedge
Driven by invisible blows,
10   The rock will split, we shall come at the wonder, we shall find the Hesperides.[1]

Oh, for the wonder that bubbles into my soul,
I would be a good fountain, a good well-head,
Would blur no whisper, spoil no expression.

What is the knocking?
What is the knocking at the door in the night?
It is somebody wants to do us harm.

No, no, it is the three strange angels.
Admit them, admit them.

[1]In Greek mythology, sisters who protected a garden in which grew a tree bearing golden apples

Bavarian Gentians

Not every man has gentians in his house
In soft September, at slow, sad Michaelmas.

Bavarian gentians, tall and dark, but dark
darkening the daytime torch-like with the smoking blueness of Pluto's gloom,
ribbed hellish flowers erect, with their blaze of darkness spread blue,
blown flat into points, by the heavy white draught of the day.

Torch-flowers of the blue-smoking darkness, Pluto's dark-blue blaze
black lamps from the halls of Dis,[1] smoking dark blue
giving off darkness, blue darkness, upon Demeter's yellow-pale day
10   whom have you come for, here in the white-cast day?

Reach me a gentian, give me a torch!
let me guide myself with the blue, forked torch of a flower
down the darker and darker stairs, where blue is darkened on blueness
down the way Persephone goes, just now, in first-frosted September.
to the sightless realm where darkness is married to dark
and Persephone herself is but a voice, as a bride,
a gloom invisible enfolded in the deeper dark
of the arms of Pluto as he ravishes her once again
and pierces her once more with his passion of the utter dark
among the splendour of black-blue torches, shedding fathomless darkness on
20   the nuptials.

Give me a flower on a tall stem, and three dark flames,
for I will go to the wedding, and be wedding-guest
at the marriage of the living dark.

[1]Dis, Dispater, the Roman name for a deity who was the same as the Greek Pluto, god of the
underworld

Ezra Pound

Ezra Pound (1885–1972) was born in Idaho, but left as an infant and grew up
in the suburbs of Philadelphia. From an early age he determined to become
a great poet and set out to educate himself to that end. After graduate work
at the University of Pennsylvania he taught briefly at Wabash College in
Crawfordsville, Indiana. He was fired when he afforded a night's shelter to a
homeless dancing girl and left almost immediately for Europe, where he spent
most of the rest of his life. A young man of extraordinary generosity, he
discovered or promoted writers as diverse as Lawrence, Eliot, Joyce, and Frost.
And as a young man he was determinedly esthetic. After the First World War
killed off many friends—young artists of great promise—he became increasingly
embittered about social matters and turned paranoid. This development led
to his admiration for Benito Mussolini, the Italian dictator, and to the act of
broadcasting on Italian radio to American troops during the Second World War.
After the war, he was accused of treason but was judged mentally unfit to stand
trial. After many years in St. Elizabeth's Hospital in Washington, D.C., under
guard, he was released as an old man to return to Italy, where he lived out his
long life.

The River-Merchant's Wife: A Letter

While my hair was still cut straight across my forehead
I played about the front gate, pulling flowers.
You came by on bamboo stilts, playing horse,
You walked about my seat, playing with blue plums.
And we went on living in the village of Chokan:
Two small people, without dislike or suspicion.

At fourteen I married My Lord you.
I never laughed, being bashful.

Lowering my head, I looked at the wall.
10   Called to, a thousand times, I never looked back.

At fifteen I stopped scowling,
I desired my dust to be mingled with yours
For ever and for ever and for ever.
Why should I climb the look out?

At sixteen you departed,
You went into far Ku-to-yen, by the river of swirling eddies,
And you have been gone five months.
The monkeys make sorrowful noise overhead.

You dragged your feet when you went out.
20   By the gate now, the moss is grown, the different mosses,
Too deep to clear them away!
The leaves fall early this autumn, in wind.
The paired butterflies are already yellow with August
Over the grass in the West garden;
They hurt me. I grow older.
If you are coming down through the narrows of the river Kiang,
Please let me know beforehand,
And I will come out to meet you
                    As far as Cho-fu-Sa.   *(By Rihaku)*[1]

[1]The Japanese name for Chinese poet Li Po, who wrote the original

from Hugh Selwyn Mauberley

IV

These fought in any case,
and some believing,
          pro domo,[1] in any case . . .

Some quick to arm,
some for adventure,
some from fear of weakness,
some from fear of censure,
some for love of slaughter, in imagination,
learning later . . .
10   some in fear, learning love of slaughter;

Died some, pro patria,[1]
          non 'dulce' non 'et decor'[1] . . .
walked eye-deep in hell
believing in old men's lies, then unbelieving
came home, home to a lie,
home to many deceits,
home to old lies and new infamy;

[1]In Latin *pro domo* means "for home." Pound is alluding to a poem by the Roman poet Horace, whom he quotes (and later contradicts), who wrote that it is "sweet and fitting" (*dulce et decor* [*um*]) to die "for one's country" (*pro patria*).

usury age-old and age-thick
and liars in public places.

20 Daring as never before, wastage as never before.
Young blood and high blood,
fair cheeks, and fine bodies;

fortitude as never before

frankness as never before,
disillusions as never told in the old days,
hysterias, trench confessions,
laughter out of dead bellies.

V

There died a myriad,
And of the best, among them,
30 For an old bitch gone in the teeth,
For a botched civilization,

Charm, smiling at the good mouth,
Quick eyes gone under earth's lid,

For two gross of broken statues,
For a few thousand battered books.

H.D. (Hilda Doolittle)

Hilda Doolittle (1886–1961) attended Bryn Mawr College and knew William
Carlos Williams and Ezra Pound when all three poets were young. (It was at
Pound's suggestion that she began signing her poems with her initials only.)
She began as an imagist poet; later in life she wrote long philosophic poems.

Sea Rose

Rose, harsh rose,
marred and with stint of petals,
meagre flower, thin,
sparse of leaf,

more precious
than a wet rose,
single on a stem—
you are caught in the drift.

Stunted, with small leaf,
10 you are flung on the sand,
you are lifted
in the crisp sand
that drives in the wind.

Can the spice-rose
drip such acrid fragrance
hardened in a leaf?

Robinson Jeffers

Robinson Jeffers (1887–1962) settled with his family in California when he was sixteen years old. His third book, *Tamar and Other Poems* (1924), brought him to readers' attention. As he grew older he became progressively more misanthropic, with a passionate and romantic love for the natural world, which found man pathetic and inadequate in comparison to its natural grandeurs. He built his own house out of stone in Carmel.

Hurt Hawks

I

The broken pillar of the wing jags from the clotted shoulder,
The wing trails like a banner in defeat,
No more to use the sky forever but live with famine
And pain a few days: cat nor coyote
Will shorten the week of waiting for death, there is game without talons.
He stands under the oak-bush and waits
The lame feet of salvation; at night he remembers freedom
And flies in a dream, the dawns ruin it.
He is strong and pain is worse to the strong, incapacity is worse.
10 The curs of the day come and torment him
At distance, no one but death the redeemer will humble that head,
The intrepid readiness, the terrible eyes.
The wild God of the world is sometimes merciful to those
That ask mercy, not often to the arrogant,
You do not know him, you communal people, or you have forgotten him;
Intemperate and savage, the hawk remembers him;
Beautiful and wild, the hawks, and men that are dying, remember him.

II

I'd sooner, except the penalties, kill a man than a hawk; but the great
    redtail[1]
Had nothing left but unable misery
From the bone too shattered for mending, the wing that trailed under his talons
20   when he moved.
We had fed him six weeks, I gave him freedom,
He wandered over the foreland hill and returned in the evening, asking for
    death,
Not like a beggar, still eyed with the old
Implacable arrogance. I gave him the lead gift in the twilight. What fell was
    relaxed,
Owl-downy, soft feminine feathers; but what
Soared: the fierce rush: the night-herons by the flooded river cried fear at its
    rising
Before it was quite unsheathed from reality.

[1]Red-tailed hawk

Marianne Moore

Marianne Moore (1887–1972) was born in St. Louis, graduated from Bryn Mawr, and taught school in Pennsylvania, but lived most of her life in Brooklyn. As editor of *The Dial* from 1925 to 1929 she published many of the best modern poets. Her own poems are original and even eccentric. Her intricate descriptions are scrupulous in detail, shaped into prosaic lines that achieve a singular music.

A Grave

Man looking into the sea,
taking the view from those who have as much right to it as you have to it
    yourself,
it is human nature to stand in the middle of a thing,
but you cannot stand in the middle of this;
the sea has nothing to give but a well excavated grave.
The firs stand in a procession, each with an emerald turkey foot at the top,
reserved as their contours, saying nothing;
repression, however, is not the most obvious characteristic of the sea;
the sea is a collector, quick to return a rapacious look.
There are others besides you who have worn that look—
whose expression is no longer a protest; the fish no longer investigate them
for their bones have not lasted:
men lower nets, unconscious of the fact that they are desecrating a grave,
and row quickly away—the blades of the oars
moving together like the feet of water spiders as if there were no such thing as
    death.
The wrinkles progress among themselves in a phalanx—beautiful under
    networks of foam,
and fade breathlessly while the sea rustles in and out of the seaweed;
the birds swim through the air at top speed, emitting catcalls as heretofore—
the tortoise shell scourges about the feet of the cliffs, in motion beneath them;
and the ocean, under the pulsation of lighthouses and noise of bell buoys,
advances as usual, looking as if it were not that ocean in which dropped things
    are bound to sink—
in which if they turn and twist, it is neither with volition nor consciousness.

Edwin Muir

Edwin Muir (1887–1959) was born in the Orkneys, off the coast of Scotland. After his father was evicted from an island farm, young Muir grew up in the slums of Glasgow. His poetry built upon the contrast between the pastoral and the industrial. He and his wife Willa lived by their wits most of their lives, and are Kafka's translators. Muir is author of an excellent *Autobiography* as well as the neglected *Collected Poems*.

The Horses

Barely a twelvemonth after
The seven days war that put the world to sleep,
Late in the evening the strange horses came.

By then we had made our covenant with silence,
But in the first few days it was so still
We listened to our breathing and were afraid.
On the second day
The radios failed; we turned the knobs; no answer.
On the third day a warship passed us, heading north,
10   Dead bodies piled on the deck. On the sixth day
A plane plunged over us into the sea. Thereafter
Nothing. The radios dumb;
And still they stand in corners of our kitchens,
And stand, perhaps, turned on, in a million rooms
All over the world. But now if they should speak,
If on a sudden they should speak again,
If on the stroke of noon a voice should speak,
We would not listen, we would not let it bring
That old bad world that swallowed its children quick
20   At one great gulp. We would not have it again.
Sometimes we think of the nations lying asleep,
Curled blindly in impenetrable sorrow,
And then the thought confounds us with its strangeness.
The tractors lie about our fields; at evening
They look like dank sea-monsters couched and waiting.
We leave them where they are and let them rust:
'They'll moulder away and be like other loam.'
We make our oxen drag our rusty ploughs,
Long laid aside. We have gone back
30   Far past our fathers' land.
                                And then, that evening
Late in the summer the strange horses came.
We heard a distant tapping on the road,
A deepening drumming; it stopped, went on again
And at the corner changed to hollow thunder.
We saw the heads
Like a wild wave charging and were afraid.
We had sold our horses in our fathers' time
To buy new tractors. Now they were strange to us
40   As fabulous steeds set on an ancient shield
Or illustrations in a book of knights.
We did not dare go near them. Yet they waited,
Stubborn and shy, as if they had been sent
By an old command to find our whereabouts
And that long-lost archaic companionship.
In the first moment we had never a thought
That they were creatures to be owned and used.
Among them were some half-a-dozen colts
Dropped in some wilderness of the broken world,
50   Yet new as if they had come from their own Eden.
Since then they have pulled our ploughs and borne our loads
But that free servitude still can pierce our hearts.
Our life is changed; their coming our beginning.

T. S. Eliot

Thomas Stearns Eliot (1888–1965) was born in St. Louis, Missouri, into a family two generations removed from Boston that had created its own small Boston in St. Louis. Eliot went to prep school in Massachusetts, to Harvard, and then abroad. After some time in Europe on fellowships (he expected to finish a doctorate in philosophy at Harvard) he married an Englishwoman and settled in England, dedicating himself to the life of a poet. For a time he taught school, for a longer time he worked in a bank, and finally he became a publisher, overseer of the best poetry list in England, at Faber & Faber. His early work, derived largely from French sources, was notable for its irony and for the desolation of its landscape. This work culminated in the great modernist poem *The Waste Land* in 1922. Toward the end of that decade, Eliot converted to Anglo-Catholicism and most of the rest of his poetry was dedicated to exploring the implications of conversion. "Journey of the Magi" is one record. *The Four Quartets* is the last of his great work in poetry, though he wrote verse plays for the West End and Broadway afterward, with success more commercial than poetical. He was awarded the Nobel Prize in 1948, was widely celebrated as a critic, and was the leading literary figure of the English-speaking world during the first half of the twentieth century.

The Love Song of J. Alfred Prufrock

S'io credesse che mia risposta fosse
A persona che mai tornasse al mondo,
Questa fiamma staria senza piu scosse.
Ma perciocche giammai di questo fondo
Non torno vivo alcun, s'i'odo il vero,
Senza tema d'infamia ti rispondo.[1]

Let us go then, you and I,
When the evening is spread out against the sky
Like a patient etherized upon a table;
Let us go, through certain half-deserted streets,
The muttering retreats
Of restless nights in one-night cheap hotels
And sawdust restaurants with oyster-shells:
Streets that follow like a tedious argument
Of insidious intent
10 To lead you to an overwhelming question . . .
Oh, do not ask, "What is it?"
Let us go and make our visit.

In the room the women come and go
Talking of Michelangelo.

The yellow fog that rubs its back upon the window-panes,
The yellow smoke that rubs its muzzle on the window-panes
Licked its tongue into the corners of the evening,

---

[1]The Italian epigraph, from Dante's *Inferno*, is the speech of one who is dead and damned, whose punishment is to be wrapped in a constantly burning flame. He believes his hearer also will remain in Hell and thus says: "If I thought my reply were to someone who could ever return to the world, this flame would waver no more [i.e., I would speak no more]. But since, I'm told, nobody ever escapes from this pit, I'll tell you without fear of ill fame."

Lingered upon the pools that stand in drains,
Let fall upon its back the soot that falls from chimneys,
20   Slipped by the terrace, made a sudden leap,
And seeing that it was a soft October night,
Curled once about the house, and fell asleep.

And indeed there will be time
For the yellow smoke that slides along the street,
Rubbing its back upon the window-panes;
There will be time, there will be time
To prepare a face to meet the faces that you meet;
There will be time to murder and create,
And time for all the works and days of hands
30   That lift and drop a question on your plate;
Time for you and time for me,
And time yet for a hundred indecisions,
And for a hundred visions and revisions,
Before the taking of a toast and tea.

In the room the women come and go
Talking of Michelangelo.

And indeed there will be time
To wonder, "Do I dare?" and, "Do I dare?"
Time to turn back and descend the stair,
40   With a bald spot in the middle of my hair—
[They will say: "How his hair is growing thin!"]
My morning coat, my collar mounting firmly to the chin,
My necktie rich and modest, but asserted by a simple pin—
[They will say: "But how his arms and legs are thin!"]
Do I dare
Disturb the universe?
In a minute there is time
For decisions and revisions which a minute will reverse.

For I have known them all already, known them all:—
50   Have known the evenings, mornings, afternoons,
I have measured out my life with coffee spoons;
I know the voices dying with a dying fall
Beneath the music from a farther room.
    So how should I presume?

And I have known the eyes already, known them all—
The eyes that fix you in a formulated phrase,
And when I am formulated, sprawling on a pin,
When I am pinned and wriggling on the wall,
Then how should I begin
60   To spit out all the butt-ends of my days and ways?
    And how should I presume?

And I have known the arms already, known them all—
Arms that are braceleted and white and bare
[But in the lamplight, downed with light brown hair!]

Is it perfume from a dress
That makes me so digress?
Arms that lie along a table, or wrap about a shawl.
   And should I then presume?
   And how should I begin?

     . . . . .

70   Shall I say, I have gone at dusk through narrow streets
And watched the smoke that rises from the pipes
Of lonely men in shirt-sleeves, leaning out of windows? . . .

   I should have been a pair of ragged claws
Scuttling across the floors of silent seas.

     . . . . .

And the afternoon, the evening, sleeps so peacefully!
Smoothed by long fingers,
Asleep . . . tired . . . or it malingers,
Stretched on the floor, here beside you and me.
Should I, after tea and cakes and ices,
80   Have the strength to force the moment to its crisis?
But though I have wept and fasted, wept and prayed,
Though I have seen my head [grown slightly bald] brought in upon a platter,
I am no prophet—and here's no great matter;
I have seen the moment of my greatness flicker,
And I have seen the eternal Footman hold my coat, and snicker,
And in short, I was afraid.

   And would it have been worth it, after all,
After the cups, the marmalade, the tea,
Among the porcelain, among some talk of you and me,
90   Would it have been worth while,
To have bitten off the matter with a smile,
To have squeezed the universe into a ball
To roll it toward some overwhelming question,
To say: "I am Lazarus, come from the dead,
Come back to tell you all, I shall tell you all"—
If one, settling a pillow by her head,
   Should say: "That is not what I meant at all.
   That is not it, at all."

   And would it have been worth it, after all,
100   Would it have been worth while,
After the sunsets and the dooryards and the sprinkled streets,
After the novels, after the teacups, after the skirts that trail along the floor—
And this, and so much more?—
It is impossible to say just what I mean!
But as if a magic lantern threw the nerves in patterns on a screen:
Would it have been worth while
If one, settling a pillow or throwing off a shawl,
And turning toward the window, should say:
   "That is not it at all,
110   That is not what I meant, at all."

. . . . .

No! I am not Prince Hamlet, nor was meant to be;
Am an attendant lord, one that will do
To swell a progress, start a scene or two,
Advise the prince; no doubt, an easy tool,
Deferential, glad to be of use,
Politic, cautious, and meticulous;
Full of high sentence, but a bit obtuse;
At times, indeed, almost ridiculous—
Almost, at times, the Fool.

120   I grow old . . . I grow old . . .
I shall wear the bottoms of my trousers rolled.

Shall I part my hair behind? Do I dare to eat a peach?
I shall wear white flannel trousers, and walk upon the beach.
I have heard the mermaids singing, each to each.

I do not think that they will sing to me.

I have seen them riding seaward on the waves
Combing the white hair of the waves blown back
When the wind blows the water white and black.

We have lingered in the chambers of the sea
130   By sea-girls wreathed with seaweed red and brown
Till human voices wake us, and we drown.

Journey of the Magi

'A cold coming we had of it,
Just the worst time of the year
For a journey, and such a long journey:
The ways deep and the weather sharp,
The very dead of winter.'
And the camels galled, sore-footed, refractory,
Lying down in the melting snow.
There were times we regretted
The summer palaces on slopes, the terraces,
10   And the silken girls bringing sherbet.
Then the camel men cursing and grumbling
And running away, and wanting their liquor and women,
And the night-fires going out, and the lack of shelters,
And the cities hostile and the towns unfriendly
And the villages dirty and charging high prices:
A hard time we had of it.
At the end we preferred to travel all night,
Sleeping in snatches,
With the voices singing in our ears, saying
20   That this was all folly.

Then at dawn we came down to a temperate valley,
Wet, below the snow line, smelling of vegetation;
With a running stream and a water-mill beating the darkness,

And three trees on the low sky,
And an old white horse galloped away in the meadow.
Then we came to a tavern with vine-leaves over the lintel,
Six hands at an open door dicing for pieces of silver,
And feet kicking the empty wine-skins.
But there was no information, and so we continued
30   And arrived at evening, not a moment too soon
Finding the place; it was (you may say) satisfactory.

     All this was a long time ago, I remember,
And I would do it again, but set down
This set down
This: were we led all that way for
Birth or Death? There was a Birth, certainly,
We had evidence and no doubt. I had seen birth and death,
But had thought they were different; this Birth was
Hard and bitter agony for us, like Death, our death.
40   We returned to our places, these Kingdoms,
But no longer at ease here, in the old dispensation,
With an alien people clutching their gods.
I should be glad of another death.

John Crowe Ransom

John Crowe Ransom (1888–1974) grew up in Tennessee and was a Rhodes
scholar at Oxford. A leader in the Agrarian movement (a group of Southern
writers in the late 1920s and the 1930s) he went to Kenyon College as a
professor in 1937, edited the highly successful *Kenyon Review*, and wrote
criticism as well as poetry.

Captain Carpenter

Captain Carpenter rose up in his prime
Put on his pistols and went riding out
But had got wellnigh nowhere at that time
Till he fell in with ladies in a rout.

It was a pretty lady and all her train
That played with him so sweetly but before
An hour she'd taken a sword with all her main
And twined him of his nose for evermore.

Captain Carpenter mounted up one day
10   And rode straightway into a stranger rogue
That looked unchristian but be that as may
The Captain did not wait upon prologue.

But drew upon him out of his great heart
The other swung against him with a club
And cracked his two legs at the shinny part
And let him roll and stick like any tub.

Captain Carpenter rode many a time
From male and female took he sundry harms
He met the wife of Satan crying "I'm
20   The she-wolf bids you shall bear no more arms."

Their strokes and counters whistled in the wind
I wish he had delivered half his blows
But where she should have made off like a hind
The bitch bit off his arms at the elbows.

And Captain Carpenter parted with his ears
To a black devil that used him in this wise
O Jesus ere his threescore and ten years
Another had plucked out his sweet blue eyes.

Captain Carpenter got up on his roan
30   And sallied from the gate in hell's despite
I heard him asking in the grimmest tone
If any enemy yet there was to fight?

"To any adversary it is fame
If he risk to be wounded by my tongue
Or burnt in two beneath my red heart's flame
Such are the perils he is cast among.

"But if he can he has a pretty choice
From an anatomy with little to lose
Whether he cut my tongue and take my voice
40   Or whether it be my round red heart he choose."

It was the neatest knave that ever was seen
Stepping in perfume from his lady's bower
Who at this word put in his merry mien
And fell on Captain Carpenter like a tower.

I would not knock old fellows in the dust
But there lay Captain Carpenter on his back
His weapons were the old heart in his bust
And a blade shook between rotten teeth alack.

The rogue in scarlet and grey soon knew his mind
50   He wished to get his trophy and depart
With gentle apology and touch refined
He pierced him and produced the Captain's heart.

God's mercy rest on Captain Carpenter now
I thought him Sirs an honest gentlemen
Citizen husband soldier and scholar enow
Let jangling kites eat of him if they can.

But God's deep curses follow after those
That shore him of his goodly nose and ears
His legs and strong arms at the two elbows
60   And eyes that had not watered seventy years.

The curse of hell upon the sleek upstart
That got the Captain finally on his back
And took the red red vitals of his heart
And made the kites to whet their beaks clack clack.

Archibald MacLeish

Archibald MacLeish (1892–   ) attended Yale, went to law school at Harvard, practiced law briefly, and then moved to France as an American expatriate in the 1920s. When the Depression hit the United States he returned to this country, where he became increasingly political. He worked for *Fortune*, wrote on political subjects, and eventually allied himself with President Franklin D. Roosevelt. He was Librarian of Congress, and toward the end of Roosevelt's life became an Assistant Secretary of State. When Roosevelt died, MacLeish left government. He taught at Harvard for some years, beginning in 1949, and returned to the writing of poetry.

You, Andrew Marvell

And here face down beneath the sun
And here upon earth's noonward height
To feel the always coming on
The always rising of the night:

To feel creep up the curving east
The earthy chill of dusk and slow
Upon those under lands the vast
And ever climbing shadow grow

And strange at Ecbatan the trees
10   Take leaf by leaf the evening strange
The flooding dark about their knees
The mountains over Persia change

And now at Kermanshah the gate
Dark empty and the withered grass
And through the twilight now the late
Few travelers in the westward pass

And Baghdad darken and the bridge
Across the silent river gone
And through Arabia the edge
20   Of evening widen and steal on

And deepen on Palmyra's street
The wheel rut in the ruined stone
And Lebanon fade out and Crete
High through the clouds and overblown

And over Sicily the air
Still flashing with the landward gulls
And loom and slowly disappear
The sails above the shadowy hulls

And Spain go under and the shore
30   Of Africa the gilded sand
And evening vanish and no more
The low pale light across that land

Nor now the long light on the sea:

And here face downward in the sun
To feel how swift how secretly
The shadow of the night comes on . . .

Wilfred Owen

Wilfred Owen (1893–1918) was a poet of the First World War. Like most young
Englishmen in 1914, he had cherished a romantic notion of battle. He lived
long enough—before the war killed him, just a few days before the armistice—
to write bitter and antiromantic poems of real modern war.

Dulce et Decorum Est[1]

Bent double, like old beggars under sacks,
Knock-kneed, coughing like hags, we cursed through sludge,
Till on the haunting flares we turned our backs,
And towards our distant rest began to trudge.
Men marched asleep. Many had lost their boots,
But limped on, blood-shod. All went lame, all blind;
Drunk with fatigue; deaf even to the hoots
Of gas-shells dropping softly behind.

Gas! Gas! Quick, boys!—An ecstasy of fumbling,
10   Fitting the clumsy helmets just in time,
But someone still was yelling out and stumbling
And floundering like a man in fire or lime.—
Dim through the misty panes and thick green light,
As under a green sea, I saw him drowning.

In all my dreams before my helpless sight
He plunges at me, guttering, choking, drowning.

If in some smothering dreams, you too could pace
Behind the wagon that we flung him in,
And watch the white eyes writhing in his face,
20   His hanging face, like a devil's sick of sin;
If you could hear, at every jolt, the blood
Come gargling from the froth-corrupted lungs,
Bitter as the cud
Of vile, incurable sores on innocent tongues,—
My friend, you would not tell with such high zest
To children ardent for some desperate glory,
The old Lie: Dulce et decorum est
Pro patria mori.[1]

[1]The Roman poet Horace wrote that it "is sweet and fitting" (*dulce et decorum est*) "to die for
one's country" (*pro patria mori*).

E. E. Cummings

Edward Estlin Cummings (1894–1962) grew up in Cambridge, Massachusetts, and attended Harvard before becoming a volunteer ambulance driver in the First World War. He wrote a prose book about this experience, *The Enormous Room*, and began to publish books of poems in 1923. His typographical innovations tended to conceal a diction which, much of the time, was traditional and romantic. The bitter humor of his satires proved his best work in poetry.

Poem, or Beauty Hurts Mr. Vinal

take it from me kiddo
believe me
my country, 'tis of

you, land of the Cluett
Shirt Boston Garter and Spearmint
Girl With The Wrigley Eyes(of you
land of the Arrow Ide
and Earl &
Wilson
10   Collars) of you i
sing:land of Abraham Lincoln and Lydia E. Pinkham,
land above all of Just Add Hot Water And Serve—
from every B.V.D.

let freedom ring

amen. i do however protest, anent the un
-spontaneous and otherwise scented merde which
greets one (Everywhere Why) as divine poesy per
that and this radically defunct periodical. i would
suggest that certain ideas gestures
20   rhymes, like Gillette Razor Blades
having been used and reused
to the mystical moment of dullness emphatically are
Not To Be Resharpened.(Case in point

if we are to believe these gently O sweetly
melancholy trillers amid the thrillers
these crepuscular violinists among my and your
skyscrapers—Helen & Cleopatra were Just Too Lovely,
The Snail's On The Thorn enter Morn and God's
In His andsoforth

30   do you get me?)according
to such supposedly indigenous
throstles Art is O World O Life
a formula:example, Turn Your Shirttails Into
Drawers and If It Isn't An Eastman It Isn't A
Kodak therefore my friends let
us now sing each and all fortissimo A-
mer
i

ca, I
40   love,
You. And there're a
hun-dred-mil-lion-oth-ers, like
all of you successfully if
delicately gelded(or spaded)
gentlemen(and ladies)—pretty

littleliverpill-
hearted-Nujolneeding-There's-A-Reason
americans(who tensetendoned and with
upward vacant eyes, painfully
50   perpetually crouched, quivering, upon the
sternly allotted sandpile
—how silently
emit a tiny violetflavored nuisance:Odor?

ono.
comes out like a ribbon lies flat on the brush

next to of course god america i

"next to of course god america i
love you land of the pilgrims' and so forth oh
say can you see by the dawn's early my
country 'tis of centuries come and go
and are no more what of it we should worry
in every language even deafanddumb
thy sons acclaim your glorious name by gorry
by jingo by gee by gosh by gum
why talk of beauty what could be more beaut-
10   iful than these heroic happy dead
who rushed like lions to the roaring slaughter
they did not stop to think they died instead
then shall the voices of liberty be mute?"

He spoke. And drank rapidly a glass of water

Charles Reznikoff

Charles Reznikoff (1894–1975), a leading Objectivist poet, was born in New
York City, where he lived most of his life. He wrote poems about the people he
observed in the place where he lived. He also wrote some excellent poems out
of his reading about American labor history, about the holocaust, and about
biblical subjects.

A Deserter

Their new landlord was a handsome man. On his rounds to collect rent she
      became friendly
Finally, she asked him in to have a cup of tea. After that he came often.

Once his mouth jerked, and turning, she saw her husband in the doorway.
She thought, One of the neighbors must have told him.
She smiled and opened her mouth to speak, but could say nothing.
Her husband stood looking at the floor. He turned and went away.

She lay awake all night waiting for him.
In the morning she went to his store. It was closed.
She sent for his brothers and told them he had not been home.
10   They went to the police. Hospitals and morgues were
        searched. For weeks they were called to identify drowned men.

His business had been prosperous; bank account and all were untouched. She
    and their baby girl were provided for.
In a few years they heard of him. He was dead.
He had been making a poor living in a far off city. One day he stepped in front of
    a street-car and was killed.
She married again. Her daughter married and had children. She named none
    after her father.

Jean Toomer

Jean Toomer (1894–1967) wrote in *Cane* a combination of poetry and prose
that was an early contribution to the literature of the black American.

Reapers

Black reapers with the sound of steel on stones
Are sharpening scythes. I see them place the hones
In their hip-pockets as a thing that's done,
And start their silent swinging, one by one.
Black horses drive a mower through the weeds,
And there, a field rat, startled, squealing bleeds,
His belly close to ground. I see the blade,
Blood-stained, continue cutting weeds and shade.

Robert Graves

Robert Graves (1895–   ) fought in the First World War directly upon
graduation from English public school. He was one of the survivors, and later
wrote, in his autobiographical *Good-Bye to All That,* one of the great accounts of
that war. He has written many novels, including *I, Claudius,* and collections
of essays and humor, but he has been first and foremost a poet throughout a
long and prolific career. His mythic system, concerned with the muse of poetry,
was described in *The White Goddess,* and he has remained faithful to his Muse
through many poems, revised many times, in the many volumes of his *Collected
Poems.*

In Broken Images

He is quick, thinking in clear images;
I am slow, thinking in broken images.

He becomes dull, trusting to his clear images;
I become sharp, mistrusting my broken images.

Trusting his images, he assumes their relevance;
Mistrusting my images, I question their relevance.

Assuming their relevance, he assumes the fact;
Questioning their relevance, I question the fact.

When the fact fails him, he questions his senses;
10   When the fact fails me, I approve my senses.

He continues quick and dull in his clear images;
I continue slow and sharp in my broken images.

He in a new confusion of his understanding;
I in a new understanding of my confusion.

To Juan at the Winter Solstice

There is one story and one story only
That will prove worth your telling,
Whether as learned bard or gifted child;
To it all lines or lesser gauds belong
That startle with their shining
Such common stories as they stray into.

Is it of trees you tell, their months and virtues,
Or strange beasts that beset you,
Of birds that croak at you the Triple will?
10   Or of the Zodiac and how slow it turns
Below the Boreal Crown,
Prison of all true kings that ever reigned?

Water to water, ark again to ark,
From woman back to woman:
So each new victim treads unfalteringly
The never altered circuit of his fate,
Bringing twelve peers as witness
Both to his starry rise and starry fall.

Or is it of the Virgin's silver beauty,
20   All fish below the thighs?
She in her left hand bears a leafy quince;
When with her right she crooks a finger, smiling,
How may the King hold back?
Royally then he barters life for love.

Or of the undying snake from chaos hatched,
Whose coils contain the ocean,
Into whose chops with naked sword he springs,
Then in black water, tangled by the reeds,
Battles three days and nights,
30   To be spewed up beside her scalloped shore?

Much snow is falling, winds roar hollowly,
The owl hoots from the elder,
Fear in your heart cries to the loving-cup:

Sorrow to sorrow as the sparks fly upward.
The log groans and confesses:
There is one story and one story only.

Dwell on her graciousness, dwell on her smiling,
Do not forget what flowers
The great boar trampled down in ivy time.
40   Her brow was creamy as the crested wave,
Her sea-grey eyes were wild
But nothing promised that is not performed.

Louise Bogan

Louise Bogan (1897–1970) was born in Maine and lived most of her life in New York City. She was an excellent critic, her letters and journals extraordinary—and her poems were few, spare, and perfect.

Cartography

As you lay in sleep
I saw the chart
Of artery and vein
Running from your heart,

Plain as the strength
Marked upon the leaf
Along the length,
Mortal and brief,

Of your gaunt hand.
10   I saw it clear:
The wiry brand
Of the life we bear

Mapped like the great
Rivers that rise
Beyond our fate
And distant from our eyes.

Hart Crane

Hart Crane (1899–1932) published his first book of poems, *White Buildings,* in 1926.
The Bridge (1930), a long poem centering on the Brooklyn Bridge, was an attempt
to provide a myth of America. Alcoholic and homosexual, prone to binges and fights,
Crane lived a short and turbulent life, ended by suicide when he jumped from a ship
taking him from Mexico back to New York in 1932.

from The Bridge

To Brooklyn Bridge

How many dawns, chill from his rippling rest
The seagull's wings shall dip and pivot him,
Shedding white rings of tumult, building high
Over the chained bay waters Liberty—

Then, with inviolate curve, forsake our eyes
As apparitional as sails that cross
Some page of figures to be filed away;
—Till elevators drop us from our day . . .

I think of cinemas, panoramic sleights
10   With multitudes bent toward some flashing scene
Never disclosed, but hastened to again,
Foretold to other eyes on the same screen;

And Thee, across the harbor, silver-paced
As though the sun took step of thee, yet left
Some motion ever unspent in thy stride,—
Implicitly thy freedom staying thee!

Out of some subway scuttle, cell or loft
A bedlamite speeds to thy parapets,
Tilting there momently, shrill shirt ballooning,
20   A jest falls from the speechless caravan.

Down Wall, from girder into street noon leaks,
A rip-tooth of the sky's acetylene;
All afternoon the cloud-flown derricks turn . . .
Thy cables breathe the North Atlantic still.

And obscure as that heaven of the Jews,
Thy guerdon . . . Accolade thou dost bestow
Of anonymity time cannot raise:
Vibrant reprieve and pardon thou dost show.

O harp and altar, of the fury fused,
30   (How could mere toil align thy choiring strings!)
Terrific threshold of the prophet's pledge,
Prayer of pariah, and the lover's cry,—

Again the traffic lights that skim thy swift
Unfractioned idiom, immaculate sigh of stars,
Beading thy path—condense eternity:
And we have seen night lifted in thine arms.

Under thy shadow by the piers I waited;
Only in darkness is thy shadow clear.
The City's fiery parcels all undone,
40   Already snow submerges an iron year . . .

O Sleepless as the river under thee,
Vaulting the sea, the prairies' dreaming sod,
Unto us lowliest sometime sweep, descend
And of the curveship lend a myth to God.

from Voyages

II

And yet this great wink of eternity,
Of rimless floods, unfettered leewardings,
Samite sheeted and processioned where
Her undinal vast belly moonward bends,
Laughing the wrapt inflections of our love;

Take this Sea, whose diapason knells
On scrolls of silver snowy sentences,
The sceptred terror of whose sessions rends
As her demeanors motion well or ill,
10   All but the pieties of lovers' hands.

And onward, as bells off San Salvador
Salute the crocus lustres of the stars,
In these poinsettia meadows of her tides,—
Adagios of islands, O my Prodigal,
Complete the dark confessions her veins spell.

Mark how her turning shoulders wind the hours,
And hasten while her penniless rich palms
Pass superscription of bent foam and wave,—
Hasten, while they are true,—sleep, death, desire,
20   Close round one instant in one floating flower.

Bind us in time, O Seasons clear, and awe.
O minstrel galleons of Carib fire,
Bequeath us to no earthly shore until
Is answered in the vortex of our grave
The seal's wide spindrift gaze toward paradise.

Allen Tate

Allen Tate (1899–1979) was born in Kentucky and attended Vanderbilt University in Nashville, Tennessee. He was a founding editor of *The Fugitive* and, along with John Crowe Ransom, a leader of the Southern writers called the Fugitive Group. Best known as a poet, Tate was also one of the most prominent critics of an era labeled The Age of Criticism in the American 1930s and 1940s.

In connection with this poem see "For the Union Dead" (pages 298–299) by Tate's younger friend from New England, Robert Lowell.

Ode to the Confederate Dead

Row after row with strict impunity
The headstones yield their names to the element,
The wind whirrs without recollection;
In the riven troughs the splayed leaves
Pile up, of nature the casual sacrament
To the seasonal eternity of death;
Then driven by the fierce scrutiny
Of heaven to their election in the vast breath,
They sough the rumour of mortality.

10   Autumn is desolation in the plot
Of a thousand acres where these memories grow
From the inexhaustible bodies that are not
Dead, but feed the grass row after rich row.
Think of the autumns that have come and gone!—
Ambitious November with the humors of the year,
With a particular zeal for every slab,
Staining the uncomfortable angels that rot
On the slabs, a wing chipped here, an arm there:
The brute curiosity of an angel's stare
20   Turns you, like them, to stone,
Transforms the heaving air
Till plunged to a heavier world below
You shift your sea-space blindly
Heaving, turning like the blind crab.

Dazed by the wind, only the wind
The leaves flying, plunge

You know who have waited by the wall
The twilight certainty of an animal,
Those midnight restitutions of the blood
30   You know—the immitigable pines, the smoky frieze
Of the sky, the sudden call: you know the rage,
The cold pool left by the mounting flood,
Of muted Zeno and Parmenides.
You who have waited for the angry resolution
Of those desires that should be yours tomorrow,
You know the unimportant shrift of death

And praise the vision
And praise the arrogant circumstance
Of those who fall
40 Rank upon rank, hurried beyond decision—
Here by the sagging gate, stopped by the wall.

    Seeing, seeing only the leaves
    Flying, plunge and expire

Turn your eyes to the immoderate past,
Turn to the inscrutable infantry rising
Demons out of the earth—they will not last.
Stonewall, Stonewall, and the sunken fields of hemp,
Shiloh, Antietam, Malvern Hill, Bull Run.
Lost in that orient of the thick-and-fast
50 You will curse the setting sun.

    Cursing only the leaves crying
    Like an old man in a storm

You hear the shout, the crazy hemlocks point
With troubled fingers to the silence which
Smothers you, a mummy, in time.
                The hound bitch
Toothless and dying, in a musty cellar
Hears the wind only.
             Now that the salt of their blood
60 Stiffens the saltier oblivion of the sea,
Seals the malignant purity of the flood,
What shall we who count our days and bow
Our heads with a commemorial woe
In the ribboned coats of grim felicity,
What shall we say of the bones, unclean,
Whose verdurous anonymity will grow?
The ragged arms, the ragged heads and eyes
Lost in these acres of the insane green?
The gray lean spiders come, they come and go;
70 In a tangle of willows without light
The singular screech-owl's tight
Invisible lyric seeds the mind
With the furious murmur of their chivalry.

    We shall say only the leaves
    Flying, plunge and expire

We shall say only the leaves whispering
In the improbable mist of nightfall
That flies on multiple wing;
Night is the beginning and the end

80   And in between the ends of distraction
      Waits mute speculation, the patient curse
      That stones the eyes, or like the jaguar leaps
      For his own image in a jungle pool, his victim.
      What shall we say who have knowledge
      Carried to the heart? Shall we take the act
      To the grave? Shall we, more hopeful, set up the grave
      In the house? The ravenous grave?

                                        Leave now
      The shut gate and the decomposing wall:
90   The gentle serpent, green in the mulberry bush,
      Riots with his tongue through the hush—
      Sentinel of the grave who counts us all!

Mr. Pope

      When Alexander Pope strolled in the city
      Strict was the glint of pearl and gold sedans.
      Ladies leaned out more out of fear than pity
      For Pope's tight back was rather a goat's than man's.

      Often one thinks the urn should have more bones
      Than skeletons provide for speedy dust,
      The urn gets hollow, cobwebs brittle as stones
      Weave to the funeral shell a frivolous rust.

      And he who dribbled couplets like a snake
10   Coiled to a lithe precision in the sun
      Is missing. The jar is empty; you may break
      It only to find that Mr. Pope is gone.

      What requisitions of a verity
      Prompted the wit and rage between his teeth
      One cannot say. Around a crooked tree
      A moral climbs whose name should be a wreath.

Robert Francis

Robert Francis (1901–   ) has lived most of his life in Massachusetts, mostly in a house called Fort Juniper in the countryside outside Amherst. He has written an autobiography, some fiction, and some satirical prose. A poet of reticence and quiet, he has lived without much attention from critics and prizegivers, writing his finished poems one at a time.

Three Woodchoppers

      Three woodchoppers walk up the road.
      Day after day it is the same.
      The short man always takes the lead
      Limping like one a trifle lame.

And number two leans as he goes
And number three walks very straight.
I do not time them but I know
They're never early, never late.

10 So I have seen them for a week,
Have seen them but have heard no sound.
I never saw one turn to speak.
I never saw one look around.

Out of a window to the south
I watch them come against the light.
I cross the room and to the north
I watch till they are out of sight.

Langston Hughes

Langston Hughes (1902–1967) was leader of the Harlem renaissance of black American literature and often used folk sources in his poetry, especially the forms, diction, and rhythm of blues. He also wrote fiction, essays, and drama.

Hope

Sometimes when I'm lonely,
Don't know why,
Keep thinkin' I won't be lonely
By and by.

Bad Luck Card

Cause you don't love me
Is awful, awful hard.
Gypsy done showed me
My bad luck card.

There ain't no good left
In this world for me.
Gypsy done tole me—
Unlucky as can be.

I don't know what
10 Po' weary me can do.
Gypsy says I'd kill my self
If I was you.

Homecoming

I went back in the alley
And I opened up my door.
All her clothes was gone:
She wasn't home no more.

I pulled back the covers,
I made down the bed.
A *whole* lot of room
Was the only thing I had.

Richard Eberhart

Richard Eberhart (1904–   ) attended Dartmouth College in New Hampshire and
went from there to Cambridge University in England, where he first published. He
taught at a preparatory school, served in the Navy (some of his poems of the Second
World War are deservedly famous), and for many years taught at Dartmouth.

The Groundhog

In June, amid the golden fields,
I saw a groundhog lying dead.
Dead lay he; my senses shook,
And mind outshot our naked frailty.
There lowly in the vigorous summer
His form began its senseless change,
And made my senses waver dim
Seeing nature ferocious in him.
Inspecting close his maggots' might
10   And seething cauldron of his being,
Half with loathing, half with a strange love,
I poked him with an angry stick.
The fever arose, became a flame
And Vigour circumscribed the skies,
Immense energy in the sun,
And through my frame a sunless trembling.
My stick had done nor good nor harm.
Then stood I silent in the day
Watching the object, as before;
20   And kept my reverence for knowledge
Trying for control, to be still,
To quell the passion of the blood;
Until I had bent down on my knees
Praying for joy in the sight of decay.
And so I left; and I returned
In Autumn strict of eye, to see
The sap gone out of the groundhog,
But the bony sodden hulk remained.
But the year had lost its méaning,
30   And in intellectual chains
I lost both love and loathing,
Mured up in the wall of wisdom.
Another summer took the fields again
Massive and burning, full of life,
But when I chanced upon the spot
There was only a little hair left,
And bones bleaching in the sunlight
Beautiful as architecture;
I watched them like a geometer,
40   And cut a walking stick from a birch.
It has been three years, now.
There is no sign of the groundhog.

I stood there in the whirling summer,
My hand capped a withered heart,
And thought of China and of Greece,
Of Alexander in his tent;
Of Montaigne in his tower,
Of Saint Theresa in her wild lament.

Louis Zukovsky

Louis Zukovsky (1904–   ) is one of the founders of Objectivism, a school of poets
that declared the poem itself an object, and natural objects the material of poetry. He
began as a follower of Ezra Pound, published widely in the 1930s, and then survived
in obscurity until a group of younger poets, following a similar esthetic, rediscovered
him in the 1960s.

"In Arizona"

In Arizona
          (how many years in the mountains)
The small stumped bark of a tree
Looks up
          in the shape of an adored pup

The indians do not approach it
The round indian tents
                    remain where they are
The tanned whites
                    are never seen by it
And one can imagine its imploring eyes

The skies
          it seems to look up to
                         blue
The same sun that warms the desert
Warms what one
          can imagine to be its ears.

Robert Penn Warren

Robert Penn Warren (1905–   ) attended Vanderbilt University and then Oxford
University as a Rhodes Scholar. He was the youngest member of the Fugitive Group
of Southern writers, along with Allen Tate and John Crowe Ransom. Author with
Cleanth Brooks of *Understanding Poetry,* a most influential textbook, he is an eminent
critic and novelist—*All the King's Men* won the Pulitzer Prize for fiction in 1947—as
well as a poet. His books of poems have earned him two Pulitzer Prizes and a
National Book Award.

Gold Glade

Wandering, in autumn, the woods of boyhood,
Where cedar, black, thick, rode the ridge,
Heart aimless as rifle, boy-blankness of mood,

I came where ridge broke, and the great ledge,
Limestone, set the toe high as treetop by dark edge

Of a gorge, and water hid, grudging and grumbling,
And I saw, in mind's eye, foam white on
Wet stone, stone wet-black, white water tumbling,
And so went down, and with some fright on
10   Slick boulders, crossed over. The gorge-depth drew night on,

But high over high rock and leaf-lacing, sky
Showed yet bright, and declivity wooed
My foot by the quietening stream, and so I
Went on, in quiet, through the beech wood:
There, in gold light, where the glade gave, it stood.

The glade was geometric, circular, gold,
No brush or weed breaking that bright gold of leaf-fall.
In the center it stood, absolute and bold
Beyond any heart-hurt, or eye's grief-fall.
20   Gold-massy in air, it stood in gold light-fall,

No breathing of air, no leaf now gold-falling,
No tooth-stitch of squirrel, or any far fox bark,
No woodpecker coding, or late jay calling.
Silence: gray-shagged, the great shagbark
Gave forth gold light. There could be no dark.

But of course dark came, and I can't recall
What county it was, for the life of me.
Montgomery, Todd, Christian—I know them all.
Was it even Kentucky or Tennessee?
30   Perhaps just an image that keeps haunting me.

No, no! in no mansion under earth,
Nor imagination's domain of bright air,
But solid in soil that gave it its birth,
It stands, wherever it is, but somewhere.
I shall set my foot, and go there.

Kenneth Rexroth

Kenneth Rexroth (1905–   ) was born in Indiana and has lived for many years in San Francisco, where he was an elder figure behind the Beat Generation. Anarchist in politics, broad in learning, he has published essays and translations as well as original poems.

The Signature of All Things

My head and shoulders, and my book
In the cool shade, and my body
Stretched bathing in the sun, I lie

Reading beside the waterfall—
Boehme's "Signature of all Things."[1]
Through the deep July day the leaves
Of the laurel, all the colors
Of gold, spin down through the moving
Deep laurel shade all day. They float
10   On the mirrored sky and forest
For a while, and then, still slowly
Spinning, sink through the crystal deep
Of the pool to its leaf gold floor.
The saint saw the world as streaming
In the electrolysis of love.
I put him by and gaze through shade
Folded into shade of slender
Laurel trunks and leaves filled with sun.
The wren broods in her moss domed nest.
20   A newt struggles with a white moth
Drowning in the pool. The hawks scream,
Playing together on the ceiling
Of heaven. The long hours go by.
I think of those who have loved me,
Of all the mountains I have climbed,
Of all the seas I have swum in.
The evil of the world sinks.
My own sin and trouble fall away
Like Christian's bundle, and I watch
30   My forty summers fall like falling
Leaves and falling water held
Eternally in summer air.

Deer are stamping in the glades,
Under the full July moon.
There is a smell of dry grass
In the air, and more faintly,
The scent of a far off skunk.
As I stand at the wood's edge,
Watching the darkness, listening
40   To the stillness, a small owl
Comes to the branch above me,
On wings more still than my breath.
When I turn my light on him,
His eyes glow like drops of iron,
And he perks his head at me,
Like a curious kitten.
The meadow is bright as snow.
My dog prowls the grass, a dark

[1]*The Signature of All Things* is one of the major works of German religious mystic writer Jakob Boehme (1575–1624), whose thought influenced such later philosophers as Hegel and Schopenhauer.

Blur in the blur of brightness.
50   I walk to the oak grove where
The Indian village was once.
There, in blotched and cobwebbed light
And dark, dim in the blue haze,
Are twenty Holstein heifers,
Black and white, all lying down,
Quietly together, under
The huge trees rooted in the graves.

When I dragged the rotten log
From the bottom of the pool,
60   It seemed heavy as stone.
I let it lie in the sun
For a month; and then chopped it
Into sections, and split them
For kindling, and spread them out
To dry some more. Late that night,
After reading for hours,
While moths rattled at the lamp—
The saints and the philosophers
On the destiny of man—
70   I went out on my cabin porch,
And looked up through the black forest
At the swaying islands of stars.
Suddenly I saw at my feet,
Spread on the floor of night, ingots
Of quivering phosphorescence,
And all about were scattered chips
Of pale cold light that was alive.

William Empson

William Empson (1906–   ) is known for his criticism, especially *Seven Types of Ambiguity* (1930), and for his ambiguous poems. He taught in China for many years, now lives and teaches in Sheffield, England.

Villanelle

It is the pain, it is the pain, endures.
Your chemic beauty burned my muscles through.
Poise of my hands reminded me of yours.

What later purge from this deep toxin cures?
What kindness now could the old salve renew?
It is the pain, it is the pain, endures.

The infection slept (custom or change inures)
And when pain's secondary phase was due
Poise of my hands reminded me of yours.

10 How safe I felt, whom memory assures,
Rich that your grace safely by heart I knew.
It is the pain, it is the pain, endures.

My stare drank deep beauty that still allures.
My heart pumps yet the poison draught of you.
Poise of my hands reminded me of yours.

You are still kind whom the same shape immures.
Kind and beyond adieu. We miss our cue.
It is the pain, it is the pain, endures.
Poise of my hands reminded me of yours.

W. H. Auden

Wystan Hugh Auden (1907–1973) began to publish at the end of the 1920s
and in the next decade became the spokesman of a generation. Marxist,
psychological, he wrote a poetry of ideas; then his ideas changed. Just before
the Second World War he emigrated to America and lived in New York for most
of the remainder of his life, becoming an Anglo-Catholic and altering his old
political concepts.

Musée des Beaux Arts[1]

About suffering they were never wrong,
The Old Masters: how well they understood
Its human position; how it takes place
While someone else is eating or opening a window or just walking dully along;
How, when the aged are reverently, passionately waiting
For the miraculous birth, there always must be
Children who did not specially want it to happen, skating
On a pond at the edge of the wood:
They never forgot
10 That even the dreadful martyrdom must run its course
Anyhow in a corner, some untidy spot
Where the dogs go on with their doggy life and the torturer's horse
Scratches its innocent behind on a tree.

In Brueghel's *Icarus,*[2] for instance: how everything turns away
Quite leisurely from the disaster; the ploughman may
Have heard the splash, the forsaken cry,
But for him it was not an important failure; the sun shone
As it had to on the white legs disappearing into the green
Water; and the expensive delicate ship that must have seen
20 Something amazing, a boy falling out of the sky,
Had somewhere to get to and sailed calmly on.

---

[1]Museum of Fine Arts   [2]Pieter Brueghel the Elder (1520?–1569) was a major sixteenth-century
Flemish painter. His *The Fall of Icarus,* to which Auden alludes here, is in the Musée des Beaux
Arts in Brussels.

In Memory of W. B. Yeats

(d. Jan. 1939)

1

He disappeared in the dead of winter:
The brooks were frozen, the airports almost deserted,
And snow disfigured the public statues;
The mercury sank in the mouth of the dying day.
O all the instruments agree
The day of his death was a dark cold day.

Far from his illness
The wolves ran on through the evergreen forests,
The peasant river was untempted by the fashionable quays;
10 By mourning tongues
The death of the poet was kept from his poems.

But for him it was his last afternoon as himself,
An afternoon of nurses and rumors;
The provinces of his body revolted,
The squares of his mind were empty,
Silence invaded the suburbs,
The current of his feeling failed: he became his admirers.

Now he is scattered among a hundred cities
And wholly given over to unfamiliar affections;
20 To find his happiness in another kind of wood
And be punished under a foreign code of conscience.
The words of a dead man
Are modified in the guts of the living.

But in the importance and noise of tomorrow
When the brokers are roaring like beasts on the floor of the Bourse,
And the poor have the sufferings to which they are fairly accustomed,
And each in the cell of himself is almost convinced of his freedom;
A few thousand will think of this day
As one thinks of a day when one did something slightly unusual.

30 O all the instruments agree
The day of his death was a dark cold day.

2

You were silly like us: your gift survived it all;
The parish of rich women, physical decay,
Yourself; mad Ireland hurt you into poetry.
Now Ireland has her madness and her weather still,
For poetry makes nothing happen: it survives
In the valley of its saying where executives
Would never want to tamper; it flows south
From ranches of isolation and the busy griefs,

40   Raw towns that we believe and die in; it survives,
    A way of happening, a mouth.

3

    Earth, receive an honored guest;
    William Yeats is laid to rest:
    Let the Irish vessel lie
    Emptied of its poetry.

    Time that is intolerant
    Of the brave and innocent,
    And indifferent in a week
    To a beautiful physique,

50   Worships language and forgives
    Everyone by whom it lives;
    Pardons cowardice, conceit,
    Lays its honors at their feet.

    Time that with this strange excuse
    Pardoned Kipling[1] and his views,
    And will pardon Paul Claudel,[2]
    Pardons him for writing well.

    In the nightmare of the dark
    All the dogs of Europe bark,
60   And the living nations wait,
    Each sequestered in its hate;

    Intellectual disgrace
    Stares from every human face,
    And the seas of pity lie
    Locked and frozen in each eye.

    Follow, poet, follow right
    To the bottom of the night,
    With your unconstraining voice
    Still persuade us to rejoice;

70   With the farming of a verse
    Make a vineyard of the curse,
    Sing of human unsuccess
    In a rapture of distress;

    In the deserts of the heart
    Let the healing fountain start,
    In the prison of his days
    Teach the free man how to praise.

---

[1]Rudyard Kipling (1865–1936), British writer born in Bombay and author of the *Jungle Books, Kim,* novels, short stories, and many poems, wrote much about the British Empire.　[2]Paul Claudel (1868–1955), French dramatist, poet, and diplomat, produced works that were highly mystical and often symbolist.

Louis MacNeice

Louis MacNeice (1907–1963) was an English poet of the 1930s associated with W. H. Auden, who collaborated with him on *Letters from Iceland*. Born in Ireland, he lived most of his life in London, where he was a producer for the BBC.

The Sunlight on the Garden

The sunlight on the garden
Hardens and grows cold,
We cannot cage the minute
Within its nets of gold,
When all is told
We cannot beg for pardon.

Our freedom as free lances
Advances towards its end;
The earth compels, upon it
10 Sonnets and birds descend;
And soon, my friend,
We shall have no time for dances.

The sky was good for flying
Defying the church bells
And every evil iron
Siren and what it tells:
The earth compels,
We are dying, Egypt, dying

And not expecting pardon,
20 Hardened in heart anew,
But glad to have sat under
Thunder and rain with you,
And grateful too
For sunlight on the garden.

Theodore Roethke (1908–1963)

See pages 520–534.

Stephen Spender

Stephen Spender (1909–   ) is the survivor of the 1930s group of English poets. He met Auden at Oxford and was influenced by him. Like Auden, he sympathized with the Loyalist side in Spain, which he visited during the Spanish Civil War. Unlike Auden, Spender remained largely in England, and made fewer poems as time passed, writing essays and representing a liberal literary consensus. He edited *Encounter* from 1953 to 1965.

What I Expected, Was

What I expected, was
Thunder, fighting,
Long struggles with men
And climbing.

After continual straining
I should grow strong;
Then the rocks would shake,
And I rest long.

What I had not foreseen
10   Was the gradual day
Weakening the will
Leaking the brightness away,
The lack of good to touch,
The fading of body and soul
—Smoke before wind,
Corrupt, unsubstantial.

The wearing of Time,
And the watching of cripples pass
With limbs shaped like questions
20   In their odd twist,
The pulverous grief
Melting the bones with pity,
The sick falling from earth—
These, I could not foresee.

Expecting always
Some brightness to hold in trust,
Some final innocence
Exempt from dust,
That, hanging solid,
30   Would dangle through all,
Like the created poem,
Or faceted crystal.

Charles Olson

Charles Olson (1910–1970) was highly influential as poet and literary thinker. His first publication was critical, a book about *Moby-Dick* called *Call Me Ishmael.* He wrote an essay on "Projective Verse" which may be regarded as the manifesto of the Black Mountain School of American poets, loosely derived from Pound and from Zukovsky's Objectivism. His long series of *Maximus Poems* is his major poetic work.

Maximus, to Gloucester, Sunday, July 19

and they stopped before that bad sculpture of a fisherman

—"as if one were to talk to a man's house,
knowing not what gods or heroes are"—

not knowing what a fisherman is
instead of going straight to the Bridge
and doing no more than—saying no more than—
in the Charybdises of the
Cut waters the flowers tear off
the wreathes

10   the flowers
turn
the character of the sea   The sea jumps
the fate of the flower   The drowned men are undrowned
in the eddies

              of the eyes
              of the flowers
              opening
              the sea's eyes

The disaster
20   is undone
What was received as alien
—the flower
on the water, that a man drowns
that he dies in water as he dies on earth, the impossible
            that this gross fact can return to us
                in this upset
on a summer day
of a particular tide

that the sensation is true,
that the transformations of fire are, first of all, sea—
30   "as gold for wares wares for gold"

        Let them be told who stopped first
        by a bronze idol

        A fisherman is not a successful man,
        he is not a famous man he is not a man
        of power, these are the damned by God

whose surface bubbles
with these gimlets
which screw-in like

potholes, caustic
40   caked earth of painted
pools, Yellowstone

Park of holes
is death the diseased
presence on us, the spilling lesion

of the brilliance
it is to be alive: to walk onto it,
as Jim Bridger the first into it,

it is more true a scabious
field than it is a pretty
50   meadow

        When a man's coffin is the sea
        the whole of creation shall come to his funeral,

it turns out; the globe
is below, all lapis

and its blue surface golded
by what happened

this afternoon: there are eyes
in this water

the flowers
60 from the shore,

awakened
the sea

Men are so sure they know very many things,
they don't even know night and day are one

A fisherman works without reference to
that difference. It is possible he also

by lying there when he does lie, jowl
to the sea, has another advantage: it is said,

'You rectify what can be rectified,' and when a man's heart
70 cannot see this, the door of his divine intelligence is shut

let you who paraded to the Cut today
to hold memorial services to all fishermen
who have been lost at sea in a year
when for the first time not one life was lost

radar sonar radio telephone good engines
bed-check seaplanes goodness over and under us

no difference
when men come back

Elizabeth Bishop

Elizabeth Bishop (1911–1979) was born in Massachusetts, attended Vassar,
and lived for many years in Brazil. Critics noticed the influence of Marianne
Moore on her first book of poems, *North and South* (1946). She won a Pulitzer
Prize in 1956 for *Poems* and later published *Questions of Travel* (1965),
Collected Poems (1969), and *Geography III* (1977).

The Fish

I caught a tremendous fish
and held him beside the boat
half out of water, with my hook
fast in a corner of his mouth.
He didn't fight.
He hadn't fought at all.
He hung a grunting weight,

battered and venerable
and homely. Here and there
10   his brown skin hung in strips
like ancient wallpaper,
and its pattern of darker brown
was like wallpaper:
shapes like full-blown roses
stained and lost through age.
He was speckled with barnacles,
fine rosettes of lime,
and infested
with tiny white sea-lice,
20   and underneath two or three
rags of green weed hung down.
While his gills were breathing in
the terrible oxygen
—the frightening gills,
fresh and crisp with blood,
that can cut so badly—
I thought of the coarse white flesh
packed in like feathers,
the big bones and the little bones,
30   the dramatic reds and blacks
of his shiny entrails,
and the pink swim-bladder
like a big peony.
I looked into his eyes
which were far larger than mine
but shallower, and yellowed,
the irises backed and packed
with tarnished tinfoil
seen through the lenses
40   of old scratched isinglass.
They shifted a little, but not
to return my stare.
—It was more like the tipping
of an object toward the light.
I admired his sullen face,
the mechanism of his jaw,
and then I saw
that from his lower lip
—if you could call it a lip—
50   grim, wet, and weaponlike,
hung five old pieces of fish-line,
or four and a wire leader
with the swivel still attached,
with all their five big hooks
grown firmly in his mouth.
A green line, frayed at the end
where he broke it, two heavier lines,

and a fine black thread
still crimped from the strain and snap
60 when it broke and he got away.
Like medals with their ribbons
frayed and wavering,
a five-haired beard of wisdom
trailing from his aching jaw.
I stared and stared
and victory filled up
the little rented boat,
from the pool of bilge
where oil had spread a rainbow
70 around the rusted engine
to the bailer rusted orange,
the sun-cracked thwarts,
the oarlocks on their strings,
the gunnels—until everything
was rainbow, rainbow, rainbow!
And I let the fish go.

Robert Hayden

Robert Hayden (1913–1980) grew up in Detroit, where he attended Wayne
State University, later studying at the University of Michigan. He taught at Fisk
in Nashville for many years and then returned to teach at Michigan. In 1976
he went to Washington as Poetry Consultant at the Library of Congress. His
poems explored areas of the black American experience, and in a time of
militancy Hayden avoided militancy. He became an adherent of the Bahai faith
when he was a young man and remained true to it.

Middle Passage

I

Jesús, Estrella, Esperanza, Mercy:

Sails flashing to the wind like weapons,
sharks following the moans the fever and the dying;
horror the corposant and compass rose.

Middle Passage:
voyage through death
to life upon these shores.

"10 April 1800—
Blacks rebellious. Crew uneasy. Our linguist says
10 their moaning is a prayer for death,
ours and their own. Some try to starve themselves.
Lost three this morning leaped with crazy laughter
to the waiting sharks, sang as they went under."

Desire, Adventure, Tartar, Ann:

Standing to America, bringing home
black gold, black ivory, black seed.

Deep in the festering hold thy father lies,
of his bones New England pews are made,
those are altar lights that were his eyes.

20   Jesus   Saviour   Pilot   Me
Over   Life's   Tempestuous   Sea

We pray that Thou wilt grant, O Lord,
safe passage to our vessels bringing
heathen souls unto Thy chastening.

Jesus   Saviour
          "8 bells. I cannot sleep, for I am sick
          with fear, but writing eases fear a little
          since still my eyes can see these words take shape
          upon the page & so I write, as one
30   would turn to exorcism. 4 days scudding,
          but now the sea is calm again. Misfortune
          follows in our wake like sharks (our grinning
          tutelary gods). Which one of us
          has killed an albatross? A plague among
          our blacks—Ophthalmia: blindness—& we
          have jettisoned the blind to no avail.
          It spreads, the terrifying sickness spreads.
          Its claws have scratched sight from the Capt.'s eyes
          & there is blindness in the fo'c'sle
40   & we must sail 3 weeks before we come
          to port."

          What port awaits us, Davy Jones'
          or home? I've heard of slavers drifting, drifting,
          playthings of wind and storm and chance, their crews
          gone blind, the jungle hatred
          crawling up on deck.

     Thou   Who   Walked   On   Galilee

          "Deponent further sayeth *The Bella J*
          left the Guinea Coast
50   with cargo of five hundred blacks and odd
          for the barracoons of Florida:

          "That there was hardly room 'tween-decks for half
          the sweltering cattle stowed spoon-fashion there;
          that some went mad of thirst and tore their flesh
          and sucked the blood:

          "That Crew and Captain lusted with the comeliest
          of the savage girls kept naked in the cabins;
          that there was one they called The Guinea Rose
          and they cast lots and fought to lie with her:

60   "That when the Bo's'n piped all hands, the flames
          spreading from starboard already were beyond

control, the negroes howling and their chains
entangled with the flames:

"That the burning blacks could not be reached,
that the Crew abandoned ship,
leaving their shrieking negresses behind,
that the Captain perished drunken with the wenches:

"Further Deponent sayeth not."

Pilot   Oh   Pilot   Me

II

70 Aye, lad, and I have seen those factories,
Gambia, Rio Pongo, Calabar;
have watched the artful mongos baiting traps
of war wherein the victor and the vanquished

Were caught as prizes for our barracoons.
Have seen the nigger kings whose vanity
and greed turned wild black hides of Fellatah,
Mandingo, Ibo, Kru to gold for us.

And there was one—King Anthracite we named him—
fetish face beneath French parasols
80 of brass and orange velvet, impudent mouth
whose cups were carven skulls of enemies:

He'd honor us with drum and feast and conjo
and palm-oil-glistening wenches deft in love,
and for tin crowns that shone with paste,
red calico and German-silver trinkets

Would have the drums talk war and send
his warriors to burn the sleeping villages
and kill the sick and old and lead the young
in coffles to our factories.

90 Twenty years a trader, twenty years,
for there was wealth aplenty to be harvested
from those black fields, and I'd be trading still
but for the fevers melting down my bones.

III

Shuttles in the rocking loom of history,
the dark ships move, the dark ships move,
their bright ironical names
like jests of kindness on a murderer's mouth;
plough through thrashing glister toward
fata morgana's lucent melting shore,
100 weave toward New World littorals that are
mirage and myth and actual shore.

Voyage through death,
> voyage whose chartings are unlove.

A charnel stench, effluvium of living death
spreads outward from the hold,
where the living and the dead, the horribly dying,
lie interlocked, lie foul with blood and excrement.

> *Deep in the festering hold thy father lies,*
> *the corpse of mercy rots with him,*
110 > *rats eat love's rotten gelid eyes.*

> *But, oh, the living look at you*
> *with human eyes whose suffering accuses you,*
> *whose hatred reaches through the swill of dark*
> *to strike you like a leper's claw.*

> *You cannot stare that hatred down*
> *or chain the fear that stalks the watches*
> *and breathes on you its fetid scorching breath;*
> *cannot kill the deep immortal human wish,*
> *the timeless will.*

120
> "But for the storm that flung up barriers
> of wind and wave, *The Amistad*, señores,
> would have reached the port of Príncipe in two,
> three days at most; but for the storm we should
> have been prepared for what befell.
> Swift as the puma's leap it came. There was
> that interval of moonless calm filled only
> with the water's and the rigging's usual sounds,
> then sudden movement, blows and snarling cries
> and they had fallen on us with machete
130 > and marlinspike. It was as though the very
> air, the night itself were striking us.
> Exhausted by the rigors of the storm,
> we were no match for them. Our men went down
> before the murderous Africans. Our loyal
> Celestino ran from below with gun
> and lantern and I saw, before the cane-
> knife's wounding flash, Cinquez,
> that surly brute who calls himself a prince,
> directing, urging on the ghastly work.
140 > He hacked the poor mulatto down, and then
> he turned on me. The decks were slippery
> when daylight finally came. It sickens me
> to think of what I saw, of how these apes
> threw overboard the butchered bodies of
> our men, true Christians all, like so much jetsam.
> Enough, enough. The rest is quickly told:
> Cinquez was forced to spare the two of us
> you see to steer the ship to Africa,

and we like phantoms doomed to rove the sea
150 voyaged east by day and west by night,
deceiving them, hoping for rescue,
prisoners on our own vessel, till
at length we drifted to the shores of this
your land, America, where we were freed
from our unspeakable misery. Now we
demand, good sirs, the extradition of
Cinquez and his accomplices to La
Havana. And it distresses us to know
there are so many here who seem inclined
160 to justify the mutiny of these blacks.
We find it paradoxical indeed
that you whose wealth, whose tree of liberty
are rooted in the labor of your slaves
should suffer the august John Quincy Adams
to speak with so much passion of the right
of chattel slaves to kill their lawful masters
and with his Roman rhetoric weave a hero's
garland for Cinquez. I tell you that
we are determined to return to Cuba
170 with our slaves and there see justice done. Cinquez—
or let us say 'the Prince'—Cinquez shall die."

The deep immortal human wish,
the timeless will:

Cinquez its deathless primaveral image,
life that transfigures many lives.

Voyage through death
to life upon these shores.

Delmore Schwartz

Delmore Schwartz (1913–1966) was a member of a generation of American poets unusually talented and unusually cursed in their private lives. Schwartz had periods of madness, and when he died in a New York hotel in 1966 he was alone and friendless; his body went unclaimed for three days. In early years his poetry carried great promise, and he published as well some exemplary fiction and criticism.

In the Naked Bed, in Plato's Cave

In the naked bed, in Plato's cave,
Reflected headlights slowly slid the wall,
Carpenters hammered under the shaded window,
Wind troubled the window curtains all night long,
A fleet of trucks strained uphill, grinding,
Their freights covered, as usual.
The ceiling lightened again, the slanting diagram

Slid slowly forth.
                          Hearing the milkman's chop,
10   His striving up the stair, the bottle's chink,
I rose from bed, lit a cigarette,
And walked to the window. The stony street
Displayed the stillness in which buildings stand,
The street-lamp's vigil and the horse's patience.
The winter sky's pure capital
Turned me back to bed with exhausted eyes.

Strangeness grew in the motionless air. The loose
Film grayed. Shaking wagons, hooves' waterfalls,
Sounded far off, increasing, louder and nearer.
20   A car coughed, starting. Morning, softly
Melting the air, lifted the half-covered chair
From underseas, kindled the looking-glass,
Distinguished the dresser and the white wall.
The bird called tentatively, whistled, called,
Bubbled and whistled, so! Perplexed, still wet
With sleep, affectionate, hungry and cold. So, so,
O son of man, the ignorant night, the travail
Of early morning, the mystery of beginning
Again and again,
                          while History is unforgiven.

John Berryman

John Berryman (1914–1972) wrote with great ambition and intensity (fiction
and essays as well as poetry) and is best known for *Homage to Mistress
Bradstreet* (1954) and *The Dream Songs* (1969).

from The Dream Songs

14

Life, friends, is boring. We must not say so.
After all, the sky flashes, the great sea yearns,
we ourselves flash and yearn,
and moreover my mother told me as a boy
(repeatingly) 'Ever to confess you're bored
means you have no

Inner Resources.' I conclude now I have no
inner resources, because I am heavy bored.
Peoples bore me,
10   literature bores me, especially great literature,
Henry bores me, with his plights & gripes
as bad as achilles,

who loves people and valiant art, which bores me.
And the tranquil hills, & gin, look like a drag

and somehow a dog
has taken itself & its tail considerably away
into mountains or sea or sky, leaving
behind: me, wag.

16
Henry's pelt was put on sundry walls
where it did much resemble Henry and
them persons was delighted.
Especially his long & glowing tail
by all them was admired, and visitors.
They whistled: This is *it!*

Golden, whilst your frozen daiquiris
whir at midnight, gleams on you his fur
& silky & black.
Mission accomplished, pal.
My molten yellow & moonless bag,
drained, hangs at rest.

Collect in the cold depths barracuda. Ay,
In Sealdah Station some possessionless
children survive to die.
The Chinese communes hum. Two daiquiris
withdrew into a corner of the gorgeous room
and one told the other a lie.

312
I have moved to Dublin to have it out with you,
majestic Shade,[1] You whom I read so well
so many years ago,
did I read your lesson right? did I see through
your phases to the real? your heaven, your hell
did I enquire properly into?

For years then I forgot you, I put you down,
ingratitude is the necessary curse
of making things new:
I brought my family to see me through,
I brought my homage & my soft remorse,
I brought a book or two

only, including in the end your last
strange poems made under the shadow of death
Your high figures float
again across my mind and all your past
fills my walled garden with your honey breath
wherein I move, a mote.

[1]A reference to William Butler Yeats

David Ignatow

David Ignatow (1914–   ) was born in Brooklyn, New York, and worked for many years in business. Since the mid-1960s he has taught at numerous universities while continuing to publish books of poems including *Facing the Tree* and *Selected Poems*, edited by Robert Bly, both in 1975. Living most of his life in the environs of New York City, Ignatow is a poet of the city.

Rescue the Dead

Finally, to forgo love is to kiss a leaf,
is to let rain fall nakedly upon your head,
is to respect fire,
is to study man's eyes and his gestures
as he talks,
is to set bread upon the table
and a knife discreetly by,
is to pass through crowds
like a crowd of oneself.
10   Not to love is to live.

To love is to be led away
into a forest where the secret grave
is dug, singing, praising darkness
under the trees.

To live is to sign your name,
is to ignore the dead,
is to carry a wallet
and shake hands.

To love is to be a fish.
20   My boat wallows in the sea.
You who are free,
rescue the dead.

Randall Jarrell

Randall Jarrell (1914–1965) was born in Tennessee and studied at Vanderbilt. He taught at Kenyon College as a young man, along with John Crowe Ransom. Robert Lowell and Peter Taylor were students there, and from this concentration of literary men emerged much American literature. Jarrell served in the Second World War and wrote about it. In the last decades of his life he lived in North Carolina, where he taught, and he wrote criticism that was possibly better known during his lifetime than his poetry.

Eighth Air Force[1]

If, in an odd angle of the hutment,
A puppy laps the water from a can
Of flowers, and the drunk sergeant shaving

[1]In World War II, the U.S. Eighth Air Force bombed Germany and occupied Europe from bases in England.

Whistles *O Paradiso!*[2]—shall I say that man
Is not as men have said: a wolf to man?

The other murderers troop in yawning;
Three of them play Pitch, one sleeps, and one
Lies counting missions, lies there sweating
Till even his heart beats: One; One; One.
10   *O murderers!* . . . Still, this is how it's done:

This is war. . . . But since these play, before they die,
Like puppies with their puppy; since, a man,
I did as these have done, but did not die—
I will content the people as I can
And give up these to them: Behold the man![3]

I have suffered, in a dream, because of him,
Many things;[4] for this last saviour, man,
I have lied as I lie now. But what is lying?
Men wash their hands, in blood, as best they can:
20   I find no fault in this just man.

[2]An aria from Meyerbeer's *L'Africaine*   [3]John 19:4–5   [4]Matthew 27:19

William Stafford

William Stafford (1914–   ) was born in Kansas and has lived most of his life in
the Pacific Northwest. His *Stories That Could Be True: Poems New and Collected*
appeared in 1977, only fifteen years after his first collection, *Travelling Through the
Dark,* won the National Book Award. His poetry is quiet, reticent, reserved,
compassionate, and ultimately happy.

Travelling Through the Dark

Travelling through the dark I found a deer
dead on the edge of the Wilson River road.
It is usually best to roll them into the canyon:
that road is narrow; to swerve might make more dead.

By glow of the tail-light I stumbled back of the car
and stood by the heap, a doe, a recent killing;
she had stiffened already, almost cold.
I dragged her off; she was large in the belly.

My fingers touching her side brought me the reason—
10   her side was warm; her fawn lay there waiting,
alive, still, never to be born.
Beside that mountain road I hesitated.

The car aimed ahead its lowered parking lights;
under the hood purred the steady engine.
I stood in the glare of the warm exhaust turning red;
around our group I could hear the wilderness listen.

I thought hard for us all—my only swerving—,
then pushed her over the edge into the river.

Returned to Say

When I face north a lost Cree
on some new shore puts a moccasin down,
rock in the light and noon for seeing,
he in a hurry and I beside him.

It will be a long trip; he will be a new chief;
we have drunk new water from an unnamed stream;
under little dark trees he is to find a path
we both must travel because we have met.

Henceforth we gesture even by waiting;
10   there is a grain of sand on his knifeblade
so small he blows it and while his breathing
darkens the steel his eyes become set

And start a new vision: the rest of his life.
We will mean what he does. Back of this page
the path turns north. We are looking for a sign.
Our moccasins do not mark the ground.

Dylan Thomas

Dylan Thomas (1914–1953) grew up in Wales and wrote prose and poetry about his childhood. He began early to write excellent lyrical poetry, and published his first book when he was only nineteen. At least half of his *Collected Poems* was written or drafted before he was twenty-two. Continually in debt, alcoholic, he lived a life with less and less poetry in it. The sparse later work remained high in quality, like the play *Under Milk Wood*, finished just as he died at the age of thirty-nine.

This Bread I Break

This bread I break was once the oat,
This wine upon a foreign tree
Plunged in its fruit;
Man in the day or wind at night
Laid the crops low, broke the grape's joy.

Once in this wind the summer blood
Knocked in the flesh that decked the vine,
Once in this bread
The oat was merry in the wind;
10   Man broke the sun, pulled the wind down.

This flesh you break, this blood you let
Make desolation in the vein,
Were oat and grape
Born of the sensual root and sap;
My wine you drink, my bread you snap.

A Refusal to Mourn the Death, by Fire, of a Child in London

Never until the mankind making
Bird beast and flower
Fathering and all humbling darkness
Tells with silence the last light breaking
And the still hour
Is come of the sea tumbling in harness

And I must enter again the round
Zion of the water bead
And the synagogue of the ear of corn
10   Shall I let pray the shadow of a sound
Or sow my salt seed
In the least valley of sackcloth to mourn

The majesty and burning of the child's death.
I shall not murder
The mankind of her going with a grave truth
Nor blaspheme down the stations of the breath
With any further
Elegy of innocence and youth.

Deep with the first dead lies London's daughter,
20   Robed in the long friends,
The grains beyond age, the dark veins of her mother,
Secret by the unmourning water
Of the riding Thames.
After the first death, there is no other.

Fern Hill

Now as I was young and easy under the apple boughs
About the lilting house and happy as the grass was green,
    The night above the dingle starry,
        Time let me hail and climb
    Golden in the heydays of his eyes,
And honoured among wagons I was prince of the apple towns
And once below a time I lordly had the trees and leaves
        Trail with daisies and barley
    Down the rivers of the windfall light.

10   And as I was green and carefree, famous among the barns
About the happy yard and singing as the farm was home,
    In the sun that is young once only,
        Time let me play and be
    Golden in the mercy of his means,
And green and golden I was huntsman and herdsman, the calves
Sang to my horn, the foxes on the hills barked clear and cold,
        And the sabbath rang slowly
    In the pebbles of the holy streams.

All the sun long it was running, it was lovely, the hay
20 Fields high as the house, the tunes from the chimneys, it was air
    And playing, lovely and watery
      And fire green as grass.
    And nightly under the simple stars
As I rode to sleep the owls were bearing the farm away,
All the moon long I heard, blessed among stables, the night-jars
    Flying with the ricks, and the horses
      Flashing into the dark.

And then to awake, and the farm, like a wanderer white
With the dew, come back, the cock on his shoulder: it was all
30   Shining, it was Adam and maiden,
      The sky gathered again
    And the sun grew round that very day.
So it must have been after the birth of the simple light
In the first, spinning place, the spellbound horses walking warm
    Out of the whinnying green stable
      On to the fields of praise.

And honoured among foxes and pheasants by the gay house
Under the new made clouds and happy as the heart was long,
    In the sun born over and over,
40   I ran my heedless ways,
    My wishes raced through the house high hay
And nothing I cared, at my sky blue trades, that time allows
In all his tuneful turning so few and such morning songs
    Before the children green and golden
      Follow him out of grace,

Nothing I cared, in the lamb white days, that time would take me
Up to the swallow thronged loft by the shadow of my hand,
    In the moon that is always rising,
      Nor that riding to sleep
50   I should hear him fly with the high fields
And wake to the farm forever fled from the childless land.
Oh as I was young and easy in the mercy of his means,
      Time held me green and dying
    Though I sang in my chains like the sea.

Gwendolyn Brooks

Gwendolyn Brooks (1917–   ) is a leading black American poet, born in
Kansas, who began publishing with *A Street in Bronzeville* in 1945. *Annie Allen*,
published in 1949, received a Pulitzer Prize. Brooks took a new life from the
vitality of the black movement of the 1960s.

The Bean Eaters

They eat beans mostly, this old yellow pair.
Dinner is a casual affair.

Plain chipware on a plain and creaking wood,
Tin flatware.

Two who are Mostly Good.
Two who have lived their day,
But keep on putting on their clothes
And putting things away.

And remembering . . .
10   Remembering, with twinklings and twinges,
As they lean over the beans in their rented back room that is full of beads
and receipts and dolls and cloths, tobacco crumbs, vases and fringes.

We Real Cool

The Pool Players.
Seven at the Golden Shovel.

We real cool. We
Left school. We

Lurk late. We
Strike straight. We

Sing sin. We
Thin gin. We

Jazz June. We
Die soon.

Robert Lowell

Robert Lowell (1917–1977) was born in Massachusetts into the eminent
literary and academic family of the Lowells, related to the poets Amy and
James Russell Lowell and to a president of Harvard. After attending Harvard
for several terms, he transferred to Kenyon College in Ohio, where he studied
with John Crowe Ransom and made the acquaintance of Allen Tate and
Randall Jarrell. His first book, *Land of Unlikeness*, was published in a small
edition in 1944, followed by *Lord Weary's Castle* in 1947, which won the
Pulitzer Prize. With *Life Studies* in 1959 his work took an abrupt turn away
from the formal stanzas and couplets of his early poetry into the painful
confessional verse that came to characterize him. In his last years he wrote
with a prolixity he had lacked as a young man and perhaps with less success,
publishing nine volumes in the last twelve years of his life, before he died of a heart
attack at the age of sixty.

After the Surprising Conversions

September twenty-second, Sir: today
I answer. In the latter part of May,
Hard on our Lord's Ascension, it began
To be more sensible. A gentleman
Of more than common understanding, strict
In morals, pious in behavior, kicked

Against our goad. A man of some renown,
An useful, honored person in the town,
He came of melancholy parents; prone
10   To secret spells, for years they kept alone—
His uncle, I believe, was killed of it:
Good people, but of too much or little wit.
I preached one Sabbath on a text from Kings;
He showed concernment for his soul. Some things
In his experience were hopeful. He
Would sit and watch the wind knocking a tree
And praise this countryside our Lord has made.
Once when a poor man's heifer died, he laid
A shilling on the doorsill; though a thirst
20   For loving shook him like a snake, he durst
Not entertain much hope of his estate
In heaven. Once we saw him sitting late
Behind his attic window by a light
That guttered on his Bible; through that night
He meditated terror, and he seemed
Beyond advice or reason, for he dreamed
That he was called to trumpet Judgment Day
To Concord. In the latter part of May
He cut his throat. And though the coroner
30   Judged him delirious, soon a noisome stir
Palsied our village. At Jehovah's nod
Satan seemed more let loose amongst us: God
Abandoned us to Satan, and he pressed
Us hard, until we thought we could not rest
Till we had done with life. Content was gone.
All the good work was quashed. We were undone.
The breath of God had carried out a planned
And sensible withdrawal from this land;
The multitude, once unconcerned with doubt,
40   Once neither callous, curious nor devout,
Jumped at broad noon, as though some peddler groaned
At it in its familiar twang: "My friend,
Cut your own throat. Cut your own throat. Now! Now!"
September twenty-second, Sir, the bough
Cracks with the unpicked apples, and at dawn
The small-mouth bass breaks water, gorged with spawn.

Skunk Hour

(For Elizabeth Bishop)

Nautilus Island's hermit
heiress still lives through winter in her Spartan cottage;
her sheep still graze above the sea.
Her son's a bishop. Her farmer

is first selectman in our village;
she's in her dotage.

Thirsting for
the hierarchic privacy
of Queen Victoria's century,
10   she buys up all
the eyesores facing her shore,
and lets them fall.

The season's ill—
we've lost our summer millionaire,
who seemed to leap from an L. L. Bean[1]
catalogue. His nine-knot yawl
was auctioned off to lobstermen.
A red fox stain covers Blue Hill.

And now our fairy
20   decorator brightens his shop for fall;
his fishnet's filled with orange cork,
orange, his cobbler's bench and awl;
there is no money in his work,
he'd rather marry.

One dark night,
my Tudor Ford climbed the hill's skull;
I watched for love-cars. Lights turned down,
they lay together, hull to hull,
where the graveyard shelves on the town. . . .
30   My mind's not right.

A car radio bleats,
"Love, O careless Love. . . ." I hear
my ill-spirit sob in each blood cell,
as if my hand were at its throat. . . .
I myself am hell;
nobody's here—

only skunks, that search
in the moonlight for a bite to eat.
They march on their soles up Main Street:
40   white stripes, moonstruck eyes' red fire
under the chalk-dry and spar spire
of the Trinitarian Church.

I stand on top
of our back steps and breathe the rich air—
a mother skunk with her column of kittens swills the garbage pail.
She jabs her wedge-head in a cup
of sour cream, drops her ostrich tail,
and will not scare.

[1]A Maine store that specializes in outdoor gear and country clothing; its label is popular among affluent city people who summer in the country.

For the Union Dead

"Relinquunt Omnia Servare Rem Publicam."[1]

The old South Boston Aquarium stands
in a Sahara of snow now. Its broken windows are boarded.
The bronze weathervane cod has lost half its scales.
The airy tanks are dry.

Once my nose crawled like a snail on the glass;
my hand tingled
to burst the bubbles
drifting from the noses of the cowed, compliant fish.

My hand draws back. I often sigh still
10   for the dark downward and vegetating kingdom
of the fish and reptile. One morning last March,
I pressed against the new barbed and galvanized

fence on the Boston Common. Behind their cage,
yellow dinosaur steamshovels were grunting
as they cropped up tons of mush and grass
to gouge their underworld garage.

Parking spaces luxuriate like civic
sandpiles in the heart of Boston.
A girdle of orange, Puritan-pumpkin colored girders
20   braces the tingling Statehouse,

shaking over the excavations, as it faces Colonel Shaw
and his bell-cheeked Negro infantry
on St. Gaudens'[2] shaking Civil War relief,
propped by a plank splint against the garage's earthquake.

Two months after marching through Boston,
half the regiment was dead;
at the dedication,
William James[3] could almost hear the bronze Negroes breathe.

Their monument sticks like a fishbone
30   in the city's throat.
Its Colonel is as lean
as a compass-needle.

He has an angry wrenlike vigilance,
a greyhound's gentle tautness;
he seems to wince at pleasure,
and suffocate for privacy.

---

[1]"They sacrifice everything to serve the republic."
[2]Sculptor Augustus Saint-Gaudens (1848–1907) made a bronze relief of Colonel Robert Shaw (1837–1863), who led a black regiment during the Civil War.
[3]William James (1842–1910), American psychologist and philosopher, professor at Harvard

He is out of bounds now. He rejoices in man's lovely,
peculiar power to choose life and die—
when he leads his black soldiers to death,
40   he cannot bend his back.

On a thousand small town New England greens,
the old white churches hold their air
of sparse, sincere rebellion; frayed flags
quilt the graveyards of the Grand Army of the Republic.

The stone statues of the abstract Union Soldier
grow slimmer and younger each year—
wasp-waisted, they doze over muskets
and muse through their sideburns . . .

Shaw's father wanted no monument
50   except the ditch,
where his son's body was thrown
and lost with his "niggers."

The ditch is nearer.
There are no statues for the last war here;
on Boylston Street, a commercial photograph
shows Hiroshima boiling

over a Mosler Safe, the "Rock of Ages"
that survived the blast. Space is nearer.
When I crouch to my television set,
60   the drained faces of Negro school-children rise like balloons.

Colonel Shaw
is riding on his bubble,
he waits
for the blessèd break.

The Aquarium is gone. Everywhere,
giant finned cars nose forward like fish;
a savage servility
slides by on grease.

Robert Duncan

Robert Duncan (1919–   ) born in Oakland, has been a San Francisco poet
for most of his life, associated with the Black Mountain group of poets. Erudite
and prolific, Duncan has been a source of energy for other poets, especially in
the Bay Area, in ideas and example.

Poetry, a Natural Thing

Neither our vices nor our virtues
further the poem. "They came up
    and died
just like they do every year
    on the rocks."

The poem
feeds upon thought, feeling, impulse,
   to breed   itself,
a spiritual urgency at the dark ladders leaping.

10   This beauty is an inner persistence
        toward the source
     striving against (within) down-rushet of the river,
        a call we heard and answer
     in the lateness of the world
        primordial bellowings
     from which the youngest world might spring,

     salmon not in the well where the
        hazelnut falls
     but at the falls battling, inarticulate,
20   blindly making it.

     This is one picture apt for the mind.

     A second: a moose painted by Stubbs,[1]
     where last year's extravagant antlers
        lie on the ground.
     The forlorn moosey-faced poem wears
        new antler-buds,
        the same,

     "a little heavy, a little contrived,"

     his only beauty to be
30   all moose.

[1]George Stubbs (1724–1806), an English artist, is best known for his animal paintings.

Howard Nemerov

Howard Nemerov (1920–   ) attended Harvard before serving in the Royal
Canadian Air Force and the United States Air Force in the Second World War.
He has taught at various American universities, currently at Washington
University in St. Louis. Over the years, he has written steadily, with
considerable skill, without drawing great attention. His *Collected Poems*
appeared in 1977.

Brainstorm

The house was shaken by a rising wind
That rattled window and door. He sat alone
In an upstairs room and heard these things: a blind
Ran up with a bang, a door slammed, a groan
Came from some hidden joist, and a leaky tap,
At any silence of the wind walked like
A blind man through the house. Timber and sap
Revolt, he thought, from washer, baulk and spike.
Bent to his book, continued unafraid

10 Until the crows came down from their loud flight
To walk along the rooftree overhead.
Their horny feet, so near but out of sight,
Scratched on the slate; when they were blown away
He heard their wings beat till they came again,
While the wind rose, and the house seemed to sway,
And window panes began to blind with rain.
The house was talking, not to him, he thought,
But to the crows; the crows were talking back
In their black voices. The secret might be out:
20 Houses are only trees stretched on the rack.
And once the crows knew, all nature would know.
Fur, leaf and feather would invade the form,
Nail rust with rain and shingle warp with snow,
Vine tear the wall, till any straw-borne storm
Could rip both roof and rooftree off and show
Naked to nature what they had kept warm.

He came to feel the crows walk on his head
As if he were the house, their crooked feet
Scratched, through the hair, his scalp. He might be dead
30 It seemed, and all the noises underneath
Be but the cooling of the sinews, veins,
Juices, and sodden sacks suddenly let go;
While in his ruins of wiring, his burst mains,
The rainy wind had been set free to blow
Until the green uprising and mob rule
That ran the world had taken over him,
Split him like seed, and set him in the school
Where any crutch can learn to be a limb.

Inside his head he heard the stormy crows.

Richard Wilbur

Richard Wilbur (1921–   ) was born in New Jersey and has lived in the
eastern United States. During the Second World War he fought in Italy and
France; he began writing poems in the Army. His work is decorative, skillful,
aimed to please and to enlighten rather than to shock or to overwhelm. He is
one of the few poets of his generation who has not undergone violent change, in
work and private life, which has earned him the disapproval of critics.

Still, Citizen Sparrow

Still, citizen sparrow, this vulture which you call
Unnatural, let him but lumber again to air
Over the rotten office, let him bear
The carrion ballast up, and at the tall

Tip of the sky lie cruising. Then you'll see
That no more beautiful bird is in heaven's height,
No wider more placid wings, no watchfuller flight;
He shoulders nature there, the frightfully free,

The naked-headed one. Pardon him, you
10   Who dart in the orchard aisles, for it is he
Devours death, mocks mutability,
Has heart to make an end, keeps nature new.

Thinking of Noah, childheart, try to forget
How for so many bedlam hours his saw
Soured the song of birds with its wheezy gnaw,
And the slam of his hammer all the day beset

The people's ears. Forget that he could bear
To see the towns like coral under the keel,
And the fields so dismal deep. Try rather to feel
20   How high and weary it was, on the waters where

He rocked his only world, and everyone's.
Forgive the hero, you who would have died
Gladly with all you knew; he rode that tide
To Ararat;[1] all men are Noah's sons.

[1]The mountain on which Noah's Ark landed

Mind

Mind in its purest play is like some bat
That beats about in caverns all alone,
Contriving by a kind of senseless wit
Not to conclude against a wall of stone.

It has no need to falter or explore;
Darkly it knows what obstacles are there,
And so may weave and flitter, dip and soar
In perfect courses through the blackest air.

And has this simile a like perfection?
10   The mind is like a bat. Precisely. Save
That in the very happiest intellection
A graceful error may correct the cave.

Philip Larkin

Philip Larkin (1922–   ) attended Oxford, wrote two early novels, and chose
the life of a professional librarian. He has written little, but his work has been
finished and fine. In the eyes of most observers, he is the best English poet
of his time. He is librarian of the University at Hull. His volumes are *The Less
Deceived* (1955), *The Whitsun Weddings* (1964), and *High Windows* (1974).

Mr. Bleaney

'This was Mr. Bleaney's room. He stayed
The whole time he was at the Bodies, till
They moved him.' Flowered curtains, thin and frayed,
Fall to within five inches of the sill,

Whose window shows a strip of building land,
Tussocky, littered. 'Mr. Bleaney took
My bit of garden properly in hand.'
Bed, upright chair, sixty-watt bulb, no hook

Behind the door, no room for books or bags—
10   'I'll take it.' So it happens that I lie
Where Mr. Bleaney lay, and stub my fags
On the same saucer-souvenir, and try

Stuffing my ears with cotton-wool, to drown
The jabbering set he egged her on to buy.
I know his habits—what time he came down,
His preference for sauce to gravy, why

He kept on plugging at the four aways[1]—
Likewise their yearly frame: the Frinton folk
Who put him up for summer holidays,
20   And Christmas at his sister's house in Stoke.

But if he stood and watched the frigid wind
Tousling the clouds, lay on the fusty bed
Telling himself that this was home, and grinned,
And shivered, without shaking off the dread

That how we live measures our own nature,
And at his age having no more to show
Than one hired box should make him pretty sure
He warranted no better, I don't know.

[1]A form of betting on English professional soccer games

Aubade

I work all day, and get half drunk at night.
Waking at four to soundless dark, I stare.
In time the curtain-edges will grow light.
Till then I see what's really always there:
Unresting death, a whole day nearer now,
Making all thought impossible but how
And where and when I shall myself die.
Arid interrogation: yet the dread
Of dying, and being dead,
10   Flashes afresh to hold and horrify.

The mind blanks at the glare. Not in remorse
—The good not done, the love not given, time
Torn off unused—nor wretchedly because
An only life can take so long to climb
Clear of its wrong beginnings, and may never;
But at the total emptiness for ever,
The sure extinction that we travel to

And shall be lost in always. Not to be here,
Not to be anywhere,
20   And soon; nothing more terrible, nothing more true.

This is a special way of being afraid
No trick dispels. Religion used to try,
That vast moth-eaten musical brocade
Created to pretend we never die,
And specious stuff that says *No rational being*
Can fear a thing it will not feel, not seeing
That this is what we fear—no sight, no sound,
No touch or taste to smell, nothing to think with,
Nothing to love or link with,
30   The anaesthetic from which none come round.

And so it stays just on the edge of vision,
A small unfocused blur, a standing chill
That slows each impulse down to indecision.
Most things may never happen: this one will,
And realisation of it rages out
In furnace-fear when we are caught without
People or drink. Courage is no good:
It means not scaring others. Being brave
Lets no one off the grave.
40   Death is no different whined at than withstood.

Slowly light strengthens, and the room takes shape.
It stands plain as a wardrobe, what we know,
Have always known, know that we can't escape,
Yet can't accept. One side will have to go.
Meanwhile telephones crouch, getting ready to ring
In locked-up offices, and all the uncaring
Intricate rented world begins to rouse.
The sky is white as clay, with no sun.
Work has to be done.
50   Postmen like doctors go from house to house.

James Dickey

James Dickey (1923–   ) was an All-Southern halfback as a young man and
then a fighter pilot during the Second World War and the Korean War. He tried
teaching and advertising and after publishing volumes of poetry returned to
teaching again. His *Collected Poems* won the National Book Award in 1966. His
novel *Deliverance* became a successful motion picture.

The Heaven of Animals

Here they are. The soft eyes open.
If they have lived in a wood
It is a wood.
If they have lived on plains
It is grass rolling
Under their feet forever.

Having no souls, they have come,
Anyway, beyond their knowing.
Their instincts wholly bloom
10 And they rise.
The soft eyes open.

To match them, the landscape flowers,
Outdoing, desperately
Outdoing what is required:
The richest wood,
The deepest field.

For some of these,
It could not be the place
It is, without blood.
20 These hunt, as they have done,
But with claws and teeth grown perfect,

More deadly than they can believe.
They stalk more silently,
And crouch on the limbs of trees,
And their descent
Upon the bright backs of their prey

May take years
In a sovereign floating of joy.
And those that are hunted
30 Know this as their life,
Their reward: to walk

Under such trees in full knowledge
Of what is in glory above them,
And to feel no fear,
But acceptance, compliance.
Fulfilling themselves without pain

At the cycle's center,
They tremble, they walk
Under the tree,
40 They fall, they are torn,
They rise, they walk again.

Anthony Hecht

Anthony Hecht (1923–   ) fought in the infantry in the Second World War and
has taught at American universities for most of his life. He is not prolific,
finishes few poems, and finishes them with an extraordinarily high gloss. *The
Hard Hours* (1967) includes a selection of early poems

The Dover Bitch: A Criticism of Life

(for Andrews Wanning)

So there stood Matthew Arnold and this girl
With the cliffs of England crumbling away behind them,
And he said to her, "Try to be true to me,

And I'll do the same for you, for things are bad
All over, etc., etc."
Well now, I knew this girl. It's true she had read
Sophocles in a fairly good translation
And caught that bitter allusion to the sea,
But all the time he was talking she had in mind
₁₀ The notion of what his whiskers would feel like
On the back of her neck. She told me later on
That after a while she got to looking out
At the lights across the channel, and really felt sad,
Thinking of all the wine and enormous beds
And blandishments in French and the perfumes.
And then she got really angry. To have been brought
All the way down from London, and then be addressed
As a sort of mournful cosmic last resort
Is really tough on a girl, and she was pretty.
₂₀ Anyway, she watched him pace the room
And finger his watch-chain and seem to sweat a bit,
And then she said one or two unprintable things.
But you mustn't judge her by that. What I mean to say is,
She's really all right. I still see her once in a while
And she always treats me right. We have a drink
And I give her a good time, and perhaps it's a year
Before I see her again, but there she is,
Running to fat, but dependable as they come.
And sometimes I bring her a bottle of *Nuit d'Amour*.

Denise Levertov

Denise Levertov (1923–   ), who was born in England, came to the United
States when she married an American soldier. Her early poems were collected
in England. After her move to the United States, she became affiliated with
the Black Mountain group of poets and her style changed considerably. She was
a leader in the antiwar movement during the Vietnam years.

October

Certain branches cut
certain leaves fallen
the grapes
          cooked and put up
for winter

mountains without one
shrug of cloud
no feint of blurred
wind-willow leaf-light

₁₀ their chins up
in blue of the eastern sky
their red cloaks
wrapped tight to the bone

John Logan

John Logan (1923–   ) was born in Red Oak, Iowa and went to school in the
Midwest. In more recent years he has lived in California, in upstate New York,
and in Hawaii, writing his poems and editing *Choice*.

The Picnic

It is the picnic with Ruth in the spring.
Ruth was third on my list of seven girls
But the first two were gone (Betty) or else
Had someone (Ellen has accepted Doug).
Indian Gully the last day of school;
Girls make the lunches for the boys too.
I wrote a note to Ruth in algebra class
Day before the test. She smiled, and nodded.
We left the cars and walked through the young corn
10   The shoots green as paint and the leaves like tongues
Trembling. Beyond the fence where we stood
Some wild strawberry flowered by an elm tree
And Jack-in-the-pulpit was olive ripe.
A blackbird fled as I crossed, and showed
A spot of gold or red under its quick wing.
I held the wire for Ruth and watched the whip
Of her long, striped skirt as she followed.
Three freckles blossomed on her thin, white back
Underneath the loop where the blouse buttoned.
20   We went for our lunch away from the rest,
Stretched in the new grass, our heads close
Over unknown things wrapped up in wax papers.
Ruth tried for the same, I forget what it was,
And our hands were together. She laughed,
And a breeze caught the edge of her little
Collar and the edge of her brown, loose hair
That touched my cheek. I turned my face in-
to the gentle fall. I saw how sweet it smelled.
She didn't move her head or take her hand.
30   I felt a soft caving in my stomach
As at the top of the highest slide
When I had been a child, but was not afraid,
And did not know why my eyes moved with wet
As I brushed her cheek with my lips and brushed
Her lips with my own lips. She said to me
Jack, Jack, different than I had ever heard,
Because she wasn't calling me, I think,
Or telling me. She used my name to
Talk in another way I wanted to know.
40   She laughed again and then she took her hand;
I gave her what we both had touched—can't
Remember what it was, and we ate the lunch.
Afterward we walked in the small, cool creek

Our shoes off, her skirt hitched, and she smiling,
My pants rolled, and then we climbed up the high
Side of Indian Gully and looked
Where we had been, our hands together again.
It was then some bright thing came in my eyes,
Starting at the back of them and flowing
50   Suddenly through my head and down my arms
And stomach and my bare legs that seemed not
To stop in feet, not to feel the red earth
Of the Gully, as though we hung in a
Touch of birds. There was a word in my throat
With the feeling and I knew the first time
What it meant and I said, it's beautiful.
Yes, she said, and I felt the sound and word
In my hand join the sound and word in hers
As in one name said, or in one cupped hand.
60   We put back on our shoes and socks and we
Sat in the grass awhile, crosslegged, under
A blowing tree, not saying anything.
And Ruth played with shells she found in the creek,
As I watched. Her small wrist which was so sweet
To me turned by her breast and the shells dropped
Green, white, blue, easily into her lap,
Passing light through themselves. She gave the pale
Shells to me, and got up and touched her hips
With her light hands, and we walked down slowly
70   To play the school games with the others.

Louis Simpson

Louis Simpson (1923–   ) was born in Jamaica and grew up there, coming to
the United States when he was seventeen. He left Columbia College to enter
the U.S. Army during the Second World War and received his citizenship at
Berchtesgaden. He has published a novel, a textbook, two books of criticism,
and numerous books of poems. *At the End of the Open Road* (1963) won a
Pulitzer Prize.

Walt Whitman at Bear Mountain

". . . life which does not give the preference to any other life, of any
previous period, which therefore prefers its own existence . . ."
                                        —*Ortega y Gasset*

Neither on horseback nor seated,
But like himself, squarely on two feet,
The poet of death and lilacs
Loafs by the footpath. Even the bronze looks alive
Where it is folded like cloth. And he seems friendly.

'Where is the Mississippi panorama
And the girl who played the piano?

Where are you, Walt?
The Open Road goes to the used-car lot.

10   'Where is the nation you promised?
These houses built of wood sustain
Colossal snows,
And the light above the street is sick to death.

'As for the people—see how they neglect you!
Only a poet pauses to read the inscription.'

'I am here,' he answered.
'It seems you have found me out.
Yet, did I not warn you that it was Myself
I advertised? Were my words not sufficiently plain?

20   'I gave no prescriptions,
And those who have taken my moods for prophecies
Mistake the matter.'
Then, vastly amused—'Why do you reproach me?
I freely confess I am wholly disreputable.
Yet I am happy, because you have found me out.'

A crocodile in wrinkled metal loafing . . .

Then all the realtors,
Pickpockets, salesmen, and the actors peforming
Official scenarios,
30   Turned a deaf ear, for they had contracted
American dreams.

But the man who keeps a store on a lonely road,
And the housewife who knows she's dumb,
And the earth, are relieved.

All that grave weight of America
Cancelled! Like Greece and Rome.
The future in ruins!
The castles, the prisons, the cathedrals
Unbuilding, and roses
40   Blossoming from the stones that are not there . . .

The clouds are lifting from the high Sierras,
The Bay mists clearing;
And the angel in the gate, the flowering plum,
Dances like Italy, imagining red.

In the Suburbs

There's no way out.
You were born to waste your life.
You were born to this middleclass life

As others before you
Were born to walk in procession
To the temple, singing.

John Haines

John Haines (1924–   ) was a homesteader in Alaska for fifteen years and now divides his time between Alaska and the continental United States.

To Turn Back

The grass people bow
their heads before the wind.

How would it be
to stand among them, bending
our heads like that . . . ?

Yes . . . and no . . . perhaps . . .
lifting our dusty faces
as if we were waiting for
the rain . . . ?

10   The grass people stand
all year, patient and obedient—

to be among them
is to have only simple
and friendly thoughts,

and not be afraid.

Donald Justice

Donald Justice (1925–   ) grew up in Florida and attended the Writers Workshop at Iowa, where he now teaches. His *Selected Poems* appeared in 1979.

Counting the Mad

This one was put in a jacket,
This one was sent home,
This one was given bread and meat
But would eat none,
And this one cried No No No No
All day long.

This one looked at the window
As thought it were a wall,
This one saw things that were not there,
10   This one things that were,
And this one cried No No No No
All day long.

This one thought himself a bird,
This one a dog,
And this one thought himself a man,
An ordinary man,
And cried and cried No No No No
All day long.

A. R. Ammons

Archie Randolph Ammons (1926–   ) worked in business for many years before he became a professor of English. He teaches at Cornell.

Working with Tools

I make a simple assertion
like a nice piece of stone
and you
alert to presence and entrance
man your pick and hammer

and by chip and deflection
distract simplicity
and cut my assertion
back to mangles, little heaps:

10   well, baby, that's the way
you get along: it's all right,
I understand such
ways of being afraid:
sometimes you want my come-on

hard, something to
take in and be around:
sometimes you want
a vaguer touch: I understand
and won't give assertion up.

Robert Bly

Robert Bly (1926–   ) comes from a farm in western Minnesota, and after some time in the Navy attended Harvard, from which he graduated in 1950. Editor of an influential literary magazine—variously called *The Fifties, The Sixties,* and *The Seventies*—he has championed modernist poets of other literatures and has extended great influence on a younger generation of American poets. His own poems have been collected in *Silence in the Snowy Fields* (1962), *The Light Around the Body* (1967)—which won a National Book Award—and in seven other collections.

Hunting Pheasants in a Cornfield

I

What is so strange about a tree alone in an open field?
It is a willow tree. I walk around and around it.
The body is strangely torn, and cannot leave it.
At last I sit down beneath it.

II

It is a willow tree alone in acres of dry corn.
Its leaves are scattered around its trunk, and around me,

Brown now, and speckled with delicate black.
Only the cornstalks now can make a noise.

III

The sun is cold, burning through the frosty distances of space.
10   The weeds are frozen to death long ago.
Why then do I love to watch
The sun moving on the chill skin of the branches?

IV

The mind has shed leaves alone for years.
It stands apart with small creatures near its roots.
I am happy in this ancient place,
A spot easily caught sight of above the corn,
If I were a young animal ready to turn home at dusk.

A Man Writes to a Part of Himself

What cave are you in, hiding, rained on?
Like a wife, starving, without care,
Water dripping from your head, bent
Over ground corn . . .

    You raise your face into the rain
That drives over the valley—
Forgive me, your husband,
On the streets of a distant city, laughing,
With many appointments,
10   Though at night going also
To a bare room, a room of poverty,
To sleep among a bare pitcher and basin
In a room with no heat—

    Which of us two then is the worse off?
And how did this separation come about?

Robert Creeley

Robert Creeley (1926–   ) grew up in New England, and attended Harvard,
after which he tried chicken farming in New Hampshire, then lived on the
Spanish island of Majorca. Most recently he has alternated between Placitas,
New Mexico, and the University of Buffalo in New York. Creeley taught at Black
Mountain College and edited the *Black Mountain Review*, and as much as
anyone else formed the Black Mountain school of poetry. His *Selected Poems*
appeared in 1977.

The Rain

All night the sound had
come back again,
and again falls
this quiet, persistent rain.

What am I to myself
that must be remembered,
insisted upon
so often? Is it

10   that never the ease,
even the hardness,
of rain falling
will have for me

something other than this,
something not so insistent—
am I to be locked in this
final uneasiness.

Love, if you love me,
lie next to me.
Be for me, like rain,
20   the getting out

of the tiredness, the fatuousness, the semi-
lust of intentional indifference.
Be wet
with a decent happiness.

For My Mother: Genevieve Jules Creeley

(April 8, 1887—October 7, 1972)

Tender, semi-
articulate flickers
of your

presence, all
those years
past

now, eighty-
five, impossible to
count them

10   one by one, like
addition, sub-
traction, missing

not one. The last
curled up, in
on yourself,

position you take
in the bed, hair
wisped up

on your head, a
20   top knot, body
skeletal, eyes

closed against,
it must be,
further disturbance—

breathing a skim
of time, lightly
kicks the intervals—

days, days and
years of it,
30   work, changes,

sweet flesh caught
at the edges,
dignity's faded

dilemma. It
is *your* life, oh
no one's

forgotten anything
ever. They want
to make you

40   happy when
they remember. Walk
a little, get

up, now, die
safely,
easily, into

singleness, too
tired with it
to keep

on and on.
50   Waves break at
the darkness

under the road, sounds
in the faint
night's softness. Look

at them, catching
the light, white
edge as they turn—

always again
and again. Dead
60   one, two,

three hours—
all these minutes
pass. Is it,

was it, ever
you alone
again, how

long you kept
at it, your
pride, your

70 lovely, confusing
discretion. Mother, I
love you—for

whatever that
means,
meant—more

than I know, body
gave me my
own, generous,

inexorable place
80 of you. I feel
the mouth's sluggish-

ness, slips on
turns of things
said, to you,

too soon, too late,
wants to
go back to beginning,

smells of the hospital
room, the doctor
90 she responds

to now, the
order—get me
there. "Death's

let you out—"
comes true,
this, that,

endlessly circular
life, and we
came back

100 to see you one
last
time, this

time? Your head
shuddered,
it seemed, your

eyes wanted,
I thought,
to see

who it was.
110   I am here,
and will follow.

Allen Ginsberg

Allen Ginsberg (1926–   ) was born in New Jersey and attended Columbia in
New York City, but became known as a San Francisco poet with the publication
of *Howl* in 1956. At the forefront of the Beat Generation (he appears in several
novels by Jack Kerouac, under different names), Ginsberg has been a leader,
spiritual and political as well as poetic.

America

America I've given you all and now I'm nothing.
American two dollars and twentyseven cents January 17, 1956.
I can't stand on my own mind.
America when will we end the human war?
Go fuck yourself with your atom bomb.
I don't feel good don't bother me.
I won't write my poem till I'm in my right mind.
America when will you be angelic?
When will you take off your clothes?
10   When will you look at yourself through the grave?
When will you be worthy of your million Trotskyites?
America why are your libraries full of tears?
America when will you send your eggs to India?
I'm sick of your insane demands.
When can I go into the supermarket and buy what I need with my good looks?
American after all it is you and I who are perfect not the next world.
Your machinery is too much for me.
You made me want to be a saint.
There must be some other way to settle this argument.
20   Burroughs is in Tangiers I don't think he'll come back it's sinister.
Are you being sinister or is this some form of practical joke?
I'm trying to come to the point.
I refuse to give up my obsession.
America stop pushing I know what I'm doing.
America the plum blossoms are falling.
I haven't read the newspapers for months, everyday somebody goes on trial for
        murder.
America I feel sentimental about the Wobblies.
America I used to be a communist when I was a kid I'm not sorry.

I smoke marijuana every chance I get.
30 I sit in my house for days on end and stare at the roses in the closet.
When I go to Chinatown I get drunk and never get laid.
My mind is made up there's going to be trouble.
You should have seen me reading Marx.
My psychoanalyst thinks I'm perfectly right.
I won't say the Lord's Prayer.
I have mystical visions and cosmic vibrations.
America I still haven't told you what you did to Uncle Max after he came over
    from Russia.

I'm addressing you.
Are you going to let your emotional life be run by Time Magazine?
40 I'm obsessed by Time Magazine.
I read it every week.
Its cover stares at me every time I slink past the corner candystore.
I read it in the basement of the Berkeley Public Library.
It's always telling me about responsibility. Businessmen are serious.
    Movie producers are serious. Everybody's serious but me.
It occurs to me that I am America.
I am talking to myself again.

Asia is rising against me.
I haven't got a chinaman's chance.
50 I'd better consider my national resources.
My national resources consist of two joints of marijuana millions of genitals an
    unpublishable private literature that goes 1400 miles an hour and
    twentyfive-thousand mental institutions.
I say nothing about my prisons nor the millions of underprivileged who live in
    my flowerpots under the light of five hundred suns.
I have abolished the whorehouses of France, Tangiers is the next to go.
My ambition is to be President despite the fact that I'm a Catholic.

American how can I write a holy litany in your silly mood?
I will continue like Henry Ford my strophes are as individual as his automobiles
    more so they're all different sexes.
America I will sell you strophes $2500 apiece $500 down on your old strophe
America free Tom Mooney
America save the Spanish Loyalists
60 America Sacco & Vanzetti must not die
America I am the Scottsboro boys.
America when I was seven momma took me to Communist Cell meetings they
    sold us garbanzos a handful per ticket a ticket costs a nickel and the
    speeches were free everybody was angelic and sentimental about the
    workers it was all so sincere you have no idea what a good thing the party
    was in 1835 Scott Nearing was a grand old man a real mensch Mother
    Bloor made me cry I once saw Israel Amter plain. Everybody must have
    been a spy.
America you don't really want to go to war.
America it's them bad Russians.
Them Russians them Russians and them Chinamen. And them Russians.

The Russia wants to eat us alive. The Russia's power mad. She wants to take
  our cars from out our garages.
Her wants to grab Chicago. Her needs a Red Readers' Digest. Her wants our
  auto plants in Siberia. Him big bureaucracy running our fillingstations.
That no good. Ugh. Him make Indians learn read. Him need big black niggers.
  Hah. Her make us all work sixteen hours a day. Help.
America this is quite serious.
America this is the impression I get from looking in the television set.
America is this correct?
I'd better get right down to the job.
It's true I don't want to join the Army or turn lathes in precision parts factories,
  I'm nearsighted and psychopathic anyway.
America I'm putting my queer shoulder to the wheel.

James Merrill

James Merrill (1926–   ) attended Amherst and now alternates between a
house in Greece and a house in Connecticut. He has published two novels; his
books of poems have twice won the National Book Award.

After Greece

Light into the olive entered
And was oil. Rain made the huge pale stones
Shine from within. The moon turned his hair white
Who next stepped from between the columns,
Shielding his eyes. All through
The countryside were old ideas
Found lying open to the elements.
Of the gods' houses only
A minor premise here and there
Would be balancing the heaven of fixed stars
Upon a Doric capital. The rest
Lay spilled, their fluted drums half sunk in cyclamen
Or deep in water's biting clarity
Which just barely upheld me
The next week, when I sailed for home.
But where is home—these walls?
These limbs? The very spaniel underfoot
Races in sleep, toward what?
It is autumn. I did not invite
Those guests, windy and brittle, who drink my liquor.
Returning from a walk I find
The bottles filled with spleen, my room itself
Smeared by reflection on to the far hemlocks.
I some days flee in dream
Back to the exposed porch of the maidens
Only to find my great-great-grandmothers
Erect there, peering
Into a globe of red Bohemian glass.
As it swells and sinks, I call up

30 Graces, Furies, Fates, removed
To my country's warm, lit halls, with rivets forced
Through drapery, and nothing left to bear.
They seem anxious to know
What holds up heaven nowadays.
I start explaining how in that vast fire
Were other irons—well, Art, Public Spirit,
Ignorance, Economics, Love of Self,
Hatred of Self, a hundred more,
Each burning to be felt, each dedicated
40 To sparing us the worst; how I distrust them
As I should have done those ladies; how I want
Essentials: salt, wine, olive, the light, the scream—
No! I have scarcely named you,
And look, in a flash you stand full-grown before me,
Row upon row, Essentials,
Dressed like your sister caryatids
Or tombstone angels jealous of their dead,
With undulant coiffures, lips weathered, cracked by grime,
And faultless eyes gone blank beneath the immense
50 Zinc and gunmetal northern sky . . .
Stay then. Perhaps the system
Calls for spirits. This first glass I down
To the last time
I ate and drank in that old world. May I
Also survive its meanings, and my own.

Frank O'Hara

Frank O'Hara (1926–1966) was a poet of vast influence; the naturalness of O'Hara's language has earned him many followers. He attended Harvard and then worked at the Museum of Modern Art in New York, where he held an important position at the time of his accidental death in 1966. His *Collected Poems* came out in 1971.

The Day Lady Died

It is 12:20 in New York a Friday
three days after Bastille day, yes
it is 1959 and I go get a shoeshine
because I will get off the 4:19 in Easthampton
at 7:15 and then go straight to dinner
and I don't know the people who will feed me

I walk up the muggy street beginning to sun
and have a hamburger and a malted and buy
an ugly NEW WORLD WRITING to see what the poets
10 in Ghana are doing these days
                    I go on to the bank
and Miss Stillwagon (first name Linda I once heard)
doesn't even look up my balance for once in her life
and in the GOLDEN GRIFFIN I get a little Verlaine

for Patsy with drawings by Bonnard although I do
think of Hesiod, trans. Richmond Lattimore or
Brendan Behan's new play or *Le Balcon* or *Les Nègres*

of Genet, but I don't, I stick with Verlaine
after practically going to sleep with quandariness

20   and for Mike I just stroll into the PARK LANE
Liquor Store and ask for a bottle of Strega and
then I go back where I came from to 6th Avenue
and the tobacconist in the Ziegfeld Theatre and
casually ask for a carton of Gauloises and a carton
of Picayunes, and a NEW YORK POST with her face on it

and I am sweating a lot by now and thinking of
leaning on the john door in the 5 SPOT
while she whispered a song along the keyboard
to Mal Waldron and everyone and I stopped breathing

Why I Am Not a Painter

I am not a painter, I am a poet.
Why? I think I would rather be
a painter, but I am not. Well,

for instance, Mike Goldberg[1]
is starting a painting. I drop in.
"Sit down and have a drink" he
says. I drink; we drink. I look
up. "You have SARDINES in it."
"Yes, it needed something there."
10   "Oh," I go and the days go by
and I drop in again. The painting
is going on, and I go, and the days
go by. I drop in. The painting is
finished. "Where's SARDINES?"
All that's left is just
letters, "It was too much," Mike says.

But me? One day I am thinking of
a color: orange. I write a line
about orange. Pretty soon it is a
20   whole page of words, not lines.
Then another page. There should be
so much more, not of orange, of
words, of how terrible orange is
and life. Days go by. It is even in
prose, I am a real poet. My poem
is finished and I haven't mentioned
orange yet. It's twelve poems, I call
it ORANGES. And one day in a gallery
I see Mike's painting, called SARDINES.

[1]A contemporary American painter

W. D. Snodgrass

William DeWitt Snodgrass (1926–   ), born in Pennsylvania, attended the
Writers Workshop at Iowa, where he wrote his first book, *Heart's Needle*.
Credited by Robert Lowell with the invention of confessional verse, Snodgrass
in his own work has moved on to the use of dramatic monologue.

April Inventory

The green catalpa tree has turned
All white; the cherry blooms once more.
In one whole year I haven't learned
A blessed thing they pay you for.
The blossoms snow down in my hair;
The trees and I will soon be bare.

The trees have more than I to spare.
The sleek, expensive girls I teach,
Younger and pinker every year,
Bloom gradually out of reach.
The pear tree lets its petals drop
Like dandruff on a tabletop.

The girls have grown so young by now
I have to nudge myself to stare.
This year they smile and mind me how
My teeth are falling with my hair.
In thirty years I may not get
Younger, shrewder, or out of debt.

The tenth time, just a year ago,
I made myself a little list
Of all the things I'd ought to know,
Then told my parents, analyst,
And everyone who's trusted me
I'd be substantial, presently.

I haven't read one book about
A book or memorized one plot.
Or found a mind I did not doubt.
I learned one date. And then forgot.
And one by one the solid scholars
Get the degrees, the jobs, the dollars.

And smile above their starchy collars.
I taught my classes Whitehead's[1] notions;
One lovely girl, a song of Mahler's.[2]
Lacking a source-book or promotions,
I showed one child the colors of
A luna moth and how to love.

---

[1]Alfred North Whitehead (1861–1947), English philosopher and mathematician   [2]Gustav Mahler (1860–1911), Austrian composer and conductor, wrote several songs and song cycles in addition to nine monumental symphonies.

I taught myself to name my name,
To bark back, loosen love and crying;
To ease my woman so she came,
40   To ease an old man who was dying.
I have not learned how often I
Can win, can love, but choose to die.

I have not learned there is a lie
Love shall be blonder, slimmer, younger;
That my equivocating eye
Loves only by my body's hunger;
That I have forces, true to feel,
Or that the lovely world is real.

While scholars speak authority
50   And wear their ulcers on their sleeves,
My eyes in spectacles shall see
These trees procure and spend their leaves.
There is a value underneath
The gold and silver in my teeth.

Though trees turn bare and girls turn wives,
We shall afford our costly seasons;
There is a gentleness survives
That will outspeak and has its reasons.
There is a loveliness exists,
60   Preserves us, not for specialists.

Lobsters in the Window

First, you think they are dead.
Then you are almost sure
One is beginning to stir.
Out of the crushed ice, slow
As the hands of a schoolroom clock,
He lifts his one great claw
And holds it over his head;
Now, he is trying to walk.

But like a run-down toy;
10   Like the backward crabs we boys
Splashed after in the creek,
Trapped in jars or a net,
And then took home to keep.
Overgrown, retarded, weak,
He is fumbling yet
From the deep chill of his sleep

As if, in a glacial thaw,
Some ancient thing might wake
Sore and cold and stiff
20   Struggling to raise one claw
Like a defiant fist;

Yet wavering, as if
Starting to swell and ache
With that thick peg in the wrist.

I should wave back, I guess.
But still in his permanent clench
He's fallen back with the mass
Heaped in their common trench
Who stir, but do not look out
30   Through the rainstreaming glass,
Hear what the newsboys shout,
Or see the raincoats pass.

John Ashbery

John Ashbery (1927–   ) attended Harvard, overlapping with Robert Creeley, Robert Bly, Adrienne Rich, and Frank O'Hara. He spent ten years in Paris, writing for an American newspaper there, and later worked for *Art News* in New York. For many years his poetry has attracted a small but enthusiastic group of readers. In 1975, his latest volume won the Pulitzer Prize, the National Book Award, and the award of the National Book Critics Circle.

Rivers and Mountains

On the secret map the assassins
Cloistered, the Moon River was marked
Near the eighteen peaks and the city
Of humiliation and defeat—wan ending
Of the trail among dry, papery leaves
Gray-brown quills like thoughts
In the melodious but vast mass of today's
Writing through fields and swamps
Marked, on the map, with little bunches of weeds.
10   Certainly squirrels lived in the woods
But devastation and dull sleep still
Hung over the land, quelled
The rioters turned out of sleep in the peace of prisons
Singing on marble factory walls
Deaf consolation of minor tunes that pack
The air with heavy invisible rods
Pent in some sand valley from
Which only quiet walking ever instructs.
The bird flew over and
20   Sat—there was nothing else to do.
Do not mistake its silence for pride or strength
Or the waterfall for a harbor
Full of light boats that is there
Performing for thousands of people
In clothes some with places to go
Or games. Sometimes over the pillar
Of square stones its impact
Makes a light print.

So going around cities
30   To get to other places you found
It all on paper but the land
Was made of paper processed
To look like ferns, mud or other
Whose sea unrolled its magic
Distances and then rolled them up
Its secret was only a pocket
After all but some corners are darker
Than these moonless nights spent as on a raft
In the seclusion of a melody heard
40   As though through trees
And you can never ignite their touch
Long but there were homes
Flung far out near the asperities
Of a sharp, rocky pinnacle
And other collective places
Shadows of vineyards whose wine
Tasted of the forest floor
Fisheries and oyster beds
Tides under the pole
50   Seminaries of instruction, public
Places for electric light
And the major tax assessment area
Wrinkled on the plan
Of election to public office
Sixty-two years old bath and breakfast
The formal traffic, shadows
To make it not worth joining
After the ox had pulled away the cart.

Your plan was to separate the enemy into two groups
60   With the razor-edged mountains between.
It worked well on paper
But their camp had grown
To be the mountains and the map
Carefully peeled away and not torn
Was the light, a tender but tough bark
On everything. Fortunately the war was solved
In another way by isolating the two sections
Of the enemy's navy so that the mainland
Warded away the big floating ships.
70   Light bounced off the ends
Of the small gray waves to tell
Them in the observatory
About the great drama that was being won
To turn off the machinery
And quietly move among the rustic landscape
Scooping snow off the mountains rinsing
The coarser ones that love had

Slowly risen in the night to overflow
Wetting pillow and petal
80   Determined to place the letter
On the unassassinated president's desk
So that a stamp could reproduce all this
In detail, down to the last autumn leaf
And the affliction of June ride
Slowly out into the sun-blackened landscape.

Galway Kinnell

Galway Kinnell (1927–   ) grew up in Rhode Island and attended Princeton University. For many years he supported himself by teaching correspondence courses, spending a year teaching in Iran and an occasional term at an American university while he devoted himself to literary work. He has published one novel, and translations of Villon and the contemporary French poet Yves Bonnefoy. The *Book of Nightmares*, probably his best-known book of poems, appeared in 1971.

The Bear

1

In late winter
I sometimes glimpse bits of steam
coming up from
some fault in the old snow
and bend close and see it is lung-colored
and put down my nose
and know
the chilly, enduring odor of bear.

2

I take a wolf's rib and whittle
10   it sharp at both ends
and coil it up
and freeze it in blubber and place it out
on the fairway of the bears.

And when it has vanished
I move out on the bear tracks,
roaming in circles
until I come to the first, tentative, dark
splash on the earth.

And I set out
20   running, following the splashes
of blood wandering over the world.
At the cut, gashed resting places
I stop and rest,
at the crawl-marks
where he lay out on his belly

to overpass some stretch of bauchy ice
I lie out
dragging myself forward with bear-knives in my fists.

3

On the third day I begin to starve,
at nightfall I bend down as I knew I would
at a turd sopped in blood,
and hesitate, and pick it up,
and thrust it in my mouth, and gnash it down,
and rise
and go on running.

4

On the seventh day,
living by now on bear blood alone,
I can see his upturned carcass far out ahead, a scraggled,
steamy hulk,
the heavy fur riffling in the wind.

I come up to him
and stare at the narrow-spaced, petty eyes,
the dismayed
face laid back on the shoulder, the nostrils
flared, catching
perhaps the first taint of me as he
died.

I hack
a ravine in his thigh, and eat and drink,
and tear him down his whole length
and open him and climb in
and close him up after me, against the wind
and sleep.

5

And dream
of lumbering flatfooted
over the tundra,
stabbed twice from within,
splattering a trail behind me,
splattering it out no matter which way I lurch,
no matter which parabola of bear-transcendence,
which dance of solitude I attempt,
which gravity-clutched leap,
which trudge, which groan.

6

Until one day I totter and fall—
fall on this

stomach that has tried so hard to keep up,
to digest the blood as it leaked in,
to break up
and digest the bone itself: and now the breeze
70   blows over me, blows off
the hideous belches of ill-digested bear blood
and rotted stomach
and the ordinary, wretched odor of bear,

blows across
my sore, lolled tongue a song
or screech, until I think I must rise up
and dance. And I lie still.

7

I awaken I think. Marshlights
reappear, geese
80   come trailing again up the flyway.
In her ravine under old snow the dam-bear
lies, licking
lumps of smeared fur
and drizzly eyes into shapes

with her tongue. And one
hairy-soled trudge stuck out before me,
the next groaned out,
the next,
the next,
90   the rest of my days I spend
wandering: wondering
what, anyway,
was that sticky infusion, that rank flavor of blood, that poetry, by which I lived?

W. S. Merwin

William Stanley Merwin (1927–   ) attended Princeton with Galway Kinnell
and lived for some years in Spain, where for a while he tutored Robert Graves's
children. He has translated from French and from Spanish especially. In recent
years he has written short, symbolic prose, collected into two volumes. He has
published eight books of his poems.

Something I've Not Done

Something I've not done
is following me
I haven't done it again and again
so it has many footsteps
like a drumstick that's grown old and never been used

In late afternoon I hear it come closer
at times it climbs out of a sea
onto my shoulders
and I shrug it off
10   losing one more chance

Every morning
it's drunk up part of my breath for the day
and knows which way
I'm going
and already it's not done there

But once more I say I'll lay hands on it
tomorrow
and add its footsteps to my heart
and its story to my regrets
20   and its silence to my compass

Charles Tomlinson

Charles Tomlinson (1927–   ) was born in an industrial English town and
attended Cambridge. He teaches at Bristol and is a painter as well as a poet.
In some of his poetry he has learned from American sources, especially Wallace
Stevens and the Black Mountain poets.

Paring the Apple

There are portraits and still-lifes.

And there is paring the apple.

And then? Paring it slowly,
From under cool-yellow
Cold-white emerging. And . . .?

The spring of concentric peel
Unwinding off white,
The blade hidden, dividing.

There are portraits and still-lifes
10   And the first, because 'human'
Does not excel the second, and
Neither is less weighted
With a human gesture, than paring the apple
With a human stillness.

The cool blade
Severs between coolness, apple-rind
Compelling a recognition.

James Wright

James Wright (1927–1980) grew up among the coal mines and steel mills of
Ohio and attended Kenyon College, where he studied with John Crowe
Ransom. His first book was *The Green Wall*, which made him the Yale Younger
Poet in 1957. *To a Blossoming Pear Tree*, his eighth book, appeared in 1977.

The First Days

Optima dies prima fugit[1]

The first thing I saw in the morning
Was a huge golden bee ploughing
His burly right shoulder into the belly
Of a sleek yellow pear
Low on a bough.
Before he could find that sudden black honey
That squirms around in there
Inside the seed, the tree could not bear any more.
The pear fell to the ground
10   With the bee still half alive
Inside its body.
He would have died if I hadn't knelt down
And sliced the pear gently
A little more open.
The bee shuddered, and returned.
Maybe I should have left him alone there,
Drowning in his own delight.
The best days are the first
To flee, sang the lovely
20   Musician born in this town
So like my own.
I let the bee go
Among the gasworks at the edge of Mantua.

[1]"The best day is the first to flee," a line from the Roman poet Vergil, who was born near Mantua

Philip Levine

Philip Levine (1928–   ) grew up in Detroit and attended the Writers
Workshop at Iowa. His work was formal at the beginning, restrained and
delicate, and has acquired strength and vitality as he has grown older. His
volumes include *They Feed They Lion* (1972) and *1933: Poems* (1974).

Salami

Stomach of goat, crushed
sheep balls, soft full
pearls of pig eyes,
snout gristle, fresh earth,

worn iron of trotter, slate
of Zaragoza, dried cat heart,
cock claws. She grinds
them with one hand and
with the other fists
10   mountain thyme, basil,
paprika, and knobs of garlic.
And if a tooth of stink thistle
pulls blood from the round
blue marbled hand
all the better for
this ruby of Pamplona,
this bright jewel of Vich,
this stained crown
of Solsona, this
20   salami.
          The daughter
of mismatched eyes,
36 year old infant smelling
of milk. Mama, she cries, mama,
but mama is gone,
and the old stone cutter
must wipe the drool
from her jumper. His puffed fingers
unbutton and point her
30   to toilet. Ten, twelve hours
a day, as long as the winter sun
holds up he rebuilds
the unvisited church
of San Martin. Cheep cheep
of the hammer high above
the town, sparrow cries
lost in the wind or lost
in the mind. At dusk he leans
to the coal dull wooden Virgin
40   and asks for blessings on
the slow one and peace
on his grizzled head, asks
finally and each night
for the forbidden, for
the knowledge of every
mysterious stone, and
the words go out on
the overwhelming incense
of salami.
50   A single crow
passed high over the house,
I wakened out of nightmare.
The winds had changed,
the Tremontana was tearing

out of the Holy Mountains
to meet the sea winds
in my yard, burning and
scaring the young pines.
The single poplar wailed
60   in terror. With salt,
with guilt, with the need
to die, the vestments
of my life flared, I
was on fire, a stranger
staggering through my house
butting walls and falling
over furniture, looking
for a way out. In the last room
where moonlight slanted
70   through a broken shutter
I found my smallest son
asleep or dead, floating
on a bed of colorless light.
When I leaned closer
I could smell the small breaths
going and coming, and each
bore its prayer for me,
the true and earthy prayer
of salami.

Anne Sexton

Anne Sexton (1928–1974) did not begin to write poems until she was in her late twenties, attending poetry workshops. Then she wrote prolifically and with great energy for many years, combating psychosis and an urge to suicide. Her books include *To Bedlam and Part Way Back* (1960), *Live or Die* (1967), and *The Awful Rowing Towards God* (1975).

Wanting to Die

Since you ask, most days I cannot remember.
I walk in my clothing, unmarked by that voyage.
Then the almost unnameable lust returns.

Even then I have nothing against life.
I know well the grass blades you mention,
the furniture you have placed under the sun.

But suicides have a special language.
Like carpenters they want to know *which tools.*
They never ask *why build.*

10   Twice I have so simply declared myself,
have possessed the enemy, eaten the enemy,
have taken on his craft, his magic.

In this way, heavy and thoughtful,
warmer than oil or water,
I have rested, drooling at the mouth-hole.

I did not think of my body at needle point.
Even the cornea and the leftover urine were gone.
Suicides have already betrayed the body.

Still-born, they don't always die,
20   but dazzled, they can't forget a drug so sweet
that even children would look on and smile.

To thrust all that life under your tongue!—
that, all by itself, becomes a passion.
Death's a sad bone; bruised, you'd say,

and yet she waits for me, year after year,
to so delicately undo an old wound,
to empty my breath from its bad prison.

Balanced there, suicides sometimes meet,
raging at the fruit, a pumped-up moon,
30   leaving the bread they mistook for a kiss,

leaving the page of the book carelessly open,
something unsaid, the phone off the hook
and the love, whatever it was, an infection.

Edward Dorn

Edward Dorn (1929–   ) attended Black Mountain College and studied with
Robert Creeley and Charles Olson. One of Olson's didactic pamphlets is a
bibliography addressed to Ed Dorn. Perhaps his best work is the long poem
originally called *Gunslinger*, now shortened to *Slinger*.

On the Debt My Mother Owed to Sears Roebuck

Summer was dry, dry the garden
our beating hearts, on that farm, dry
with the rows of corn the grasshoppers
came happily to strip, in hordes, the first
thing I knew about locust was they came
dry under the foot like the breaking of
a mechanical bare heart which collapses
from an unkind an incessant word whispered
in the house of the major farmer
10   and the catalogue company,
from no fault of anyone
my father coming home tired
and grinning down the road, turning in
is the tank full? thinking of the horse
and my lazy arms thinking of the water
so far below the well platform.

On the debt my mother owed to sears roebuck
we brooded, she in the house, a little heavy
from too much corn meal, she
20 a little melancholy from the dust of the fields
in her eye, the only title she ever had to lands—
and man's ways winged their way to her through the mail
saying so much per month
so many months, this is yours, take it
take it, take it, take it
and in the corncrib, like her lives in that house
the mouse nibbled away at the cob's yellow grain
until six o'clock when her sorrows grew less
and my father came home

30 On the debt my mother owed to sears roebuck?
I have nothing to say, it gave me clothes to
wear to school,
and my mother brooded
in the rooms of the house, the kitchen, waiting
for the men she knew, her husband, her son
from work, from school, from the air of locusts
and dust masking the hedges of fields she knew
in her eye as a vague land where she lived,
boundaries, whose tractors chugged pulling harrows
40 pulling discs, pulling great yields from the earth
pulse for the armies in two hemispheres, 1943
and she was part of that *stay at home army* to keep
things going, owing that debt.

Thom Gunn

Thom Gunn (1929–   ) grew up in England, son of a successful journalist,
attended Cambridge, and came to California in 1954. He lives in San
Francisco, where he has spent most of the time since leaving England.

On the Move

'Man, you gotta Go.'

The blue jay scuffling in the bushes follows
Some hidden purpose, and the gust of birds
That spurts across the field, the wheeling swallows,
Have nested in the trees and undergrowth.
Seeking their instinct, or their poise, or both,
One moves with an uncertain violence
Under the dust thrown by a baffled sense
Or the dull thunder of approximate words.

On motorcycles, up the road, they come:
10 Small, black, as flies hanging in heat, the Boys,
Until the distance throws them forth, their hum
Bulges to thunder held by calf and thigh.

In goggles, donned impersonality,
In gleaming jackets trophied with the dust,
They strap in doubt—by hiding it, robust—
And almost hear a meaning in their noise.

Exact conclusion of their hardiness
Has no shape yet, but from known whereabouts
They ride, direction where the tires press.
20 They scare a flight of birds across the field:
Much that is natural, to the will must yield.
Men manufacture both machine and soul,
And use what they imperfectly control
To dare a future from the taken routes.

It is a part solution, after all.
One is not necessarily discord
On earth; or damned because, half animal,
One lacks direct instinct, because one wakes
Afloat on movement that divides and breaks.
30 One joins the movement in a valueless world,
Choosing it, till, both hurler and the hurled,
One moves as well, always toward, toward.

A minute holds them, who have come to go:
The self-defined, astride the created will
They burst away; the towns they travel through
Are home for neither bird nor holiness,
For birds and saints complete their purposes.
At worst, one is in motion; and at best,
Reaching no absolute, in which to rest,
40 One is always nearer by not keeping still.

X. J. Kennedy

X. J. Kennedy (1929–   ) is the only poet in this book with a pen-initial. His
name is Joseph Kennedy, but he felt that there had been enough Joseph
Kennedys in the news. He is the author of poems for children, successful
textbooks, and two books of poems.

In a Prominent Bar in Secaucus One Day

(To the tune of 'The Old Orange Flute' or the tune of 'Sweet Betsy from Pike')

In a prominent bar in Secaucus one day
Rose a lady in skunk with a topheavy sway,
Raised a knobby red finger—all turned from their beer—
While with eyes bright as snowcrust she sang high and clear:

'Now who of you'd think from an eyeload of me
That I once was a lady as proud as could be?
Oh I'd never sit down by a tumbledown drunk
If it wasn't, my dears, for the high cost of junk.

'All the gents used to swear that the white of my calf
10 Beat the down of the swan by a length and a half.
In the kerchief of linen I caught to my nose
Ah, there never fell snot, but a little gold rose.

'I had seven gold teeth and a toothpick of gold,
My Virginia cheroot was a leaf of it rolled
And I'd light it each time with a thousand in cash—
Why the bums used to fight if I flicked them an ash.

'Once the toast of the Biltmore, the belle of the Taft,
I would drink bottle beer at the Drake, never draught,
And dine at the Astor on Salisbury steak
20 With a clean tablecloth for each bite I did take.

'In a car like the Roxy I'd roll to the track,
A steel-guitar trio, a bar in the back,
And the wheels made no noise, they turned over so fast,
Still it took you ten minutes to see me go past.

'When the horses bowed down to me that I might choose,
I bet on them all, for I hated to lose.
Now I'm saddled each night for my butter and eggs
And the broken threads race down the backs of my legs.

'Let you hold in mind, girls, that your beauty must pass
30 Like a lovely white clover that rusts with its grass.
Keep your bottoms off bar stools and marry you young
Or be left—an old barrel with many a bung.

'For when time takes you out for a spin in his car
You'll be hard-pressed to stop him from going too far
And be left by the roadside, for all your good deeds,
Two toadstools for tits and a face full of weeds.'

All the house raised a cheer, but the man at the bar
Made a phonecall and up pulled a red patrol car
And she blew us a kiss as they copped her away
40 From that prominent bar in Secaucus, N.J.

Adrienne Rich

Adrienne Rich (1929–   ) grew up in Baltimore and attended Radcliffe
College. She was Yale Younger Poet in her senior year at college and two years
later received a Guggenheim Fellowship. Her second volume—*The Diamond
Cutters*—followed in 1955 and then there was a gap of some years, while she
had three sons in rapid succession. Her work has changed considerably, losing
its decorativeness, becoming starker, tighter, tougher, and more emotional.
Her prose book, *Of Woman Born* (1977), is a monument of the feminist
movement.

From an Old House in America

1.

Deliberately, long ago
the carcasses

of old bugs crumbled
into the rut of the window

and we started sleeping here
Fresh June bugs batter this June's

screens, June-lightning batters
the spiderweb

I sweep the wood-dust
10   from the wood-box

the snout of the vacuum cleaner
sucks the past away

2.

Other lives were lived here:
mostly un-articulate

yet someone left her creamy signature
in the trail of rusticated

narcissus straggling up
through meadowgrass and vetch

Families breathed close
20   boxed-in from the cold

hard times, short growing season
the old rainwater cistern

hulks in the cellar

3.

Like turning through the contents of a drawer:
these rusted screws, this empty vial

useless, this box of watercolor paints
dried to insolubility—

but this—
this pack of cards with no card missing

30   still playable
and three good fuses

and this toy: a little truck
scarred red, yet all its wheels still turn

The humble tenacity of things
waiting for people, waiting for months, for years

4.

Often rebuked, yet always back returning
I place my hand on the hand

of the dead, invisible palm-print
on the doorframe

40   spiked with daylilies, green leaves
catching in the screen door

or I read the backs of old postcards
curling from thumbtacks, winter and summer

fading through cobweb-tinted panes—
white church in Norway

Dutch hyacinths bleeding azure
red beach on Corsica

set-pieces of the world
stuck to this house of plank

50   I flash on wife and husband
embattled, in the years

that dried, dim ink was wet
those signatures

5.

If they call me man-hater, you
would have known it for a lie

but the *you* I want to speak to
has become your death

If I dream of you these days
I know my dreams are mine and not of you

60   yet something hangs between us
older and stranger than ourselves

like a translucent curtain, a sheet of water
a dusty window

the irreducible, incomplete connection
between the dead and living

or between man and woman in this
savagely fathered and unmothered world

6.

The other side of a translucent
curtain, a sheet of water

70   a dusty window, Non-being
utters its flat tones

the speech of an actor learning his lines
phonetically

the final autistic statement
of the self-destroyer

All my energy reaches out tonight
to comprehend a miracle beyond

raising the dead: the undead to watch
back on the road of birth

7.

80   I am an American woman:
I turn that over

like a leaf pressed in a book
I stop and look up from

into the coals of the stove
or the black square of the window

Foot-slogging through the Bering Strait
jumping from the *Arbella* to my death

chained to the corpse beside me
I feel my pains begin

90   I am washed up on this continent
shipped here to be fruitful

my body a hollow ship
bearing sons to the wilderness

sons who ride away
on horseback, daughters

whose juices drain like mine
into the *arroyo* of stillbirths, massacrès

Hanged as witches, sold as breeding-wenches
my sisters leave me

100   I am not the wheatfield
nor the virgin forest

I never chose this place
yet I am of it now

In my decent collar, in the daguerrotype
I pierce its legend with my look

my hands wring the necks of prairie chickens
I am used to blood

When the men hit the hobo track
I stay on with the children

110   my power is brief and local
but I know my power

I have lived in isolation
from other women, so much

in the mining camps, the first cities
the Great Plains winters

Most of the time, in my sex, I was alone

8.

Tonight in this northeast kingdom
striated iris stand in a jar with daisies

120 the porcupine gnaws in the shed
fireflies beat and simmer

caterpillars begin again
their long, innocent climb

the length of leaves of burdock
or webbing of a garden chair

plain and ordinary things
speak softly

the light square on old wallpaper
where a poster has fallen down

Robert Indiana's LOVE
130 leftover of a decade

9.

I do not want to simplify
Or: I would simplify

by naming the complexity
It was made over-simple all along

the separation of powers
the allotment of sufferings

her spine cracking in labor
his plow driving across the Indian graves

her hand unconscious on the cradle, her mind
140 with the wild geese

his mother-hatred driving him
into exile from the earth

the refugee couple with their cardboard luggage
standing on the ramshackle landing-stage

he with fingers frozen around his Law
she with her down quilt sewn through iron nights

—the weight of the old world, plucked
drags after them, a random feather-bed

10.

Her children dead of diphtheria, she
150 set herself on fire with kerosene

(O Lord I was unworthy
Thou didst find me out)

she left the kitchen scrubbed
down to the marrow of its boards

"The penalty for barrenness
is emptiness

my punishment is my crime
what I have failed to do, is me . . ."

—Another month without a show
160   and this the seventh year

O Father let this thing pass out of me
I swear to You

I will live for the others, asking nothing
I will ask nothing, ever, for myself

11.

Out back of this old house
datura tangles with a gentler weed

its spiked pods smelling
of bad dreams and death

I reach through the dark, groping
170   past spines of nightmare

to brush the leaves of sensuality
A dream of tenderness

wrestles with all I know of history
I cannot now lie down

with a man who fears my power
or reaches for me as for death

or with a lover who imagines
we are not in danger

12.

If it was lust that had defined us—
180   their lust and fear of our deep places

we have done our time
as faceless torsos licked by fire

we are in the open, on our way—
our counterparts

the pinyon jay, the small
gilt-winged insect

the Cessna throbbing level
the raven floating in the gorge

the rose and violet vulva of the earth
190 filling with darkness

yet deep within a single sparkle
of red, a human fire

and near and yet above the western planet
calmly biding her time

13.
They were the distractions, lust and fear
but are

themselves a key
Everything that can be used, will be:

the fathers in their ceremonies
200 the genital contests

the cleansing of blood from pubic hair
the placenta buried and guarded

their terror of blinding
by the look of her who bore them

If you do not believe
that fear and hatred

read the lesson again
in the old dialect

14.
But can't you see me as a human being
210 he said

What is a human being
she said

I try to understand
he said

what will you undertake
she said

will you punish me for history
he said

what will you undertake
220 she said

do you believe in collective guilt
he said

let me look in your eyes
she said

15.

Who is here. The Erinyes.[1]
One to sit in judgment.

One to speak tenderness.
One to inscribe the verdict on the canyon wall.

If you have not confessed
230   the damage

if you have not recognized
the Mother of reparations

if you have not come to terms
with the women in the mirror

if you have not come to terms
with the inscription

the terms of the ordeal
the discipline   the verdict

if still you are on your way
240   still She awaits your coming

16.

"Such women are dangerous
to the order of things"

and yes, we will be dangerous
to ourselves

groping through spines of nightmare
(*datura* tangling with a simpler herb)

because the line dividing
lucidity from darkness

is yet to be marked out

250   Isolation, the dream
of the frontier woman

leveling her rifle along
the homestead fence

still snares our pride
—a suicidal leaf

laid under the burning-glass
in the sun's eye

Any woman's death diminishes me

---

[1]The Furies; in Greek mythology, terrible winged goddesses who avenge unpunished crime.

Gregory Corso

Gregory Corso (1930–   ), born in New York, has worked as a manual laborer, a merchant seaman, and a teacher. Two of his early books were published by City Lights Books in San Francisco, where he belonged to the Beat Generation.

Marriage

Should I get married? Should I be good?
Astound the girl next door with my velvet suit and faustus hood?
Don't take her to movies but to cemeteries
tell all about werewolf bathtubs and forked clarinets
then desire her and kiss her and all the preliminaries
and she going just so far and I understanding why
not getting angry saying You must feel! It's beautiful to feel!
Instead take her in my arms lean against an old crooked tombstone
and woo her the entire night the constellations in the sky—

10   When she introduces me to her parents
back straightened, hair finally combed, strangled by a tie,
should I sit knees together on their 3rd degree sofa
and not ask Where's the bathroom?
How else to feel other than I am,
often thinking Flash Gordon soap—
O how terrible it must be for a young man
seated before a family and the family thinking
We never saw him before! He wants our Mary Lou!
After tea and homemade cookies they ask What do you do for a living?
20   Should I tell them? Would they like me then?
Say All right get married, we're losing a daughter
but we're gaining a son—
And should I then ask Where's the bathroom?

O God, and the wedding! All her family and her friends
and only a handful of mine all scroungy and bearded
just wait to get at the drinks and food—
And the priest! he looking at me as if I masturbated
asking me Do you take this woman for your lawful wedded wife?
And I trembling what to say say Pie Glue!
30   I kiss the bride all those corny men slapping me on the back
She's all yours, boy! Ha-ha-ha!
And in their eyes you could see some obscene honeymoon going on—
Then all that absurd rice and clanky cans and shoes
Niagara Falls! Hordes of us! Husbands! Wives! Flowers! Chocolates!
All streaming into cozy hotels
All going to do the same thing tonight
The indifferent clerk he knowing what was going to happen
The lobby zombies they knowing what
The whistling elevator man he knowing
40   The winking bellboy knowing
Everybody knowing! I'd be almost inclined not to do anything!

Stay up all night! Stare that hotel clerk in the eye!
Screaming: I deny honeymoon! I deny honeymoon!
running rampant into those almost climactic suites
yelling Radio belly! Cat shovel!
O I'd live in Niagara forever! in a dark cave beneath the Falls
I'd sit there the Mad Honeymooner
devising ways to break marriages, a scourge of bigamy
a saint of divorce—

50   But I should get married I should be good
How nice it'd be to come home to her
and sit by the fireplace and she in the kitchen
aproned young and lovely wanting my baby
and so happy about me she burns the roast beef
and comes crying to me and I get up from my big papa chair
saying Christmas teeth! Radiant brains! Apple deaf!
God what a husband I'd make! Yes, I should get married!
So much to do! like sneaking into Mr Jones' house late at night
and cover his golf clubs with 1920 Norwegian books
60   Like hanging a picture of Rimbaud on the lawnmower
like pasting Tannu Tuva postage stamps all over the picket fence
like when Mrs Kindhead comes to collect for the Community Chest
grab her and tell her There are unfavorable omens in the sky!
And when the mayor comes to get my vote tell him
When are you going to stop people killing whales!
And when the milkman comes leave him a note in the bottle
Penguin dust, bring me penguin dust, I want penguin dust—

Yet if I should get married and it's Connecticut and snow
and she gives birth to a child and I am sleepless, worn,
70   up for nights, head bowed against a quiet window, the past behind me,
finding myself in the most common of situations a trembling man
knowledged with responsibility not twig-smear nor Roman coin soup—
O what would that be like!
Surely I'd give it for a nipple a rubber Tacitus
For a rattle a bag of broken Bach records
Tack Della Francesca all over its crib
Sew the Greek alphabet on its bib
And build for its playpen a roofless Parthenon

No, I doubt I'd be that kind of father
80   not rural not snow no quiet window
but hot smelly tight New York City
seven flights up, roaches and rats in the walls
a fat Reichian wife screeching over potatoes Get a job!
And five nose running brats in love with Batman
And the neighbors all toothless and dry haired
like those hag masses of the 18th century
all wanting to come in and watch TV
The landlord wants his rent
Grocery store Blue Cross & Electric Knights of Columbus

90 Impossible to lie back and dream Telephone snow, ghost parking—
No! I should not get married I should never get married!
But—imagine If I were married to a beautiful sophisticated woman
tall and pale wearing an elegant black dress and long black gloves
holding a cigarette holder in one hand and a highball in the other
and we lived high up in a penthouse with a huge window
from which we could see all of New York and ever farther on clearer days
No, can't imagine myself married to that pleasant prison dream—

O but what about love? I forget love
not that I am incapable of love
100 it's just that I see love as odd as wearing shoes—
I never wanted to marry a girl who was like my mother
And Ingrid Bergman was always impossible
And there's maybe a girl now but she's already married
And I don't like men and—
but there's got to be somebody!
Because what if I'm 60 years old and not married,
all alone in a furnished room with pee stains on my underwear
and everybody else is married! All the universe married but me!

Ah, yet well I know that were a woman possible as I am possible
110 then marriage would be possible—
Like SHE in her lonely alien gaud waiting her Egyptian lover
so I wait—bereft of 2,000 years and the bath of life.

Ted Hughes

Ted Hughes (1930–   ) attended Cambridge University, where he met and
married Sylvia Plath. His poems have been continually difficult, obdurate, and
violent, often about animals—real or mythical. He is concerned to discover and
explore instinctual life.

Thrushes

Terrifying are the attent sleek thrushes on the lawn,
More coiled steel than living—a poised
Dark deadly eye, those delicate legs
Triggered to stirrings beyond sense—with a start, a bounce, a stab
Overtake the instant and drag out some writhing thing.
No indolent procrastinations and no yawning stares,
No sighs or head-scratchings. Nothing but bounce and stab
And a ravening second.

Is it their single-mind-sized skulls, or a trained
10 Body, or genius, or a nestful of brats
Gives their days this bullet and automatic
Purpose? Mozart's brain had it, and the shark's mouth
That hungers down the blood-smell even to a leak of its own

Side and devouring of itself: efficiency which
Strikes too streamlined for any doubt to pluck at it
Or obstruction deflect.

With a man it is otherwise. Heroisms on horseback,
Outstripping his desk-diary at a broad desk,
Carving at a tiny ivory ornament
20   For years: his act worships itself—while for him,
Though he bends to be blent in the prayer, how loud and above what
Furious spaces of fire do the distracting devils
Orgy and hosannah, under what wilderness
Of black silent waters weep.

Gary Snyder

Gary Snyder (1930–   ) grew up on the West Coast and attended Reed
College. He did graduate work in Oriental languages at Berkeley and has lived
many years in Japan, studying Zen Buddhism in Kyoto. Now he lives in a house
of his own construction called Kitkitdizze, north of Sacramento, and practices
the life he preaches.

Above Pate Valley

We finished clearing the last
Section of trail by noon,
High on the ridge-side
Two thousand feet above the creek—
Reached the pass, went on
Beyond the white pine groves,
Granite shoulders, to a small
Green meadow watered by the snow,
Edged with Aspen—sun
10   Straight high and blazing
But the air was cool.
Ate a cold fried trout in the
Trembling shadows. I spied
A glitter, and found a flake
Black volcanic glass—obsidian—
By a flower. Hands and knees
Pushing the Bear grass, thousands
Of arrowhead leavings over a
Hundred yards. Not one good
20   Head, just razor flakes
On a hill snowed all but summer,
A land of fat summer deer,
They came to camp. On their
Own trails. I followed my own
Trail here. Picked up the cold-drill,
Pick, singlejack, and sack
Of dynamite.
Ten thousand years.

Geoffrey Hill

Geoffrey Hill (1932–   ) grew up in a Midlands English town, where his father was the local policeman. He attended Oxford, and after earning two degrees there went to Leeds, where he has become a professor. He writes his poems slowly and produces little, but his work has great power and originality.

Merlin

I will consider the outnumbering dead:
For they are the husks of what was rich seed.
Now, should they come together to be fed,
They would outstrip the locusts' covering tide.

Arthur, Elaine, Mordred; they are all gone
Among the raftered galleries of bone.
By the long barrows of Logres they are made one,
And over their city stands the pinnacled corn.

Orpheus and Eurydice

Though there are wild dogs
    Infesting the roads
We have recitals, catalogues
    Of protected birds;

And the rare pale sun
    To water our days.
Men turn to savagery now or turn
    To the laws'

Immutable black and red.
10   To be judged for his song,
Traversing the still-moist dead,
    The newly-stung,

Love goes, carrying compassion
    To the rawly-difficult;
His countenance, his hands' motion,
    Serene even to a fault.

Sylvia Plath

Sylvia Plath (1932–1963) attended Smith College, and wrote with a professional skill from an early age. She attended Cambridge University on a fellowship, where she met and married the English poet Ted Hughes. After the birth of their second child, when Plath and Hughes were separated, her work abandoned its skillful surfaces and became profoundly emotional, angry, brilliant, and disturbing. There was a brief moment of great poetry, ended by her suicide. The posthumous *Ariel* (1965) collects her best poetry.

Poppies in October

Even the sun-clouds this morning cannot manage such skirts.
Nor the woman in the ambulance
Whose red heart blooms through her coat so astoundingly—

A gift, a love gift
Utterly unasked for
By a sky

Palely and flamily
Igniting its carbon monoxides, by eyes
Dulled to a halt under bowlers.

10   O my God, what am I
That these late mouths should cry open
In a forest of frost, in a dawn of cornflowers.

Lady Lazarus

I have done it again.
One year in every ten
I manage it—

A sort of walking miracle, my skin
Bright as a Nazi lampshade,
My right foot

A paperweight,
My face a featureless, fine
Jew linen.

10   Peel off the napkin
O my enemy.
Do I terrify?—

The nose, the eye pits, the full set of teeth?
The sour breath
Will vanish in a day.

Soon, soon the flesh
The grave cave ate will be
At home on me

And I a smiling woman.
20   I am only thirty.
And like the cat I have nine times to die.

This is Number Three.
What a trash
To annihilate each decade.

What a million filaments.
The peanut-crunching crowd
Shoves in to see

Them unwrap me hand and foot—
The big strip tease.
30   Gentleman, ladies,

These are my hands,
My knees.
I may be skin and bone,

Nevertheless, I am the same, identical woman.
The first time it happened I was ten.
It was an accident.

The second time I meant
To last it out and not come back at all.
I rocked shut

40   As a seashell.
They had to call and call
And pick the worms off me like sticky pearls.

Dying
Is an art, like everything else.
I do it exceptionally well.

I do it so it feels like hell.
I do it so it feels real.
I guess you could say I've a call.

It's easy enough to do it in a cell.
50   It's easy enough to do it and stay put.
It's the theatrical

Comeback in broad day
To the same place, the same face, the same brute
Amused shout:

"A miracle!"
That knocks me out.
There is a charge

For the eyeing of my scars, there is a charge
For the hearing of my heart—
60   It really goes.

And there is a charge, a very large charge,
For a word or a touch
Or a bit of blood

Or a piece of my hair or my clothes.
So, so, Herr Doktor.
So, Herr Enemy.

I am your opus,
I am your valuable,
The pure gold baby

70   That melts to a shriek.
I turn and burn.
Do not think I underestimate your great concern.

Ash, ash—
You poke and stir.
Flesh, bone, there is nothing there—

A cake of soap,
A wedding ring,
A gold filling.

Herr God, Herr Lucifer,
80   Beware
Beware.

Out of the ash
I rise with my red hair
And I eat men like air.

Death & Co.

Two, of course there are two.
It seems perfectly natural now—
The one who never looks up, whose eyes are lidded
And balled, like Blake's,
Who exhibits

The birthmarks that are his trademark—
The scald scar of water,
The nude
Verdigris of the condor.
10   I am red meat. His beak

Claps sidewise: I am not his yet.
He tells me how badly I photograph.
He tells me how sweet
The babies look in their hospital
Icebox, a simple

Frill at the neck,
Then the flutings of their Ionian
Death-gowns,

Then two little feet.
20   He does not smile or smoke.

The other does that,
His hair long and plausive.
Bastard
Masturbating a glitter,
He wants to be loved.

I do not stir.
The frost makes a flower,
The dew makes a star,
The dead bell,
30   The dead bell.

Somebody's done for.

Etheridge Knight

Etheridge Knight (1933–   ) was wounded in Korea and later became
addicted to heroin. He supported his habit by stealing, which left him in the
Indiana State Prison. He began to write poems in prison, where Gwendolyn
Brooks visited and encouraged him. His first volume was called *Poems from
Prison*. Since his release he has taught poetry at various colleges and conducted
workshops all over the United States.

Hard Rock Returns to Prison from the Hospital for the Criminal Insane

Hard Rock was "known not to take no shit
From nobody," and he had the scars to prove it:
Split purple lips, lumped ears, welts above
His yellow eyes, and one long scar that cut
Across his temple and plowed through a thick
Canopy of kinky hair.

The WORD was that Hard Rock wasn't a mean nigger
Anymore, that the doctors had bored a hole in his head,
Cut out part of his brain, and shot electricity
10   Through the rest. When they brought Hard Rock back,
Handcuffed and chained, he was turned loose,
Like a freshly gelded stallion, to try his new status.
And we all waited and watched, like indians at a corral,
To see if the WORD was true.

As we waited we wrapped ourselves in the cloak
Of his exploits: "Man, the last time, it took eight
Screws to put him in the Hole." "Yeah, remember when he
Smacked the captain with his dinner tray?" "He set
The record for time in the Hole—67 straight days!"
20   "Ol Hard Rock! man, that's one crazy nigger."
And then the jewel of a myth that Hard Rock had once bit
A screw on the thumb and poisoned him with syphilitic spit.

The testing came, to see if Hard Rock was really tame.
A hillbilly called him a black son of a bitch
And didn't lose his teeth, a screw who knew Hard Rock
From before shook him down and barked in his face.
And Hard Rock did *nothing*. Just grinned and looked silly,
His eyes empty like knot holes in a fence.

And even after we discovered that it took Hard Rock
30 Exactly 3 minutes to tell you his first name,
We told ourselves that he had just wised up,
Was being cool; but we could not fool ourselves for lóng,
And we turned away, our eyes on the ground. Crushed.
He had been our Destroyer, the doer of things
We dreamed of doing but could not bring ourselves to do,
The fears of years, like a biting whip,
Had cut grooves too deeply across our backs.

2 Poems for Black Relocation Centers

I

Flukum couldn't stand the strain. Flukum
wanted inner and outer order, so
he joined the army where U.S. Manuals made
everything plain—even how to button his shirt,
and how to kill the yellow men. (If Flukum
ever felt hurt or doubt about who his enemy
was, the Troop Information Officer or the Stars
and Stripes[1] straightened him out.)
Plus, we must not forget
10 that Flukum was paid well to let the Red
Blood. And sin? If Flukum ever thought about sin
or Hell for squashing the yellow men, the good Chaplain
(Holy by God and by Congress) pointed out with
Devilish skill that to kill the colored men was not
altogether a sin.

Flukum marched back from the war, straight and tall,
and with presents for all: a water pipe for daddy,
teeny tea cups for mama, sheer silk for tittee, and
a jade inlaid dagger for me. But, with a smile
20 on his face in a place just across the bay,
Flukum, the patriot, got shot that same day,
got shot in his great wide chest, bedecked with good
conduct ribbons. He died surprised, he had thought
the enemy far away on the other side of the sea.

(When we received his belongings they took away my dagger.)

---

[1]Newspaper published for U.S. service personnel overseas

II
Dead. He died in Detroit, his beard
was filled with lice; his halo glowed
and his white robe flowed magnificently
over the charred beams and splintered glass;
30   his stern blue eyes were rimmed with red,
and full of reproach; and the stench: roasted rats
and fat baby rumps swept up his nose that
had lost its arch of triumph. He died outraged,
and indecently, shouting impieties and betrayals.
And he arose out of his own ashes. Stripped.
A faggot in steel boots.

Imamu Amiri Baraka

Imamu Amiri Baraka (LeRoi Jones) (1934–   ) is a leading black playwright
and poet. He has also published short stories and polemical prose. He began
publishing as an integrated black writer and edited a magazine in collaboration
with white editors. In later years his politics have moved from black
separatism to Marxism-Leninism.

Watergate

"Dead Crow" is an ol ugly
eagle
i know
run a "eagle
laundry"
wash
eagles
over & over
this eagle wash
10   hisself
like lady macbeth
blood mad & sterile
hooked teeth
pulled
out
in a flag costume
just stripes
no stars

Careers

What is the life
of the old lady
standing
on the stair
print flowered
housedress

        gray and orange
        hair
        bent
10   on a rail
        eyes open for
        jr.
        bobby
        jb, somebody
        to come, and carry her
        wish
        slow
        cripple woman, still does
        white folks work
20   in the mornings she get up
        creeps into a cadillac
        up into the florient lilac titty valleys
        of blind ugliness, you think the woman loves
        the younger white woman
        the woman she ladles soup for
        the radio she turns on when the white lady nods
        she carries them in her bowed back hunched face
        my grandmother workd the same
        but stole things for jesus' sake
30   we wore boss rags in grammar school
        straight off the backs of straight up americans
        used but groovy and my grandmother when she returned at night
        with mason jars and hat boxes full of goods
        probably asked for forgiveness on the bus
        i think the lady across from me must do the same
        though she comes back in a cab, so times, it seems,
        have changed.

Wendell Berry

Wendell Berry (1934–   ) was born in Kentucky, lived in New York briefly, and returned to Kentucky, where for a time he taught at the University. Increasingly Berry has turned to farming his own land and to writing about "culture and agriculture." He has written novels and books of essays as well as poems. With Gary Synder, he is a poet whose work and life serve to preserve the planet.

The Wild Geese

        Horseback on Sunday morning,
        harvest over, we taste persimmon
        and wild grape, sharp sweet
        of summer's end. In time's maze
        over the fall fields, we name names
        that went west from here, names
        that rest on graves. We open

a persimmon seed to find the tree
that stands in promise,
10   pale, in the seed's marrow.
Geese appear high over us,
pass, and the sky closes. Abandon,
as in love or sleep, holds
them to their way, clear,
in the ancient faith: what we need
is here. And we pray, not
for new earth or heaven, but to be
quiet in heart, and in eye
clear. What we need is here.

Mark Strand

Mark Strand (1934–   ) was born in Canada and attended colleges in the United
States, where he has settled. He lives in Salt Lake City, Utah.

Pot Roast

I gaze upon the roast,
that is sliced and laid out
on my plate
and over it
I spoon the juices
of carrot and onion.
And for once I do not regret
the passage of time.

I sit by a window
10   that looks
on the soot-stained brick of buildings
and do not care that I see
no living thing—not a bird,
not a branch in bloom,
not a soul moving
in the rooms
behind the dark panes.
These days when there is little
to love or to praise
20   one could do worse
than yield
to the power of food.
So I bend

to inhale
the steam that rises
from my plate, and I think
of the first time
I tasted a roast
like this.

30   It was years ago
      in Seabright,
      Nova Scotia;
      my mother leaned
      over my dish and filled it
      and when I finished
      filled it again.
      I remember the gravy,
      its odor of garlic and celery,
      and sopping it up
40   with pieces of bread.

      And now
      I taste it again.
      The meat of memory.
      The meat of no change.
      I raise my fork in praise,
      and I eat.

Charles Wright

Charles Wright (1935–   ) comes from Virginia and lives in California, where he teaches at the University of California at Irvine.

Virgo Descending

    Through the viridian (and black of the burnt match),
    Through ox-blood and ochre, the ham colored clay,
    Through plate after plate, down
    Where the worm and the mole will not go,
    Through ore-seam and fire-seam,
    My grandmother, senile and 89, crimpbacked, stands
    Like a door ajar on her soft bed,
    The open beams and bare studs of the hall
    Pink as an infant's skin in the floating dark;
10 Shavings and curls swing down like snowflakes across her face.

    My aunt and I walk past. As always, my father
    Is planning rooms, dragging his lame leg,
    Stroke-straightened and foreign, behind him,
    An aberrant 2-by-4 he can't fit snug.
    I lay my head on my aunt's shoulder, feeling
    At home, and walk on.
    Through arches and door jambs, the spidery wires
    And coiled cables, the blueprint takes shape:
    My mother's room to the left, the door closed;
20 My father's room to the left, the door closed—

    Ahead, my brother's room, unfinished;
    Behind, my sister's room, also unfinished.
    Buttresses, winches, block-and-tackle: the scale of everything

Is enormous. We keep on walking. And pass
My aunt's room, almost complete, the curtains up,
The lamp and the medicine arranged
In their proper places, in arm's reach of where the bed will go . . .
The next one is mine, now more than half done,
Cloyed by the scent of jasmine
30   White-gummed and anxious, their mouths sucking the air dry.

Home is what you lie in, or hang above, the house
Your father made, or keeps on making,
The dirt you moisten, the sap you push up and nourish . . .
I enter the living room, it, too, unfinished, its far wall
Not there, opening on to a radiance
I can't begin to imagine, a light
My father walks from, approaching me,
Dragging his right leg, rolling his plans into a perfect curl.
That light, he mutters, that damned light.
40   We can't keep it out. It keeps on filling your room.

Charles Simic

Charles Simic (1938–   ) was born in Yugoslavia and came to the United States in 1949. He lives in New Hampshire and has published four books of poems.

Fork

This strange thing must have crept
Right out of hell.
It resembles a bird's foot
Worn around the cannibal's neck.

As you hold it in your hand,
As you stab with it into a piece of meat,
It is possible to imagine the rest of the bird:
Its head which like your fist
Is large, bald, beakless and blind.

Seamus Heaney

Seamus Heaney (1939–   ) was born in County Derry in the North of Ireland, and now lives in Dublin with his wife and three children. He has visited the United States on many occasions and currently teaches one term a year at Harvard University. *Field Work* (1979) is his fourth book of poems. In 1980 he published *Preoccupations: Selected Prose* and reissued his first three books as *Poems 1965–1975*.

A Drink of Water

She came every morning to draw water
Like an old bat staggering up the field:

The pump's whooping cough, the bucket's clatter
And slow diminuendo as it filled,
Announced her. I recall
Her grey apron, the pocked white enamel
Of the brimming bucket, and the treble
Creak of her voice like the pump's handle.
Nights when a full moon lifted past her gable
10   It fell back through her window and would lie
Into the water set out on the table.
Where I have dipped to drink again, to be
Faithful to the admonishment on her cup,
Remember the Giver fading off the lip.

Song

A rowan like a lipsticked girl.
Between the by-road and the main road
Alder trees at a wet and dripping distance
Stand off among the rushes.

There are the mud-flowers of dialect
And the immortelles of perfect pitch
And that moment when the bird sings very close
To the music of what happens.

Tom Clark

Tom Clark (1941–   ) was born in Illinois, attended the University of Michigan, and studied at Cambridge University in England. He writes books on baseball: *Champagne and Baloney* about Charles Finley, *No Big Deal* about Mark Fidrych.

Poem

Like musical instruments
Abandoned in a field
The parts of your feelings

Are starting to know a quiet
The pure conversion of your
Life into art seems destined

Never to occur
You don't mind
You feel spiritual and alert

10   As the air must feel
Turning into sky aloft and blue
You feel like

You'll never feel like touching anything or anyone
Again
And then you do

Louise Glück

Louise Glück (1943–   ) lives in Vermont and has published three collections of her poems, including *The House on the Marshland* (1975) and *Descending Figure* (1980).

Gratitude

Do not think I am not grateful for your small
kindness to me.
I like small kindnesses.
In fact I actually prefer them to the more
substantial kindness, that is always eying you,
like a large animal on a rug,
until your whole life reduces
to nothing but waking up morning after morning
cramped, and the bright sun shining on its tusks.

Gregory Orr

Gregory Orr (1947–   ) published two books of poems, *Burning the Empty Nests* and *Gathering the Bones Together,* while still in his twenties, and has followed most recently with *The Red House* (1980). He was born in upper New York state and attended Antioch College and Columbia University. He teaches at the University of Virginia. See also pages 30 and 36.

The Sweater

I will lose you. It is written
into this poem the way
the fisherman's wife knits
his death into the sweater.

Joyce Peseroff

Joyce Peseroff (1948–   ) grew up in New York City, studied writing at the University of California at Irvine, and lives outside Boston.

The Hardness Scale

Diamonds are forever so I gave you quartz
which is #7 on the hardness scale
and it's hard enough to get to know anybody these days
if only to scratch the surface
and quartz will scratch six other mineral surfaces:
it will scratch glass
it will scratch gold
it will even
scratch your eyes out one morning—you can't be
10 too careful.
Diamonds are industrial so I bought
a ring of topaz
which is #8 on the hardness scale.

I wear it on my right hand, the way it was
supposed to be, right? No tears and fewer regrets
for reasons smooth and clear as glass. Topaz will scratch glass,
it will scratch your quartz,
and all your radio crystals. You'll have to be silent
the rest of your days
20   not to mention your nights. Not to mention
the night you ran away very drunk very
very drunk and you tried to cross the border
but couldn't make it across the lake.
Stirring up geysers with the oars you drove the red canoe
in circles, tried to pole it but
your left hand didn't know
what the right hand was doing.
You fell asleep
and let everyone know it when you woke up.
30   In a gin-soaked morning (hair of the dog) you went
hunting for geese,
shot three lake trout in violation of the game laws,
told me to clean them and that
my eyes were bright as sapphires
which is #9 on the hardness scale.
A sapphire will cut a pearl
it will cut stainless steel
it will cut vinyl and mylar and will probably
cut a record this fall
40   to be released on an obscure label known only to aficionados.
I will buy a copy.
I may buy you a copy
depending on how your tastes have changed.
I will buy copies for my friends
we'll get a new needle,
a diamond needle,
which is #10 on the hardness scale
and will cut anything.
It will cut wood and mortar,
50   plaster and iron,
it will cut the sapphires in my eyes and I will bleed
blind as 4 A.M. in the subways when even degenerates
are dreaming, blind as the time
you shot up the room with a new hunting rifle
blind drunk
as you were.
You were #11 on the hardness scale
later that night
apologetic as
60   you worked your way up
slowly from the knees
and you worked your way down
from the open-throated blouse.
Diamonds are forever so I give you softer things.

Writing About Poems

1. General advice

One way to learn about anything is to write about it. We can test our ability to read poems by writing essays that explain or argue or compare or evaluate. Writing a paper we clarify our ideas—to ourselves and to others—as we describe how we understand. If our goal in studying poetry is to arrive at sound taste and just discrimination, we write papers on poems in order to examine and clarify the means by which we arrive at judgment.

For general advice, there is none better at the start than *use your intelligence*. Many people beginning to write about literature feel that they should show themselves responding ("I cried when I finished this sonnet") instead of applying their brains and looking closely at the words in front of them. Second, *be forthright* in stating an opinion; we learn by making a thesis and defending it, even if later we discover that we have erred. A noncommittal paper usually has less to say than a paper that is vigorous but mistaken. Third, while writing and revising a paper, continually *question whether it serves the poem* written about. Do not digress into subjects that lead away from the work itself. Writing about Theodore Roethke's poem "Orchids," one student displayed only botanic research into the flower; another who read up on Roethke's life offered information about his childhood in a greenhouse. Neither served the poem itself.

A. Ways of writing about poems

1. Concentration on the text

Most teachers, when they assign papers, ask their students to concentrate on the texts themselves—not on the lives of the authors, or the authors' historical eras, or the context of literary history or influence. Most assignments ask for an explication, an analysis, or a comparison and contrast.

a. Explication

The word *explication* originally means "unfolding." When we explicate a literary work we unfold its intricate layers of theme and form, showing its construction as if we spread it out upon a table. In writing about poetry, we most often use the tool of explication, because poems are usually dense and concentrated; we take the poem word by word or line by line. Explication's goal is to lay out in critical prose everything the author has done in a short poem or brief passage of a longer poem; the best explication goes the furthest toward that goal.

Explication does not concern itself with the poet's life or times; it treats the work of art almost as if it were anonymous. The poet's historical period, however, may determine the definitions of words. If the work is a century or more old, some of its words will have changed in their meanings. Because the explicator's task is to make explicit what the author *may* have put into the work—not assuming conscious intentions, but aware of possibilities—the explicator must keep in mind the time when the work was written and the altering definitions of words. Thus when an eighteenth-century writer like Alexander Pope speaks of "science," we must notice that the word meant something like "general knowledge" and not that branch of knowledge we study as chemistry, physics, and biology. In order to determine the meaning of a word in a particular era, it is useful to consult the *Oxford English Dictionary* (see page 19).

Use common sense when explicating. It is tempting to go too far, to follow particular words down rabbit holes into Wonderland, using ingenuity more than intelligence. One student explicated a couplet of Robert Frost:

> The old dog barks backward without getting up.
> I can remember when he was a pup.

Desperate to write four hundred words about two lines—having chosen the wrong poem to write four hundred words about—the student noticed that Frost had elsewhere written about Sirius the Dog Star, and that *dog* was "God" spelled backward, and wrote four hundred words to confuse astrology and theology into a pair of lines about aging and the passage of time. The general advice must govern the explicator as well as all other critics: write so that you make sense of the whole work considered; do not entertain fascinating improbabilities.

For an example of explication, look again at the poems explained in the first chapter—Frost's "Stopping by Woods on a Snowy Evening" and Williams's "so much depends." These explications are longer and more detailed than most teachers will expect from students beginning a study of literature, but they give notions of method and range. Remember that when we explain a poem or a passage in poetry, we should attend to form as well as to content; we must not simply indicate intellectual understanding by paraphrase, but account for the shape and sound of a poem as well as its paraphrasable content.

Paraphrase is a necessary *part* of explication; it is not the whole thing. Many critics beginning an explication find it useful to summarize the action and theme of the poem as a prelude, giving a brief account of the whole before concentrating on the parts. This summary is like the beginning of a speech in a debate, which tells us the general conclusion the argument will lead to. With explication as with argument, the proof is in the pudding. The step-by-step explanation of the use and function of particular words is the pudding of explication.

To write a paper of explication, we should always pick a poem which pleases us and which we find fascinating. It will not serve to choose something we do not respond to, or something about which we find little intriguing. It is all right (it is possibly even good tactics) if something in the poem either displeases us or remains puzzling. When we have chosen a poem to write about, or narrowed choice down to a few, we should read and reread and reread. Read with a pencil or pen in hand, taking notes both of observations about the poem and about puzzlements. After many readings, with note-taking, it is wise to refresh the mind about the elements of poetry and reread again to notice matters possibly ignored. Everyone is naturally more sensitive to certain elements than to others. Perhaps we find ourselves sensitive to the poem's structure as argument, if it is a poem that structures an argument. Perhaps we need to look harder to pick up the poem's images and their connections. Use the elements of poetry, as noted in the chapters of this text, as a checklist suggesting what to look for. Not all poems will satisfy all items on the checklist of chapters. But it is our task as explicators to make ourselves aware of everything that is there.

Here is a paper by a student named Mary Lois Goldberg, who picked a short poem by Robert Frost for explication.

Mistaking Snow

Only eight lines long, Robert Frost's "A Patch of Old Snow" appears as slight as it is brief. Close reading of the poem, however, reveals that its off-hand manner or tone conceals something more serious than first appears. In this disparity between appearance and reality, between apparent lightness and real seriousness, we see a poem typical of Frost.

The title gives us no problem, because the poem's primary subject is simply "a patch of old snow." Somebody might try to work something out of the dictionary definition of "patch" as a "piece of material . . . to conceal or reinforce. . ."[1] Perhaps the poem in its playful tone acts as a concealment of its own seriousness—but really I don't think the title expresses an idea of hiding. The snow is "a patch" because it is smaller than the earth it lies on.

One of the first things I noticed about this poem was its rhyme, which is really good! They are rhymes which you would never expect. First, a verb with an -ed ending—"guessed," which we pronounce the same as "guest" really—is rhymed with the noun "rest." Just because they are spelled differently, and maybe because they are different parts of speech, they seem as if they should not go together, but they do. Then the second rhyme is a rhyme of two syllables, which is unusual in itself: "overspread it" and "read it." Although the parts of speech are the same—a verb followed by a pronoun object—the first of the verbs has three syllables and the second has one. This difference contributes to the surprise of the rhyme, and the surprise gives part of the poem's pleasure.

The poem is written not only in rhyme but in meter. The first and third lines of each stanza have three feet and the second and fourth have two. (Trimeter and dimeter). Some of the feet are three-syllable ($\breve{}\breve{}'$) and some are two-syllable ($\breve{}'$). I don't know whether to call the meter anapestic or iambic. Here is my scansion:

---

[1] *American Heritage Dictionary,* William Morris, ed., American Heritage Publishing Co. Inc. & Houghton Mifflin Co.: Boston, 1969.

There's a patch | of old snow | in a corner
   That I should | have guessed
Was a blow | away pap | er the rain
   Had brought | to rest.

It is speck | led with grime | as if
   Small print | overspread it
The news | of a day | I've forgotten—
   If I ev | er read it.

Thirteen of the twenty feet are anapestic and seven are iambic; maybe we should call the meter anapestic with iambic tendencies. Of the eight lines, *half* have feminine endings, including the last line of the poem.

Having written all this about meter, I am not sure what to say about it. I wonder if the tentativeness or uncertainty of the meter—all those extra syllables, or all those syllables cut away—might combine with the surprise of the rhyme to pull you along feeling that you are not just sure where you are going. But with the direct (if surprising) rhyme, and the foot-numbers staying the same, when you come to the end you know that this is the only place you could have come to.

Each stanza is composed of one sentence, and each sentence also seems tentative or uncertain at first, and finally conclusive. Frost built the sentences so that they stick together (which is like the direct rhyme and count of feet) but so that it's hard to see how they stick together (which is like the witty rhymes and mixed feet). The "I should have guessed" in the second line is an interruption to "that . . . was"—except that without the interruption the sentence would not make any sense because it would mix present and past tenses. Therefore the sentence looks at first as if it were careless or off-hand, but when you put it together, you see that all the parts fit and are necessary.

Finally I want to talk about the meaning or theme in the poem, and I come to it only now because I think that the poem needs its own sound-shape and sentence-shape to say what it has to say. The statement of the poem is easy enough to paraphrase: I see a piece of snow and at first I think it is a piece of newspaper because it looks like one, but it is a small matter anyhow. But the poem seems to me to imply something more.

There are two things I want to notice, one in each stanza. First is "paper," which could be wrapping paper or waxpaper but turns out to be newspaper. I think that the delay in discovering the kind of paper is a teasing which is like the surprise of the rhymes. Then in the second stanza, "speckled with grime" is an accurate image for old snow—and when I notice this I suddenly realize that this poem about something visible has hardly any images in it. The title, "A Patch of Old Snow," is an image, but not a vivid one. If this poem does not end in description, then what does it end in?

I think this poem is about a casual, unremarkable visual mistake—and then it says, "So what; it doesn't matter." At first the poet reports that he "should have guessed" that a clump of old snow was a piece of paper. We give easy assent to the comparisons: yes, in April a piece of dirty snow does look like a newspaper. Then in the second stanza Frost explains that grime is speckled on snow *as* print overspreads paper, almost as if he needs to say: look; this mistake was easy to make! Then, as if he felt that he had protested too much, he says that the newspaper (which does not exist except as a mental error) probably did not have any news important to him anyway, because he would have forgotten it. As his withdrawal seems complete, he withdraws further: "If I ever read it." He has made a mistake and explained, and then said it's not worth worrying about, but at the same time he has shown himself worrying about it—a lot!

Another student in the same class decided that *patch* was a key word, that it implied diminishment, concealment, and despair in the poem—and wrote a good paper to defend her ideas.

b. Analysis

To analyze something is to separate it into parts in order to understand it. Explication deals exhaustively with something small; analysis deals with a part of something—perhaps the repetition of certain phrases in D. H. Lawrence's "Bavarian Gentians" or Robert Frost's characterization in "The Death of the Hired Man." Attending to one part of a poem, the analyst must relate that part to the work as a whole. In analysis we thus use summary or paraphrase to establish the whole of which we analyze a part. If an analysis fails to relate part to whole, the paper will seem pointless. We want to know not only that the poet repeats the word *blue* twenty-seven times in thirty-nine lines but what this repetition accomplishes in the poem.

When we write about poems of any length, analysis allows us to limit our topic. Never try to analyze a whole long work, any more than you would try to explicate a whole long work. Find ways to limit your topic by analysis—by the isolation of parts. No one can write a decent six-hundred-word theme on the whole of Adrienne Rich's "From an Old House in America." Nor would an analysis of the theme of that poem be possible in less than several thousand words. Analysis discovers part within part. It would be possible to analyze the role of place in that poem.

When we consider writing an analytical paper, we begin by thinking analytically about what we have read. Looking at several poems by Robert Frost, fascinated by "Design" with its white flower that should have been blue, we might analyze "Color in Three Poems by Robert Frost." Thinking about this subject, we must come to some sort of conclusion. For an analytical paper to hold together, it will assert and defend a *thesis* that can usually be reduced to a single sentence. A thesis is not the same as a topic—"Robert Frost Using Colors"—nor should it merely describe or report: "Robert Frost often uses imagery of color in his poetry. . . ." Instead it must conclude and assert a purpose: "For Robert Frost, in these poems, color disguises reality and suggests a malignancy of matter or maker."

In the text of "To Read a Poem" many poems or passages are analyzed for one element—for the use of language, imagery, metaphor, for allusion, symbolism, rhythm, assonance and alliteration, and meter. For examples, look at the metaphorical analysis of a Shakespearean sonnet on pages 38–39, or the analysis of allusion in Louise Bogan's epigram on pages 55–56.

Students writing analytical papers often limit their topics by concentrating on one part of an element. Theodore Roethke's "The Meadow Mouse" (pages 163–164) includes so many images that "Imagery in 'The Meadow Mouse' " would make a long paper; one student narrowed it to " 'My Thumb of a Child': Infant Images in 'The Meadow Mouse.' " Writing about Frost's "Stopping by Woods on a Snowy Evening," a student might analyze "The Tone of Frost's Speaker," or "Frost's Smart Horse in 'Stopping by Woods . . .,' " or "Images of Cold and Comfort." Dealing with a longer poem, a writer might isolate one character: "The Characterization of the Hired Man in Frost's 'Death of the Hired Man' "; or analyze a part of theme: "Definitions of 'Home' in Frost's 'Death of the Hired Man.' "

Writing analysis, we remain aware that everything is related to everything else. If we speak of images, it is hard not to mention metaphor, because many images make metaphors. Discussing the metaphorical structure of a sonnet, we will notice that some of the linkage among metaphors is accomplished by images. Sometimes we can lose track of our topic by noticing too closely the interrelationships of many elements. We need, sometimes, to mention a rhyme when we are discussing characterization, if the rhyme makes a point of character. But we should not be sidetracked into a discussion of rhyme just because the subject comes up. We must keep watch of ourselves, as we write, that we do not lose track. A clear thesis can be the North Star to guide us through the wilderness of analysis.

In making a thesis, it is best to look for an element that has relevance to the whole poem. Sometimes we can fall into an analysis which records accurately some facts about a poem but stops short of showing the relevance of these facts. A formal analysis of a sonnet that only disclosed the existence of sonnet form would be trivial, too elementary for the name of analysis. However, a good analytical paper could be written which showed how sonnet form reflected itself in the poem's shapely argument, sorting itself out into the quatrains (if the sonnet is Shakespearean) and into octave and sestet.

Here is Mark O'Malley's analysis of Theodore Roethke's "The Meadow Mouse." (The poem is on pages 163–164.)

"My Thumb of a Child": Infant Images in "The Meadow Mouse"

In Theodore Roethke's "The Meadow Mouse," the speaker finds a tiny mouse, feeds it and protects it, then finds it missing and worries over it. At the beginning, the poem seems to be a simple, affectionate story about caring for a little animal; by the end the poet raises the emotional pitch, and we feel pity for everything—human as well as animal, adult as well as infantile—"innocent, hapless, forsaken."

This emotional widening, this enlargement of compassion, derives from Roethke's skillful and touching uses of imagery associated with infancy, that era of life (whether of man or beast) that most demands our protectiveness. The poem is full of images, and many of them suggest the miniature. In the first stanza we have the adjectives "baby," "little," "small," "little" again, and finally "miniscule." Contrasts of size emphasize the mouse's tininess and connect his tininess to infancy. He is "cradled" in my hand: in relation to this mouse, my hand is in shape and size like a cradle to a baby. When his whiskers are compared to those of a "cartoon mouse," perhaps we recollect small children watching cartoons; at any rate, the notion of a "cartoon mouse" belongs to the world of the child.

At the beginning of the second stanza occurs the most touching contrast of size. In relation to a big animal (horse, cow), the mouse is like a bottle top to a watering trough. This mouse is little! Then the mouse is described anatomically as if his body were distorted like a human baby's, where the head is proportionately large and the stomach puffs out after eating: "His belly big / as his head."

In the second part of the poem, when the mouse is discovered missing, we find the most startling image of smallness and infancy: "My thumb of a child. . . ." I think that the image works two ways; first, this mouse is no bigger than a child's thumb—thus we insist on the small while continuing to associate the mouse with childhood. Or, second, we could paraphrase it: "This child the size of my [grown-up] thumb." (We have heard this kind of language before: the phrase "this dog of an infidel" or "my prince of a friend" equates dog and infidel, prince and friend.) In this second reading, the mouse becomes "this child," almost the speaker's child, as anxiety increases tenderness.

Toward the end of the poem we read of another baby animal, "the nestling fallen"; this ends the series of images of infancy. From the alternate baby animal the poem moves to the presumably adult turtle and to the presumably human "paralytic stunned in the tub," and finally to the general lamentation of the great concluding line. The many images of infancy begin and sustain the pity which becomes general at the end.

c. Comparison and Contrast

A third kind of paper is the comparison and contrast of two texts, usually in connection with a specific theme, a formal device, or a technical element of the genre. A teacher might invite a comparison of Shakespeare's use of the sonnet form with Robert Frost's, for instance. (When we compare two objects, we make notes of likeness and unlikeness; henceforth we will speak only of comparing, implying contrast.) The process of comparison requires analysis of each work, with notice of similarities and differences in the matters analyzed. We need not repeat here our remarks on analysis.

In writing comparison and contrast our troubles are likely to be structural. We may generate the materials for a decent analysis of two different poems but find it difficult to organize these materials. Here is a passage from a student's draft:

> In the sonnet by Shakespeare every four lines is a whole separate idea, then the last two lines is another unit that is complete to itself. In Milton's the first part is eight lines and the second is six, without further subdivision. Shakespeare's rhyming separates the parts, not just the ideas. Milton's rhyming is more difficult, using just two rhymes in the octave (ABBAABBA) but therefore making the eight lines a smooth whole. Shakespeare . . .

These rapid oscillations are nervous; the reader's head snaps back and forth, as if watching a ping-pong game; after a while we forget which poet is which, and who has the serve.

In a short paper of comparison, a writer may be able to write a paragraph or two of similarities, a paragraph or two of dissimilarities, and reach a conclusion in the final paragraph. But such simplicity of structure is rare. More likely, we will need to make a structure something like this:

1. Statement of comparability
2. First similarity
   Work A
   Work B
3. Second similarity
   Work A
   Work B
4. First dissimilarity
   Work A
   Work B
5. Second dissimilarity
   Work A
   Work B
6. Conclusion based on evidence: thesis

Sometimes the grammar of the complex sentence can avoid the ping-pong monotony of compounds that flick our heads and back and forth on our necks. Instead of saying "Work A is seven stanzas of 11 lines making the whole poem 77 lines long, and Work B is 13 stanzas of six lines each which makes 78 lines in all," we can sound more various: "While Work A displays its 77 lines into seven stanzas of 11 lines each, Work B spreads its 76 into 19 four-line stanzas."

A different structure takes a topic and then looks at each work two ways:

First item (like the use of color symbolism)
   Similarities between Works A and B
   Dissimilarities between Works A and B
Second item (like the means used for indicating symbolism)
   Similarities between Works A and B
   Dissimilarities between Works A and B

The material we collect for a paper determines its best form. Always decide on a thesis before writing. If we start writing in the sweet hope that a thesis will solidify from the air of our prose, we write a disorganized paper.

Mostly, we find the differences between two works with obvious similarities: the two sonnets are each fourteen lines long, each within iambic pentameter, each rhymed throughout—and then the differences begin: structure of thought, rhyme, rhythm, metaphor, diction. One paper might end by asserting that despite all the differences between them these two sonnets will share many qualities. Another might with equal justice argue that the differences outweighed the similarities. The conclusions will supply the writers' theses.

We illustrate analyzed elements of poems by comparing and contrasting them. Sometimes we find within one poet's work a habit of writing or thinking: "Emily Dickinson's Imagery of Animals." Such a paper might compare and contrast parts of three or four Dickinson poems to investigate her use of animal images. Not only images, but structural devices, recurrent symbols, and themes may provide material for comparative analysis.

On the other hand, sometimes we contrast two or more poets. "Poets and Flowers: Two Strategies in Roethke and Frost" compares Frost's "Design" with Roethke's "Orchids." Any comparison and contrast, within one poet's work or among different poets, will require separate analyses or small explications, and judgment on likeness or difference.

2. Concentration on Context

Sometimes in studying poetry, and in writing papers about it, we concentrate not so much on the text as on the context of the work—the historical, personal, or literary backgrounds out of which the poem came. This kind of criticism usually suggests cause and effect. We argue that the work has characteristics that derive from causes or sources in the author's society, personal life, or reading. To establish these characteristics the critic must usually analyze or explicate; but then, having described these characteristics, the writer will shift emphasis from text to context.

a. History and Society

Whatever we do, we express the times we live in. When poets write, they reflect their own era by deploring it, by celebrating it, or even by writing to escape it. Social criticism sometimes supports philosophical positions. Some critics find literary form and content dominated and determined by economics; this criticism draws a line of causation from economic force to literary result. Other social criticism relates literature to theories of nationality and national history. Often the social or historical critic tries to illuminate meaning by understanding the social and historical conditions under which older work was written, helping the modern reader to understand how it seemed to its contemporaries. When we read ancient poetry, we would be ignorant if we identified a queen as a figure resembling Queen Elizabeth II.

Because this sort of criticism requires historical knowledge, a student writing about the historical sources of a text must do research. In the library we can find, for example, what critics and historians have discovered about the relationship of Elizabethan culture to the sonnet sequence. Often we can find books that give backgrounds to different literary periods, setting forth the dominating philosophical, political, and religious ideas of an era. Basil Willey's *Eighteenth Century Background* is an example. But we need not write about remote times when we write social or historical papers. A student could connect some poems by William Butler Yeats with the political situation of Yeats's Ireland by reading in the history of modern Ireland.

b. Biography

If a work of art cannot help but reflect its era, equally it cannot help but reflect the life of the man or woman who wrote it.

This statement is easy enough to make, but it is often difficult to demonstrate the connection between life and work. Things are subtler than they seem. For instance, a poet may speak of himself overtly—Yeats wrote the line "I, the poet William Yeats . . ."—yet make statements that are not historically true. If we take the poet's word, we are often deceived. Writers frequently make up a self to speak from, and make great literature out of this fabrication. Walt Whitman constructed a character called "Walt Whitman" who was rough, manly, vigorous, brave, noisy; apparently the man himself was shy, and when he read his poems aloud spoke so softly that no one could hear him past the first row. On the other hand, T. S. Eliot proclaimed the impersonality of the artist, said that literature was a flight from personality, and proclaimed these doctrines when he had written "The Waste Land," which critics have begun to understand as the most personal of poems. By noticing disparities between the poet's proclamations and realities we begin to investigate the biographical context.

The student who undertakes biographical criticism should therefore take warning. Perhaps no other approach to literature requires more sophistication. Like historical criticism it requires research as well as subtlety, psychological acumen, and modesty. The last quality may be the most urgent; we may suspect a biographical connection and suggest it by inference, but we seldom *know*. We know only the obvious: reading a biography of D. H. Lawrence, we can trace his imagery of flowers to the landscape he grew up in; but if we derive his ideas of evil from a childhood experience, we must be very careful.

c. The Literary History

If a literary work is a big river, we know the names of many of the tributaries that go to form it. There is the language an author grows up among, the common speech; there are the politics, economics, and social structure of a poet's historical period and social class; there are a poet's own psyche, upbringing, relationships with parents and siblings, even inheritance of characteristics. Another large tributary is the poetry that the poet has learned from.

Everything a writer has read—like everything that has happened in the life—can contribute to the work done. As athletes learn their moves from watching other athletes, as a guitar player learns chords from another musician, writers learn their craft from observing, analyzing, and loving earlier literary work. For this reason literature has a history, a sequence if not a progress. Progress would imply that literature was getting better all the time, a proposition difficult to support.

To write a paper in literary history, the critic must know earlier literature, something we may not wish to demand in an introductory course.

Although we have separated these approaches to literature's context in order to describe them, they are not mutually exclusive. To write about influence on Keats, we read his letters and consult his biographers. We need to use explication and analysis, within the historical or biographical or literary methods, to establish claims about the text discussed. It is most important to know what we are doing when we are doing it, and not to confuse our methods.

3. Common Pitfalls in Writing about Poetry

A few common errors of method occur again and again.

a. The Personal Error

Many of the pitfalls that threaten us when we write about poetry take one shape: we do not regard the work itself or its context, but some irrelevant matter from the outside. One of the most frequent irrelevancies is our personal histories and beliefs.

To write a theme about one's personal experience can be a fine thing, but such a theme is *not* about literature. Perhaps because it seems easier to write out of personal experience, many people fall into the personal error. Taking the title of D. H. Lawrence's "Bavarian Gentians," they tell about their experience of gardens. Writing about Robert Frost's "Stopping by Woods on a Snowy Evening," they confide that they respond to this poem with special pleasure because they are so fond of horses.

Even without personal narrative, there is danger of sanctifying personal response. It is a commonly held notion in the modern world that one person's opinion is as good as anybody else's. The defense of misreading is usually a smug "That is how *I* see it, and everyone is entitled to their own opinion." Democratic and egalitarian as the idea appears, it is an idea we hold to only so long as it conveniences us. The same student who holds that his opinion of Plato is as worthy as his philosophy professor's is unlikely to consider his professor's opinion of automobile repair as good as his own. Although there are many possible ways to understand a poem, it is demonstrable that some interpretations are wrong; the text denies them. No one should go to jail for having a wrong opinion—but *opinions can be wrong*. Poetry is not a series of cloud shapes into which we can imagine all sorts of castles.

Be governed by the text. Learn to submit to the text, to test all ideas and interpretations to the scrutiny of the text, and discard ideas that do not fit. This attitude requires humility before the fact of literature and expels or denies that conceit which says "Whatever *I* discover in the text is right for *me*." There is more of I/me in such reading than there is of poetry.

b. The Historical Error

A less egotistical fallacy equally an impediment to good reading is the biographical and historical error that looks past a work of the imagination to find events in the poet's life or times of which the poem is a representation or to which it responds. This error uses the text as a pretext for discourse, not about the work of art but about history or biography. I do not mean to attack the good criticism that legitimately connects the work and the life, and the work to the times. Too often, readers pick on some portion of a poem, trust it as a piece of reality, and run away from literature to speak of history or biography. Yeats's poem "The Second Coming" (page 229) speaks of a time of chaos and turbulence, when "the center does not hold. / Mere anarchy is loosed upon the world. . . ." One student, noticing Yeats's dates (1865–1939) decided that Yeats was referring to the Great War of 1914–1918, and wrote:

> As Yeats predicted, the great empires came apart, the German and especially the Austro-Hungarian, but really it was not "mere anarchy" because out of parts of

these empires Czechoslovakia was created, and the Treaty of Versailles which followed the war determined exactly who had authority over what territory. It is true that the League of Nations . . .

Here the historical error has run away with the paper, and the student has taken a few lines from the poem as a text for a summary of world history. Information is used not to illuminate the poem but to escape from it. As a matter of fact, this poem was written after World War I at the time of the Civil War in Ireland.

Never assume, when the poet uses *I,* that the poet speaks in his or her own person. First, many poets like Robert Browning write dramatic monologue, in which they assume the mask (sometimes called a *persona*) of an imagined or historical personage; the poem resembles a speech from a play. Second, as we observed earlier, writers often make up a self, called by their own names, that remains an imaginary and unhistorical creature.

Our uninformed guesses are as likely to be wrong as right. When a writer undertakes a work, some of the material doubtless comes from the author's experience and observation, as true as a photograph or a verbatim account; and doubtless some of the material is imagined, made up in the service of a truth-telling broader than representation. For the most part, we cannot determine what is imagined and what reported, and it does not matter. Our job as readers is not to determine the one from the other but to read the whole as a work of art.

c. The Error of Influence

The error of influence blights some papers in literary history. There is a logical fallacy for which there is a Latin phrase, *post hoc ergo propter hoc:* "after the fact, therefore on account of the fact," describing the human tendency to mistake sequence for cause and effect. Many poor themes assume an influence on tenuous evidence. But even when the influence is genuine, it is not always important. It may be useful to notice that Robert Frost learned this or that from Wordsworth, or that Robert Creeley is indebted to the example of William Carlos Williams. In each case the causes are clear and the effects significant. But it does not follow that every literary phenomenon can usefully be discussed in terms of literary genealogy. Walt Whitman's style was a shock to the literary world it assaulted. We have learned that it derives partly from old Hebrew poetry translated by the scholars of the King James version of the Bible. Yet for the most part Whitman's style remains Whitman's invention. Anyone asserting literary influence ought to ask the question: If what I assert is true, what of it? It seems true enough, for instance, that the style of D. H. Lawrence's poetry altered after he had read Walt Whitman . . . but what of it? One student, noticing not only the influence but the background suggested by Whitman's style, came up with a notion of connection:

> Lawrence's rhythm and his use of parallel constructions changed only after he had studied Whitman in order to write his celebrated essay upon him. Such a fact, true

enough, is merely a detail of influence. Whitman's rhythms apparently unleashed something in Lawrence, but what did they unleash? I want to suggest a connection which I cannot demonstrate. We know that much of Whitman's grammar, and therefore rhythm, came from the translations of Hebrew poetry, in its parallel syntactic structures, as rendered by the King James translators of the seventeenth century. We know from Lawrence's fiction and essays that he grew up listening to Bible readings and biblical oratory. Especially in his late work about the Book of Revelation, he reveals how essential to his emotional youth were the accents of prophecy. I suggest that Whitman affected Lawrence's poetry by way of the Bible. Whitman's rhythms showed Lawrence how to tap a source of feeling in himself.

Notice that this student takes a subject which has a factual base, and that he uses biographical information and inference. We know that Lawrence read Whitman with great attention because Lawrence wrote a famous essay about him. Sometimes, influence-hunters have argued the influence of X on Y where it has been virtually certain that Y was wholly unaware of X, or could not possibly have read more than a story or two. Even more embarrassing, on occasion a critic has described the influence of A on B—when B died before A was born.

4. Reading the Critics

If students are asked to write about history, biography, or literary influence, they are expected to use the library, to read historians, biographers, critics, and scholars.

Here we must address a question: If we explicate or analyze only—not requiring background information—how much do we use the library, how much do we refer to critics who have published analyses and explications of the poems we write about?

Some teachers find it useful to ask their students to check out the critics, to test their own notions against the published work of professionals. Other teachers ask their students *not* to consult critics; some even forbid the practice. Many teachers feel that reading professional criticism inhibits their students and keeps them from developing their own ideas, from making mistakes and learning to correct their mistakes, from finding their own ways to evaluate and interpret. With an exaggerated respect for the printed word, these teachers argue, students become passive when they read critics; they assume that published work must be correct and parrot it back in their own papers. On the other hand, students doing their own work without help or interference from professional critics, knowing that fellow students also work alone, do their best work.

B. Writing the theme

1. Before Writing: Getting Ideas

Whether the topic is assigned or free, we need to gather ideas as the first stage of the paper-writing process, long before beginning a first draft.

Generally we will know which poems we are to write about. If we have a choice, we should pick the poem that fascinates us most, even if we feel we do not understand it thoroughly. It is a deadly mistake to pick something uninteresting because we think it is simple or easy. If we are not interested we will never write well about it. The poem or poems chosen, we must then undertake a series of thorough readings, pencil in hand. If the book is our own, we can write in the margins or underline. (If the book belongs to a library or someone else, do not make a mark on it.) Some notes will spill over the page, and we should keep a notebook beside the chair we read in. At first, we should not look for anything in particular, but take note of everything that strikes us—a pun, a piece of wit, a linebreak, a rhyme, an ambiguity, a curious tone, a word to look up, a striking image, a puzzling repetition. We should make note not only of what we enjoy but of what puzzles or annoys us. We should read aggressively, demanding of each word or line that it reveal its function and usefulness. We should note big and note little, note outside and inside. If a poem is fourteen lines long, we should remember that it can be embarrassing to write five pages on a brief poem without having mentioned that it is a sonnet.

We should read, taking notes, for one long session, then put the theme out of our minds for a day before we return to read again. It is astonishing how much thinking we do when we do not know we are thinking.

The next stage is to assemble notes toward a conclusion. If we are writing an explication, we may use all the notes that continue to look sensible, that contribute to understanding and elucidating the meaning and form of the text. If we are writing analysis, we will need to narrow the topic, which will probably mean discarding many notes. Look for a topic large enough to be worth the time and effort, small enough to be handled in the space assigned.

2. Writing and Revising

Notes make a blueprint for constructing the paper. It helps to make an informal outline, a recognition of what needs to follow what in order to demonstrate a thesis. These notes can be numbered in a notebook, or transferred to three-by-five-inch cards and stacked in order, or cut from long sheets and piled in appropriate piles. Probably many notes will refer to lines of the text, for the heart of literary criticism is intelligent quotation. No amount of good argument will persuade the reader so much as the brief, accurate example: an image; a rhyme. Any paper will need to assert a thesis, list occasions, and exemplify.

We should always try to spend at least one day away from our paper, between a draft and a revision. Revising, we should check for good, complete sentences, fresh language, logic, accurate quotation, and correct spelling. Revising, we should try for conciseness. We all use too many adjectives, and for that matter we may find that we can drop a whole paragraph here and there. If we leave big margins in typing a first draft, or type it triple-space, we will be grateful for the correcting space. Revising, we fill out paragraphs that remain thin; we find more reasons, more examples, and bolster our points. We examine the order of ideas, arguments, and examples.

3. Manuscript Form

Teachers sometimes require particular form for papers. In the absence of other directions, the notes that follow should serve in most circumstances.

a. Paper, Margins, etc.

Use 8½-by-11-inch-paper.

Type if you can, double space. Avoid erasable typing paper, which smudges. If you write by hand, use paper with deep lines, or write every other line on narrow-lined paper. Use only one side of a piece of paper.

Put your name, your teacher's name, class and section number, and date in the upper right-hand corner of your paper.

Leave margins of 1¼ inches at top, bottom, and sides. Always make a copy— a carbon or a photocopy—before you hand your paper in.

Number your pages.

Staple your pages together in the upper left-hand corner.

b. Titles

Put quotation marks around titles of poems shorter than book length ("Stopping by Woods on a Snowy Evening"). A book length poem's title is underlined (The Iliad). Note that titles underlined in papers will be *italicized* in print.

c. Quotations

Use quotation marks around excerpts from literature that you quote within sentence and paragraph:

> When William Carlos Williams looked at a primitive piece of farm machinery, he saw something which he made important through the power of his seeing; he saw it "glazed with rain / water . . ." He saw it "beside the white / chickens . . ." But seeing was not the only sense the doctor . . .

(We use a /, when quoting a poem, to indicate a line break.) But when we separate a quotation from sentence and paragraph—indenting it and typing it single space—we do not use quotation marks because we have indicated quotation by the spacings of the typography:

> When William Carlos Williams looked at a primitive piece of farm machinery, he saw something important because of the power of his seeing:
>
> glazed with rain
> water
>
> beside the white
> chickens
>
> But seeing was not the only sense that the doctor employed in making his poems. . . .

These two ways of quoting are appropriate to different lengths of quotation. When we are quoting only a few words, we include the quotation within the paragraph, and put quotation marks around it. When we quote more than a few words, we indent the quotation, single-space it, and omit quotation marks— except when the quoted passage itself has already used quotation marks.

d. Footnotes

When we clearly quote from the text under discussion, as in an explication, there is no point in footnoting.

Often we can note the source of a quotation, without a footnote, in the text of the paper: "Not until the fifth line does Frost use an image of sight . . ." When we find it awkward to include such information in the flow of sentences, a parenthesis can be used; sometimes it is easiest, if there is likely to be any confusion, simply to footnote a reference. Always be certain that the reader knows what he or she is reading.

When we quote or paraphrase from a critic, scholar, biographer, or historian— or even from the *Encyclopaedia Britannica—we must always footnote our sources.* If we take full notes when we read and remain scrupulous in noting the sources of our ideas or words, no one will ever accuse us of plagiarism; plagiarism is stealing, borrowing, or otherwise appropriating other people's ideas or sentences.

To quote from a book, copy the quotation accurately, put quotation marks around it, and put a number slightly higher than the line of words:[1]. Number sequentially throughout your paper; i.e., do not begin a new series of numbers on each page. Footnoting from a book, give this information in this order: author's name, book's title, edition number if any, city and publisher, date, and the number of the page quoted from. Here is one example:

[1]X.J. Kennedy, *Literature,* 2nd ed. (Boston: Little, Brown, 1979), pp. 1386–1387.

When quoting from a magazine article, use the volume number and date in place of the edition number, city, publisher, and date. Here is an example:

[12]Howard Norman, "Dry Tomb," *Westigan Review,* vol. 3, no. 4 (Fall 1978), 10.

When we refer again, later in the paper, to a source quoted earlier, we can shorten the reference to the writer's name and give the different page number:

Kennedy, 1385.

But if we refer to two different books by Kennedy, or poems by Norman, we would need to use full footnote form, and in further references distinguish between the two sources by quoting title as well as author.

e. Bibliography

When we have consulted books or magazines in order to write a paper, we should list everything consulted on a separate sheet at the end of the paper, in a *bibliography*. We should list material consulted even if we have not footnoted the source as a quote or a paraphrase. Arrange the list alphabetically by the author's last name. We list anonymous works alphabetically by title.

A book:

Newman, Edwin. *Strictly Speaking*. New York: Warner Books, 1975.

An article in a book:

Hamill, Pete. "The Language of the New Politics." In *Language in America*. Ed. Neil Postman, Charles Weingartner, and Terence P. Moran. New York: Pegasus, 1969.

An article in a magazine:

Middleton, Christopher. "Notes on a Viking Prow," *PN Review,* 10, Vol. 6, No. 2, 6–8.

An anonymous article from an encyclopedia:

"Geisha." *The Columbia Encyclopedia*. 1963.

Acknowledgments

A. R. Ammons. "Working with Tools" from *Briefings: Poems Small and Easy* by A. R. Ammons is reprinted by permission of W. W. Norton & Company, Inc. Copyright © 1971 by A. R. Ammons.

John Ashbery. "Rivers and Mountains" from *Rivers and Mountains* by John Ashbery; copyright © 1962, 1963, 1964, 1966 by John Ashbery. Reprinted by permission of Georges Borchardt, Inc.

W. H. Auden. "In Memory of W. B. Yeats" and "Musée des Beaux Arts" from *W. H. Auden: Collected Poems* by W. H. Auden, edited by Edward Mendelson; copyright 1940 and renewed 1968 by W. H. Auden; reprinted by permission of Random House, Inc., and from *Collected Shorter Poems 1927–1957* by W. H. Auden, reprinted by permission of Faber and Faber Limited.

Amiri Baraka (LeRoi Jones). "Watergate" and "Careers" from *Selected Poetry of Amiri Baraka/ LeRoi Jones*; copyright © 1979 by Imamu Amiri Baraka. Reprinted by permission of William Morrow & Company.

Wendell Berry. "The Wild Geese" from *The Country of Marriage* by Wendell Berry; copyright © 1971 by Wendell Berry. Reprinted by permission of Harcourt Brace Jovanovich, Inc.

John Berryman. "Dream Song #14," "Dream Song #16," and "Dream Song #312," from *The Dream Songs* by John Berryman; copyright © 1959, 1962, 1963, 1964, 1965, 1966, 1967, 1968, 1969 by John Berryman. Reprinted by permission of Farrar, Straus & Giroux, Inc.

Elizabeth Bishop. "The Pink Dog" by Elizabeth Bishop; copyright © 1979 by Alice Methfessel, Executrix of the Estate of Elizabeth Bishop. This poem originally appeared in *The New Yorker*. "The Monument" from *Complete Poems* by Elizabeth Bishop; copyright © 1939, 1969 by Elizabeth Bishop, copyright renewed © 1967 by Elizabeth Bishop. Both reprinted by permission of Farrar, Straus & Giroux, Inc.

Robert Bly. "Taking the Hands . . . ," "Hunting Pheasants in a Cornfield," and "A Man Writes to a Part of Himself" from *Silence in the Snowy Fields,* Wesleyan University Press, Middletown, Conn., 1962; copyright © 1960, 1961, 1962 by Robert Bly and reprinted with his permission. "The Dead Seal Near McClure's Beach" from *The Morning Glory* by Robert Bly; copyright © 1975 by Robert Bly and reprinted with his permission.

Louise Bogan. "Cartography" and "To An Artist, to Take Heart" from *The Blue Estuaries* by Louise Bogan; copyright © 1964, 1965 by Louise Bogan. Reprinted by permission of Farrar, Straus & Giroux, Inc.

Gwendolyn Brooks. "The Bean Eaters" and "We Real Cool. The Pool Players. Seven at the Golden Shovel" from *The World of Gwendolyn Brooks* by Gwendolyn Brooks; copyright © 1959 by Gwendolyn Brooks. Reprinted by permission of Harper & Row, Publishers.

Tom Clark. "Stones" from *Stones*; © Tom Clark. Reprinted by permission of the author.

Gregory Corso. "Marriage" from *The Happy Birthday of Death* by Gregory Corso; copyright © 1960 by New Directions Publishing Corporation. Reprinted by permission of New Directions.

Hart Crane. "Voyages, I and II" and lines from "The Bridge" from *The Complete Poems and Selected Prose and Poetry of Hart Crane*; copyright 1933, 1958, 1966 by Liveright Publishing Corporation. Reprinted by permission of Liveright Publishing Corporation.

Robert Creeley. "The Rain" and "The Hill" from *For Love: Poems 1950–1960* by Robert Creeley; copyright © 1962 by Robert Creeley. "For My Mother: Genevieve Jules Creeley" from *Selected Poems* by Robert Creeley; copyright © 1976 by Robert Creeley. Reprinted by permission of Charles Scribner's Sons.

E. E. Cummings. "1(a" from *Complete Poems 1913–1962* by E. E. Cummings; copyright © 1958 by E. E. Cummings. Reprinted by permission of Harcourt Brace Jovanovich, Inc. "next to of course god america i" and "Poem, or Beauty Hurts Mr. Vinal" from *IS 5, poems by E. E. Cummings*; copyright 1926 by Boni & Liveright; copyright renewed 1953 by E. E. Cummings. Reprinted by permission of Liveright Publishing Corporation.

J. V. Cunningham. Two epigrams by J. V. Cunningham, reprinted by permission of the Ohio University Press.

James Dickey. "The Heaven of Animals" from *Poems 1957–1967*; copyright © 1961 by James Dickey. Reprinted by permission of Wesleyan University Press. "The Heaven of Animals" first appeared in *The New Yorker*.

Emily Dickinson. "After great pain, a formal feeling comes—," "The first Day's Night had come—," "Me from Myself—to banish—," "My Life had stood—a Loaded Gun—," "The Province of the Saved," and "A still—Volcano—Life—" from *The Complete Poems of Emily Dickinson,* edited by Thomas H. Johnson. Reprinted by permission of Little, Brown and Company. "Because I could not stop for Death—," "I cannot live with You—," "I'm ceded—I've stopped being Theirs—," "I felt a Cleaving in my Mind—," "He fumbles at your Soul," "I heard a Fly buzz—when I died—," "Much Madness is divinest Sense—," "A narrow Fellow in the Grass," "He put a Belt around my life—," "Severer Service of myself—," "The Soul has Bandaged moments," and "I would not paint—a picture—" reprinted by permission of the publishers and the Trustees of Amherst College from *The Poems of Emily Dickinson,* edited by Thomas H. Johnson, Cambridge, Mass.: The Belknap Press of Harvard University Press; copyright © 1951, 1955 by the President and Fellows of Harvard College.

H. D. "Heat" and "The Sea Rose" from *Selected Poems* by Hilda Doolittle; copyright © 1925, 1953, 1957 by Norman Holmes Pearson. Reprinted by permission of New Directions.

Edward Dorn. "On the Debt My Mother Owed to Sears Roebuck"; reprinted by permission of the author.

Robert Duncan. "Poetry, A Natural Thing" from *The Opening of the Field* by Robert Duncan; copyright © 1960 by Robert Duncan. Reprinted by permission of New Directions.

Richard Eberhart. "The Groundhog" from *Collected Poems 1930–1976* by Richard Eberhart; copyright © 1960, 1976 by Richard Eberhart. Reprinted by permission of Oxford University Press, Inc. and of Chatto & Windus Ltd.

Russell Edson. "Bringing a Dead Man Back to Life" from *The Intuitive Journey and Other Works* by Russell Edson; copyright © 1976 by Russell Edson. Reprinted by permission of Harper & Row, Publishers.

T. S. Eliot. "The Love Song of J. Alfred Prufrock" and "Journey of the Magi" from *Collected Poems 1909–1962* by T. S. Eliot; copyright 1936 by Harcourt Brace Jovanovich, Inc.; copyright © 1963, 1964 by T. S. Eliot. Reprinted by permission of Harcourt Brace Jovanovich and of Faber and Faber Limited.

William Empson. "Villanelle" from *Collected Poems of William Empson*; copyright 1949, 1977 by William Empson. Reprinted by permission of Harcourt Brace Jovanovich, Inc. and of Chatto & Windus Ltd.

Ian Hamilton Finlay. "Homage to Malevich" from *Poems to Hear and See* by Ian Hamilton Finlay; copyright © 1971 by Ian Hamilton Finlay. Reprinted by permission of Macmillan Publishing Co., Inc.

Robert Francis. "Hogwash," copyright © 1965 by Robert Francis, and "Three Woodchoppers," copyright © 1944, 1972 by Robert Francis, from *Robert Francis: Collected Poems, 1936–1976,* University of Massachusetts Press, 1976.

Robert Frost. "Acquainted with the Night," "After Apple-Picking," "Birches," "Come In," "Desert Places," "Design," "The Draft Horse," "To Earthward," "Ends," "The Gift Outright," "Home Burial," "The Most of It," "Mowing," "The Need of Being Versed in Country Things," "Neither Out Far Nor In Deep," "Once by the Pacific," "Out, Out—," "The Pasture," "The Road Not Taken," "The Silken Tent," and "Stopping by Woods on a Snowy Evening" from *The Poetry of Robert Frost,* edited by Edward Connery Lathem. Copyright 1916, 1923, 1928, 1930, 1934, 1939, © 1967, 1969 by Holt, Rinehart and Winston; copyright 1936, 1942, 1944, 1951, © 1956, 1958, 1962 by Robert Frost; copyright © 1964, 1967, 1970 by Lesley Frost Ballantine. Reprinted by permission of Holt, Rinehart and Winston. "In White" from *The Dimensions of Robert Frost* by Reginald L. Cook; copyright © 1958 by Reginald L. Cook. Reprinted by permission of Holt, Rinehart and Winston.

Allen Ginsberg. "America," copyright © 1956, 1959 by Allen Ginsberg, and "First Party at Ken Kesey's with Hell's Angels," copyright © 1968 by Allen Ginsberg. Reprinted by permission of City Lights Books.

Louise Glück. "Gratitude" from *The House on the Marshland* by Louise Glück; copyright © 1975 by Louise Glück. Reprinted by permission of The Ecco Press.

Edward Gorey. Excerpt from "The Listing Attic" from *Amphigory* by Edward Gorey; copyright © 1954, 1972 by Edward Gorey. Reprinted by permission of Candida Donadio & Associates, Inc. "The Listing Attic" was first published by Duell, Sloan, & Pearce–Little, Brown.

Robert Graves. "In Broken Images" from *Poems 1929*, copyright 1929 by Robert Graves, published by the Seizin Press, and "To Juan at the Winter Solstice" from *Poems 1938–1945,* copyright 1945 by Robert Graves, published by Cassell and Company, Ltd. Reprinted by permission of Curtis Brown, Ltd., and from *Collected Poems* by permission of A. P. Watt Ltd.

Edgar A. Guest. "The Rough Little Rascal" from *Collected Verse of Edgar A. Guest,* copyright 1934. Reprinted by permission of Contemporary Books, Inc., Chicago.

Thom Gunn. "On the Move" from *The Sense of Movement* by Thom Gunn. Reprinted by permission of Faber and Faber Ltd.

John Haines. "To Turn Back" from *Winter News* by John Haines; copyright © 1964 by John Haines. Reprinted by permission of Wesleyan University Press.

Thomas Hardy. "During Wind and Rain," "Epitaph on a Pessimist," "The Man He Killed," "The Oxen," "The Ruined Maid," and "Transformations" from *Collected Poems of Thomas Hardy,* published by the Macmillan Publishing Co., Inc., New York, 1953.

Robert Hayden. "Middle Passage" from *Angle of Ascent, New and Selected Poems* by Robert Hayden; copyright © 1975, 1972, 1970 by Robert Hayden. Reprinted by permission of Liveright Publishing Corporation.

Seamus Heaney. "A Drink of Water" and "Song" from *Field Work,* copyright © 1979 by Farrar, Straus & Giroux, Inc.

Anthony Hecht. "The Dover Bitch," copyright © 1960 by Anthony E. Hecht, and "Samuel Sewall" from *The Hard Hours* by Anthony Hecht, copyright 1954 by Anthony E. Hecht. Reprinted by permission of Atheneum Publishers.

Geoffrey Hill. "Merlin" and "Orpheus and Eurydice" from *Somewhere Is Such a Kingdom* by Geoffrey Hill; copyright © 1975 by Geoffrey Hill. Reprinted by permission of Houghton Mifflin Company.

A. E. Housman. "To an Athlete Dying Young" from *A Shropshire Lad,* Authorized Edition, from *The Collected Poems of A. E. Housman* by A. E. Housman; copyright 1939, 1940, © 1965 by Holt, Rinehart and Winston. Copyright © 1967, 1968 by Robert E. Symons. "Eight O'Clock" from *The Collected Poems of A. E. Housman* by A. E. Housman; copyright 1922 by Holt, Rinehart and Winston. Copyright 1950 by Barclays Bank Ltd. Reprinted by permission of Holt, Rinehart and Winston; The Society of Authors as the literary representative of A. E. Housman; and Jonathan Cape Ltd., publishers of A. E. Housman's *Collected Poems.*

Langston Hughes. "Bad Luck Card" from *Selected Poems of Langston Hughes* by Langston Hughes; copyright 1927 by Alfred A. Knopf, Inc. renewed 1955 by Langston Hughes. "Homecoming" from *Selected Poems of Langston Hughes* by Langston Hughes; copyright © 1959 by Langston Hughes. "Hope" from *Selected Poems of Langston Hughes* by Langston Hughes; copyright 1942 by Alfred A. Knopf, Inc., renewed 1970 by Arna Bontemps and George Houston Bass. Reprinted by permission of Alfred A. Knopf, Inc. "On the Road" by Langston Hughes; copyright © 1934, 1952, 1962 by Langston Hughes. Reprinted by permission of Harold Ober Associates. "On the Road" first appeared in *Esquire* magazine.

Edwin Arlington Robinson. "Eros Turannos" from *Collected Poems* by Edwin Arlington Robinson; copyright 1916 by Edwin Arlington Robinson, renewed 1944 by Ruth Nivison. Reprinted by permission of Macmillan Publishing Co., Inc.

Theodore Roethke. "Cuttings," copyright 1948 by Theodore Roethke; "Big Wind," copyright 1947 by The United Chapter of Phi Beta Kappa; "Dolor," copyright 1943 by Modern Poetry Association, Inc.; "Elegy for Jane," copyright 1950 by Theodore Roethke; "I Knew a Woman," copyright 1954 by Theodore Roethke; "Journey to the Interior," copyright © 1961 by Beatrice Roethke as Administratrix of the Estate of Theodore Roethke; "The Lost Son," copyright 1947 by Theodore Roethke; "The Meadow Mouse," copyright © 1963 by Beatrice Roethke as Administratrix of the Estate of Theodore Roethke; "My Papa's Waltz," copyright 1942 by Hearst Magazines, Inc.; "Orchids," copyright 1948 by Theodore Roethke; "The Rose," copyright © 1963 by Beatrice Roethke as Administratrix of the Estate of Theodore Roethke; "The Sloth," copyright 1950 by Theodore Roethke; "The Visitant," copyright 1950 by Theodore Roethke. All from *The Collected Poems of Theodore Roethke*. Reprinted by permission of Doubleday & Company, Inc.

Carl Sandberg. "Chicago" from *Chicago Poems* by Carl Sandberg; copyright 1916 by Holt, Rinehart and Winston; copyright 1944 by Carl Sandberg. Reprinted by permission of Harcourt Brace Jovanovich, Inc.

Delmore Schwartz. "In the Naked Bed, in Plato's Cave" from *Selected Poems: Summer Knowledge* by Delmore Schwartz; copyright 1938 by New Directions. Reprinted by permission of New Directions.

Anne Sexton. "Wanting to Die" from *Live or Die* by Anne Sexton; copyright © 1966 by Anne Sexton. Reprinted by permission of Hougton Mifflin Company.

Charles Simic. "Fork" from *Dismantling the Silence* by Charles Simic. Reprinted by permission of George Braziller, Inc.

Louis Simpson. "Early in the Morning" from *The Good News of Death and Other poems* by Louis Simpson; copyright 1950, 1951, 1952, 1953, 1954, 1955 by Louis Simpson. Reprinted by permission of Charles Scribner's Sons.

W. D. Snodgrass. "April Inventory" from *Heart's Needle* by W. D. Snodgrass; copyright © 1957 by W. D. Snodgrass. Reprinted by permission of Alfred A. Knopf, Inc. "Lobster in the Window" from *After Experience* by W. D. Snodgrass; copyright © 1963 by W. D. Snodgrass. Reprinted by permission of Harper & Row, Publishers. Originally appeared in *The New Yorker*.

Gary Snyder. "Above Pate Valley" and "Hay for the Horses" by Gary Snyder. Reprinted by permission of the author.

Gary Soto. "Field," "Wind," "Stars," "Rain," and "Fog" from "The Elements of San Joaquin" by Gary Soto; copyright © 1977 by Gary Soto, reprinted by permission of the author, the University of Pittsburgh Press, and *Poetry*. These poems first appeared in *Poetry*.

Stephen Spender. "What I Expected, Was" from *Collected Poems 1928–1953* by Stephen Spender; copyright 1934 and renewed 1962 by Stephen Spender. Reprinted by permission of Faber and Faber Ltd. and Random House, Inc.

William Stafford. "Returned to Say" from *Stories That Could Be True* by William Stafford; copyright 1962. "Traveling through the Dark" by William Stafford; copyright 1960 by William Stafford. Reprinted by permission of Harper & Row, Publishers.

Wallace Stevens. "Disillusionment of Ten O'Clock," "The Emperor of Ice-Cream," "The Snow Man," and "Sunday Morning" from *The Collected Poems of Wallace Stevens;* copyright 1923 and renewed 1951 by Wallace Stevens. Reprinted by permission of Alfred A. Knopf, Inc.

Mark Strand. "Pot Roast" from *The Late Hour* by Mark Strand; copyright © 1973, 1975, 1976, 1977, 1978 by Mark Strand. Reprinted by permission of Atheneum Publishers. Originally published in *The New Yorker*.

Allen Tate. "Ode to the Confederate Dead" and "Mr. Pope" from *The Swimmers,* copyright © 1970 by Charles Scribner's Sons. Reprinted by permission of Oxford University Press.

Dylan Thomas. "And Death Shall Have No Dominion," "This Bread I Break," "Fern Hill," and "A Refusal to Mourn . . ." from *The Poems* by Dylan Thomas; copyright 1939, 1943, 1946 by New

Directions Publishing Corporation. Also published by J. M. Dent & Sons Ltd. Reprinted by permission of New Directions and David Higham Associates Limited.

Edward Thomas. "The Owl" from *Collected Poems* by Edward Thomas; first American edition published 1974 by W. W. Norton & Company, Inc. Also published by Faber and Faber Ltd. Reprinted by permission of W. W. Norton & Company and of Myfanwy Thomas.

Charles Tomlinson. "Paring the Apple"; reprinted by permission of the author.

Jean Toomer. "Reapers" from *Cane* by Jean Toomer; copyright 1923 by Boni & Liveright, renewed 1951 by Jean Toomer. Reprinted by permission of Liveright Publishing Corporation.

Robert Penn Warren. "Gold Glade" from *Promises,* copyright © 1957 by Random House, Inc.

Richard Wilbur. "Museum Piece" and "Still, Citizen Sparrow" from *Ceremony and Other Poems* by Richard Wilbur; copyright 1950, 1978 by Richard Wilbur. "Mind" from *Things of This World* by Richard Wilbur; copyright 1956 by Richard Wilbur. "Tywater" from *The Beautiful Changes and Other Poems* by Richard Wilbur; copyright 1947, 1975 by Richard Wilbur. Reprinted by permission of Harcourt Brace Jovanovich, Inc.

William Carlos Williams. "Nantucket," "Poem," "The Red Wheelbarrow," "Spring and All," and "This Is Just to Say" from *Collected Earlier Poems* by William Carlos Williams; copyright 1938 by New Directions Publishing Corporation. Reprinted by permission of New Directions.

Charles Wright. "Virgo Descending" from *Bloodlines* by Charles Wright; copyright © 1975 by Charles Wright. Reprinted by permission of Wesleyan University Press.

James Wright. "The First Days" from *To a Blossoming Pear Tree* by James Wright; copyright © 1974, 1979 by James Wright. Reprinted by permission of Farrar, Straus & Giroux, Inc. "A Blessing" and "Lying in a Hammock at William Duffy's Farm in Pine Island, Minnesota" from *Collected Poems* by James Wright; copyright © 1961 by James Wright. Reprinted by permission of Wesleyan University Press. "A Blessing" first appeared in *Poetry.*

William Butler Yeats. The following poems from *Collected Poems* by William Butler Yeats are reprinted by permission of Macmillan Publishing Co., Inc., A. P. Watt Ltd., The Macmillan Company of Canada, and Michael and Anne Yeats: "Among School Children," "Leda and the Swan," "Sailing to Byzantium" (copyright 1928 by Macmillan Publishing Co., Inc., renewed 1956 by Georgia Yeats); "The Apparitions" (copyright 1940 by Georgia Yeats, renewed 1968 by Bertha Georgia Yeats, Michael Butler Yeats, and Anne Yeats); "Crazy Jane Talks with the Bishop" (copyright 1933 by Macmillan Publishing Co., Inc., renewed 1961 by Bertha Georgia Yeats); "The Lamentation of the Old Pensioner," two lines from "When You Are Old," "Who Goes With Fergus?", four lines from the fourth version of "Cradle Song" (copyright 1906 by Macmillan Publishing Co., Inc., renewed 1934 by William Butler Yeats); "The Magi" (copyright 1916 by Macmillan Publishing Co., Inc., renewed 1944 by Bertha Georgia Yeats); "The Second Coming" (copyright 1924 by Macmillan Publishing Co., Inc., renewed 1952 by Bertha Georgia Yeats); 1890 text of "The Old Pensioner" and Versions 2 and 3 of the last stanza of "Cradle Song" from *The Variorum Edition of the Poems of W. B. Yeats,* edited by Peter Allt and Russell K. Alspach (copyright 1957 by Macmillan Publishing Co., Inc.)

Louis Zukofsky. "In Arizona" from *Collected Short Poems, 1923–1964* by Louis Zukofsky; copyright © 1971, 1966, 1965 by Louis Zukofsky. Reprinted by permission of W. W. Norton & Company, Inc.

Photo Credits

The Bettmann Archive: pages 116, 130, 139

Gloria Karlson/Portogallo Photographic Services: cover

James O. Sneddon: page 150; from Roethke, *Selected Letters,* University of Washington Press

Index

Index

Page numbers in italic type show location of biographical information

A Guide to Literary Terms

These are basic literary terms and important words from the genre of poetry. The page numbers will guide you quickly to definitions. To find these words elsewhere in the text, check the index.